I Killed
Bette Davis

I Killed Bette Davis

And Other Confessions of Heinous Crimes Committed in the Name of Moviemaking

Larry Cohen

Foreword by John Landis

Sticking Place Books
2025

ISBN 979-8-89976-044-0

Table of Contents

Foreword by John Landis   ix
Introduction   xiii

1:   All About Bette   1
2.   Backstory   27
3.   Enter the Boy Director   37
4.   Those Glorious Pageboy Days   55
5.   The Big Break Comes—and Goes   65
6.   Early Days in Hollywood   77
7.   Starting from Scratch   81
8.   Writers vs. Directors (The War That Never Ends)   97
9.   The Making (and Unmaking) of *Bone*   105
10.   At Last—A Hit!   113
11.   Me and My Baby   137
12.   Mr. Cohen Goes to Washington   157
13.   Why I Love Actors   183
14.   The Art of Getting Fired   203
15.   It's All in the Casting   215
16.   I Love a Parade   221
17.   Tricks of the Trade, Part 1   227
18.   The Ones That Got Away   235
19.   Happenings and Chance Meetings   247
20.   More Narrow Escapes   253
21.   Winging the Serpent   265
22.   Beware of Compliments   275
23.   The Greats (and Near Greats), Part 1   279
24.   The Greats (and Near Greats), Part 2   287
25.   The Greats (and Near Greats), Part 3   301
26.   Going West   315
27.   Chance Encounters   321
28.   A Kindred Spirit   329
29.   With Friends Like These…   339
30.   Trials and Tribulations   351
31.   All About Laurene   359

32. Terms of Endearment   371
33. Making Waves   379
34. Three Leading Ladies   397
35. Tricks of the Trade, Part 2   407
36. The World's Smallest Movie   413
37. A Sniper Intervenes   437
38. *It's Alive* Lives Again   443
39. Analyzing Larry Cohen   451

Appendix: Memo (for the Internet)   461

Larry Cohen wrote these memoirs several years before his death, which is why they don't cover the final act of his life—the release of Steve Mitchell's spirited documentary *King Cohen*, for instance, or the shocking murder of his sister, Ronni Chasen. But these are his memoirs: unsparingly honest, fiercely funny, and written with the same maverick energy that powered his films. What you have here is Larry in full flight—recounting his Bronx childhood, his apprenticeship in television, his ascension as New York's preeminent independent filmmaker, his two happy marriages, and his decades of jousting with other directors who dared tinker with his scripts. It's pure Cohen: opinionated, impatient with nonsense, and forever convinced that his next great idea was just around the corner.

Some light editing has been done for clarity and context, but no attempt has been made to reshape the material or invent the "missing" last chapters Larry never wrote—or perhaps never wanted to write. To do so would have been to tidy up a life defiantly untidy by design.

It has been a joy and an honor to help shepherd this project into the world—and to work with the Cohen family, private collectors, and the remarkable visual legacy Larry left behind. In assembling the filmic parade that surrounded him—photos, posters, and ephemera that radiate his irrepressible showman's spirit—I've tried to give readers a sense of the world Larry created, and the one he never stopped hustling to conquer. Few filmmakers promoted themselves with the flair and audacity that Larry did, and the images here reflect that swagger, serving as a visual counterpart to his voice: bold, funny, and unmistakably his own. And for those who finish these pages still hungry for more Larry Cohen, *Headhunter*—an unproduced script brimming with his trademark wit and nerve—is being published simultaneously by Sticking Place Books.

I am deeply grateful to my friend and fellow film scholar Derek Davidson, whose discerning eye and guidance on the visual materials throughout have been invaluable.

Many thanks are also extended to Cynthia Cohen, Melissa Cohen (not least for her photographs), Gavin Smith and John Landis.

Cohen was a one-man film industry, a carnival barker with a typewriter, and a living argument for a kind of wild imagination only the craziness of New York could ignite. His movies never waited for permission—they simply leapt into motion and dared the world to keep up. Cohen's irrepressible energy, that blend of street smarts, self-promotion, and cinematic nerve, animates every page of this book.

James Kenney

Foreword by John Landis

I first met Larry Cohen through George Folsey Jr., whose father, George Sr., was the cinematographer on Larry's first movie, *Bone*, made in 1972. George Jr. was *Bone*'s film editor. George Sr. was in his mid-80s when he was the DP on Larry's first picture. His first job in the movie business had been as an office boy for Adolph Zukor at the Paramount building in New York. Those were the days when they shot Westerns in New Jersey! He became a cameraman working at Paramount with directors like Ernst Lubitsch and shooting the Marx Brothers first film (an early talkie), *Coconuts*, before moving to MGM, where he worked for the next fifty years before retiring. Larry was lucky (and smart) to get him for *Bone*.

George Jr. edited and served as executive producer on my first film, *Schlock* (aptly titled). We went on to collaborate on many more movies, with him first as my editor and later as my producer. George also cut *Black Caesar* for Larry, and one of the films George and I collaborated on featured Larry as an actor. In *Spies Like Us* there are four very suspicious CIA Spooks armed and standing guard at an abandoned drive-in in the Arizona desert: Michael Apted, Martin Brest, B. B. King and Larry Cohen. And just to get to these guys, you had to pass the scary, scruffy guards played by Joel Coen and Sam Raimi!

Larry was always great fun. He told terrific stories about his time as an NBC page in the early days of live television. You can still feel his youthful excitement as he writes about it in this book. He was always a writer and always a hustler. He even sold several scripts for *The Defenders*, the distinguished TV series starring E. G. Marshall, when he was in the army, stationed in Virginia in 1964.

Larry had a long and successful career in television, but my special fondness for Larry's work is centered on his wild and very independent movies. His black exploitation pictures starring Fred Williamson shot on the streets of New York (usually without permits) and at his home in Beverly Hills (also without

Larry Cohen in John Landis' *Spies Like Us.*

permits) are energetic and move forward in a sort of hell or high water way. At the end of *Black Caesar*, Larry put hidden cameras on Fifth Avenue across the street and in a parked and a moving car in front of Tiffanys to capture Fred Williamson's dying steps as he staggers down the sidewalk, gunshot and bloodied, with the soundtrack wailing away. It's hard not to notice the well-meaning pedestrians on the sidewalks of New York offering this poor fellow help. You can almost hear Fred's stage whisper, "Get the fuck away from me, mister—we're making a movie!"

Once, when I was directing a commercial on the streets of Manhattan, the two NYPD motorcycle cops with us suddenly shouted, "Someone is firing machine guns at the Chrysler Building!" They roared off, sirens blazing. I later learned that Larry was filming *Q,* and had his movie cops firing guns from the top of the Chrysler Building as a helicopter circled, shooting the plates for Jim Danforth's winged serpent in flight. And, of course, with no permits!

Perhaps the most remarkable thing about *Q* is the extraordinary performance of Michael Moriarty. He is brilliant, and it's a testament to Larry and Moriarty that they could create a character so sad and so compelling in such a wacky movie.

It's Alive, Larry's mutant killer baby movie, manages to generate tremendous sympathy for the parents of the Rick Baker monstrosity (Rick's then wife Elaine wore the mutant baby mask for the close-ups). And again, Larry gets unexpect-edly powerful performances from John P. Ryan and Sharon Farrell as the traumatized father and mother.

In *The Private Files of J. Edgar Hoover*, Larry's spot-on casting of Broderick Crawford and Dan Daley as J. Edgar Hoover and his longtime Associate Director Clyde Tolson gives the picture a gravitas and sense of reality that Clint East-wood's later film, *J. Edgar*, completely lacked. As the FBI had just moved out of its old building in Washington D.C. and into its new headquarters, Larry and his crew waltzed into the old building and filmed away. They even shot in Hoover's old office! And, say it with me: WITH NO PERMISSION OR PERMITS!

Larry was a constant source of ideas and stories. *The Stuff*, *Special Effects*, *Maniac Cop 1, 2 & 3*, *The Ambulance*, *Phone Booth*—the list is long. *God Told Me To* is, I genuinely believe, a unique and excellent film. It deals with religion, family, space aliens, New York, and, as Dr. Pretorius says in *Bride of Frankenstein*, "a world of Gods and Monsters." There is a sequence shot (or rather stolen) in a sea of police officers marching in the Saint Patrick's Day Parade that ends with chaos and murder. If you haven't seen it, you should. And yes, as always, no permit.

Larry Cohen was outrageous. Larry Cohen was a hustler. Larry Cohen was a maverick. And Larry Cohen was a visionary. I miss him.

Introduction

With Bette Davis on the set of *Wicked Stepmother.*

Alright, the title got your attention. But this isn't a confession of homicide. My crime is not punishable by law, though it did end the life of Hollywood's greatest female star.

I never meant Bette Davis any harm. Just the opposite. It began as an effort to help her resurrect her dormant career and ended with the final nail in the coffin of a legend.

There's no question that sometimes people you admire are better off being left alone. Butting into their life and trying to change things for the better can have the opposite effect. Bette might have been lucky if I hadn't seen her that night appearing as a presenter at the 1986 Golden Globes. If my heart hadn't gone out to the outrageous lady who limped on stage dragging one leg and struggling with partial facial paralysis. But the moment Bette spoke, there was no mistaking her—the commanding Queen of Warner Bros., a powerhouse of versatility who reigned at the studio during an era dominated by men. She carried films such as *Mrs. Skeffington*, *Dark Victory*, and *Now, Voyager*, and secured her place in screen history with eleven Academy Award nominations and two wins, for *Jezebel* and *All About Eve*. Undefeatable, I thought.

I was to be proved wrong.

As of that night, I was determined to create a project that would bring Bette back. I'd write a script especially tailored for her. A part nobody else could play. And I wouldn't give up until she agreed to do it. The title of the film was *Wicked Stepmother*.

My motive was to do good for someone who'd given so many generations of moviegoers such enjoyment. Instead, I did her much harm—and made it impossible for her to ever work again. Bette lived only to act. Once robbed of that, she could only relax her grip on life and surrender to the cancer that she'd resisted for so long.

What makes what occurred even more tragic is that Bette and I had grown fond of each other during the preparations for *Wicked Stepmother*. We loved hanging out together and she gave me such pleasure with anecdotes of her golden years as the highest-paid woman in America. How she loved lounging around my house off Coldwater Canyon in Beverly Hills—and I have the cigarette burns on the furniture to prove it.

Bette Davis presenting Sydney Pollack with a Golden Globe
at the 1986 ceremony.

Months after Bette dropped out of the film because of "creative differences" with me, she was quoted in the *New York Times* as saying, "I have dealt with so many directors," but with me she had finally met her "Waterloo." According to her, I was the guy who had finally defeated Bette Davis.

But the truth was otherwise.

She laid the blame on her director, and having learned all the facts, as you will see, I was willing at the time to take the rap.

That was my final gesture of admiration and friendship. I knew it wouldn't do my career as a filmmaker much good to have the great Bette Davis berating me on *Entertainment Tonight* twice in one week, but I was willing to live with it in hopes that Bette would get another shot at acting in some future movie. In my heart I knew she couldn't live if she didn't work again. When she told those fibs about me it was out of pure fear—not malice. And, after all, I was to blame for getting her into this mess.

Why didn't I just mind my own business and let her alone? What right did I have to meddle in her life? She never asked for my help. Bette Davis never asked for *anyone's* help. That wasn't her style. In a film she'd recently completed, Lindsay Anderson's *The Whales of August*, co-starring Lillian Gish and Vincent Price, the producers had built a special ramp leading up to the porch of the house which was the principal location in order that Bette might avoid mounting steps each day. Bette was outraged at the gesture and refused to ever set foot on that ramp. She gave me hell when I'd had a comfortable bed put in her dressing room, and insisted she never had to lie down between takes.

Instead, I charmed her into signing on, got her a $250,000 paycheck, and let her have cast approval for all the other parts. I even gave Bette's secretary an associate producer credit. Everything to make her happy.

And what happened made her miserable.

Sure, I killed Bette Davis by meddling in her life.

But I've only scratched the surface of what happened. And I'd hate for you to miss out on all the sordid details. So it's all laid out for you here—all the fun and the fiascos, all the memories, the pain and the pleasures of working with a woman who is undeniably one of the screen's immortals. And beyond Bette, this book takes you through the rest of my journey: the films, the battles, the triumphs and misadventures that defined my career.

As a child I did my best to enrage my father whenever possible. Early on I learned the magic words that would throw dad into a fury and propel him down the narrow hallways of our Washington Heights apartment in hot pursuit. Fortunately there was a latch on the bathroom door and I spent much of my childhood locked safely inside. I must admit I enjoyed having the power to wreak havoc within the family at my sole discretion.

I went on in my career to deliberately provoke those who positioned themselves as my superiors—even though I never accepted them as such. I knew what buttons to push and delighted in the result, even if it infrequently led to my dismissal as writer or director. It was always about being in control. That's why I eventually wrote, produced and directed most of my own films. Though I often courted disaster, I never acknowledged any possibility of failure.

Walking a tightrope, I refused to look down. Not only did I survive the treacherous rapids of the entertainment industry, but I also seemed to pick up momentum. While the careers of many of my highly-regarded contemporaries began to fizzle, I found greater acceptance late in my career, finally becoming a hot writer and being paid more for a script than I was accustomed to receiving for delivering an entire movie.

It's been a ride on a rollercoaster, and I chose to sit in the first car, standing up without any safety bar. I venture to say I've had more fun in this wacky business than anyone I know. I hope you'll enjoy reliving some of it with me.

You admit to sneaking into FBI headquarters in Washington and shooting The Private Files of J. Edgar Hoover *there without permission?*

I grabbed a few scenes in the Attorney General's office, too.

You don't deny firing dozens of machine guns at the top of the Chrysler Building and causing panic in the streets below for Q?

Guilty as charged.

Or staging an impromptu gunfight for God Told Me To *in the middle of the Saint Patrick's Day Parade on Fifth Avenue?*

Andy Kaufman played the part of the crazed killer.

How about the time you ran the Staten Island Ferry up on a sandbar in the middle of New York Harbor for Deadly Illusion, *a movie you were later fired from?*

I guess I did a lot of damage to my favorite city, didn't I?

And somehow you managed to insult and abuse just about every Hollywood big shot—from Barry Diller on down?

They still loved me.

I suppose you enjoyed trading punches in a knock-down, drag-out brawl with the future president of CBS?

It was all over a beautiful woman.

Was it really a smart idea to sue Nixon's appointee to be Director of the IRS?

I won, didn't I?

And you still found time to write 37 produced screenplays, direct 20 of them, produce 24 movies, and create eight network television series and four stage plays?

Imagine what I could have accomplished if I'd gotten along with people better.

Including Phone Booth, *a thriller that all takes place inside a telephone booth?*

Which I originally cooked up for Hitchcock.

You must be Larry Cohen!

Want to know how it all happened? Buy the book.

Chapter 1
All About Bette

I only got a ringside table at the 1986 Golden Globes awards because I showed up with my sister, Ronni Chasen, who'd become one of the industry's foremost publicists. At one point in the program it was announced that Bette Davis would be presenting the next award. There was thunderous applause — which changed into waves of shock as she appeared onstage, dragging one withered leg behind her. Bette couldn't have weighed more than 80 pounds and she was clearly recovering from a stroke. Yet she insisted on being seen in public. As Miss Davis reached the microphone, I cast a glance to the next table where fellow legend Barbara Stanwyck sat with her hand clasped over her mouth, suppressing an audible gasp. She couldn't believe the condition of Bette Davis. Nor could anyone else.

But when she spoke, it was the unmistakable Bette Davis, as challenging as ever. She was daring the audience not to look at her.

Many months after that, I saw Miss Davis on some television talk shows and her condition seemed to have improved. It seemed to me that she was making public appearances in hopes that someone would take notice and offer her a job. In truth, she hadn't made a theatrical feature in over ten years. Her career, even before the series of strokes, had been relegated to appearances in television movies.

Apparently, Bette's strategy worked because I read that she'd finally been cast with Lillian Gish in *The Whales of August*. She was playing a blind woman confined to a wheelchair so she could remain more or less immobile. Soon afterwards, her new book came on the market. It was entitled *This 'n That*. While reading it, I got the idea for a Bette Davis movie. The horrendous condition she was in would work for and not against us in this comedy about a happily married young couple who return from a vacation to discover that the wife's widowed father had gotten married in their absence. My God, he's married Bette Davis and she's already moved in! It's a variation on the classic *The Man Who Came to Dinner* theme—the unwelcome house guest who won't go away. In this case it's even worse, because she insists on being called "mom"!

I could easily imagine having to live under the same roof with a vitriolic Bette Davis, and from there on, the screen-play began to write itself. I seemed to hear Bette's voice in my head, and by the time the week was over, I'd already finished the script, which I promptly sent to Bette's agent. It was called *Wicked Stepmother* and it was instantly rejected. I later learned that Bette had never even seen the material. Knowing my previous credits, her agents had assumed it was a horror movie and passed on it, unread.

I couldn't give up, however, since there was no one else who could play the part other than Bette.

Months dragged on before my publicist, Milt Kahn, casually mentioned that he knew Robert Osborne (who had recently gained fame as the primary host of Turner Classic Movies). Osborne not only lived in the same apartment building as Bette, but was a confidante as well.

Through Bob Osborne, my script was resubmitted on an informal basis. She called a few days later. I knew it was Bette because there was smoke coming out of the telephone. Her voice crackled over the line like sparks from a frayed old electrical cord just before it burns your house to the ground.

"Well, I certainly got a few laughs thanks to you last night," she snapped. "Am I mistaken, or did you write this especially for me?"

She was clearly flattered and was interested in meeting me. Would I drop by her place on Havenhurst for a cocktail? Naturally I jumped at the opportunity, and brought along my agent, Peter Sabiston. He was a charming gentleman in his seventies, and I thought Bette might take a liking to him. As it was, all her attention was riveted on me.

Her home was a large, sprawling condominium in a pre-World War II building not far off Sunset. Contrary to expectations, there was no memorabilia of her career visible. No posters, no photos with celebrities, no trace of the two Oscars she'd won.

On one wall I did notice a tiny charcoal sketch of a person most wouldn't recognize. It was George Arliss, the noted stage star who'd made films for Warner Bros. in the 1930s. He had actually discovered Bette Davis and insisted she appear in his movie, *The Man Who Played God.*

Warners had intended to drop her contract at that time, and it was only through Arliss' intervention that the studio relented. Within a few years, Bette Davis would be the queen of Warner Bros. and the highest salaried woman in America. She had never forgotten what George Arliss had done for her. She held few others in such esteem.

I was also surprised to discover framed photographs of Bette's estranged daughter, B. D. Hyman, prominently displayed—despite the fact that she'd written a scathing memoir, *My Mother's Keeper*, which painted her mother in the most unflattering terms. Bette had been devastated upon its publication. Taking notice of my interest in the photos, Bette quickly commented, "If your children like you, you can't have been a very good mother."

Joining Bette at our initial meeting was her assistant, Kathryn Sermak, a trim brunette who radiated efficiency. Kathryn had become virtually a surrogate daughter to Bette, one who would someday inherit half of her estate. As Bette would later inform me, Kathryn had recently "lost her man" and was therefore able to devote her full attention to the legendary actress.

There was no question that Bette loved my script and wanted to do it. Not many people were tailoring material for her at this stage of her career. She would be leaving shortly to appear at the Kennedy Center Honors where she was again being celebrated.

There were many such honors in the offing, but no employment. She indicated that *The Whales of August* had been an unpleasant shoot. The weather was horrid and she hadn't gotten on with Lillian Gish. Many attached to the production would claim that Bette took advantage of the fact that Miss Gish's hearing was impaired. The scuttlebutt was that Bette had deliberately lowered her voice during their scenes so that Lillian Gish wouldn't be able to hear her cues. Bette angrily responded to these rumors, telling me, "It's a total lie. Miss

Gish was stone deaf. She couldn't have heard the cues if I'd shouted them through a bullhorn."

After we'd gone over the material, Bette asked Kathryn to uncork a bottle of white wine. It was her tradition to offer a toast: "Let's hope we like each other at the finish as much as we do at the start."

We then relaxed together as she generously regaled us with tales of her career, particularly at Warners, about how Errol Flynn was habitually late on the set and how his trailer would rock visibly back and forth as he entertained young starlets during the break between set-ups. But, she concluded, "Boy, was he handsome!"

Somehow, the subject of Edward G. Robinson came up. It seemed that Kay Francis, a statuesque star of the 1930s, never wanted to play opposite Robinson because he was so short he'd have to stand on a box. None of the actresses at Warners were anxious to do love scenes with him. A contingent of them, led by Bette, had gone to Jack Warner, begging him not to force them to kiss Robinson on screen. "He had those awful purple lips," she explained. It was a blast hearing her sound off on her contemporaries like that. She complained she never got to play opposite most of the great male stars. Jack Warner knew it wasn't necessary to pay top dollar for a male lead when Bette was big enough to carry a movie on her own. Her great success and box-office appeal sabotaged her efforts to co-star with Clark Gable or Gary Cooper. Warner knew that audiences would still turn out if Bette's name alone appeared on the marquee.

When Bette inquired if there might be a job for Kathryn on my film, I suggested that she become associate producer—not just assume a title, but have major responsibilities—which is exactly what Kathryn wanted. Bette couldn't have been more affectionate as she walked us to the door. On the way out, taking note of her furnishings, I focused on an embroidered cushion which lay on her sofa. The lettering read "Old Age is not for Sissies." Bette might as well have been a poster girl for this slogan. The two mastectomies and the two strokes had taken their toll.

As soon as we'd left the apartment, Pete pulled me aside, saying, "How can you even consider making a movie with a woman in her condition?"

I knew it was foolhardy, but just meeting Bette had been such a moving experience that I couldn't let go. Sure, she was infirm, but the same spirit was there as always. And, after all, wasn't she was supposed to be playing an old hag? In the story she would turn out to be a witch: a particularly appropriate role for a woman who once named her New England home "Witch's Way." Bette had often been accused of being a witch, or something along those lines.

But soon, difficulties arose in the person of her attorney and long-time manager, Harold Schiff.

Having checked me out, Mr. Schiff was not sure he wanted Bette to appear in a Larry Cohen movie. After all, I'd been associated with too many exploitation films with titles like *Hell Up in Harlem* and *It's Alive*. He realized Bette didn't have many pictures left in her and thought it would be better that *The Whales of August* be her last film rather than *Wicked Stepmother*.

I had no choice but to fly to New York and try to convince Mr. Schiff to change his opinion. My friend Fifi Oscard, a prominent New York agent, arranged a breakfast meeting and I must've charmed the hell out of him because he completely reversed himself and we quickly closed a deal for Bette to receive $250,000 for five weeks' work.

Now I had a binding commitment to pay Bette a quarter of a million dollars but no studio to finance the picture. I made my next move—taking a full-page ad in *Variety* proclaiming "Bette is bad again. Bette Davis is THE WICKED STEPMOTHER." I also enlisted the aid of my long-time pal, Robert Littman, to join me as producer. Bobby had important connections, one of which paid off. Alan Ladd, Jr., who then headed MGM, agreed to finance our picture to the tune of $2,500,000.

The pre-production period with Bette was consistently amusing. She visited my home off Coldwater Canyon and took a liking to the place. She was constantly dropping her cigarettes or flicking ashes. I considered the property damage to be a memento of our working relationship. I could point out the holes in the sofa and say, "Bette Davis did that."

One afternoon, Bette happened to take notice of a half-dozen small, gold-plated replicas of a director's chair that lined a shelf in my living room. "Well, I see you've won more than a few awards yourself," she purred.

I didn't have the heart to tell her that these were nothing more than place settings from the annual DGA award dinners I'd attended that I'd brought home as souvenirs. I simply nodded humbly, allowing her to go on thinking that I was up there in her league.

Bette got into the habit of phoning me day or night with any thoughts that might have occurred to her, quickly stating an opinion then hanging up without even saying goodbye. For example, I'd pick up the phone and hear that unmistakable rasp,

"Larry, I've decided that my character must have red hair rather than my normal color... Click." And she'd be gone.

She wanted costumer Julie Weiss to do her wardrobe. I handed Julie my credit card and told her to go out and spend $25,000 on Bette's clothes... just to make Bette happy. When the picture was over, she could keep it all.

Bette decided she wanted Lionel Stander, best known now for his role as majordomo to Robert Wagner and Stefanie Powers on the long-running series *Hart to Hart*, to play her husband, and I thought he was an excellent choice. We had readings at my house to select an actress to play Mr. Stander's daughter and Bette quickly settled on Colleen Camp, who had previously starred in Peter Bogdanovich's *They All Laughed* and Jonathan Lynn's film adaptation of the board game *Clue*. For some reason, while seated in my living room with Colleen, Bette began to reminisce on the subject of Samuel Goldwyn, for whom she'd worked on *The Little Foxes*. She began to compare the old man with his son, Sam Goldwyn, Jr., whom she dismissed as a total incompetent.

Bette Davis and Lionel Stander on the set of *Wicked Stepmother*.

After Colleen left, I told Bette, "I'm sure you didn't realize that Colleen is John Goldwyn's wife. You were just maligning her father-in-law."

Bette threw her head back in laughter. "Well, that's one on me, isn't it?"

After receiving her Kennedy Center award, Bette had returned from Washington in a fury. "Whoever heard of an award where the recipient isn't allowed to speak?"

She was outraged that she had to remain in a box with the other honorees and the President, and was limited to simply taking a bow. She also detested the award: "What is this thing? It looks like a sash! Am I supposed to wear it?" She tossed it in a closet, out of sight.

One afternoon, Bette invited me to her apartment to show me the wigs she'd purchased. I found her seated at her kitchen table with several copies of my script and a yellow highlighter pen, making her notes in the margins just like any working actress.

After approving the wigs, I offered to reimburse her, and she handed me a bill for only $180. She had gotten a huge discount. I put two hundred-dollar bills on the mantlepiece and left. I'd only been home a few minutes when the phone rang. It was Bette. "Well, now I feel like a kept woman."

With Colleen Camp on the set of *Wicked Stepmother*.

I never once heard Bette curse. Her favorite expletive was "Oh, brother!" One day she confided that she'd always wanted to say "shit" in a movie. She'd been disappointed in not getting to play Martha in *Who's Afraid of Virginia Woolf?* on screen— a role notorious for its foul-mouthed tirades—and wanted to throw a few curse words. I promised I'd try to work some in.

The house I'd selected to film in was located in Hollywood's Hancock Park district. It had a sumptuous guest cottage which could serve as Bette's dressing room. It had its own kitchen, TV, stereo system, and even that bed, which offended Bette. "I will have no occasion to lie down."

I began escorting her through the house, describing how the scenes would be played, taking care to include Kathryn in on everything. Before we left, Bette grabbed both my hands, digging in her nails, and whispered, "Why are you addressing Kathryn all the time and not me?" I responded that Kathryn was associate producer and I was showing her the appropriate respect.

Bette dug in even deeper as she looked up into my eyes with great sincerity. "I don't want you to be afraid of me. Many directors have been, but you don't have to be. I think you're a great guy, and I want you to know that."

I explained to Bette that I'd directed other celebrated stars of her era like Sylvia Sidney and Celeste Holm. To me, she was just an actress—and a very good one. At that point she kissed me on the cheek. This became a tradition whenever she arrived for work and when she departed. There was always that mandatory display of affection.

It wasn't until Bette finally reported for work on a full-time basis that I realized the extent of her addiction to cigarettes. She smoked one-hundred Vantage cigarettes every day. Before she arrived, five packs would be broken open and their contents placed in cups. Wherever she went, Kathryn would follow Bette around with this supply of cigarettes. She was never without one.

I suppose it took a lot of nerve to point out that all this smoking was bad for her. She replied, "Oh, Larry, I know. But if I didn't have a cigarette in my hand, I wouldn't know what to do with myself."

Before actual production began, we shot some test footage of Bette at my home to see how she'd look in the wig and the costumes. She was extremely nervous. "Don't make me speak if we're not recording sound. I hate to see myself on the screen with my mouth moving and not hear anything."

Just before the tests were shot, I'd gotten a phone call from my cameraman, Daniel Pearl. He'd been summoned to Bette's apartment, and she had insulted him, threatening to have him fired if she wasn't completely satisfied with his photography. Daniel considered her a horrible old woman and was refusing to work with her. He was quitting. I immediately called Bette. Her first words were, "I met your DP, and Daniel's a wonderful guy. I just loved him." Needless to say, Daniel stayed on.

For some reason, Bette was extremely wary of my 19-year-old daughter Jill. Each time she visited my home, her eyes would dart around, and she would quickly ask, "Where's Jill?" Somehow, she sensed that Jill was out to provoke her. One day as she sat at my dining room table running lines, Jill approached. "Oh, Miss Davis, I'm having my birthday party here on Friday night. Will you come?" Those Bette Davis eyes flared. "No, Jill, I won't." There was no apology and no good wishes. Bette knew she was being bullshitted and she put an immediate end to it.

On the other hand, when visitors dropped by our filming location, Bette gladly spent time with them, signed autographs, and seemed pleased to be in their company. Although she had an elaborate dressing room, she insisted on coming onto the set early and having a chair placed in the midst of the crew who were balanced above her on ladders hanging lights. She usually situated herself in the most precarious spot. "It'd be safer to wait in your dressing room 'til we're ready," I suggested. "I just like to see what's going on," she said. I was afraid somebody might drop a piece of equipment on her as she sat there, puffing away, giving all the crew members the eye.

A movie set *can* be a dangerous place. There are criss-crossing cables everywhere and I was concerned Bette would trip over one of them. One day my worst fears were realized. The PA came running with the report that Bette had fallen in the yard behind the house. I hurried to the window and saw her stretched out on the ground, with Kathryn kneeling

Lionel Stander, Bette Davis, Colleen Camp and David Rasche.

beside her. A few other crew people had come to her aid, but she was violently shooing them away. She refused to be helped up, and so several apple boxes were brought and placed next to her. Using them for leverage, she managed to struggle to her knees and then to her feet, virtually unassisted. I was about to step outside and get involved, and then I realized how embarrassed she'd be for me to see her in this condition.

I remained out of sight—or so I thought. But Bette had an eagle eye. Somehow, she caught a glimpse of me, and when I finally came to her dressing room to offer sympathy, she let me know that she'd seen me "hiding" when she was in distress. I explained that I'd tried to spare her any extra embarrassment. She finally agreed that had been the best approach.

I offered to let her go home for the day, but she refused. We had scenes to be shot on the second floor of the house. Originally, Bette said she'd allow several of the grips to lift her up and carry her to the top of the stairs. But now that she'd fallen, she was determined to walk up the stairs herself. And she did.

With Tom Bosley on the set of *Wicked Stepmother.*

In dealing with Bette, I found that holding my ground was the best tactic. Prior to production, she'd staged a fashion show for me at Western Costume to model her new wardrobe. She had Julie Weiss and her staff running around like chickens without heads while she tried on a dozen outfits.

When she was finished, I had to offer my critique. "I'm sorry, but they all look alike. Everything's black. You're a small woman and the clothes make you appear even smaller. We need something to brighten this all up—a colorful sash here, a handkerchief there, a belt…"

Bette's head reared back. For a moment I was in the presence of Jezebel or a vengeful Queen Elizabeth. "Very well, then we'll throw everything out and start all over!" she snapped.

I replied, without a beat, "No, we won't, Bette. We'll keep what we've got and touch it up—give it more contrast, make each outfit distinctly individual." I addressed myself to Julie, telling her exactly what to do while Bette stood there seething. Finally I turned back to Bette, "You invited me here because you wanted my opinion. Well, I'm giving it to you." That seemed to calm Bette down. The matter was closed. I think she secretly liked having somebody in charge.

At first, she informed us that she wished to be called "Miss Davis." Later she decided she preferred "BD." I always called her Bette. She tried calling me "Mr. Cohen," but I wouldn't let her get away with it.

Shooting a scene for *Wicked Stepmother*.

She knew I liked hearing anecdotes about the old days at Warners. When a plane flew over the house while we were filming, ruining the take, Bette murmured "George Brent." I asked her what she meant, and she explained that George Brent (who had been her real-life lover and leading man in classics like *Jezebel* and *Dark Victory*) owned his own plane and enjoyed flying. When Jack Warner suspended him and barred him from the lot, George Brent simply piloted his private aircraft low over the studio soundstage in Burbank, circling endlessly. No one could shoot sound while Brent continued to harass, and he was quickly rehired at full salary. Thereafter, every time a plane passed over our location, I would shout, "George Brent" and Bette would break up.

To bring Bette Davis to a boil all you need to do was mention Faye Dunaway. The two had formed a mutual hate society when shooting the 1976 TV movie *The Disappearance of Aimee.* As Bette explained it, Miss Dunaway was totally unprofessional. She would arrive on the set inexcusably late and deplorably unprepared. During a crowd sequence, she kept several hundred extras waiting for well over an hour. Finally Bette took it upon herself to entertain and amuse them all by putting on an impromptu performance. She sang the song, "I'm Getting a Letter from Daddy," from her mega-hit *Whatever Happened to Baby Jane?*, then answered questions from the extras and spun endless anecdotes. When Miss Dunaway finally deigned to show up, Bette waded into her like a bantamweight fighter in front of the entire crew. And that was one of the good days!

Bette was a total pro, and she expected the same from everyone around her. The best thing she could say about Humphrey Bogart, the *Casablanca* star with whom she appeared in more than a half-dozen films, was that Bogart was truly a professional, although he wasn't given to much small talk. "We didn't pal around much on the set. He was all business."

Despite—or perhaps because of—her great success, her love life had proved a shambles. She chose husbands who were hardly competitive. There was an unsuccessful musician, followed by a desk clerk at a New England hotel. She even had a romance with an Army sergeant whom she met at the Hollywood Canteen, which she co-founded with John Garfield.

There wasn't any question that she was flirting with me throughout our rehearsals, always leaning against me and whispering in my ear. If we'd met at a different time and place, there's no doubt some sparks would've flown.

At first Bette insisted she was from "the old school" and resisted any improvisation. But after a day or two, she came around to trying it my way, and actually seemed to enjoy it. Being extemporaneous was something new and challenging.

Still, it was clear to me that all through the first week, Bette was suffering. It wasn't just the fall. She seemed genuinely uncomfortable and her line-readings were odd. She would take pauses in the midst of sentences that were uncalled for. She began begging me to see the dailies. I resisted until one afternoon she beckoned me into an empty room in the house, sat down on the bed, and burst into tears. I couldn't believe Bette Davis was crying. Maybe this was just another tactic, but I couldn't resist. I agreed to have dailies shown to her on Saturday.

Later that afternoon, she had another unfortunate accident with a self-igniting cigarette. One of Bette's powers as a witch was the ability to light her own cigarettes without a match. They would simply burst into flame at will. To create this effect, a young special effects wizard had to rig a cigarette attached to a wire which would run up Bette's arm to a battery pack behind her. On cue, he would make a connection and the cigarette would ignite.

While rigging Bette, he confided that he'd written a 65-page thesis on her films as his term paper in college. Bette seemed totally taken with this chap and I felt myself getting jealous. Then the moment of ignition arrived. At first try, her devoted fan gave her such a paralyzing electric shock that she actually screamed. He couldn't stop apologizing and begged for another chance to make the gag work—serving only to give Bette a second and even worse dose.

Now I was determined to cancel the effect entirely. "We'll do this in post-production," I suggested. But Bette refused. She was not to be cowed in front of cast and crew. Finally, after much work, our young man announced that the problem had been solved.

We tried a third take, during which the cigarette ignited with incendiary force. There was a flash of fire and Bette was clasping both hands over her right eye, which apparently had been scorched. The faulty effects artist was instantly banished from the set. Minutes later, Bette recovered, never complaining about any further discomfort. But I was to hear more of this later.

Throughout the production, she continued to demonstrate absolute respect for me as her director. There was a question of whether Bette should be standing or seated in one particular sequence. As I continued to debate the blocking with her, another actor, David Rasche, chimed in. "I think Bette's right…"

That's all he got to say. Bette turned on him in a fury. "Larry's directing this picture, not you! Keep out of this!"

I turned to catch Rasche's reaction, but all I saw was his foot clearing the doorway. He'd made one of the quickest exits in history. And he never interfered again.

Another evening while we were trying to film in Hancock Park, the teenagers next door deliberately turned up their stereo so as to harass us. It would be impossible to record sound with all that racket coming from next door.

Bette approached me. "Want me to go over and tell them to turn it off?" she inquired.

I could just see it—opening your front door to see Bette Davis standing there, ordering you to shut off your boom box.

I thanked Bette but chose to send a production assistant over with a crisp one-hundred-dollar bill. The music soon stopped. But I was amused at Bette's willingness to pitch in.

I'd bought her a birthday present prior to the start of production—an antique charm bracelet—and she wore it to the set regularly, always waving her wrist in the air and jiggling the bracelet to make sure I noticed she had it on.

We spent much of our downtime, while cameras were being positioned, in animated discussion. I asked her opinion of those who'd directed her in the past. She had little good to say about Vincent Sherman, who helmed *Mr. Skeffington* and *Old Acquaintance*, both successes starring Davis, or, in fact, most of the other Warner contract directors. "I had to direct myself," she insisted.

She did remain enamored of three-time Oscar winner William Wyler, an arch disciplinarian who made her descend a staircase for 45 takes during the filming of *Jezebel*. With Wyler she always knew who was boss.

I pointed out to her that in *The Letter*, Wyler had her play a great deal of her most dramatic dialogue with her back to the camera. "Yes," she laughed. "Willie told me no matter how good you are, the audience gets sick of looking at you. Besides, the audience wanted me to turn around, and when I finally did, there was great impact. It's the idea of withholding something from them—and then finally giving it to them."

Each day at the conclusion of her last scene, I'd notice Bette pooching her lips in my direction, demanding our traditional goodbye kiss. Sometimes the Assistant Director would tell me that she'd signed out but had waited a full 20 minutes before leaving because she had to personally say goodnight. I'd locate her, lean over, and she'd plant a wet one on my cheek before heading home. She did so on her very last day of production. I had no idea she'd never be coming back.

Unbeknownst to me, Bette had been having trouble with her dentures prior to the start of principal photography. Her bridge had cracked and she attempted to repair it herself. When it slipped, she'd push it back in place with her tongue and hope for the best. It sounds comedic but it's also tragic. She was acting while trying to keep her teeth in.

When she showed up at the projection room that Saturday and saw how she looked in the dailies, she was appalled and became despondent, so much so that the bridge dislodged entirely, and Kathryn Sermak had to search around under the seats in the dark to retrieve the broken pieces. Can anybody blame poor Bette for not wanting to come back to work?

There was wide speculation within the industry as to why Bette Davis left the production of *Wicked Stepmother*. For a while, her attorney Harold Schiff claimed that she'd been mistreated, citing the fall, the accident with the special effects, and even faulting my direction. The final truth came to light on June 24, 1988 before a notary public of the state of New York. To her credit, in her sworn statement to the attorneys for the insurance and completion bond companies who needed to accurately ascertain blame for the shutdown and delay in the production of *Wicked Stepmother*, Bette finally owned up to the truth and completely absolved me of any responsibility for her premature departure. The following is quoted verbatim from her deposition:

QUESTION: On or about the 25th of April, do you have an opinion as to the state of your health at the time you began filming?

BETTE DAVIS: I was having an absolutely wicked problem with my two dentures, yes. It was up to me to make a decision, but I thought I could manage them. Otherwise I would have had to postpone the film. So I made the decision that I could cope with it, that I could manage it during shooting, yes.

QUESTION: How long prior to the beginning of photography had you been having this problem?

BETTE DAVIS: The first denture broke one night in a restaurant. The lower one broke and I… they mended that temporarily before I started.

QUESTION: Did the problem with your dentures become worse as filming went along?

BETTE DAVIS: Yes, indeed. You do not really like a close-up camera on you if half your upper denture is falling down during shooting. When I saw some of the film, it was so evident, which is a disgrace really to be filming that way, I was not able to cope with it. The uppers kept slipping down during my lines. It was nerve-wracking trying to act under these circumstances. It was kind of embarrassing, besides.

It wasn't a Larry Cohen problem. It was a dental problem. Knowing it would delay the picture—perhaps for months, while her New York dentists worked on her—Bette convinced herself that she could get through the filming while struggling to hold the broken dentures in place.

I believe it was partially her desire not to let me down that led her to make such a foolish decision. Or perhaps it was the fear that MGM would cancel the whole picture if she appeared in any way infirm.

So she tried to fake it, and failed. No one was more aware of this than Bette herself. She could barely get the lines out because of the necessary pauses to readjust the bridge with her tongue. For a perfectionist like her, this was pure hell. And yet, she never leveled with me. If she had, I certainly would have closed down for a month and re-shot the early scenes upon her return. Sadly, despite the closeness of our relationship, she still didn't trust me enough to reveal her problem—which I agree was insurmountable.

After seeing herself in the dailies that Saturday, she'd rushed to New York to the one dentist she trusted. He informed her that several more teeth needed to be extracted and it would take weeks to create her new set of dentures.

In her condition, she could never have faced the camera. But she couldn't admit that publicly. To have left the movie for medical reasons might've made her uninsurable in future. Without insurance she'd never work again, and Bette Davis lived to work. That's a fair explanation of why she chose to pretend she'd left the film solely because of creative differences.

I'd spoken to her briefly when she called me to say she wasn't coming back. "I made a terrible mistake, Larry," she said. "I have to leave the picture." She sounded terribly sad. On the edge of being apologetic.

I didn't argue or try to change her mind. I simply wished her well. The following week was spent negotiating with Harold Schiff while I continued to shoot additional scenes in which Bette's character did not appear. I thought, surely, that I would get her back.

I should have remembered how Bette wriggled her way out of Josh Logan's musical *Miss Moffat*, which was still on tour, by faking a back problem. Or how she got out of an earlier Broadway musical revue, *Two's Company*, by claiming a medical disability. Instead, I preferred to recall how she'd walked off the set of *The Little Foxes* after a dispute with William Wyler—but had dutifully returned nearly a month later to do a brilliant job.

Then, on June 1, 1988, I received the following note from Bette's New York dentist, Theodore Tyberg: "Ms. Davis has lost approximately 15 pounds and now weighs 75 pounds and is therefore exhausted."

At this point, I had no choice but to pull the plug. I had meetings with both the completion guarantor and the insurance company. There was an effort to hire a replacement, Lucille Ball. We found that Lucy was in the hospital herself and near death. An MGM executive suggested Carol Burnett, but my position was that she had no box-office clout.

I argued, "Bette Davis can't sell any tickets at the movies either, but she's popular on video. Every store has a Bette Davis section. With her name on the box, we'll sell thousands of videos and recoup the studio's entire investment."

With Bette, the picture would also have a life on television and cable. I'd salvage the footage she'd shot and rewrite the script to accommodate her disappearance. Fortunately, Bette played a witch so she could transform herself into a beautiful young woman at will. Barbara Carrera who previously starred in *I, the Jury*, a film I'd been fired from, was appearing in the film playing Bette's daughter, so I switched it. She'd play the ravishing creature that Bette becomes. Everything else in the script could remain the same. We'd be back in production in ten days.

Directing Barbara Carrera in front of a blue screen
for *Wicked Stepmother*.

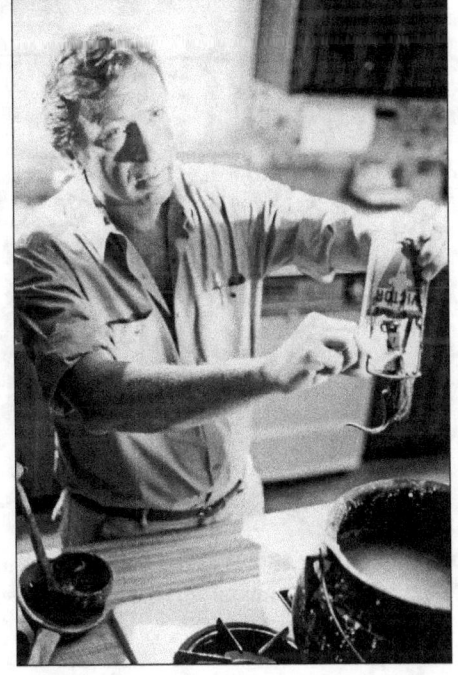

Here was a way for the insurance company and the completion guarantor to avoid eating a $2.5 million loss. If they dumped the picture, all the contracts would be honored in full and I would have been paid my entire fee, so I had nothing to gain financially. I simply wanted to salvage what I was certain would be Bette's final screen appearance and save everyone concerned from financial disaster. I was trying to create order out of chaos.

Since Bette had worked only one week—one-fifth of her commitment—she'd receive only $50,000. The rest of her salary would be plowed back into the movie to cover the cost of additional special effects.

I hate to say it, but the best parts of *Wicked Stepmother* are those in which Bette Davis does not appear. The rest of the cast was excellent. But when Bette comes on screen, her physical condition is so shocking that the audience is in no mood to laugh. Still, it would have been a shame to toss her final performance in the scrap heap. I enjoyed every minute I worked with her, and I wanted to preserve the experience.

With Colleen Camp and Barbara Carrera
on the set of *Wicked Stepmother*.

I did many interviews prior to the release of the picture after Bette went public about her reaction to the film (which she hadn't seen). Though she fabricated stories about how I'd mistreated her, I spoke of her only with admiration, emphasizing my opinion that she could make many more films and that dental problems could befall anyone at any age. I was saying what I thought she'd want me to say.

In an attempt to keep my word, I contacted Kathryn Sermak and invited her to pick up Bette's entire wardrobe from the film. It consisted of $25,000 worth of clothes that Bette would surely enjoy. I could've sold them to a celebrity gift shop, but I chose to be generous.

Eventually, Kathryn did show up to claim the garments and to inform me that Bette said, "Thanks." Then she had the nerve to add, "I hope you realize that Ms. Davis was always ready to come back—until you pulled the rug out from under her." I'm sure Bette made herself believe that. If it made her feel better, the hell with reality.

The following year I was in Tanzania on a safari when my wife Cynthia and I heard radio reports that Bette Davis had died in a Paris hospital. Apparently, her body was found to be riddled with cancer. It later became clear that when she took the medical exam as required before appearing in any movie, she'd so bamboozled the doctor that he never actually touched her. She knew that if she underwent any serious examination, her true condition would be revealed. Probably no one but Bette Davis could have gotten away with this ploy, but people were accustomed to being terrified of her. I wasn't.

Sometime thereafter, a memorial to Bette was held on a soundstage at Warner Bros. Studios. I could've attended but I thought it more proper to phone Kathryn first. I didn't want to show up if it'd make her uncomfortable. I expressed my desire to be there because of my genuine affection for Bette. Kathryn responded that she'd rather I didn't come.

I stayed away, but spent the afternoon watching a few Bette Davis movies and wishing that I'd known her in her prime and had the opportunity to direct her when she was still in possession of all her faculties. In all honesty, I had to admit that at her peak, Ms. Davis would never have appeared in one of my pictures. It was a trade-off, and I suppose I still got the best of the bargain.

Wicked Stepmother remains an entertaining little comedy with an excellent cast of players. It's far from the worst movie Bette made after her 1960s comeback with *Whatever Happened to Baby Jane?* In retrospect, even knowing what would lie ahead, I still would've made the picture with Bette. It was worth it for the memories.

When I'd complained to the producers of *Entertainment Tonight* that they'd aired only Bette's side of the story, they went back and ran a clip from her interview the following evening. In it she was a bit more generous to me. When asked what she thought of my retaining her 15 minutes of footage in the finished picture, she responded, "Mr. Cohen is a very clever and inventive fellow. I'm interested to see what he did."

The fact that she always positioned herself close beside me, held my hand and planted those loving kisses, still makes me believe that she genuinely liked me. But when her career was threatened, she thought nothing of damaging my reputation to protect her own. She was treating me like a character in one of her movies.

Doing postproduction on *Wicked Stepmother*
(Barbara Carrera onscreen).

David Rasche, Shawn Donohue and Bette Davis
in *Wicked Stepmother.*

Publicly, I never disputed her, but usually replied, "Everybody else gives Bette dinners. I gave her a job."

And that, of course, was undeniable.

Many perceived this film as being a financial failure. Apparently not. I ran into the attorney for the insurance company several years back, who informed me that he'd just received a check for $780,000 in profits. The completion guarantor, Film Finances, got a similar amount. I'm sure they've been issued additional checks since, which means they've recouped their entire investment and are happily in the black. All thanks to me. Had I simply thrown in the towel and collected my salary, the studio, the insurance company and the guarantor would have eaten the entire budget.

I said to the attorney, "Don't you think you people ought to buy me a car as a way of saying thanks?"

He immediately beat a hasty retreat.

Chapter 2
Backstory

My grandmother was a tough cookie. She had started work wrapping packages in the Ludwig Baumann Department Store on West 36th Street in Manhattan when she was 12 years old. She went on to become a store detective. I called her the Old Flatfoot.

She hated my father, who reciprocated. Every day after he left for work, she would unlock the door to our Washington Heights apartment using her own key, and enter, wearing a house dress and ready to go to work. Although she couldn't stand my dad, she did his laundry, vacuumed his floors, changed his sheets, and did his ironing. Grandma Julie put in a full day's work, then waited by the window until she saw my father arrive back in the late afternoon. She always timed it so that she left the building just as he was crossing the street after parking his car. She made certain he'd see her heading off up the block.

Dad would then storm into the apartment and bark, "Was your mother here today?" Mom would lie blatantly to his face. He'd reply that he'd just seen her going up the street and demanded to know if she had her own key. All he got were more lies. Grandma would comment, "Who does he think comes in here and cleans the place?" Clearly not my mother, who could usually be found shopping for bargains on Fordham Road in the Bronx. These purchases would usually be passed through our first-floor window and hidden under the bed so dad wouldn't see them. I always hated being part of the conspiracy.

Grandma Julie was born Julia Florence Phaelan to an Irish Catholic family. Her five brothers were tough cops, one of whom rose to the rank of captain. Another brother became an undertaker who was always amply supplied with corpses by his siblings. In those days, the motto of the NYPD was shoot first, ask questions later.

There were also several sisters in the family, but all took a back seat to Julia, who became the self-appointed disciplinarian. Though her brothers were all the size of Brian Dennehy, Julia kept them in line, often resorting to violence. According to her, she once attacked one of her brothers with the jagged edge of an open tin can when he tried to defy her authority in the household. She was nicknamed Portions because she stringently doled out the food at the table, guaranteeing that no one got more than their fair share. Her father, a veterinarian, had died prematurely after being kicked by a horse.

The tradition in those times was that grown children continued to live at home. After they married, their spouses moved in with the family.

Grandma ended up ruling this enormous roost. She was so busy bossing everyone around it was probably assumed that she would never marry—until she met Bill Collins on the boardwalk in Atlantic City. The heel of her high-button shoe became caught between the slats and this dapper gentleman came to her rescue, kneeling and undoing the buckles for her. He escorted her around town for months before she discovered that his real name was Moses Loewenstein. "Collins" was the stage name Grandpa had used when he toured the West as part of an eccentric banjo act. He and his brother Arthur had eventually become black-faced minstrels portraying Mr. Bones and Mr. Tambo, the end men who did all the jokes. (Odd, isn't it, that the grandson of a minstrel and the son of a Harlem slumlord should go on to make several black exploitation movies?)

The two brothers rode the rails, even playing a saloon owned by former outlaw Frank James. They later moved on to vaudeville, appearing on the bill with Clayton, Jackson & Durante, which all came to an end when, on her deathbed, Grandpa's mother made him promise to give up the stage. He kept his word. Much to my disappointment, he never played the banjo again. It sat in a closet in his apartment with only one string left intact. I begged him so many times to get the banjo restrung and perform for me, but it was clearly painful for him to remember the sense of freedom and joy he'd experienced during his life as a performer. He declined to talk much about his experiences on the road.

He and Grandma opened a gents' furnishings store on the then-fashionable 125th Street in Manhattan. Moe Loewenstein was such a generous soul, Grandma had to police the premises to make sure he didn't give away shirts, collars and neckties to anyone with a hard-luck story.

My mother, Carolyn, grew up stagestruck since her parents took her to all of the vaudeville shows and the latest movies. She was beautiful enough to have had a theatrical career, but my grandma wouldn't permit it. Mom did have a marked resemblance to Lana Turner, and she was always impeccably dressed and groomed.

Throughout my childhood, she loved coming back from the movies and relating the entire plot of the film in vivid detail. She could summarize an entire 90-minute movie in seven or eight minutes. It was an amazing talent, which she continued to possess until the very end of her life at the age of 88. I can vividly recall her telling me the story of *Key Largo*, *Random Harvest* and *Mildred Pierce*. Once you'd listened to her, you felt like you'd already seen the picture.

My mom was only in her early twenties when she married Irving Cohen, who would soon find employment under another name. In those days, Davega camera stores would not hire Jews.

Dad was a brilliant photographer and could have been a great success, but he was raised in the tradition that a man's labor is only honorable if it brings him constant unhappiness. It was sinful to enjoy your work. Every day had to be torture. Finally he took a job with his father, managing low-cost housing in Harlem.

During World War II, rent control came into effect. Tenants were paying $33 a month for four-bedroom apartments, while the cost of oil and maintenance skyrocketed. It was a miserable way to make a living, and dad's only happy moments were when he was out shooting with his Rolleiflex camera. It appears that I inherited my pictorial sense from my dad and my love of story from my mother.

At first, when they married, dad had moved in with Carolyn's parents and Grandma Julie did her best to make his life miserable. She even had a boxer dog that attacked him every time he entered the apartment. I also seemed to have developed an aversion to dad from birth. Every time he walked into my room I would vomit, and the smell would permeate the premises for the entire evening. Finally, he'd had enough and grabbed me out of my crib, placing my mouth under the bathtub spigot and turning on the cold water. It was described by Grandma as child abuse, but it had its effect. I never threw up again.

Finally, mom and dad struck out on their own, attempting to escape Grandma Julie. But whatever apartment they rented, she and grandpa moved around the corner. I remember Grandpa Moses as a quiet and dignified gentleman who looked like a cross between silent film pioneer D. W. Griffith and General MacArthur. I was his favorite. In later years we would watch our Brooklyn Dodger baseball games together on his small 10-inch RCA television. I loved being in his company.

The best times of my childhood were at Grandma and Grandpa's because there I was accepted without criticism. At home, dad found it necessary to take out his frustrations on us after returning from another miserable day in Harlem. There was usually an explosion at the dinner table and I'd be sent to my room where I could listen to my radio programs and read my comics in peace.

Although dad was merciless in his criticism of me, I always loved him. Somehow, I sensed his torment. His one opportunity to escape might have been being drafted during World War II, but sadly his ulcer kept him from participating in one of the great adventures of our century. With his photographic skills, he would certainly have been assigned to the Signal Corps. It would have been the most liberating experience of his life. But it was not to happen. Many of those exempted from military service stayed on the home front and amassed fortunes during the war. Not my dad, who found a way to pass up every opportunity for success.

He did nothing to encourage me in my career as a writer. When I spent countless hours in my room creating my own comic books, he'd complain, "You're only in there drawing all day because you have no friends." Yet when I brought kids to the house, he always did his best to embarrass me in front of them. Nobody wanted to come back.

He'd had a miserable relationship with his own father. There was a period of ten years during which they never spoke. Dad probably thought this was the proper relationship between father and son and was doing his best to perpetuate it. I, on the other hand, was always offering him advice, which would only serve to drive him into a frenzy. Before we sat down at the dinner table, I'd suggest that he take the phone off the hook to avoid being called by an irate tenant in the midst of his meal. He'd ignore my suggestion and then, naturally, the phone would ring bringing inevitable bad news. Someone had thrown a porcelain toilet seat out the window onto Edgecombe Avenue. I would then chime in, "I knew this was gonna happen." When he tried to reach across the table to smack me, my mother would always block the blow, sometimes with her head.

This was mom's usual practice when we rode in the car on Sundays. She'd always be seated between me and my father in the front seat of his Pontiac. I'd have the effrontery to ask, "Where are we going?" which would precipitate a tirade which usually began with the words, "You half-wit…"

The fact is dad never knew where we were going. He simply felt it imperative that we take a ride in the car on Sundays. After all, he'd been polishing it all week long. We'd drive aimlessly for hours until we found ourselves in the midst of some monumental traffic jam. Motorists would be pulled to the side of the road with steam hissing from under their hoods, and dad inevitably found it necessary to shout out the window at them, "Imbecile, get yourself a car that runs!" These unfortunates would stare at him in disbelief as we rode by.

In the city he always drove with the window down, the better to insult other motorists. "Jerk—who taught you to drive?" He had to vent his anger, and I was happy to hear someone else being called names.

Throughout my childhood I recall Grandma Julie warning my father not to continually hit me in the head. "You'll make an idiot of him," was her catchphrase. This in no way deterred dear old Grandma herself from hurling a Gerber's baby food jar halfway across the kitchen with unerring accuracy and shattering one of my permanent front teeth. Apparently, she'd taken exception to my behavior while she was feeding my baby sister Ronni and had put the first object at hand to use. When my father came home that night and viewed the damage, he simply turned to Grandma and quietly remarked, "Ma, don't hit him in the head."

Today, whenever I look at that chipped tooth in the mirror, I think fondly of Grandma.

I vividly recall buying my first Broadway theater tickets at a dollar each for balcony seats to four plays at the City Center, all to star José Ferrer. From the first row of the second balcony, I thrilled to *Cyrano*, *Richard III*, *Charley's Aunt* and *The*

Shrike, never realizing that someday I would direct Joe Ferrer in a movie.

Following my bar mitzvah at age 13, I expected to spend the rest of the summer goofing around Manhattan, but my parents had other ideas. They booked me into a summer camp although the season was half over. I resisted going, realizing that I'd be an outsider. Everyone would have picked their friends and teams would have been chosen up long before my arrival. I couldn't have been more correct. Everybody at camp hated me and I soon began plotting my escape. One night I failed to return to the bunk. Instead, I hid out in a crawl space beneath the mess hall and watched as the search slowly began for the missing camper.

Scores of flashlights were cutting through the night (which in the future would inspire shots in my movie *It's Alive*). Everyone had been awakened and divided into search parties and local police were arriving to participate in the hunt for the lost boy. Then I heard someone say that they'd have to drain the lake. All I could think of was how much money this would cost my father, so I climbed out of hiding, stumbled into view, and tried to make everybody believe that I had tripped, fallen, and blacked out.

The next day the rabbi, who was head counselor, gave me his word that he would return my father's tuition if I would only tell the truth. So I admitted I just hated it there and soon dad showed up to bring me home. We drove only a few miles before he pulled over to the side of the road and whacked the hell out of me, saying, "You're not going back to the city to go to the movies every day. You're going to Grandma Cohen's."

A chilling thought! This was his mother, a Romanian immigrant who wore too much make-up and left lipstick stains on your cheek. She was usually doused with perfume, which also turned me off. Though she was always dolled up and well-coiffed, rumor had it that she could neither read nor write. Her husband, Grandpa Sam, a fellow Romanian whom she hated, seldom spoke at all, but could usually be counted upon for a crisp five-dollar bill which would be clasped in his palm when he offered a goodbye handshake.

Actually, my tenure at their bungalow colony proved to be memorable because of a girl in the next adjoining bungalow named Joan. She was 16. She didn't have many companions to choose from, so she settled on me, spending the rest of the month of August teaching me all about sex. I guess I fell in love with her, but she warned me that she could never see me in the city. If her friends in high school knew she was going around with a 13-year-old, she'd be ostracized.

She was as good a teacher as I was an apt pupil. It would be a long time before I would have the opportunity to put my education to use again. After all, I lived with my parents, traveled on the bus or subway, and had an allowance of three dollars a week. Where was a guy to go to get laid?

My term of ecstasy with Joan was brought to a jarring conclusion when one day I stepped into the bungalow and the screen door closed silently behind me. I walked to the kitchen sink where Grandma was preparing a meal and tapped her, lightly, on the shoulder. She screamed and had a heart attack. Soon my father appeared to bring me back to the sweltering city. Another brief drive, another pull to the curb, another beating. Followed by freedom.

By the last ten days in August I was back at the movies in Manhattan again.

It was late that summer when I wrote my first piece of material and submitted it to Hollywood. It was an original routine for Abbott and Costello which I mailed to them care of Universal Studios. I never heard a word in return. It was 45 years later when I finally picked up a cassette recording of some of Abbott and Costello's classic radio programs. I was astonished to hear the exact routine that I had sent them. It'd been broadcast without my ever knowing about it. One of their writers had apparently seen my material and stolen it verbatim. I was amazed to realize that I'd been writing for Abbott and Costello when I was 13 years old. If only they'd acknowledged the material and brought me to Hollywood, I could've become the boy genius of comedy!

As it was, any inclination I had to enter show business continued to be received with scorn, especially by dad. My mother's cousin, Truman Gaige, was an actor whose only claim to fame was that he'd once roomed with Cary Grant. It was clear to everyone that Truman was gay. My father referred to him as "a fairy nice person." Any mention of my entering show

business was greeted with, "He's another Truman Gaige." I found it smarter to keep my aspirations to myself. When I began slipping out of the house in later years to do my night-club act, I never mentioned where I was going. Nor did I ever invite my parents to see me perform.

In 1959, after I'd sold a few scripts, I bought my father a color television console as a gift and had it delivered to his apartment in Riverdale. Dad just couldn't accept it graciously. "What do I need this for? Suppose something goes wrong with it? Who's going to pay for the repairs?"

I assured him that the set came with a full year's service contract included, but he still continued to grumble that there was nothing good on in color. He didn't like *Bonanza* or *The Dinah Shore Chevy Show*. Why should he be forced to watch them just because they were in color? Yet as the sole owner of a color television in the neighborhood, he became something of a celebrity. Eventually he mellowed and we became friends, and I forgave him because I realized the pain he'd passed on to me was simply his own pain.

I saw what could happen to a man if he didn't pursue his dream, if he settled for mediocrity. That's what impelled me to continue on, even when I met with so much disappointment early on, I couldn't afford to give up and live my father's life all over again.

My father died before I achieved any great success. Had he been around, he probably would have grumbled over the mansion I bought with several acres of land and 24 rooms, and he certainly would have objected to my marrying a girl from Texas who already had three small children. But I think he was on the verge of being proud of me before death overtook him.

Although only 53, he carried his disappointment heavily through the years and looked at least ten years older. He and my mother grew closer, but it all came too late. His life was winding down. As I pass his award-winning photographs that line my walls, I think of him every day and wish our life together had been more loving. Those gorgeous black-and-white studies of people and landscapes are the true soul of my father.

On the other hand, if dad had understood what I was trying to achieve and offered me his kindness and support, it might have lessened the compulsion I felt to overcome all obstacles. Thanks to him, I became immunized to criticism. Without being exposed to Dad's constant negativity, I might have given up too easily. Show business is full of rejection, but I was accustomed to that. I'm certain there are others equally talented who simply opted out after slamming into a blank wall once too often. I never gave a thought to surrendering to failure. I was also determined not to follow in the footsteps of Grandpa Moses, who had turned his back on his beloved career in vaudeville.

Chapter 3
Enter the Boy Director

"JOSEPH STALIN DEAD" read the headline in the *Daily News*. As a movie-crazed sixth grader, I could only see this newspaper as a fantastic prop. It would be central to the 8mm suspense masterpiece I would create utilizing dad's Bell & Howell camera. Espionage, betrayal and finally pursuit through the Cloisters, the reconstructed monastery the Rockefellers had erected at the highest point in Manhattan's Fort Tryon Park. For my cast I would recruit schoolmates, bribed into making their movie debut with an offer of a free comic book culled from my extensive collection. Since I had no facility for cutting, the entire film would have to be pre-edited in the camera as it was being shot. I'd shoot a wide angle, then immediately a close-up, then a reverse. I had already visualized the completed movie. All I need do was reproduce what already existed in my mind.

After years of hanging out at matinees, I had developed a near perfect eye for matching action and a sense of camera placement. What was sent back from the laboratory and threaded into the projector amazed even me! The key sequence worked on several complex levels: the Communist spy has had a change of heart since Stalin's death and now wants to destroy the crucial microfilm. He's rolled it up and secreted it in the barrel of his own gun which has now fallen into the hands of the leader of the espionage network, whom he tries to provoke into pulling the trigger. By dying, he will deny the master spy access to those crucial military secrets.

Not a bad story for a nine-year-old to conjure up. I'd sell a similar yarn to *The Defenders* 15 years later. What's really odd is that I'd inadvertently stumbled upon the actual drop site Communist agents were using in Washington Heights. High-ranking Soviet spies were eventually arrested in that very park exchanging microfilm!

Of course, hardly anyone saw my movie—already I was having distribution problems... In order to get kids to come to my house and watch it, I had to part with still more comic books. Luckily, I had an endless supply.

My father's camera operated off of a spring. You wound it up tightly and it would run for 45 seconds, which was the maximum duration of any one shot. Even then I was into quick cutting. I didn't get permission for the chase around the parapets of the Cloisters, I simply waited until the solitary security guard wasn't looking. From the outset I was stealing movies.

My mother tells me that when she took me to my very first movie, *Winter Carnival*, with Ann Sheridan, the picture was already on. It was a skiing sequence with the camera careening down a snow swept slope. I took one look at the enormous screen and all that motion and immediately began to scream at the top of my lungs. She quickly removed this hysterical 4-year-old from the theater, daring to bring me back only months later when *The Wizard of Oz* was playing. This time she took no chances and escorted me to my seat while the lights were still up. She noticed I was somewhat fearful when the theater darkened, but then as the film began, so did my lifelong love affair.

During my childhood there were two great movie chains: the RKO Circuit and Loew's—or as we called it "LOEEEZ." In those days every picture played locally on a double feature. Usually a film would open on Wednesday and play only through Sunday. On Monday and Tuesday, low-budget programmers would fill in. Westerns with Roy Rogers and Gene Autry, or crime series like *Boston Blackie* or *The Whistler*, and often a Frankenstein or Dracula film. Then on Wednesday another major studio release would arrive, coupled with a Blondie and Dagwood comedy or a Charlie Chan mystery. Usually I liked the second feature as much as the first.

Besides the two cinema palaces, there was the tiny Alpine Theater on Dyckman Street where RKO product would play a week after its initial run at the more expensive Coliseum on 181st Street. The Alpine became my favorite hangout because it hosted Warner Bros. pictures with the stars that I much preferred, like Bogart, Cagney, Edward G. Robinson and, yes, Bette Davis. When I first began going to the movies, the children's price was just 12 cents, 14 cents on Saturday. Years later when it went up to 18 cents I was outraged. All theaters programmed continuous shows without intermission. Whatever time people arrived at the theater they would simply buy their tickets and enter. A uniformed usher with a flashlight would find them a seat in the dark. They'd watch both films through and then usually exclaim, "This is where we came in."

The first movie I saw all by myself was *The Princess and the Pirate* starring Bob Hope and Virginia Mayo (with whom I immediately fell in lust). I'd also become hooked on radio dramas. There were shows especially designed for kids: *Dick Tracy*, *Hop Harrigan America's Ace of the Airwaves*, *Captain Midnight and the Secret Squadron*, *The Adventures of Tom Mix* (sponsored by Shredded Ralston) and *Terry and the Pirates*. Listening to them stimulated my imagination.

One afternoon in 1945, my programs were interrupted by an urgent bulletin: President Roosevelt had succumbed to a stroke at Warm Springs, Georgia. This was big news and I rushed out onto the street to announce it to the world. In a predominantly democratic neighborhood, this was news that people did not want to hear or believe. The response to my shouts of "FDR'S DEAD!" was usually, "Shut your dirty mouth, sonny—don't you dare say that!" Neighbors poked their heads out the window hollering at me not to spread such nasty lies. What kind of a boy was I, anyway? Apparently, FDR was immortal. We were in the midst of a war, and he was our leader. This made me a traitor.

A bunch of bigger kids on the block also took exception and began to chase me down an alley with the intention of beating me to a pulp, while none of the adults witnessing the event did anything to prevent them from meting out the maximum punishment. I continued to protest that FDR was indeed a goner and nothing they could do to me would bring him back. I was taking a tremendous pounding when someone reliable ventured outside and corroborated my story. By the time I had staggered home in torn clothes, black and blue with a bloody nose, all thoughts of becoming a future newscaster had vanished.

I was in sixth grade when one of our assignments was to read a magazine called *Consumer Reports* and select one particular product which was critiqued in the publication. We were then to prepare an oral report to present to the entire class. Naturally I paid no attention to the assignment until the morning it was due. Then, over breakfast, I simply flipped the magazine open, picked the first article at random, and began copying notes on an index card, listing vital statistics. Unfortunately, the product I had selected was female absorbent napkins. I had no idea what these things were, but I did notice that when I began my oral dissertation, our teacher's mouth was hanging open—almost to the floor—and the girls in the class were staring at me with abject horror and disbelief. I droned on and on for at least ten minutes, comparing the absorbent quality of these pads, never having the slightest inkling of what their application entailed. Finally, after finishing, I heard no questions, just gasps. It wasn't until the break between classes that one of my fellow students, Chick Kodick, took me aside and clued me in. The truth is that I got most of my sexual education from Chick, who always seemed to know the score. My report soon became the talk of the school, and I was something of a hero. Everyone thought I'd done it on purpose—although the girls in my class avoided eye contact for a long time afterwards.

Dad and I never found much time to do things together, but that changed once a television set came into our house. For years he'd resisted buying a TV, claiming, "It hasn't been perfected yet." The real reason for his reluctance was his refusal to pay $3 a month to the landlord for the privilege of mounting an antenna on the roof. Finally, when everyone else in the building already had television, he relented. Rather than getting a famous make like RCA or Zenith, dad brought home a Pilot television set, a brand nobody had heard of. Even with the tall antenna installed on the rooftop six stories above our ground floor apartment, our reception was dreadful.

In those days, the television stations in New York transmitted from different locations. If Channel 2 came in clearly, then Channel 4 had ghosts (double images). The only solution to this problem was to rotate the antenna. So if we were watching NBC and then wanted CBS, dad would send me up to the roof to swivel the pole in every direction possible until we got some semblance of a picture down in Apartment 1F. He would communicate with me by screaming out the window, "More to the right, you dummy. No, the other direction, halfwit!"

All our neighbors regularly heard me referred to as ignoramus, imbecile, and any other term of endearment that might come to mind. I'd heard it so often that it didn't bother me, but it became the talk of the building.

As months went on and the reception got no better, dad came up with the brilliant notion of mounting the antenna on an even higher pole. After all, it was the same $3 to the landlord no matter how tall the antenna was. To prevent the new elongated pole from bending in the wind, guide wires would be attached.

Of course, dad and I were to install it ourselves. And so on one fateful Saturday afternoon, we proceeded to the roof where we fastened together several more lengths of pipe and then began to hoist the entire apparatus straight up, with the safety wires dangling loosely prior to being hooked to the walls for added support.

No sooner did dad get the antenna up than it began to sway violently, buckling in the middle. Dad was gripping it with both arms, holding tight, and suddenly I saw him being propelled across the roof, first in one direction and then the other. I'd never seen his feet move so fast. It was a scene worthy of Buster Keaton. He didn't dare let go of the thing lest it topple into the street below and kill some innocent bystander or my poor mother, who had her head poked out of the window six stories below. All she heard were shouts and screams. My God, dad was headed for the edge of the roof! He was just going over when I dived at him, seizing him around the waist and adding my weight to his. We both nearly went over. Then, mercifully, the antenna stabilized. "What are you waiting for? Hook up the goddamn guide wires, moron!" was my reward.

Hours later, our duties completed, we returned to the apartment below and found the reception marginally improved. Now the ghosts were much sharper. My nightly task remained the same, constantly climbing to the rooftop to turn the antenna clockwise or counterclockwise as per the shouted commands from below. I spent as much time on the roof as I did watching television.

Dad never publicly thanked me for saving his life that day, but he never denied it when I recounted the story — which I did as often as possible.

Maybe I was an idiot as my dad so often proclaimed, but my memories are nevertheless of a happy childhood. I felt safe, well fed and optimistic about the future. Even then I saw the humor in everyone's behavior.

There was so much petty bickering over money at home that I felt badly asking for movie money. Instead, I collected empty soda pop bottles which could be redeemed for two cents apiece. During the war it was required that the metal cap also be returned in order to receive the full deposit. Sometimes the shopkeepers would try to make my life miserable, realizing that I didn't intend to buy anything.

"Those aren't our bottles!" one clerk shouted at me. To which I replied, "Gee, I'm sorry!" as I dropped all the bottles to the floor watching them shatter before dashing off down the street with the store manager in hot pursuit. I later found it quicker and easier to carry packages for customers of the local Safeway or Grand Union markets. I'd wait until some elderly woman would emerge struggling with a heavy bundle and offer to lug her purchases home. Sometimes to a sixth-floor walk-up. Usually I'd get a dime. It didn't take long to amass sufficient tips to purchase my movie ticket. To make the admission price seem more of a bargain, I'd sit through the features twice. The second time around I'd be studying the techniques utilized by Hollywood's great writers and directors.

I'd begun drawing my own comic books as a hobby and I transferred much of what I learned at the movies to my illustrations. My comics ran 64 pages in length with six panels to a page. Each was actually a camera angle. Telling a dramatic story in a cartoon form wasn't much different from presenting a story on film. I was actually creating story-boards. Oddly enough, when I finally began to direct, I didn't use storyboards, preferring to have the freedom to create in the moment.

After my Russian spy movie I didn't make many others. My interest had shifted to comedy. I'd always been the clown of the class and based most of my friendships on my ability to crack the other kids up. I might not have been the best second baseman in school, but I was certainly the funniest wise guy. Getting laughs gave me acceptance, and I started to believe I could be a professional comic.

By the time I reached my teens, I was already doing amateur shows and club dates around the city—usually talent contests for little or no pay. I'd learned where the comedians hung out—Hansen's Drug Store, next door to the Winter Garden Theater. The building directly above, 1650 Broadway, housed many of the booking agents for variety acts. Milton Berle had his office there.

I began to haunt that street corner, which was just a subway ride downtown from Washington Heights. Pocket money was hard to come by, but the B&G Coffee Shop located beside Hansen's offered the "bottomless cup"—as many refills as you demanded. Not far away at the automat I could use ketchup, hot water and plenty of salt to make myself free tomato soup. Customers would always leave saltine crackers unopened in their original wrappers. These could be crumbled up into the soup to provide some semblance of nourishment. The lemons that had been set out to supplement the tea service could be squeezed into a glass and converted into lemonade with plenty of sugar added. On occasion I would spring for a crock of baked beans or some macaroni and cheese for 15 cents, just to allow the automat to make a little profit on the deal.

I tried selling jokes to comics since I was deemed too young to be performing professionally. I'd auditioned for the *Horn and Hardart Children's Hour* but hadn't made the grade. My delivery was acerbic, and they wanted "cute." Some of the local comics paid for my jokes, most stiffed me. One threatened to throw me out of the ninth-floor window of his manager's office.

In retrospect, I'd have been better off making my 8mm movies and refining my cinematic skills, but I had to get comedy out of my system. Part of my problem was that I was too damned creative, always finding it necessary to come up with a brand-new routine. Once the jokes got laughs, I grew tired of them. Most performers did the same act for years, sometimes a lifetime. I had the delusion I was on television and needed an entirely new repertoire for each appearance. It was a case of wasted energy. I never stuck with any routine long enough to refine it to perfection.

My interest in cinema was undiminished. I saw everything. Now I could catch the movies in their first run at a downtown showcase like the Strand or Loew's State or the Roxy (where I would someday soon find employment as an usher). I had to be there opening day, even if it meant ditching school. There was usually a star-studded stage show which accompanied the film.

I saw Danny Kaye at the Roxy and sat through three straight shows. Jack Benny graced that same stage along with Rochester, Phil Harris, and his entire entourage. I remember vividly how Mr. Benny tried to play his violin throughout the show only to be continuously interrupted by Dennis Day and the others. Finally, at the close, just as Jack finally launched into his solo, the curtains behind him opened and the *News of the Day* came on screen. Benny continued to ignore this, fiddling away while the newsreel drowned him out. That's how the show ended. No bows, no goodbyes, just Jack's silhouette against the Fox Movietone News. It was a fabulous finish.

Seeing such performers live on stage proved to be more of an education than I was getting at George Washington High (the same school, incidentally, from which fellow director Samuel Fuller was expelled).

Not able to afford tickets to legitimate Broadway shows, I found a way to sneak in during the intermission. This was called second-acting. I figured that the second act always had to be better than the first. When the audience stepped outside for a smoke, I'd mingle, then help myself to a program and search for a seat that hadn't been occupied. Only occasionally was I thrown out on my ear. Actually, I preferred standing room and still do. When I'm comfortable in my expensive orchestra seat and the curtain comes up, my eyelids often droop, particularly if the show doesn't grab me.

With upwards of 50 plays running at one time, New York was a wonderland to grow up in, particularly for a star-struck kid.

It was assumed that I'd go on to college, and, to my father's relief, I managed to get accepted at City College of New York, where tuition consisted of a $15 per term bursar's fee. Still, dad had to cough up for books and carfare. But he figured that since the campus was located in the middle of Harlem, I could collect rents for him between classes. I'd be earning my keep for a change. Dad, who resembled actor Keenan Wynn, was what is commonly known as a slumlord. Although he really tried hard to make the buildings livable, it was a losing battle. Costs kept going up and rent control prevented him from making even a fair profit on his investment. Little wonder he always seemed so frustrated.

Memories of my years at CCNY always bring back a warm glow. It was there that I fully developed my love of theater, performing small roles in school productions and working as a slave doing tech work backstage. When it became apparent to me that the Dramatic Society was ruled by a small clique that would never accept me, I simply formed my own theatrical troupe, putting on plays and variety shows. I played Mephistopheles in a capsule version of *Faust* and the blind prophet in *Oedipus* under the kindly guidance of our faculty advisor Samuel Sumberg.

Each Thursday during the free period between twelve and two, I would also host a complete comedy review performed in Townsend Harris auditorium on the school campus. I'd open the show with a topical monologue based on recent news events followed by original comedy sketches in which I'd always play top banana supported by my two sidekicks: Paul Kagan (who would later become renowned as the president of Paul Kagan Associates, one of the leading research organizations in the media industry) and my other comedy partner Vic Ziegel (who would become a noted sports columnist for New York newspapers). In this era, it was unheard of for comedians to be appearing on college campuses. That all came later. I suppose I was pioneering something that could've become lucrative had I stuck with it. However, the smart material that went over so well at CCNY fell on deaf ears when it was performed in the Catskill Mountains or in the lesser nightclubs around the city.

I'd been doing club dates for some time and appearing in talent contests, teamed up with Tommy James, a heavy-set black kid who worked at the City Morgue by day. We did terrible impersonations. Tommy would announce, "And now ladies and gentlemen, Mr. Louis Armstrong." Then he would step aside as I moved to the microphone and did "Satchmo," while he glared at me with an outraged expression. Sometimes this act went over well. Often it bombed.

After that I partnered with friend Ogden Nield, appearing at the Café Wha? in Greenwich Village. Finally, I began doing a solo act at the Upstairs at the Duplex off Sheridan Square. I usually went on just ahead of a bespectacled young comedian who looked extremely unhappy to be performing at all. He never laughed at anything I said, and I swore that if I could break this guy up, I'd know I was a success. This never happened. Naturally the withdrawn young comic had to be Woody Allen.

I'd become the official master of ceremonies at all City College events and was now billed as "The Clown Prince of CCNY." Another guy I vainly attempted to amuse was the cadet commanding officer of my ROTC unit, a fellow student who really took the military life seriously. He had his hands full dealing with my pranks, but finally realized that if he'd smile once in a while, I'd probably shut up and take orders.

We both had a yen for the hot salted pretzels which the bagel man sold off a pushcart just outside the campus gate. When we'd run into each other there, he would be more relaxed and prone to laughter—and I took full advantage of the situation. I loved to break him up. The cadet's name? Colin Powell.

I was scheduled to appear in the CCNY Carnival Show, which was the big event of the school year. Comedienne Martha Raye would be the celebrity headliner, but at the last minute she canceled and I had to fill her spot. I was on for a full half hour and reached my performing peak that night, absolutely bringing down the house.

When the audience streamed out of the tent, which had been erected in Lewisohn Stadium on the campus of the City College of New York, I found myself sitting on the apron of the stage alone, a bit stunned at my own success. I looked up to

Performing at City College of New York, 1958.

see a beautiful brunette towering over me. She must have been at least six feet and had been introduced from the audience as a special guest. Stars from the Broadway stage often appeared at CCNY functions to help promote their productions. This girl was featured as Stupefying Jones in the musical *Li'l Abner*. Her name was Julie Newmar, and she had waited around especially to meet me.

I couldn't believe it as she lavished praise and even gave me her home telephone number. Wow! I soon became a regular backstage at *Li'l Abner*, where she shared a dressing room with Tina Louise. I couldn't believe they let me hang around and watch them change from their costumes into their street clothes. Dating Julie Newmar, who later portrayed Catwoman in the 1960s television series *Batman*, was the thrill of my young life.

Some months later I got a taste of reality when, while in her apartment, I noticed her unemployment insurance booklet on the dresser. *Li'l Abner* had closed, and she was at liberty. By the following season, however, she was starring on Broadway with Claudette Colbert and Charles Boyer in *The Marriage-Go-Round*.

Julie Newmar in the 1959 film version of *Li'l Abner*.

I couldn't help bragging to a friend that I was currently romancing Julie Newmar, a fact that he wouldn't believe. I took him to the stage entrance of her theater after the final curtain and waited for Julie to emerge. She wasn't wearing her glasses that night and walked straight past and into a waiting limo, ignoring me completely.

I phoned her at home later that night and she was totally apologetic. "I didn't even see you. If I had I would've taken you to the party with me."

Over the years I noted that all the really tall girls I knew had terribly bad eyesight. Maybe I should write a scientific paper on the subject.

Julie eventually went off to Hollywood to film *The Marriage-Go-Round* and we lost track of one another. Today, when I occasionally meet her at a party, she seems to have forgotten our time together. But I still retain fond memories of her as a wonderful friend. Being with her gave me the confidence to always go after the prettiest girls. That's been my policy since. Julie once confided in me, "If my father knew I was going out with a Jew, he'd kill me." I'd hear the same comment from quite a few girls in the years that followed. They'd say it, but it would never deter them from hopping into your bed. I suppose they were simply trying to be honest.

While at City College, I was thrilled to learn that the great Paul Robeson was scheduled to speak, and I canceled my own Thursday performance so I could be there to see him. At the last moment, the university withdrew permission for his appearance on the grounds that he was a Communist. This was the period of the McCarthy hearings, which most of the student body followed on a small TV screen in the basement of Army Hall.

The Cold War and the Korean conflict had the country bitterly divided. CCNY had long been tainted by association with Communists. It was even being referred to as "The Little Red Schoolhouse" and the administration was trying to reverse that image. Paul Robeson, however, decided to visit the campus, even if he was forbidden to speak. He strolled through our college cafeteria, a large, brooding figure who instantly dominated the entire room. A few of us ventured over to shake his large but gentle hand and marvel at the sound of that deeply resonant voice.

Several days later I was scheduled to emcee a school show. I decided to take on the Paul Robeson controversy in my opening monologue. When I came to the microphone, my first words were, "I want to thank CCNY President Buell Gallagher for allowing me to speak here tonight." There was a moment of silence and then a roar went up, followed by deafening applause. Even President Buell Gallagher was grinning. I commented, "He's smiling but he's burning," to still another roar. Instantly I had become the school hero.

A constant companion in the CCNY cafeteria was my buddy Herb Stempel, a down-at-the-heels army veteran who'd become a celebrity since his appearance on the NBC game show *Twenty-One*. Herb was engaged in a weekly battle of wits against Charles Van Doren for the big prize money, but he advised me that he was destined to lose. This was preordained since the show was fixed. I couldn't believe what I was hearing. Stempel told me that the show's producer, Dan Enright, was feeding contestants the answers. Even though he thought he could beat Van Doren fair and square, Herb had been instructed to miss the big question the following week. He wanted to do something about it.

Stempel had tried blowing the whistle but, so far, no one would believe him. I suggested he call the *New York Post*. I even went to the phone booth with him and stood beside him as he told his tale to a *Post* reporter—who was too afraid to write the story.

True to his prediction, Herb did lose the following week, as per instructions. Later, incidents finally precipitated an investigation of all the quiz shows and eventually, Herb's testimony made headlines. Barry and Enright's *Twenty-One* was removed from the airwaves and Herb Stempel was quickly forgotten until John Turturro played him in Robert Redford's *Quiz Show* 45 years later. But Herb was nothing like the fool he was made out to be in that film. He was as honorable as he was intelligent. One of the good guys.

Most summers I escaped the New York heat by performing as a comedian and social director in the Catskill Mountains. There are only four or five hotels left today, but in the Sixties there may have been over a hundred resorts and an equal number of bungalow colonies scattered around the lakesides of Monticello, South Fallsburg and Kiamesha, New York. There were the quality hotels such as Grossinger's and the Concord, which presented veteran headliners like Sophie Tucker and Eddie Cantor. Then there were the second and third level hotels which usually booked acts that would double or triple on a weekend. A comedian needed to own a car and be willing to drive the girl singer up to the mountains. Since I didn't drive, I had to hook up with a singer who had wheels.

A comic would usually sign with an agent for a set price. Then the agent would book him for as many shows as he possibly could manage. Some comics would triple, playing six engagements over one weekend.

Late one night, I bumped into Zero Mostel, who was doing a third show at Brown's Hotel. He went on at one o'clock in the morning and the showroom was practically empty. Even so, I felt I was in the presence of a formidable talent. He was also a fellow graduate of City College. After the show we hung out and even sang the school anthem together. Zero had been blacklisted and this was the best job he could get. But he was a pro, and he went out and did his very best under the worst circumstances. That was a lesson to me. No matter what the conditions, do the job!

I would usually sign on as emcee at some second-string hotel and then try to drum up as many outside club dates as I could. I didn't last at any one resort for an entire season. My material was too geared to topical events and satire. I was writing new material by day and breaking it in at night. Unfortunately, Catskill audiences preferred comics who told stories with the punchline in Yiddish.

After a few weeks I would usually discover another hungry comedian prowling the grounds and it would dawn on me that I was about to be canned. I'd ask the other comic what hotel *he'd* been fired from and then run over there and get his job. The hotel owners could be cruel and had no compunctions about locking you out of your room when they were through with you.

Back in the city I settled for a $28 a week job as a Roxy usher and stood inspection every morning in full uniform. Again I couldn't take the discipline and got fired for wearing brown socks instead of black. I continued to peddle fresh material to the comedians who congregated around 1650 Broadway. The problem with most performers was that they refused to try out the routine in its entirety. If the first few lines didn't get a laugh, they'd run for cover and revert to their old stuff. I kept trying to direct them, to give them confidence and the encouragement to do the entire act even if it meant going into the ground. It always took time to break in fresh stuff.

I had one final and disastrous summer as MC at Pine Hill Lodge in Mount Freedom, New Jersey (affectionately known as The Whore House). I had replaced a comic who'd been there for over ten years. He wasn't very funny, but the hotel guests reveled at throwing food at him and tossing him in the pool with his clothes on.

My first night on stage I was interrupted by two New Jersey police officers who handcuffed me in front of the audience and hauled me off to spend the night in jail—all to the merriment of the crowd. Was this show business?

Another evening I had just begun my monologue when someone jumped up and yelled "It's 8:30." En masse, the entire audience rose up and walked up the aisle into the lobby, leaving me to perform to an empty house. I couldn't figure out what happened until I followed everyone out and saw them crowded around the television screen, watching *The $64,000 Question*. A shoemaker was competing for the big prize and there was no way a young comic like me could compete with the drama being played out on that television screen. Maybe it was time to give up performing.

By then I'd completed my documentary filmmaking courses at CCNY, having studied editing under the tutelage of Gene Milford (who'd cut *On the Waterfront*). During my screenwriting course, I'd usually shown up with a blank notebook and simply ad-libbed my scenes aloud to the class. Winging it came naturally to me.

Otto Preminger visited class once but stayed only a few minutes, storming out in anger when one of the students arose to insist he was a long-lost nephew. That was the last we saw of Otto.

Saturday Review film critic Arthur Knight was another of our teachers. His book, *The Liveliest Art*, was just about the only text on filmmaking available in any bookstore. Today there seem to be hundreds, maybe thousands, of books available, and filmmaking seems to be one of the most sought after of all professions.

Chapter 4
Those Glorious Pageboy Days

Speaking of professions, I was moonlighting now as an NBC page at 30 Rockefeller Plaza.

My mother had first brought me to these studios during her brief addiction to quiz shows. She'd been picked as a contestant several times and had won a few small prizes. To her it seemed a great way to spend an afternoon at no cost except carfare and she often took me along for company. I was more or less casing the joint, waiting for the day when I'd be old enough to slip back in unnoticed and watch some of the great NBC dramatic shows in rehearsal. I'd learned that upstairs in Studio 8G, the *Philco Television Playhouse* rehearsed all weekend for a live Sunday night telecast. *The Robert Montgomery Show* rehearsed next door in Studio 8H for its Monday night presentation. On Wednesdays, *The Kraft Playhouse* was in prep on the third floor. All I needed to do was penetrate the RCA building. In those days, security was extremely lax.

I couldn't have been more than 16 years old when I began trespassing, strolling directly past the page boy in the lobby with a phony script in my hand and murmuring, "It's okay." Nobody ever stopped me or asked me what was okay.

I'd take the elevator up to nine and hurry down the fire stairs to the eighth-floor studios. Since I showed up religiously, I soon became a fixture, a familiar face following the director around the set. I recall one dour assistant director on the Robert Montgomery show who constantly seemed suspicious of me. This was young Dominick Dunne, but then he always had that suspicious look about him. At the outset of each week's show, a voice would be heard shouting, "One minute, Mr. Montgomery." The star would then appear on camera saying, "Thank you, Nick, and good evening!" Nick was Dominick Dunne.

Across the hall in 8-G, I watched Rod Steiger and Nancy Marchand rehearse the live production of Paddy Chayevsky's

Marty, and later E. G. Marshall and Eva Marie Saint blocking Chayevsky's *Middle of the Night*. Lillian Gish performed *A Trip to Bountiful* while I looked on. This was truly television's golden age. I was absorbing more here on weekends than I'd ever pick up in any directing class.

What a thrill one day when I walked into a radio studio and encountered Jimmy Stewart, bigger than life, recording a Theater Guild production. Jimmy turned out to be every bit as nice in person as the characters he played on screen. Slipping onto the set of a Ginger Rogers TV special, I ran into a surprisingly talkative Trevor Howard and chatted with him for most of the afternoon. I figured if I was seen schmoozing with the star, I wouldn't be thrown out. Nobody knew who the hell I was, but they had to assume that this jerky kid had some legitimate reason to be around.

I even ventured over to Studio 6-B, strictly forbidden territory, where Milton Berle starred in and directed his *Texaco Star Theater*, television's number-one-rated program. Here, visitors were notoriously unwelcome. Berle himself would come running up and down the aisle wearing a suede jacket with a whistle dangling around his neck and mopping his face with a towel. He was continually shouting that it was too cold in the studio and yet he kept perspiring. If Milton saw anyone unfamiliar seated out front, he'd confront them personally and demand to know their business. Then he'd invariably kick them out.

I would remain seated, a stupid kid wearing a pork pie hat, staring straight ahead and absolutely terrified as the biggest star in TV glared over at me. I refused to make eye contact and Milton never spoke a word. He would simply bypass me and move on to pick on someone else. I was never ejected from Uncle Miltie's studio. Maybe he felt sorry for me.

By the time I began working in these same NBC studios as a page boy, Milton Berle's star had faded. His weekly show had been canceled and he was seeking a comeback. The Emmy Awards were to be telecast from Studio 8-H where I was then stationed. Early in the afternoon of the show, I looked up to see Milton Berle approaching. He asked me to escort him through the studio and show him the set for that night's telecast. I guided him between the tables that had been set up to create a nightclub atmosphere and up onto the stage.

Milton Berle.

I remained beside him while he worked out what he intended to do. It was scheduled to be a brief appearance, but Milton had other plans. Once on, they'd never get him off. That night he'd deliver an astonishing performance, one of the most memorable of his career. Based on that one single shot, he was given another 30-minute time slot on NBC.

I hadn't told Milton how much he meant to me as a kid, or that I'd worked as a comic. I did, however, ask him what performer had influenced him the most in regard to his own style. Who had his idol been? He replied, "That's easy. I took my attitude from Ted Healy."

Very few would've remembered who Ted Healy was. He'd died young but had made his mark in vaudeville with an act called "Ted Healy and his Three Stooges." Yes, the same Three Stooges—Moe, Shemp and Larry. If you watch Ted Healy work in classic old movies, you can recognize the mannerisms that Berle copied and refined: the turned-up hat, the wagging cigar, the boisterous come-on.

Eventually, NBC decided to get rid of Milton Berle and assigned him to host the humiliating *Jackpot Bowling*, which was enough to convince anyone to break their contract. This was a sad lesson to be learned. When they no longer want you, they'll find a way to get rid of you.

One of my continuing duties as an NBC page had been to work *The Howdy Doody Show*, one of the most popular children's shows in early television. Howdy was marionette whose human counterpart, Buffalo Bob Smith, created and hosted the show.

Parents would bring their children to sit in the studio audience, which was known as the "peanut gallery." Once surrendering their kids, the parents would then be ushered upstairs to watch the program in a separate screening room.

Once Buffalo Bob had the kids to himself, he'd begin to amuse his camera crew by making off-color remarks. The sexual innuendos he tossed at the kids evoked howls of laughter from the exclusively male staff. I wondered what would happen if any of the parents accidentally strayed back into the room. Children's radio star Uncle Don was run out of broadcasting when, rumor has it, a microphone was accidentally left open, and he was heard to say "We're off? Good, that ought to hold the little bastards." Surely Buffalo Bob would have been drummed out of television had anyone ratted him out.

During my tenure as a page, I got to hang around with such celebrities as heavyweight champion Joe Louis, director John Huston, actresses Lauren Bacall and Anne Bancroft, and even Louis Armstrong.

One morning, resplendent in my blue uniform with its gold trim, I stepped into an elevator at NBC and found myself face to face with none other than Bob Hope. "Well Packy East,"

I exclaimed, citing Hope's name when he was an amateur boxer in his late teens. "Would you please autograph my uniform?" I thought I'd seize this opportunity to become a gag writer for "Rapid Robert."

Bob took a liking to me and invited me to a private screening of the rough cut of his newest movie, *Paris Holiday*, which was to be held that evening. He suggested that I assemble a contingent of the page staff and the guidettes, and bring them along. I must admit that Hope's movie, in which he co-starred with the French comedian Fernandel, was dreadful.

After we'd assembled in the small Fox projection room, Bob appeared for a typical introductory speech. "Before we run the picture, I've got to point out that the color doesn't match from scene to scene, a lot of the story doesn't make sense yet and the cutting is disjointed, but you've got to realize that this is—" He was about to say, "a work print" but before he could finish his sentence I chimed in, "It's a Bob Hope movie!" It got a solid laugh from the group, but not from Bob. My opportunity to write jokes for Bob Hope ended at that moment. Once again, my big mouth had gotten the better of me.

I suppose that proved my good fortune. Had Hope hired me as a gag writer, I would've become part of his anonymous writing staff rather than doing the individual work which proved so rewarding over the years.

I've talked to writers who worked for Hope and some of them described how he, on occasion, would simply toss their checks out of the second-floor window of his offices. The writers would have to scurry about the courtyard, picking up their week's wages. There were always a dozen or more writers on salary. The theory was that if there are too many writers, there are, in effect, no writers. Comedians would like to have the public believe that they come up with all the jokes themselves. A writer for a top comic is virtually an invisible man, so wisecracking my way out of a career with Bob Hope was a blessing in disguise.

How can I fail to mention a youthful encounter with Marilyn Monroe? There I was at Madison Square Garden, 20 years of age, brandishing a phony NBC press pass in an attempt to crash the opening night of the Ringling Bros. Barnum & Bailey Circus.

Celebrities were to appear as part of a charity event, and I was desperately trying to bullshit my way in. The security people at the stage door were more than a bit skeptical of my credentials. Then suddenly, all conversation stopped as the stage door opened and in stepped Marilyn. She was dressed in pink tights with matching stockings, glittering with spangles. A beige trench coat hung over her shoulders and she was flanked by bodyguards. I must say that Marilyn Monroe was not photogenic. To see her in person was to realize how truly beautiful she was. Even the camera couldn't capture her love-liness or the electricity that she generated. There was imme-diate eye contact and she walked straight up to me. "Hi," she said, in that unmistakable breathy voice. For some reason I felt completely at ease with her. "Hi, Marilyn, I hear you're going to ride a pink elephant tonight."

"I'm going to try."

"Well, don't fall off."

"I'll try not to."

The security people and the bodyguards were all kept waiting while she spoke to me just above a whisper. "So what are you doing here?"

"I'm trying to crash this party, but I'm not having much luck. Did you ever crash a party?"

"I always got somebody to take me. But I bet I could get you in."

Then she took my arm and escorted me down the passageway into Madison Square Garden as if we were old friends. Once inside she was descended upon by the Press representatives and whisked away. "I guess you're on your own now," she said, and then she was gone.

Since I had no place to sit, I had to circulate around the Garden, keeping in perpetual motion and one step ahead of the ushers. Marilyn did ride the pink elephant that night. And she didn't fall off.

My $39 a week salary from NBC enabled me to share the rent of a basement apartment on the West Side of Central Park with two of my pageboy friends. There were certain perils to living in this so-called garden apartment, which was located adjacent to the garbage room. If perchance one of us happened to leave the door unlocked, it was inevitable some tenant would open it in error and heave a large sack of refuse directly into our living room. On more than one occasion, a paper bag would come sailing in and split open spewing trash everywhere. At that point we'd have to determine who'd left the door unlocked and make them responsible for the clean-up. Such an occurrence took place while I was making out on the couch with a beautiful NBC guidette—totally shattering the romantic mood.

Even so, I loved that little basement apartment where I passed so many happy days. We often threw a BYOL (Bring Your Own Liquor) party where the price of admission was a six pack, and I've never had a better time. Everything lay ahead of us, and we had no responsibilities except to survive.

One day I was home in the apartment recovering from a terrible case of the flu. There was a polite knock on the door, and I answered it to discover one of the most beautiful girls I'd ever seen smiling at me. I couldn't have looked worse, but she didn't seem to mind. She was trying to locate a tenant who had moved out. I saw my chance and quickly invited her in for a cold drink. Marla was Greek and had only been in the country a few months. She seemed to have no guile. She was generous and openhearted, and she glowed with youthful beauty. For the first time in my life, I fell in love. She'd shown up on my doorstep like a gift from heaven. The texture of her skin and the smell of her long dark hair was unlike anything I'd experienced before. She demanded nothing and offered herself in total friendship. I'd never felt so relaxed with any woman before.

Our relationship had lasted less than a month when she came to me with the bad news—she was getting married. The fact that she'd never met the man was beside the point. Their parents were lifelong friends in Greece and had strong business ties. The groom-to-be was arriving by ship and the wedding would be in a few weeks. I couldn't believe that arranged marriages still existed, but she seemed completely content. It was not in her nature to rebel against her family. We had a few remaining days together and then she was gone, my beautiful dark-haired Greek girl. She appeared from nowhere and vanished just as quickly.

Some 30 years later I was to meet another beautiful Greek girl and fall in love all over again. This was Cynthia Costas, and I was not about to allow her to escape my clutches. Eventually we were married, and she's proved to be a most loving companion. It's not often you get a second chance in one lifetime. It seems more like fiction than fact that there is such a marked resemblance between Cynthia and my mysterious Greek girl.

Upon graduating college, I still hadn't entirely abandoned the hope of breaking through as a comedian. Then, at the moment of my biggest triumph as a performer, my career came crashing down around me. Not having an important theatrical agent, I had created one out of my own imagination. I began calling up bookers, pretending to be the non-existent "Nat Jacoby" of the William Morris Agency. Speaking in guttural tones with a slight accent, I extolled the virtues of a young comedian, Larry Curtis, definitely a star of tomorrow.

Using this subterfuge, I began to book myself into clubs. Finally I arranged for young Curtis to appear on the George Jessel telethon, which would be broadcast live from the Ritz Theatre in New York. I didn't realize I'd be slotted to appear at 11 pm on a Saturday night. This was primetime! I was sandwiched in between two very popular singers of the day, Alan Dale and Eileen Barton. This was the chance of a lifetime, and I'd written great topical material especially for the show.

That night the audience reaction exceeded even my expectations. Every joke was followed by gales of laughter and a round of applause. It was a routine worthy of Bob Hope, and when I came off stage after a huge ovation and entered the Green Room, I was virtually mobbed. "Where did you come from?" everybody wanted to know. Alan Dale was all over me, raving about my spot. I felt like a star.

All weekend long I was walking on clouds. Then Monday morning's *New York Post* hit the newsstands and with it, Barry Gray's column. He had devoted it entirely to me. It began: "Last Saturday night on the George Jessel telethon, I witnessed the most horrendous display of anti-Semitism ever permitted on the air waves."

My routine had focused on the Arab-Israeli conflict. It was an array of harmless jokes. "The Israeli Air Force... they're the ones who wear the yarmulkas with propellers." "A late bulletin... The U.S. troops have just landed on King Farouk." (Farouk was the ruler of Egypt and weighed nearly 400 pounds). Barry Gray continued with: "As the streets of Haifa flow over with Jewish blood, a young comedian attempted to ridicule a nation in mortal danger..."

I was unaware of this blistering criticism when I arrived at Hansen's Drug Store, the resident stamping grounds for comedians. Everyone turned away from me. No one would speak or look me in the eye. I'd expected a rousing reception. Certainly everyone had seen the show and heard the studio audience respond with cheers. Then somebody handed me a copy of the *Post* and it all began to sink in. What could be worse in show biz than to be labeled an anti-Semite? Many of the performers and almost all of the agents were Jewish, not to mention the clientele of the hotels and resorts. I guess I was grateful not to be beaten up, like I was the time I announced FDR's demise.

Actually, Barry Gray did beat me up pretty good. He had a daily radio program on WNEW and continued to attack me every day for a week.

I called the station and asked for the opportunity to reply, but was denied. Barry went on grinding me to dust and when he was finished, there was no chance of my ever finding anyone to book me again. Even the imaginary Nat Jacoby wasn't speaking to me! Fortunately, my employers at NBC did not connect their eager young page boy with Larry Curtis, the notorious anti-Semite, so I continued to earn my $39 weekly for what my father described as "working as an usher."

Twenty years later, as chance would have it, I was to appear as a guest on the Barry Gray radio program to publicize the opening of my film, *The Stuff*. In the course of the show, Mr. Gray asked me how I happened to become a writer and director. It was an opportunity that I'd been waiting for all my life. "It was all because of you, Barry," I replied. "You're totally responsible for my career." Naturally he asked what I meant, giving me the opening to relate the entire sordid tale. "After you destroyed my career as a comedian, I had to find something else to do with my life."

I laid it all out in detail, but Barry Gray claimed he didn't remember any of it. He seemed happy when the half-hour program was over and he could get me out of the studio.

Chapter 5
The Big Break Comes—and Goes

While laboring at NBC, I spent my lunch hours haunting the nearby offices of every television production company listed in the yellow pages. It was one blisteringly hot day in July when I staggered into the confines of Talent Associates, Ltd. They didn't have air conditioning but there were a number of huge electric fans scattered around the small lobby. Employees were fleeing their offices to stand in front of the fans and cool off. I asked the receptionist if there were any job openings. I hoped to fill out an application.

She was unnecessarily rude to me, which worked in my favor. As I headed back to the elevator, a short man in his early fifties beckoned me over. He was in his shirtsleeves with his loosened tie and the perspiration glistening on his forehead. He apologized to me for the way the receptionist had dismissed me and identified himself as Alfred Levy, the president of the company and the co-producer of *Kraft Mystery Theatre*. "What kind of job are you looking for?" he asked. I told him I would take on anything that was available. "I don't want to hear that. Tell me what you really want to do?"

I thought fast. "I want to be a writer."

"What have you written?"

"Nothing."

"Well, how do you know you can write?"

"Just give me a shot."

Mr. Levy went into his office and came back with a copy of a television script. It was something called *Too Young to Go Steady*, and it was to be a half-hour series starring Tuesday Weld, with Don Ameche playing her father. "Read this and see if you can come up with something like it."

Two days later I again appeared at Mr. Levy's office, and he was kind enough to see me. "Have you got a question?" "No," I replied. "I finished the script."

He seemed astonished that I'd written a half-hour tele-play in 48 hours. I said I'd call him the following week, but he replied, "If you could write it that fast, I can read it faster. Call me tomorrow."

The next day he was encouraging, but this wasn't the direc-tion they were going in. He did say that the writing was prom-ising and offered me another chance. This became the procedure for months, my writing totally on spec and submitting endless material to Mr. Levy, who in turn rejected everything but not without praise. He once announced in front of his entire staff, "This kid writes dialogue like Chayevsky, and he's got story ideas like David Swift."

Still no pay, but gradually I wore him down. I could see he was starting to feel guilty, which I'd been counting on. I always remained cheerful and willing and sure enough, not long afterwards he handed me a copy of an Evan Hunter book called *Killer's Choice*, one of the first of his 87th Precinct novels, all written under the pseudonym of Ed McBain. He asked me to come up with an original story and teleplay based on the characters in the book and I'd be paid a whopping $1,500.

I immediately went back to NBC and quit my job on the page staff. They were ready to fire me anyway for clowning around and bringing the guided tour down onto the set of the *Hallmark Hall of Fame*. When I told the uptight page super-visor I was now writing for primetime, he turned several shades of purple.

The response to my first draft was terrific. I was immedi-ately accepted into the fold and finally introduced to producer David Susskind, who was Mr. Levy's partner on *Kraft Mystery Theatre*. My script was put into rehearsal and telecast live from the Brooklyn Color Studios, starring Ed Herlihy, Joan Cope-land and Salome Jens. By now I'd gone home and flashed the paycheck to my father, who didn't quite know what to say. He'd spent years trying to discourage me. Now he was merely silent. I don't know why but I felt sorry for him. Putting me down had been one of his favorite pastimes.

The local newspapers got wind of the fact that an NBC page boy had written a teleplay and my photograph soon appeared in both the *Daily News* and the *New York Post*. Mom and dad didn't much like the article because they were described as a middle-aged couple living in Riverdale.

Nearly 40 years later I would go on to write two more adaptations of the McBain characters for NBC as Sunday Night Movies, *87th Precinct: Ice* and *87th Precinct: Heatwave*. I only took these jobs because it amused me to find myself back on the same old turf after so long.

The great thrill of writing a live television show was going to the studio and seeing all the sets constructed just as you'd imagined them and actually being an active part of the rehearsal process. You'd have to write and rewrite all the way up to airtime because after the final run-through, the show would be either too long or too short and had to be padded or cut. Unlike moviemaking, the producers needed to keep you around and you always felt welcome.

During rehearsal the leading lady happened to mention that her brother was also a writer. "Oh," I replied smugly. "What's he written?"

"*All My Sons*, *Death of a Salesman* and *A View from the Bridge*."

Yes, Joan Copeland's brother was Arthur Miller. That certainly put me in my place.

My next TV script, an adaptation of the novel *Night Cry* by William L. Stuart, had even more interesting casting. While the lead was played by Jack Klugman, the whole show was stolen by an offbeat character actor making his first appearance on nighttime television. He was portraying a sleazy underworld figure, a petty informant, who tries to shake the lead character down. When the show went off the air, our control room at the Brooklyn Studios was flooded with calls, one of them from Jack O'Brian, the columnist from the *New York Journal American*, who proclaimed this actor the most fascinating underworld personality since Peter Lorre.

The next day, O'Brian's full column was devoted to Peter Falk. The producers of a movie called *Murder, Inc.* were also watching that night and immediately hired Peter to play the role of Abe Reles in their film, for which he'd eventually win an Academy Award nomination. Jackie Gleason saw my show and cast both Falk and Klugman to play kidnappers who'd abducted him on a CBS special, *The Million Dollar Incident*.

Since *Kraft Theater* was live, Peter actually never saw himself on the air. He contacted me at Talent Associates a few days later and asked if he could view a kinescope of the show and copy down some of the dialogue. He wanted to use the scene as an audition for membership in the Actors Studio and he'd lost his script. I arranged it, and a few days later Peter called to tell me that he'd failed the audition.

My very next assignment for David Susskind was to sit in on a rehearsal of another live television play with the prospect of taking over and rewriting it.

I couldn't believe Susskind would bring in smart-ass kid Larry Cohen to rewrite J. P. Miller, an acclaimed playwright who'd just scripted *Days of Wine and Roses*. Of course, nobody gave Miller any hint as to why I was present at the reading. I felt rotten about it. Early on I had begun to see how things worked and how disposable even established writers could be.

David Susskind was a volatile personality with a marvelous gift of gab. He was less of a creative producer. Susskind could easily mount a remake of any established play or movie, but he wasn't facile at developing original material. For a while, he had me exhuming old properties that belonged to MGM Studios such as *Meet Me in St. Louis*, *Mrs. Miniver* and *Valley of Decision* to be rehashed as lousy TV specials. When I noted that none of them could be made as well as the originals, he responded that they didn't have to be. The idea was that they could be sold to a sponsor. Good or bad wasn't even a consideration.

Susskind and I did not get on. The vast majority of his staff were women and his story editors, Audrey Gellen and Jacqueline Babbin, soon took a dislike to me. Talent Associates had been attempting to get a weekly series on the air for years, but nobody employed there had a clue as to what made a series work.

How could they? They didn't like series television and they didn't watch those kind of shows. I suppose I never should've pointed that out because my insolence was not forgotten. Susskind's hatchet women came after me with a vengeance. Al Levy tried to protect me. After all, I was his protégé, but suddenly all opportunities to write seemed to dry up. I became Mr. Levy's $200-a-week development guy. I finally did manage to script a

David Susskind.

half-hour episode of Roald Dahl's fantasy series *Way Out*. It turned out to be the most widely remembered segments of the series, and somewhat of a classic. It was called "False Face" and dealt with an actor who specialized in playing grotesque roles on stage. He is about to open in a production of *The Hunchback of Notre Dame* and wants to pattern his Quasimodo on some real person, so he tours the Bowery, studying the faces of derelicts until he finally finds who he considers to be the ugliest man on earth. He brings the unfortunate creature back to the theater and applies his own makeup to copy the fellow's looks to absolute perfection, then takes to the stage on opening night to thunderous applause. But upon returning to his dressing room, he finds himself unable to remove the makeup. It is stuck

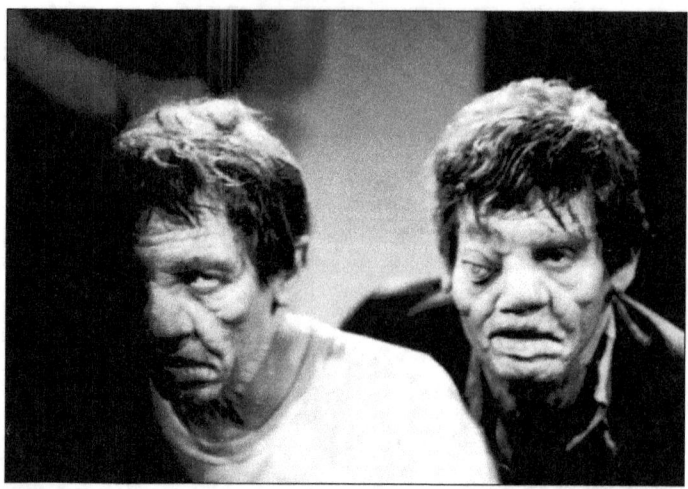

"False Face."

solid to his face. He tears at his own flesh trying to remove it, and then, in a panic, rushes back to the flop house where he had first seen the derelict. The homeless man is lying face down on a bunk as the actor seizes him, shaking him and screaming, "Give me back my face! Give me back my face!" He then rolls the derelict's body over, only to see that he now possesses the actor's handsome features. Worse yet, the derelict is dead.

As you may gather, I'm extremely proud of this show. It was chilling and well acted, and make-up wizard Dick Smith (who later did the effects for *The* Exorcist) created a memorable monster face which he later marketed as a Monster Make-Up Kit. An entire generation of young make-up wizards first cut their teeth on this kit as children.

But even this success couldn't put me back in the good graces of the two story editors who'd already brought a quick end to my meteoric rise in television. Al Levy still kept me on as his sounding board. He always described himself as a dying man, which was a self-fulfilling prophecy. He'd married a much younger, quite lovely woman named Ruth, but did not accompany her on ski vacations and the like. He talked about leaving her plenty of money when he died, which seemed to be his primary goal.

Though he and Susskind had once been very close and shared the same office, they were currently situated at opposite ends of the hall and seemed to have little to say to one another. Susskind was now a self-styled celebrity and appearing on talk shows seemed to be as important to him as producing good drama.

Without Al's intervention, I surely would have been fired from Talent Associates. As it was, I was offered only odd jobs, such as attending the 1958 opening night of the Betty Comden and Adolph Green show at the Golden Theater and escorting them in a limo to a New Jersey studio, where they'd appear live on Susskind's *Open End* TV program. Many of their friends showed up to watch the telecast and, afterwards, Susskind instructed me to lead the entire entourage to Billy Gwam's Chinese restaurant in the mid-50s for an after-show party. He would join us later.

A parade of limousines carried us all to the restaurant where I suddenly found myself as the host, entertaining such guests as Jule Styne, the composer of *Gypsy* and movie stars Margaret Leighton and Laurence Harvey. British director Peter Glenville was also in attendance along with other prestigious figures of stage and screen.

There I sat in the center of the table, ordering lavishly from the menu, selecting wines and holding court. Nobody could figure out who the hell this kid was, but after a few drinks I relaxed and began playing my role with panache. I was trying to look like I'd done this before. Actually I had about seven dollars in my pocket and David Susskind had still not made an appearance. I wondered who was going to foot this enormous bill. And still the liquor flowed and the parade of Asian delicacies continued to appear.

Finally I confided to Jule Styne, "I've got to find Susskind because I can't pay this bill."

Jule began questioning the other guests, hoping someone would have a clue as to David's whereabouts. Maybe he'd picked up a broad. Word filtered back to try Reuben's Delicatessen on 59th Street, which was open all night. (Closed not long afterward by the Health Department, this was the eatery where the Reuben sandwich originated.)

Excusing myself, I went to a phone booth and dialed Reuben's, finally getting Susskind to the phone. I have no idea why he chose to miss his own party, but he finally appeared just in time to grab the check. I've never been called upon to host such a gala event since. As the chic crowd departed, they all thanked me profusely, still unsure of my identity.

In all the time I knew him, David Susskind gave me only one good piece of advice. "Don't change your name. You'll always be ashamed of yourself later on if you do."

So I remained Larry Cohen, and for that I thank him.

I survived on my weekly paycheck from Talent Associates but also accumulated a few additional credits as a writer. I kept running into old friends who'd demand, "When's your next show coming on?"

I had nothing to announce. In some ways it was worse than when I'd been on the page staff. Having had so much publicity upon my writing debut, I couldn't just go back to being an usher at NBC again. After all that hoopla, how could I take an ordinary day job?

Even with all its intrigues, there were certain perks at Talent Associates. The girls! The place was crawling with women and the majority of them seemed to be shacking up with Susskind, who had a bizarre relationship with his wife.

I'd begun dating a few of the girls in Susskind's office, many of whom lived in the suburbs. Occasionally they'd tell me they were staying over in Manhattan and that I could meet them at some hotel suite. I'd find them waiting patiently for me and they'd order me room service and invite me to spend the night. It took me a long time to realize that Susskind had departed shortly before my arrival and that I was getting what was then commonly known then as "sloppy seconds." Whether David knew I was sleeping with his girlfriends or not, I'll never know but soon I'd be replaced on his staff by a bright young newcomer named Bob Rafelson, later the director of *Five Easy Pieces*, who would henceforth develop the new programming for the company and keep his hands off David's women. I was out of a job, and with no prospects of selling a script.

What was left but to go into the army? I owed the government six months of active duty under my Reserve agreement.

I'd been fortunate to join a Reserve Unit which exempted me from being drafted. At the time, it was virtually impossible to get into one of these units. I'd journeyed down 42nd Street and Ninth Avenue to the Reserve Headquarters and made a pitch to a civilian in charge. He was a heavy-set Italian fellow, and he was totally unresponsive until I mentioned I was a writer. "Is that so? I'm a writer, too. I wrote two books. They didn't sell, but I wrote them." He reached into his desk drawer and took out a novel entitled *The Dark Arena* which he handed to me. He wanted my opinion on it. Suddenly we were brothers. I did read his book, and it was pretty damn good. After that we had many conversations about the hardships of writing. Not only did he get me in the Unit, but he also told me I needn't show up every Monday night for drill. He was in charge of keeping the attendance records and would simply sign me in. Later he asked me if I cared to attend summer camp for two weeks of rigorous training. When I replied that I'd rather not, he found a way to slip my name out of the files and then replace it at the end of the summer.

Once he called me up and asked me to join him for lunch at the Port Authority Bus Terminal coffee shop. It was there that he told me he'd been offered the chance to write a porno movie. It would put several thousand dollars in his pocket, but he was afraid it'd ruin his reputation. I told him to write it under another name.

Years later, when I got to Hollywood and created my first television series, *Branded*, I immediately thought of calling my old pal and having him come out. I could throw a few jobs his way. But Mario had a wife and kids and a steady job working for the Department of the Army. Suppose I gave him false encouragement and ended up ruining his life? It was too big a responsibility to assume and so I left him alone. A few months later I came across his feature article in *The New York Times* magazine section about Italian Americans and their association with organized crime. A year later I read that his new book had been optioned by Paramount Pictures. And Mario Puzo went on to become known throughout the world as a best-selling novelist. Just think… if I'd dragged him out to Hollywood to write a Western series, it's possible *The Godfather* might never have been written.

Years later, Mario and I were to meet again on the beach at Malibu where we were both renting homes. He had leased the biggest house in the Colony with a tennis court. It was always overflowing with people, wining and dining and watching sports on television. They came and went, and even Mario didn't know who most of them were. But he remembered me well and we became even better friends. I even introduced him to his lifelong attorney, Bert Fields, who represented me at the time.

Mario was struggling with his latest novel, *Fools Die*, and he decided to use my wife Janelle's name as the principal female character, a beautiful but cold-blooded lesbian. Mario scribbled in the autographed copy he signed for us: "To Janelle, who gave me the name, but I swear not the character. Love, Mario."

Puzo now had a couple of secretaries and an office to work in, but the juices didn't flow as they had when he was writing his original novels in the kitchen of his home in Bayshore, Long Island. When he was working on the screenplay for *The Godfather Part II*, he'd hike down the beach and ask me for feedback. "I'm trying to come up with something like the horse's head in the first book. Michael Corleone has gotta pay back this U.S. Senator who's giving the family grief. We need a payoff, a shocker!"

I didn't have any really clever ideas, so I came up with a pretty lame one. I suggested that the senator wake up and find himself in the sack with a dead hooker, which is exactly what was used.

It was at Fort Dix, New Jersey, during my basic training, that I first met Jim Dixon, who'd soon become a good friend. At first, I couldn't stand him. He was constantly harassing me, driving me nuts and enjoying it. If we went for a ten-mile hike, Jimmy would somehow position himself in the ranks behind me, and after a few miles I'd suddenly feel my entire 40-pound backpack fall off with my mess kit and all my other equipment scattering in every direction. It was just another prank from that freckle-faced Irishman whom I nicknamed The Dalmation. He called me The Centipede because I seemed to be walking in two directions at once in the ill-fitting army boots they'd issued me.

Longtime Cohen associate James Dixon in *Wicked Stepmother*.

The fact was, those boots rubbed my feet bloody, and when the unit marched off on a 12-mile hike with full gear, I knew I'd never make it. After an hour of agony, I dropped out of formation and hid in the bushes. Once the unit had gone, I emerged and hailed a passing taxi—climbing in with rifle, pack and helmet. Within a few minutes, the cab had caught up with the unit and passed it. Jimmy Dixon spotted me riding by and nearly collapsed with laughter. I reached the final destination of the march long before my troop and took a nap in the nearby woods. When the company arrived, I rejoined them, and trucks mercifully showed up to carry us back to the base. Pulling that number got me Jimmy's respect.

But it wasn't until the day when we were working KP together, hosing out garbage cans, that Jim revealed he'd worked for the Authors League and that he was deeply interested in show business. When I explained that I was a writer with a few TV credits, our friendship was immediately cemented. And it has lasted for 45 years. I couldn't have made most of my movies without Jimmy's constant support. He was always there with his humor, his wisdom and his ability to get along with people. In addition, he's proved to be an excellent actor and a gifted screenwriter.

Chapter 6
Early Days in Hollywood

On my first trip to the West Coast, I made my home at Hollywood's Montecito Hotel, which charged only $150 a month for a very charming room with full maid service. I truly loved being in the company of all the celebrities that lived there. The Montecito was the headquarters for New Yorkers who were only on the West Coast for a brief stay.

Irish playwright Brendan Behan instantly became a pal when we met poolside one afternoon. After his swim, he'd slip into a robe, strip off his swimsuit, and allow everything to hang out, arousing numerous complaints, to which he responded, "Christ, in Ireland even the nuns take off their wet suits on the beach." Brendan had the most oversized navel I'd ever seen on any human being. It was easily the size of a golf ball. I tried not to stare.

He was a warm-hearted and generous fellow who loved to gab. One day, driving up Cherokee Avenue to the hotel, Brendan turned to wave hello to me and smashed his car straight into a telephone pole. Somehow, I felt to blame.

Carroll O'Connor became another buddy, but I'll swear that in these days he spoke with an affected British accent. He'd been doing classical plays and hadn't yet entered his Archie Bunker phase. Martin Balsam was staying there while shooting *Psycho* and ruined the movie for me by telling me the ending. Mel Brooks was always around, usually in a sour mood and perpetually arguing with the front desk. I even ran into Percy Kilbride (Pa Kettle) in the elevator and Tuesday Weld was the talk of the place — a 16-year-old shacking up with veteran actor John Ireland. Elderly Oscar winner Paul Lukas amazed me at the pool, pulling on a bathing cap and swimming a hundred laps. Every day brought new friendships.

One resident in particular showed me a great deal of love and kindness. Her name was Siri, and she was a legendary New York showgirl who'd starred at Billy Rose's Diamond

Horseshoe, where she'd been billed as "Siri, The Six-Foot Swede."

For some reason, tall girls seem to take a liking to me. Siri must have been 20 years older than me, but she'd kept herself in fabulous shape. She'd also undergone a very primitive version of breast implant surgery. Her breasts were massive, but when she took me to bed, she always begged me to be gentle and not to squeeze. Apparently, they hurt like hell. Touching her breasts was like caressing two enormous grapefruits with nipples on them. And, of course, they never moved.

At the same time she was seeing me, Siri was also dating Bruce Cabot, who'd starred in the original *King Kong*. I'd see her one night and Bruce Cabot would make off with her the next. She was another of those gals who told me that her family would disown her if they knew she was sleeping with a Jew—although it didn't seem to inhibit her any.

I wish my career in Hollywood had progressed as well as my love life. I was still taking the bus to downtown Los Angeles to collect my weekly unemployment insurance. Somebody in the hotel finally sold me a car for $50. It was a 1941 Ford with Merc-O-matic shift—whatever that meant. Hell, I couldn't even drive an automatic transmission. A former friend from the NBC page staff, Curt Sanders, took me to the parking lot at the Hollywood Bowl during the afternoon when no one was around to teach me to drive the damn thing—with disastrous results. Then Peter Falk reemerged in my life and offered to buy the car, which could have been considered a collector's item. It was perfect for the kind of roles Peter was playing in movies at that time. Humphrey Bogart would have looked fine climbing out of this vehicle. It was pure film noir.

I might've learned how to drive if my father hadn't suffered a heart attack. I rushed back to New York but got there too late. Dad had never been diagnosed with heart problems, but it was the familiar story of a man getting up to shave in the morning and collapsing in the bathroom. He struggled for a few hours but couldn't hold out. He was only 53 when he died. For years, dad had suffered from ulcers and the treatment at that time was to prescribe cream wafers, which the patient would take several times a day to line his stomach. They also advised eating as much ice cream as possible, and my mother would always serve him up a pint just before bedtime. I'm sure it was the cholesterol that killed him. I've never had much faith in doctors since.

I'd fled from Hollywood after eight months having earned a grand total of $350 for a story soon to be produced on Dick Powell's *Zane Grey's Theater*, a 30-minute Western anthology. I wasn't even considered competent enough to write the teleplay, so they simply bought my plot idea and gave it to other writers. There was no reason to rush back to Los Angeles and there was my family to consider. My mom and sister needed me.

Eventually, I obtained an east coast assignment writing a one-hour teleplay for the *U.S. Steel Hour*. It was a semi-autobiographical drama about becoming a comedian in the Catskills. The program was produced by the Theater Guild, and they were clearly concerned that the characters and their background not be too Jewish. To portray me they hired Keir Dullea, who later gained fame as the star of *2001: A Space Odyssey*. You couldn't find a more gentile young man.

Keir was a wonderful guy and we got along famously. But he was simply miscast. The female lead, a singer who worked at the hotel, was portrayed by Nancy Kovack, who later gave up her acting career to marry symphony conductor Zubin Mehta.

The one gesture toward authenticity was the addition of Henny Youngman, the famous stand-up comic, in the leading role. Henny played a broken-down comedian who can no longer find a job and, in desperation, ends up stealing the young comedian's act. The show was produced live, and everyone was concerned about whether Henny could learn an entire hour's worth of dialogue. Henny surprised everyone and gave a wonderful performance, earning an excellent review from *The New York Times*, despite one major flub. During the live telecast, Henny entered the same set in Act III as he had in Act I. He drew a blank and began doing the first act's dialogue all over again. In the control room, director Tom Donovan doubled over in agony. An ulcer attack. Then suddenly, Henny snapped out of it, picked up the correct lines, and all was saved.

It was a bittersweet story of a young man's disillusionment with show business and the shattering of his dreams. I suppose it marked my decision to bury any last hopes of becoming a performer.

I was able to eke out a living as a writer on a few more assignments. I got paid, but nothing got produced. Much of my time was spent protecting my mother against the formidable Grandma Julie, who was attempting to move back in after dad passed away. Carolyn had always been under someone's thumb all her life. Now, for the first time, she had the chance to be her own person. I'd hoped she would get a job, preferably something related to show business, which she loved. At work she could meet new people and socialize. She was only in her mid-forties and extremely attractive and she deserved to have a life. Unfortunately, she chose to take over my father's Harlem real estate and manage the buildings. This put her in contact with a few superintendents, several plumbers, and hundreds of disgruntled tenants.

I refused to let Grandma dominate my mother's life as she had before, and finally had to physically eject the old lady from our Riverdale apartment. It was painful to do because I suppose I loved Grandma more than anybody else in the world. She was the only person who'd always given and never asked for anything in return. Even when I finally became successful and tried to slip her a few dollars, she'd never accept anything. Every holiday gift I ever gave her was found after her death in its original wrappings, stored in bureau drawers. She'd never opened or used anything. I suppose she felt they were too good for everyday use.

Chapter 7
Starting From Scratch

I could only imagine dad's comments if he'd lived to see me back on unemployment insurance.

After gaining notoriety as the NBC page boy who'd written several teleplays, I had to face it: I'd had several big chances and had blown them all. I'd signed with the William Morris Agency. The placard in their lobby proudly boasted "Offices in New York, Los Angeles, London, Paris, Rome." I was suddenly out of work in five cities at once. Then Nikita Khrushchev and President Kennedy came to my rescue. The Berlin wall was erected and JFK activated the Reserves.

Heretofore, thanks to Mario Puzo, I'd avoided Reserve meetings and summer camp. But the notice to report for active duty finally reached me and I headed down to Fort Eustis, Virginia, near Colonial Williamsburg, where I was assigned to join a unit of army stevedores. Since there was nothing for the Reservists to do, they had them loading and unloading the same ship day after day.

By the time I arrived on base, the crisis was over and there were rumors that the units would all be going home. It took JFK eight months to get around to admitting he'd acted hastily. I checked in with the first sergeant only to learn that my orders had already been revoked. Unfortunately, it was too late to make an escape. My induction was in late December, and I quickly learned that the Protestant chaplain on the post was rehearsing a Christmas pageant. I rushed over to the chapel and presented my credentials. Perhaps I could help write the holiday show.

Chaplain Boggs had more than that in mind. He was preparing a weekly radio program to be broadcast locally and had me assigned on temporary duty so that I could be his personal scriptwriter. I remained on Temporary Duty for the next eight months, still assigned to a Christmas pageant. I actually spent much of that time in a tiny office in back of the chapel, turning out segments of *The Defenders*, the Emmy-award winning CBS dramatic series.

I had submitted my first storyline on spec. It struck a responsive chord with Reginald Rose (writer of *12 Angry Men*) and David Shaw, who were the showrunners. I nearly lost the job when my agent started hassling them over the money. Thankfully, my mother stepped in and ordered the Morris office to accept the offer. Reggie and David fully understood I was in the Army and arranged meetings so that I could go AWOL on Fridays and reach Manhattan for a story conference in the late afternoon.

Life at Fort Eustis offered other welcome diversions, but not with the girls at William and Mary college, who scrupulously avoided dating military personnel. They'd always spot you by your army shoes. Soldiers were considered a sub-species. This, however, did not apply to the local housewives, many of them only in their late twenties, who drove around the army base throughout the day, picking up likely prospects and bringing them home while their husbands were busy at the office.

I admit I felt guilty being taken into some poor guy's bedroom while he was out there making a living. But these beautiful, well-groomed women were virtually irresistible. Whenever possible, I avoided meeting their children, who wouldn't get home from school until later. Several of the ladies wanted me to join them for dinner with their husbands. I had the sneaking suspicion some of these gentlemen knew the score.

It was difficult to avoid such a relationship once it began. You'd be walking across the base and have one of the ladies pull up beside you in her Cadillac convertible. "Hi, Larry, hop in." How could a mere private first-class refuse?

I finally broke off all relationships when the opportunity came to join a touring show. A production of the musical *Once Upon a Mattress* was being mounted to play at bases throughout the south. I was offered the pantomime role of "the mute king," which had been originated by Jack Gilford on Broadway. I was thrilled to find Mr. Gilford's name stenciled in the lining of my costume, which had been rented from New York.

Another member of our cast was Jack Carradine, son of John Carradine, who would shortly change his name to David

Carradine and become a television star in *Kung Fu* and ultimately would star in one of my films. Jack was also working for Chaplain Boggs, painting scenery and doing minor repairs. He'd survived a court martial for stealing from the PX and had spent a great deal of his time on the base at the dentist's, getting an entire new set of teeth, courtesy of Uncle Sam. His wife, Donna, had just presented him with a baby daughter, Calista, whom they carried around the base in an apple basket.

Our tour of the Southern bases was an unforgettable experience. One evening, during a thunderstorm, all the lights failed, so the soldiers and their families, who carried flashlights, turned them on the stage. We were able to perform the balance of the production thanks to them. When the silent king finally spoke at the conclusion of the show, I made him sound exactly like the comedian Ed Wynn, which brought the house down. A few years later at 20th Century Fox, I would appear in a television pilot for *Vacation Playhouse* playing opposite Ed Wynn and the legendary Ethel Waters. The producer had heard me do my Ed Wynn imitation at a dinner party and insisted I come to the studio and audition for the star himself. They'd been seeking an actor to play Ed Wynn as a young man, and I was the only one who could come close.

When I effected his high-pitched idiotic delivery, Ed Wynn interrupted me, informing me that I was doing the "perfect fool," but that he was now a serious dramatic actor. Of course, he still sounded exactly the same. Still, I got the job, and I must have been more than competent because the entire cast and crew gave me a round of applause every time I did a take. I was so good, in fact, that at the showing of the pilot, most of the audience thought that Ed Wynn had dubbed my voice. My imitation was so perfect they couldn't imagine it wasn't him.

I recall the director, Don Taylor, approaching me on the set during filming, whispering, "The voice is great but ease up on the trembling." I inadvertently was imitating the slight tremor that Ed suffered in his later years. Ed pointed this out himself one day while complimenting me, "Oh, you've really got me down perfect now... even the shaking." Needless to say, I eliminated the shaking from then on. My experience in the army production of *Once Upon a Mattress* had paid off.

When JFK finally released the Reserves from active duty, I returned to New York to find regular employment, not only on *The Defenders* but also on *Espionage* and *The Nurses*, other shows produced by Herbert Brodkin. After writing three episodes of TV's hottest show, I was suddenly rolling in dough. I thought it was time to return to Hollywood, but when I arrived, the William Morris Agency informed me that I'd come at a very bad time. They claimed that all the TV assignments for the season had been filled.

I'd just about given up when I received a phone call from a stranger named Peter Sabiston. A mutual friend, writer James Lee, who had penned one of off-Broadway's first big hits, *Career*, had informed Peter that I was a good writer who might need help. Sabiston asked if he could take me to lunch. He showed up driving a beige Bentley and looking much like Ray Milland. It turned out this dapper fellow was the second-ranking amateur tennis player in Los Angeles and knew just about everybody. I gave him permission to find me some jobs, which he quickly accomplished. By the end of the week I had four assignments, several of them on shows that were packaged by William Morris.

I returned to the Morris office and again inquired about openings on the very shows that had already hired me. When the agents assured me they were all "locked up," I broke the news that I already had jobs on all these series—and fired them!

In no time at all, Peter Sabiston had me up for feature work and television pilot episodes. We would usually meet at the Beverly Hills Hotel's Polo Lounge in the late afternoon and take a conspicuous table. Producers and network executives would stroll in, spot us, and invariably end up offering me a job. For years I'd been pushing on doors trying to get them open, only to find out that all you had to do was pull. I wasn't chasing the offers any more, they were coming to me. From then on, the magic never stopped.

For the next 35 years I would never be without employment, and I could pick and choose what I wanted to do. All that time, Peter Sabiston remained with me, providing excellent advice and good luck, as well as consistent friendship. God bless the day he walked into my life.

Chuck Connors in *Branded*.

My Hollywood career took off for better or worse in 1964 with the sale of my first television series, *Branded*. I'd soon become the busiest writer of TV pilots in Hollywood. Of course, with success, the quality of my work would severely diminish. The problem with any series is that it's a variation of the same theme week after week, and eventually your writing suffers from repetition. Being the showrunner on a television series also entails revising everybody else's material. Some head writers become completely obsessed with the belief that they're the only ones capable of scripting the show. Writers often complain of the callous way they're treated by directors and producers, but no one can be as cruel as another writer. It's often the case of ego out of control. Not only must every line be revised, but credit must be taken as well.

It never interested me to rewrite anyone. My head was always overflowing with original ideas, so why borrow from others? With *Branded* I'd be the story editor responsible for overseeing all the scripts. There'd be virtually no prep time because the show would come on the air mid-season and no pilot was actually filmed.

The show was bought solely on the basis of a six-page treatment plus the drawing power of its star, Chuck Connors, who'd had a prior success with *The Rifleman*. It began with a meeting I had at ABC in their small upstairs offices at Hollywood and Vine. I'd come to pitch a television series to Harve Bennett but didn't have anything in particular in mind. While sitting in the waiting room, I picked up a catalogue of old 16-millimeter films available for rental and focused upon one in particular, *The Four Feathers*, an Alexander Korda Production which dealt with a young Englishman being labeled a coward and his efforts to erase that stigma through acts of heroism. By the time I walked into the meeting I'd concocted a fully developed Western series about a cavalry officer who is the sole survivor of an Indian massacre. He is branded a coward and then roams the West attempting to regain his reputation by performing acts of bravery.

As it happened, ABC did not have the opportunity to buy the show because my highly inventive agent, Peter Sabiston, took a brief outline he'd badgered me to write to Goodson-Todman Productions, a company best known for producing game shows. They'd had prior success with a half-hour western entitled *The Rebel* which starred Nick Adams. They, in turn, rushed the outline over to Procter & Gamble, who owned a time period on NBC on Sunday nights between 8:30 and 9 pm.

In those days, powerful sponsors controlled specific time slots in which they could program whatever they chose. P&G's slot immediately preceded *Bonanza*, one of the most popular programs on the air, and the lead-in for their time period was *Walt Disney Presents.*

P&G agreed to program our show if we could deliver Chuck Connors, who quickly signed on for the then unheard-of fee of $10,000 per half-hour episode. It's a ridiculously low salary now, but in those days it created a stir in the industry.

Before I could take a deep breath, we were scheduled to go on the air for a January debut. I had 16 half-hour teleplays to deliver. I came up with an idea that would set up the premise of the show. It was a song to be written by Dominic Frontiere and performed by Tex Ritter. Over the years, this theme would become more popular than the series itself. It began, "All but one man died there at Bitter Creek, and they say he ran away. Branded, marked with a coward's shame. What do you do if you're branded, will you fight for your name?"

Joseph H. Lewis was signed to direct one of the first episodes. He was a cult favorite who'd received accolades for his low budget movie *Gun Crazy*, based on a screenplay by the then blacklisted Dalton Trumbo. Joe Lewis was a tough little sonofabitch, not unlike Sam Fuller. At our initial meeting he told me, "Your first script is great, the second one's a piece of crap!" We got along fine.

The standard opening of the show depicted the court martial in which Chuck Connors was stripped of his rank in front of the entire cavalry troop. To avoid having to pay residuals to all the extras, this sequence was to be shot at a fort located in Kanab, Utah.

Frontiere flew me up there in a private Cessna. Halfway up he admitted he'd never piloted this type of plane before and wasn't exactly familiar with the controls. The landing field was a narrow strip with a torn windsock dangling from a pole, and the wreckage of a few other private aircraft was visible in the surrounding brush. After a few passes, we managed to land safely. I admit it was worth the risk to see my first series being filmed.

After a long day watching the court martial sequence unfold, I retired to my room in the only local motel and had just about dropped off to sleep when there was a pounding at the door. I opened it to find Chuck Connors—big as life—still in his cavalry uniform. "I need your help. Everybody else has gone to sleep and I can't get my boots off by myself."

Chuck wanted me to accompany him back to his room and pull off the high cavalry boots, a request which scared the shit out of me. This guy was at least six foot three, a former baseball player with a shadowy reputation of having once appeared in a male porno movie. I didn't know whether these allegations were true, and I didn't want to find out. I also couldn't risk offending my star on the very first day of production.

Once back in Chuck's room I received detailed instructions. I was to turn around while he sat in a chair with his leg between mine. Then I'd tug on the boot while he pushed his other foot against my ass. He claimed this was the traditional method. I nervously followed instructions, finally yanking so hard that Chuck came flying forward off his chair landing on the floor and smashing his head on the adjacent coffee table. He lay there for a moment sprawled on the floor not moving while I stood over him wondering if I'd killed the star of my own show. He was only stunned but it took him a minute to recover. As I helped him to his feet I joked, "They're going to love this story in *TV Guide*." He flashed me an icy stare as if he wasn't sure I was kidding.

We finished shooting in Kanab and returned to the Paramount lot to make use of their fabulous western street. As usual, my big mouth got in the way of my common sense. One day at lunch I made the mistake of telling Chuck that in my mind, *Branded* was an important series with political significance. It was really the story of a blacklisted cowboy trying to outrun the smear of false accusations. In this post-McCarthy period we'd be making an important statement. I wasn't aware of what Chuck's leanings were, but soon discovered that he was lobbying to have me kicked off the show. Politically, I had become the enemy—a left winger!

One day I strolled over to the Western street. At the far end I spotted Chuck, tall in the saddle, waiting for the next shot to be set up. He recognized me and spurred his horse to a gallop heading straight at me. I stood frozen in the center of the street as he thundered down on me. I couldn't believe he wasn't going to stop. He must've thought I'd bolt and run. When he realized I wasn't moving it was nearly too late. I felt the horse's hot breath

Chuck Connors in *Branded.*

on my face as he reined up just inches away in a cloud of dust. "I thought you were gonna run," he bellowed. I didn't say a word.

It must have been ten years later at a party on the backlot of Republic Studios (which had become the CBS Studio Center) that I was seated with Connors. By this time his career was in decline and he seemed to be a much nicer guy. He commented nostalgically, "I remember the time I tried to ride you down on the Paramount street and you held your ground. I never forgot that. You're all right!" Little did he realize that I was paralyzed with fear.

In its first two seasons, *Branded* was rated amongst the top ten. Our competition on ABC was *The F.B.I.* and on CBS *The Ed Sullivan Show*. Yet we often beat them both. Unfortunately, Chuck became testy and increasingly difficult to tolerate, particularly in his abuse of the sponsors, who expected him to do PR for certain Procter & Gamble products. He alienated them to such a degree that they finally canceled the show and never again found a program that delivered such large audiences in that time slot. What did they replace us with? An unfunny comedy called *Hey, Landlord* starring of all people, Sandy Baron, a young comic with whom I'd picketed the Barnum & Bailey Circus for the American Guild of Variety Artists years before.

Both Sandy and I were trying to get into the union when we were offered full membership plus $500 a week to join the Teamsters in picketing the circus in New England. Jackie Bright, AGVA president, took us into his private office and showed us both a scrapbook of new clippings. "ELEPHANT STAMPEDES CROWD" and "CIRCUS BIG TOP COLLAPSES" were the headlines. He cautioned us, "Whatever you see, you didn't see. Now report to Teamster Headquarters in Connecticut." Sandy had his own car and we drove up there. The Teamsters relaxed in an air-conditioned sedan all day while Sandy and I stood baking in the sun wearing picket signs. At night we were followed by roustabouts from the circus who wanted to beat us up. We had to stay with the Teamsters and pay for our own meals and rooms, which consumed much of our salary.

The second night the elderly Teamster captain got drunk and turned on Sandy. "What are you, 21? Well I'm 73 and got four grandkids and I can still beat the living shit out of you!" Which he then proceeded to do! I figured the next night would be my turn so I convinced Sandy we should split. We pretended to go for cigarettes and never came back. We kept their $500 and the AFTRA cards they'd issued us with, and nobody ever came after us.

It wasn't Sandy's fault his show replaced me, but it lasted only a few weeks and was gone.

Still, *Branded* had served its purpose. I'd been accepted in the industry as a man who could get a television program on the air without even shooting a pilot.

I soon repeated this feat in 1967 with *The Invaders*, a science fiction thriller about a man, played by Roy Thinnes,who loses his way on a country road and witnesses the landing of a flying saucer. He sees aliens descending from a spaceship, having taken human form, and he spends the entire series trying to convince others of the existence of these aliens and trying to ferret them out as they infiltrate our society.

I sold the program directly to ABC, who handed it over to Quinn Martin to produce. Quinn had obviously seen my first episode of *The Defenders* ("Kill or Be Killed") on CBS. In it, a train wreck allows an innocent man on the way to the death house to make his escape. The exact same set-up found its way into Quinn's pilot *The Fugitive*—reproduced virtually shot for shot. Quinn was always wary of me because he knew that he'd borrowed my idea and used it. And I knew it, too.

By the time *The Invaders* was announced, ABC was already underway with *Blue Light*, my spy series about an American double agent in Nazi Germany during World War II starring Robert Goulet and Christine Carere, which they decided to premiere at mid-season in January 1966. Meanwhile back in New York, producer Herbert Brodkin had sold *Coronet Blue*, a series I'd created in 1966 about a man with amnesia seeking his own identity while an assassin attempts to kill him before he can discover exactly who he is. CBS boss Jim Aubrey bought the show without a pilot and ordered it into production, but he was fired before the premiere. At the same time I wrote the initial 90-minute teleplay for the ABC/Universal courtroom drama *Arrest and Trial* (the prototype for *Law & Order* and its many derivations).

Besides Sabiston, the General Amusement Corporation was representing me on certain TV projects, and without my knowledge they sneaked over to ABC and demanded a packaging fee on *The Invaders*. I could easily have squelched that deal, but instead I proposed to the agency that they share the fee with me. For once the writer was in control, and GAC had no choice but to comply. Eventually I was paid by both ABC and the talent agency for every segment. Under my very favorable contract, cost overages on *The Invaders* were not chargeable against my definition of profits, so I've collected profits every year since.

In subsequent seasons I would develop the Fox western series for *Custer* in 1966 and in 1973 *Griff*, starring Lorne Greene, both for ABC.

Griff followed the adventures of a retired police captain who takes over his son's private detective agency after he's been murdered. While we were waiting to debut on ABC, a show with an identical pilot script premiered on CBS mid-season and

Robert Goulet throwing a punch in *Blue Light.*

scooped us. It was called *Barnaby Jones* and was again produced by Quinn Martin. I couldn't prove the format had been lifted, even though a friend to whom I'd confided the story went on to direct many episodes of that series. When my two-hour movie about *Griff* was finally aired, *TV Guide* wrote, "This was the pilot for the series *Barnaby Jones.*" And they were not far wrong. Our series with Lorne Green only lasted one season. *Barnaby Jones* went on for seven years.

When people ask me "How do you keep your ideas from being stolen?" I reply, "I don't!" *Coronet Blue*, starring Frank Converse and featuring many rising guest stars such as Alan Alda, Candice Bergen and Billy Dee Williams, vanished after only 13 shows without ever revealing the leading character's true identity. Over the years I've been asked many times for the solution to this riddle. The main character, Michael Alden, was fished out of the Hudson River with a bullet hole in his head. On the operating table he had muttered the words, "Coronet Blue…" What did it mean and who was he? He had no fingerprint records, no history of military service, no one recognized his face from newspaper photographs. The solution was this: Michael Alden was not an American, he was a Russian carefully trained to impersonate an American citizen and planted in the U.S. as part of a massive spy operation with the code-name "Coronet Blue." When he sought to defect, his spy masters tried to kill him. They continued to attempt to finish him off before he could recall who he was… and who they were.

Alan Alda guest-starring on *Coronet Blue.*

Now that I was a confirmed success as a series creator, I was approached in 1965 by Leonard Goldberg, head of ABC daytime programming. The network wanted to give me a soap opera which I would executive-produce and deliver through my own company. They were setting me up to be a supplier, offering to make me another Aaron Spelling. They were handing me a gold mine, but the only problem was I didn't want to produce other people's material, I wanted to write my own stuff. Still,

I signed the deal, set up offices, and hired a production staff whom I then did my best to avoid.

From my cavalier attitude, it was clear to the network that I wasn't interested in being a boss. My life might have taken an entirely different course had I enthusiastically taken on the role of supplier. Very few writers get offered such an opportunity. Fewer still are foolish enough to piss it away.

As it turned out, the series was doomed from the outset. *Never Too Young* was to be a teenage soap opera aimed at the youth audience. It starred Tony Dow of *Leave it to Beaver* and Tommy Rettig of *Lassie*, and featured musical performers such as Marvin Gaye and Paul Revere & the Raiders. Naturally ABC, in their wisdom, scheduled the show at two o'clock in the afternoon while its target audience was still in school. The network devised the show only to wreck it. If I'd put my heart and soul into the production I would've been extremely upset. As it was I didn't much care. After 144 episodes, it was history, to be replaced by something called *Dark Shadows.*

My writing career on television had peaked and I was to begin a new career shortly as an independent filmmaker. Certainly I'd have to deal with employees if I were to produce and direct, but only for the few weeks that the cameras were rolling. And as opposed to television, I would be in total control.

My initial movies only took 18 days to shoot. I never maintained a secretarial staff or a suite of offices but continued to work out of my house. Why get up and go to work every morning when you can create just as well in the comfort of your own home?

When I've written for the major studios, they'd assign me an office and an eager secretary, but after a several days I'd stop coming in. Then I'd get a tearful phone call from the secretary saying, "Mr. Cohen, I'm just sitting here with nothing to do. If you don't show up, they're going to send me back to the secretarial pool and I don't want to go."

So for a few mornings I'd drop by and then revert to my usual habit of working at home. There I can usually generate up to 25 pages a day in less than three hours. This leaves me with a great deal of spare time to enjoy life.

Lorne Greene and Ben Murphy starring in *Griff*.

I'm often accused of being a workaholic, but nothing could be further from the truth. When my children were young, I usually chose to write late at night, after everyone had gone to bed. My wife would fall asleep about one o'clock in the morning and then I'd slip downstairs and begin. Usually by four o'clock I was completely knocked out. I'd been operating on pure instinct for the last few hours and wouldn't even remember what I wrote until I read the stack of pages the next morning. My subconscious was doing all of the work.

I never wanted to hear my wife chiding the kids to be quiet because dad was busy working. I wanted to be fully available to them—and I was.

During these years no one ever saw me composing a script, and they wondered where it was all coming from. Was there some little gnome that came out after dark and did it all? One of the great things about being a writer is that you enter a room alone and emerge from that room with a screenplay in your hand. Unlike everyone else in the movie business, the writer does it alone. And that makes him unique. In an industry not known for any particular code of ethics, it is an honorable profession.

Chapter 8
Writers vs. Directors
(The War That Never Ends)

No one in our family had ever owned a house. I had been perfectly happy renting furnished homes in Westwood and Brentwood. Then I saw the Hearst property off Coldwater Canyon in Beverly Hills and bought it almost as a joke. It was absurd: 8700 square feet, 24 rooms inlaid with unique antique tile—most of it leftovers from the San Simeon Castle which had been built the same year in 1929 and designed by the same architect, Julia Morgan. It had long been the home of Hearst's eldest son, George. This wasn't a house, it was a mansion, situated on two acres of land with a huge swimming pool and manicured sloping lawns, plus a view of the city beyond.

I bought the place from cowboy star Clint Walker, who headlined the first ever hour-long Western series, *Cheyenne*, in 1955. Clint and his wife had no sooner moved in than began to argue about the furnishing of it. They remained camped out in the mansion living off poolside furniture until they decided to give up and get a divorce. Janelle and I had just returned from touring San Simeon when we answered an ad, saw the place, and immediately made an offer. I was scared out of my wits when it was accepted.

Soon after taking possession, I had buyer's remorse. The first time I jumped in the huge swimming pool I found a rat stuck in the drain. I came up inches away from it and recoiled in horror. Fortunately the gardener showed up and dispatched it using the tip of his shears. It was a nightmarish event, but I wrote it into my first movie, *Bone*.

The first night we spent in the house I awoke and found the basement had flooded. There were several inches of water rising around the pool table. The beautiful antique wooden floors were covered with noxious muck. The first plumbers I summoned gave me the bad news. "You've got black pipe." It was going to cost $17,000 to repair, and that was only an estimate. How could I get out of this jackpot? I'd already paid my money and I was stuck with this white elephant. What a nightmare! Thank God I had the sense to call another plumber who'd been recommended by my wife Janelle's cousin, a contractor. The second fellow was an honest man. He'd never heard of black pipe. He asked me if I'd just had some painting done in the house recently. It seemed someone had poured a good deal of the paint down the drain, and it had clogged, causing the back-up. It was strictly a roto rooter job for a few hundred dollars. I had nearly been royally rooked.

The ceilings were 50 feet high and the floors all tiled, so it was like living in a cathedral. The kids kept falling down and banging their heads and getting hurt. Janelle slipped and fell down the stairs while pregnant with Jill. I carpeted the stairs, carpeted over the tile, and eventually obliterated the echo. Gradually the place was becoming livable. Nobody could believe the size of this joint, but today it doesn't even qualify as a large house anymore. Denzel Washington's house is 50,000 square feet, and other celebs are seeking to outdo him.

Janelle and I had many happy years at 2111 Coldwater with our family before we began to spend most of our time in our New York townhouse on East 79th Street. After our divorce, when I began dating again, I found that many of the girls I went out with found the house too isolated and foreboding. They didn't like to be left there alone. My daughter Melissa played a cruel trick on one of my girlfriends whom she disliked intensely, telling her that the house was haunted, saying, "Haven't you seen the ghosts yet?" The unfortunate starlet fled the premises immediately and never returned. Melissa was triumphant. I guess she did me a favor.

In all my early years writing for TV and movies, I always pondered the question: Why do directors hate writers? The answer was simple: Because they're afraid of them.

Above all else, directors fear erosion of their authority. They'll avoid any confrontation that could make them look bad. Many directors say as little as possible, even to the actors. They try to avoid displaying their ignorance of what's going on. Instead, they hide behind a wall of silence, presenting the image of an authoritarian figure who's virtually unapproachable. If

Directing Alan Arkin in *Full Moon High*.

you don't answer any questions, you won't say anything stupid. Some directors are simply traffic cops who move the performers around from place to place without ever delving into the motivations of the characters they play.

If they've hired gifted actors who can take care of themselves, things work out well. When they use less experienced actors, it's often a disaster. Above all, the director must appear to be the captain of the ship. Even if they're lost at sea, they can't afford to admit it.

It's far more difficult for a director to bluff a writer. Invariably, when a director is brought in on a project, the tendency is to have the original screenwriter replaced. Better to engage another writer with whom they're comfortable… someone beholden to them, who will take orders. The original writer might prove confrontational. The director doesn't care to defend any of the notions they have for changing the screenplay. They simply want it done, with no room for debate. The original writer has been on the project for months, maybe even years, but they're dismissed as being "too close to the material" or "written-out."

"Let's get someone in here with a fresh point of view!" is the usual rationale. Quickly forgotten is the fact that the initial screenplay was what brought all the elements together. Someone must have liked it in order to green-light the production. But movies are the directors' medium and that often means a page-one rewrite.

On the whole, directors are uncomfortable with having only one writer on a project. Having many writers dilutes the importance of any individual who might claim credit for the success of the film. And who can blame the director? What lies ahead for them is many months of grueling labor. They'll get up at dawn and work deep into the night. Often in inclement weather... maybe knee deep in mud or snow, watching their budget climb and getting hell from both their producers and the studio executives. Who's to blame for putting them in this position? The fucking writer.

Why do I take such sadistic pleasure in making things tough on other directors? Sometimes I'll write a scene as follows: "The two detectives watch the house from directly across the street..." And then, for no reason at all, I'll add "... in a torrential rainstorm."

Nobody will ask why it has to be raining. It enhances the production values. The fact that it adds nothing whatsoever to the story and will make everyone miserable never seems to occur to the studio. I'll be home relaxing by my swimming pool, dictating another script, while the director and the crew are freezing their asses off on some distant location—up to their ankles in phony rain.

When a picture is being shot, the writers are usually long gone. They're off spending their ill-gotten gains or bilking producers out of hundreds of thousands of dollars more for some other script. They don't have to show up on the set. No one wants them there and, if the truth be known, they're secretly happy about it.

The Writers Guild has attempted to get provisions passed that would require that the writer be present throughout production. But in their heart of hearts, writers would be appalled if they were actually required to be there. Imagine standing around for 14 hours a day, with the interminable waiting, then watching your lines being butchered. It's difficult enough to visit the set for even a few minutes without making your displeasure known. You find yourself making horrible faces, as if you've just smelled something bad. If you're smart, you'll exit quickly before anybody notices.

The first thing I think of when I arrive on a set is "None of these people would be here if it wasn't for me." Which is, of course, true. Without a screenplay, no one can budget a picture, finance it, cast it or produce it. Still, when you appear on location, no one seems too excited to see you. In fact, your presence makes them nervous.

The contrary is true on the Broadway stage where the writer is king. And the same goes for television, where writers invariably run the show and assume the title of Executive Producer. (Sometimes there are eight or nine of them on one series.)

From the inception of motion pictures, the studios united to avoid letting the writer impose the same provisions of ownership and creative control that they traditionally had in the theater. On the legitimate stage, the writer has veto power over the casting and no changes in the play can be made without the writer's express permission. In addition, the writer gets a hefty percentage of all box-office receipts thanks to the Dramatists Guild contract. They're there at rehearsals and can give notes and the critics generally focus on the writing rather than the directing in their notices. Of course, there's a downside. In the theater, the author doesn't get paid more than a pittance if the show isn't a hit. In movies, writers get their cash up front.

In movies, the writer is treated like the "father" after a bitter divorce action has concluded. When they exercise their visitation rights to the set, they can't expect much of a welcome.

Though directors will certainly be upset at the analogy, there is no question that the writer is the father of the movie and the director is the mother.

The writer is the initial creator. Without them, nothing happens. But it is the director who must undergo all the pain and discomfort, all the agonizing waiting that constitutes both the production of a movie and a pregnancy. The director must deliver and nurture until finally the picture is previewed and released. All this while, the writer (papa) is seldom to be seen.

Now horror of horrors: Suppose the child emerges looking exactly like daddy? You can imagine how much the director wants that movie to be traceable back to its original author.

Today's Writers Guild regulations require that the director meet with the original writer before hiring anyone else. This rule is violated on a regular basis. Usually, the director has already chosen another writer and the meeting to which he subjects himself is no more than a sham. They know it and so do all the studio executives. Only the writer shows up in good faith, unaware that their throat has already been cut from ear to ear. At these meetings, the director is usually extremely charming and avoids going into specific detail. Instead of a work session, it's simply socializing in order to accommodate a union regulation. Everyone is smiling, but as you walk out the door, they may as well kick you in the ass. The best thing a writer can do is start spending their money and begin writing another script.

The best book ever written about the essence of being a writer is Ernest Hemingway's *The Old Man and the Sea*, which on the surface has nothing to do with literary enterprise. It's the story of an old fisherman and his battle to land a giant marlin. He makes the catch but before he can bring his trophy to shore, it's attacked by sharks that tear away all of its flesh. He has nothing to show for his victory but the skeletal remains, and the knowledge that he made that catch—all alone—without anyone's help. His struggle against the big fish and his moment of conquest are his only true reward. That sense of achievement is something he receives by performing the act itself. No one else can give it to him. No one can take it away.

The greatest moment for the writer is the moment of initial creation. Alone in your room with your typewriter, your computer, or your pencil—that's when the story comes to life. The thrill you feel as the characters take shape and begin to speak for themselves cannot be appreciated by those who haven't experienced the sensation. It's much like the moment when the artist puts brush to canvas and watches his picture emerge. It's a sublime experience.

In devising a work of fiction, writers take on a God-like role. They create beings that never existed before. They may reward them or guide them to a tragic ending. They may inflict pleasure or pain at their will. They are the lord and master of their characters. It feels good to write and then to read what you've written. The pleasure you take in your own work is all that can be expected—nothing more. The approval you seek from others may or may not materialize. You mustn't rely upon

it because, as surely as you have a success, the sharks will come and there will be very little left.

Over the years, writers have let themselves become convinced that they're second-class citizens in Hollywood. Nothing could be less true. Sure, directors get paid more, producers too, but writers are the only ones who receive their money in advance and get to keep it regardless of whether the movie is ever made. Nobody calls you and says, "By the way, we didn't produce that screenplay you sold us, so could you please send us back the money."

In a long career, the successful writer pens many more movies than most directors can ever hope to direct. A top writer will eventually earn more money than an established director because they have longevity. Some only make a picture once every two or three years while a busy writer is churning out material month after month. So don't short-change the writer. He's actually doing great.

I'm sometimes asked about my religious beliefs. I speculate that maybe God grew bored and so he created the human race for his own amusement. Rather than controlling us absolutely, he found it more entertaining to allow us free will. When we become overly tiresome to him, he sends down some catastrophe to shake us up a little. He creates bad people because what's a good story without a villain? Once in a while he might answer a prayer or two, but interfering would ruin all the fun. To God, we're just one long movie—or soap opera perhaps. In terms of initially creating and then maintaining a hands-off position, God is certainly a writer rather than a director.

On second thought, I'm being too kind to writers. As I stated earlier, no one treats a writer more miserably than another writer. This is evidenced by showrunners on network television programs who continually rewrite everybody in order to put their stamp on the show. Generally they're obsessed with the belief that they alone can write the segments. Everything must be recycled through their typewriter.

In screenwriting, there are also writers who will change anything and everything in the interest of gaining credit. They'll even alter the character names. Paramount in their mind is the credit arbitration procedure and the residuals they'll receive if they can ace the original writer out. I wish writers would be nicer to one another. Then maybe directors would be nicer, too. But don't count on it.

Taking all of the above into account, is there any doubt that I was destined to direct my own scripts? Janelle didn't have any. She bought me a director's viewfinder as a gift and encouraged me to take the leap. And in 1970, I did.

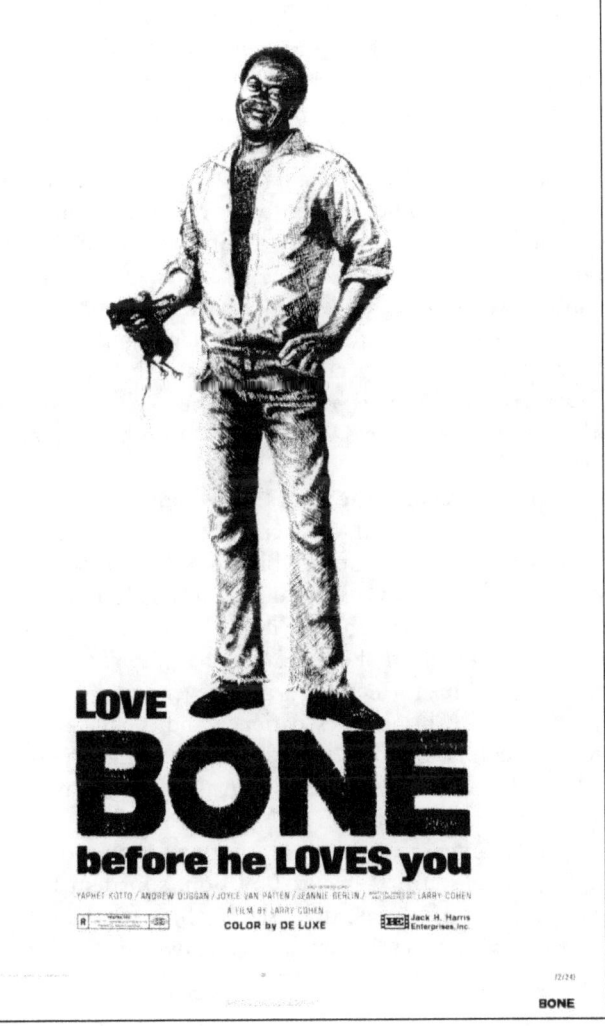

My first directorial effort, *Bone*, was originally entitled "Unreal," which should offer a clue that everything that happens in the film is a fantasy in the mind of one of the characters.

The film begins with the image of a solitary light bulb beginning to glow out of the darkness. An idea is forming. We widen to reveal the inside of a grimy cell in a Middle Eastern prison. A teenage boy lies on a straw mat staring up at the bulb, which dangles on a frayed cord.

All that follows is this boy's fantasy about the parents who abandoned him here after a drug bust and who still reside comfortably in their Beverly Hills mansion.

Bill Lenneck sells cars on local television. Bill's own fantasy about his loveless marriage is also about to unfold.

Lenore Lenneck's imagination will also be invaded—as images rising from her subconscious become a reality.

The affluent couple are by their poolside bickering when the title character, Bone, seems to materialize—a huge black man dressed in dungarees with a pack of Camels in his shirt pocket. He's a 1940s stereotype of a dangerous black buck on the prowl. He quickly crushes to death the rat that Bill has discovered caught in his pool drain. Then, without any weapon other than his blackness, he takes them both prisoner in their own home.

Upon ransacking the place, Bone finds nothing but unpaid bills and overdrawn bank statements. The Lennecks are broke. Bill's last savings account—which he's kept hidden from his wife—still has nearly five grand in it, so Bone sends Bill to withdraw the money while he holds Lenore hostage. Bill takes off with no intention of ever coming back. He's found a way to rid himself of his tormenting wife forever.

Eventually Bone loses patience and, being a man of his word, attempts to rape Lenore—a task at which he is severely lacking. He's an impotent rapist. An anachronism not unlike the colored Pullman porter or Negro shoeshine boy. Bone has lost the "nigger mystique." He is powerless and depressed. Lenore, who is at first insulted by Bone's inadequacy, decides to cheer him up—eventually seducing him. (Perhaps Lenore is Bone's own fantasy: the sex-starved and affluent white housewife.)

Yaphet Kotto, Andrew Duggan and Joyce Van Patten in *Bone*.

When Lenore realizes Bill has ditched her, she enlists Bone's aid in tracking him down and knocking him off for the insurance.

Meanwhile, Bill has taken up with a hippie shoplifter, who has disturbing fantasies of her own—identifying him with a molester who came on to her in a movie theater in her teens. When Bill makes love to her, we can see that in his mind he's thinking sensually of automotive parts.

Lenore and Bone finally catch up with Bill, but it is she alone who commits the homicide. With the deed done, she finds that Bone has vanished completely—as if he had never existed.

We leave her as she frantically rehearses lies to tell the police—still another fantasy in which a strange black man attacked her and murdered her adoring husband.

In his cell, the boy can endure no more of the haunting daydream he's concocted and finally smashes the light bulb overhead, plunging us into total darkness.

Bizarre and original, yes. Particularly since it's mostly played for comedy.

Veteran character Andrew Duggan was brilliant as Bill (I wrote the part with him in mind). Joyce Van Patten gave the performance of her career as Lenore, and Yaphet Kotto did his

Yaphet Kotto and Joyce Van Patten in *Bone*.

finest piece of film acting (in his own opinion) as Bone—who never identifies himself by that name. It's Lenore who makes it up for him.

As seed money, I'd gotten $85,000 from Nick Vanoff, the producer of TV's successful variety show *The Hollywood Palace*. It was enough to complete principal photography since I'd gotten credit from MGM labs thanks to Roger Mayer and a deferment on paying for cameras and lights. This would be my practice on all of my first dozen films: taking a token up-front payment from a backer or distributor and then putting myself on the line for the back end. It avoided bringing in a completion guarantor and having an approved budget and schedule. I enjoyed total freedom of operation.

The director of photography was George Folsey (nominated 13 times for Academy Awards for great MGM classics like *Meet Me in St. Louis*.) He'd shot the first two Marx Brothers movies. His son, George Jr., was the camera operator and later co-edited the film. He went on to produce nearly a dozen films with director John Landis.

If the making of *Bone* had been something of a kick, the marketing of it became a kick in the ass. My edited version ran to ten reels of picture and ten reels of soundtrack which

I personally transported to and from numerous screenings, all of which I insisted on attending. I wasn't about to allow studio executives to take phone calls and skip reels at their slightest whim. The buyers would have to view the picture on my terms—with me in the room. They usually balked but finally agreed.

At Warners, David Brown informed me just before the lights went down: "I may have to leave for a meeting." I knew what that meant. Ten minutes into the picture he leaned over and whispered, "I'll be staying for the whole film."

As much as he admired the movie, his studio still wouldn't release it. This was the usual response I got. Brilliantly acted and written but too off beat, too controversial. I was soon schlepping these same 20 reels to New York, in and out of taxi-cabs, wheeling them into office buildings balanced on a rickety dolly on which you'd expect to push garbage cans. This was my only color work print and I wasn't letting it out of my sight.

A few days earlier, I'd been sunbathing poolside at my Beverly Hills mansion. Now I found myself being harangued by elevator operators and ordered to use the service entrances—which were usually located somewhere around the block. My protests that I was a movie director impressed no one. To them I was a delusional delivery boy.

Getting the film into the buildings was sometimes easier than getting it out. After my second screening for Joseph E. Levine, the great film impresario took Janelle and me aside and raved about the quality of the picture, keeping us there for hours until he reluctantly admitted he had no money to fund any new acquisitions. Then why did he have us back to run it a second time? He just liked it so much he wanted to see it again. How can you get angry when a man tells you that?

But by the time Joe was done with us it was after 6.30pm. The building was closing for the weekend and the security men in the lobby wanted to see our pass to remove the boxes of film. Rushing back upstairs, I found Levine's door locked. Everyone was gone. It took a great deal of screaming, foaming at the mouth and threatening lawsuits to finally get that work print safely home. I must've run it 35 times for distributors and had a half-a-dozen nibbles that got away. Bob Shaye at New Line

Alternate release title for Larry Cohen's hard-to-market *Bone*.

Cinema was a firm "maybe" that soon developed into an even firmer "NO."

Months later, the lights came up in one Los Angeles screening room and a trim, deeply tanned gentleman named Jack H. Harris resonantly spoke those endearing words: "How much do you need to finish it?"

I always knew someone would come along. Jack made a tough deal, but he was taking a big risk.

He previewed the picture twice in Westwood to sellout crowds and excellent responses. A young Michael Douglas approached me in the lobby to offer raves and tell me that I wrote like John Guare, which was quite a compliment.

Then a third preview was set at the World Theater on Hollywood Boulevard where a black exploitation movie called *The Legend of Nigger Charley*, starring Fred Williamson, was playing. When the picture went over equally well with a predominantly black audience, I was in trouble. Jack suddenly saw *Bone* as a black action movie, although it had only one black actor and no action.

When I protested to him that this was a comedy, Jack quickly replied, "Am I going to stand in the aisle and tell them not to laugh?"

Jack's biggest hit had been _The Blob_, and that was the kind of product he understood. Still, I'm grateful to him for being there when no one else was.

After its opening, some local reviews proclaimed that _Bone_ was unintentionally funny. After all, they'd come to see a drama, hadn't they? I was always confident that it would be rediscovered. Those who saw _Bone_ years ago still remember it vividly today. After a brief revival at a Chicago art house in the year 2000, I got feedback from the theater manager that the white audience was offended by it—while blacks seemed to have no complaint. Way back in 1970, black audiences had gotten all the jokes, but whites hadn't been as upset. We may be led to believe race relations in America have come to a resolution, but _Bone_ is a litmus test. Someone once told me, "Everyone gets from your movie what they bring to it." That's why I've never given up trying to get it exhibited. From _Bone_ we learn a lot about ourselves.

When it was released on DVD in 2001, _Film Comment_ magazine selected _Bone_ as a "DVD Pick of the Month," an honor similarly bestowed by _L.A. Weekly_. They both called it a searing examination of race relations in America.

I'm pleased I made this film, but I regret that it didn't get its fair recognition at the time of its initial release. It might've altered the entire course of my career. Its success would've surely put me on the A list. But look at all the fun I would've missed.

Chapter 10
At Last—A Hit!

Sammy Davis, Jr. had a minor career in motion pictures other than playing sidekick to Sinatra and Dean Martin. He dreamed of finding a vehicle which he could carry on his own. His manager, Sy Marsh, hired me to develop a tough-guy role for Sammy and I came up with a variation on the Edward G. Robinson classic, *Little Caesar*. It would be the story of the rise and fall of a black gangster in Harlem.

Once again, the material seemed to write itself. I quickly submitted my *Black Caesar* outline, but my $10,000 fee was not forthcoming. I soon learned that Sammy was in financial difficulties, primarily with the IRS. He spent lavishly but often couldn't pay his taxes. I finally gave up trying to chase him for the money. The treatment sat idly in the trunk of Peter Sabiston's car.

Then I was called to a meeting at American International Pictures (AIP) with one of the few remaining movie moguls, the very affable Sam Arkoff. I had met Sam earlier when I'd screened *Bone* for a possible pick-up deal. AIP found the picture too controversial, but they praised the acting. Now Arkoff faced me across his wide desk and stated, "You really know how to direct those black actors."

The fact that there was only one black actor in the earlier film seemed beside the point. Arkoff wanted to make action pictures with emerging black stars, a genre which would soon become known as Blaxploitation. It took me two minutes to get down to Peter's car and locate the outline of *Black Caesar*, which I presented to Sam. He read it while I waited, and I had a deal before I left the premises. Sam had the power that no one seems to possess nowadays to make a unilateral decision. He needed no one's approval. I was to get $425,000 to deliver the entire movie. But first I had to submit an acceptable script.

I knew this would be no problem. American International was not accustomed to getting material of the quality that I was capable of turning out. The real challenge would be finding a star to cast in the principal role.

My editor, Mike Corey, took care of that by introducing me to Fred Williamson over lunch at Cyrano's restaurant. Fred was a dashing black man and a former football hero who'd played a role on the TV series *Julia* opposite Diahann Carroll and was featured in Robert Altman's *M*A*S*H*. And he had just scored in the lead role in the aforementioned *The Legend of Nigger Charley.*

Fred was acceptable to AIP, as was the screenplay. They exercised no other approvals and sent me off to make my picture.

The check Sam Arkoff gave me for the first advance was supposed to be for $200,000. On the way out of the office, I noticed it was written for only $175,000. I called the error to Sam's attention to which he replied, "You want to give me the check back?" I immediately raced to the elevator and fled.

Fred Williamson in *Black Caesar.*

I'd get more money after the first cut and the balance upon delivery of the answer print. I'd be responsible for any overages out of my own pocket.

This was the kind of arrangement I would come to love. *Total autonomy.* I was determined to give AIP more of a movie than they were paying for and I surprised them by cramming so much action onto the screen.

At this time, Larco Productions consisted of myself, my wife Janelle, and my best buddy, Jimmy Dixon, who would play one of the arch villains in the piece. There was never any budget breakdown, no production board, no cast or production insurance except on the Panavision equipment we rented.

Jimmy and I headed off to New York where Fred Williamson joined us. We had no crew, but technicians at Panavision recommended James Signorelli, a kid who would later gain renown creating filmed sequences for NBC's *Saturday Night Live* and go on to direct movies like *Easy Money* with Rodney Dangerfield. At this point, he'd shot only commercials. He wore a scruffy beard and a long ponytail. Without the facial hair, he would probably have looked 16 years old.

We had no preliminary meetings. He simply showed up in the hallway outside my friend Merv Bloch's advertising agency on East 55th Street where I'd had the camera equipment delivered. It came in large, heavy metal boxes and lined the entire corridor. I made it a practice to always deliver the camera equipment to any address other than where we intended to film. The gear would then be carted off to some other secret location where the various unions couldn't track us down.

This very first morning we piled the equipment into a yellow cab owned and operated by the superintendent of my mother's buildings in Harlem, Francisco De Grazia. Little did De Grazia realize what he was getting into.

Williamson arrived fully dressed for the role since we lacked dressing room facilities. We'd be shooting at 57th Street and Fifth Avenue, the location of Tiffanys and one of New York's busiest intersections. Jimmy Dixon had by this time donned the uniform of a New York police officer, which we'd rented from Western Costume in Hollywood. This was to be one of the most spectacular scenes in the movie, and it was to be shot by Signorelli and only one assistant. My New York agent, Alvin Ferleger, had granted me permission to get some high angle shots from the window of his offices. Taken with a hidden camera, these would greatly enhance the reality of the sequence.

Fred was supposed to emerge from Tiffanys having purchased a gift for his girl, not realizing he had been betrayed. As he crossed the street, he was to be assassinated by a hitman disguised as a New York cop.

But being unkillable, Williamson would rise to his feet and stagger wounded through the crowd. Hundreds of people would react to the situation as a now bloodied Fred would tumble and knock over a trash receptacle, regain his footing and finally hail a taxi in which to attempt an escape. This, of course, would be De Grazia's cab. Tailing Williamson would be a Cadillac, carrying more hitmen who had arrived to finish the job. The chase would head west and be blocked eventually by a garbage truck which coincidentally happened to be there. All of this was improvised, based on what we came across while heading across town. Since there was no way to bypass the garbage truck, the natural choice was to drive the taxi up onto the sidewalk.

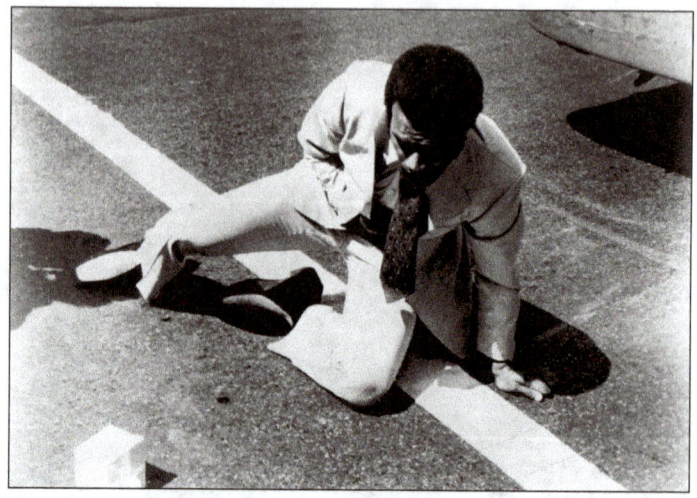

At first, Signorelli was certain he was working for a madman, but from the very first shot, his doubts begin to fade. The scene was actually working. People on the street were reacting realistically. They didn't seem to notice the cameras. After finishing a take, we'd wait for the crowd to disperse and then go back and shoot additional coverage with new people passing, and they again reacted as if they were watching a real event in progress. People actually tried to assist the seemingly wounded Williamson.

Countless police cars passed by and waved to us. They saw Jimmy Dixon dressed as a cop and thought he was assigned to duty. When necessary, Jimmy actually stopped traffic. Street vendors were even offering him free ice cream and bagels. Williamson also took encouragement from the fact that the scene was playing so beautifully. Up to that point, I'm sure he also thought I was deranged.

When it came time to pull the taxicab up onto the curb, I decided it would be best to send De Grazia out for a bite of lunch, but he sensed something sneaky was going on and doubled back, only to see his cab racing down the sidewalk, dispersing pedestrians in all directions. In order to provide some degree of security, I'd had yellow tape strung across the door-ways of all the buildings on the block so no one would simply step out into the path of the oncoming cab. In addition to this, we strapped the horn down so it would blare continuously. I figured that New Yorkers were accustomed to dodging traffic and getting out of the way of oncoming vehicles. I hoped they would do the same even if the vehicle was coming at them on the sidewalk—a supposition that proved correct. After racing the taxi up one city block, we continued the same process on the next street. Meanwhile, Williamson was doubled up in the back seat losing blood from his stomach wound and urging De Grazia on. The starstruck superintendent was now driving his own cab and playing his part to the hilt. Jimmy and his cohorts were chasing the cab on foot with guns drawn, trying to catch up as the taxi became entangled in crosstown traffic.

I should've assumed that the NYPD might take notice of men running through the streets with guns. One heavy-set black cop did rush over with his hand on his holster. Peering into the cab, he saw Williamson dripping with blood as I began yelling, "It's only a movie" and pointed to the camera. Fortunately the cop recognized Williamson from his football days and waved us on.

A few blocks closer to Broadway, I cheerfully suggested that Fred throw himself out of the back of the moving taxi into the gutter. Fred looked at me incredulously and said, "Why don't you do it first, Cohen?"

I saw no alternative but to demonstrate the stunt personally, so I immediately tossed myself out of the cab. I was in agony, but I rose, faking a smile. This would begin a pattern. I would devise a stunt, Williamson would challenge me to do it first, then he would prove that he could do it better. And neither of us would let the other know how much it hurt. I couldn't believe the scene was working and I wouldn't even consider stopping for lunch and breaking the rhythm.

Once Williamson ditched the cab and was on foot, we began racing alongside him with a handheld camera. Signorelli proved extraordinarily strong and could hold the heavy Panavision camera with an extremely steady hand. In fact, he refused to put the camera down between takes. He enjoyed lugging it around all day. When I questioned him, he claimed that carrying it strengthened him and allowed him to become more accustomed to the weight. Whatever the reason, I've never had a more proficient documentary-style camera operator in the course of my career.

The chase on foot also attracted the interest of the police. This time, four cops set off in pursuit as I tried to run interference, gesturing in the direction of the camera.

Had we been in Los Angeles, we would have immediately been arrested and the production terminated. But New York cops are far easier to deal with. They simply want to know *why*. Why are you driving a taxicab on the sidewalk? Why are you running through the streets with guns in your hands? Why is this black guy stumbling through traffic with blood all over him? As long as you can offer them an answer, they're amused and tolerant. Fortunately, nobody ever asked to see our permits—which were non-existent.

By the time we reached Times Square, the sequence was approaching its climax. For a moment, Jimmy loses track of his quarry as Williamson doubles back behind him. Using his necktie as a garrote, Fred fatally chokes his would-be assassin. It all happens beneath one of the Times Square billboards which features puffs of smoke being emitted from the lips of the Marlboro cowboy. I'd intercut the cowpoke blowing smoke rings on the sign with the slow strangulation of the hitman. A street derelict lying nearby witnesses this homicide and reacts to it. This actually happened, so we included that in the movie as well. Williamson leaves the corpse of his tormentor lying on a bench, covering his victim's face with a copy of the *Daily News*.

We'd accomplished all of this within a few short hours. On this very first day I had broken the back of the movie. I'd demonstrated that such sequences could be improvised, utilizing whatever the city had to offer. When I consider now what could've gone wrong, I shudder. When I think of how much it would've cost to prepare and stage this sequence as any rational person might've done, I realize it would have been prohibitive. At this budget, *Black Caesar* could only be made by a director in a manic state.

Jimmy and I didn't get much sleep that week. We were shooting well into the night. Still, I had to get down to the TVC laboratories by 5 am to look at the dailies on a Hazeltine Color Analyzer, which resembled a television screen but showed the film timer exactly what was on the negative, allowing him to adjust the color of the dailies accordingly. I was astonished by

Cohen and the supporting cast of *Black Caesar.*

the quality of the Tiffany sequence. It looked like a major Hollywood production. Following the dailies, Jimmy and I staggered out into the streets of the city trying to figure out what the hell to do next.

I decided it was time to venture up into Harlem, where the feature *Across 110th Street* starring Anthony Quinn and *Bone* star Yaphet Kotto had recently wrapped. This large-scale Hollywood production had been intimidated into paying big bucks for permission to park their trailers, dressing rooms and portable toilets. I'd soon face similar shakedown artists when I arrived with my cameras.

Our crew had grown to half a dozen. Once out of the van, it didn't take but a few minutes for us to be surrounded by some of the roughest looking characters I'd ever encountered. Since I had no money to pay them, I once again had to improvise. Picking out their leader, I complimented him on his look. "You're just the type of guy I need to play Fred Williamson's number one enforcer," I said, adding, "And some of your guys would look great in the movie, too." In a matter of seconds, I had them on my side. They were all going to be actors in the movie, and they'd also afford us their protection throughout Harlem, giving me license to go everywhere and do anything.

In addition, I ended up with a bunch of damn good performances. You might say these gentlemen were right for the part. They enjoyed it even more when they recognized their faces blown up on the poster displayed outside the Cinerama Theater on Broadway in Times Square, where the film opened. They'd been immortalized.

They'd also come in handy in discouraging the union organizers who'd decided to trail us past 125th Street into the depths of Harlem. If their intent was to shut us down, these Teamsters quickly changed their minds when our new-found cast members convinced them that it was most advisable to forget about bothering Larry Cohen.

This set a precedent that carried on for many years in New York in regard to the unions. Most often when they heard it was a Larry Cohen movie, they simply threw up their hands and decided to harass somebody else. I admit I lived a charmed life.

Don't get me wrong. I've got nothing against unions. I just couldn't afford their fee. At the end of the week my checks would've bounced. This was long before the unions adopted

lower rates for independent films. The choice was to make these films in my lunatic fashion or not make them at all.

While shooting *Black Caesar* I soon learned that the best way to get locations was to stroll in off the street and say, "I want to shoot a movie here." The response was usually "When?" My answer would be "Now." Before the proprietor of the store or building knew what was happening, I'd have brought the actors and equipment inside and filming was underway. I've also found that when you book a place well in advance, the chances are that the owner of the location will change his mind or jack up the price, or that when you return, there will be a crew drilling the sidewalk out front. If something can possibly go wrong, it always will. I agree that it's foolhardy to take actors and crew out in a motorcade with the expectation that you'll somehow find the proper location when you don't know where in hell you're going. While it's always proved a successful tactic for me, I don't recommend it to other filmmakers.

Once the New York shoot was completed, we hired an entirely different crew out in Los Angeles where the movie would be completed. We picked up with the storming of a mafia stronghold where a poolside party was in progress. An army of black gangsters emerge over the roof of an old Spanish mansion with machine guns blazing. The poolside buffet is blown to pieces and the bodies of the Italian mobsters tumble into the huge swimming pool.

To simplify matters, I chose to use my own house on Coldwater Canyon as the locale. We recruited many of our friends, some of them local Hollywood restaurateurs, to play the mobsters. Janelle personally catered the huge buffet. Little did she know that her prize turkey was going to be blown apart by explosives or that we would be picking turkey fragments off of our front lawn for the next six months.

One of our friends who was playing a gangster decided to take refuge underneath the buffet table when the shooting started. It was a logical thing to do, but I had a bad feeling about him being so close to the explosive charges and pulled him out. Moments later, the detonation went off, blowing a gigantic hole in the table in the exact spot where our he'd been. He would've been killed or severely injured if I hadn't had a lucky hunch.

Veteran Hollywood stuntman Paul Stader supervised the action, beginning what would be a friendship that would last for many years. And Paul wouldn't take a nickel for his work. He even allowed us to use his vintage Bugatti as a gangster car. Naturally, I had to drain my swimming pool after the sequence was completed.

This was one of the many scenes that impressed Arkoff and the AIP distribution people when they finally saw my cut. They were ready to spend some major money on the music. At first, we ran the work print for Stevie Wonder, who listened to the soundtrack while his assistants clued him in as to what was happening on screen. Stevie seemed more interested in discussing my horoscope than the content of the movie, and I assume he thought the picture to be too violent for his taste.

We then went on to James Brown, who immediately signed on. He had never composed for a movie before, but he and his manager Charles Bobbitt seemed excited about the opportunity, so I sent them a 35mm black-and-white dupe of the picture and a copy of the magnetic track, along with a detailed list of the required musical cues and the exact length of each specific cue. Some weeks later we received the tapes of Brown's recording session. He'd been overly generous. If there was a three-minute scene, he wrote five minutes of music for it. If the scene was eight minutes in duration, he wrote 12 minutes of music. The fact that the cues never fit the action seemed to have escaped him.

When I called Bobbitt about this, he shrugged it off. "The man has given you more than you need." Rather than argue,

I immediately set about the task of reediting the music to make it fit. American International was never apprised of our problem and went on to hire James Brown to score another picture, *Slaughter's Big Rip-Off*—with disastrous results. They didn't quite know how to handle it when he gave them eleven minutes of music for a six-minute scene. They swore never to employ him again.

Once the music had been added, there was nothing left but to mix the film and preview it at the Pantages Theater on Hollywood Boulevard. As was the unfortunate custom with American International, the preview was so close to the release date that there was never a chance to make any changes before the picture hit the theaters. The night of our preview, the audience seemed to enjoy the film all the way through, but suddenly, at the end, emotions changed. They hated seeing Fred Williamson beaten to death by a bunch of youthful gang members. He'd stumbled, wounded, back to the place of his origins, the tenements of Harlem where a group of black kids attacked him, stealing his gold wristwatch. They don't realize that their victim used to be Harlem's number one gang boss. It was a powerful and ironic finale, but many of the black people in the audience took offense. Fred Williamson had become their hero and they didn't want to see him die, particularly at the hands of his own people.

I was shouted at and nearly attacked in the lobby as the preview audience liberally voiced their dissatisfaction. I phoned Arkoff immediately and related the disastrous results. "I told you not to kill him," Arkoff snapped. I recalled his advice, although Sam had never been adamant about it. Now I knew that we were looking at an enormous flop. The prints had already been shipped to New York where the film would open at three major first-run theaters in only a few days.

I suggested to Sam that we change the ending. "How can you do that?" he asked. I replied, "I'll simply go to all the theaters and snip off the last scene."

The deletion would cause only a slight sound bump before the final music carried us into the end titles. With Arkoff's permission, I flew to New York, arriving at the Cinerama Theater on Broadway approximately 30 minutes before the first show was scheduled to begin. I introduced myself to the manager who brought me upstairs to the projectionist, who'd never met a director before. He was only too happy to accommodate me in clipping out the final scene and splicing on the end titles. I then proceeded across town to the RKO 59th Street, where I performed the same procedure, and then up to the RKO 86th. With these few snips, *Black Caesar* didn't die, and a looming failure was converted into a major success.

The picture, which had the tag line "Godfather of Harlem," took off from its first day of release. It was February and freezing, but lines were forming around the block and police barricades had to be erected. The management added performances so that the picture was playing practically around the clock. They also added one dollar to the price of admission, but nothing could stop audiences from pouring in. *Black Caesar* was my first big hit, and Janelle and I enjoyed going to the theater just to watch the crowds line up. We often went inside to watch key scenes which evoked an audible audience reaction. The late late shows were the most entertaining for us to visit since pimps usually brought along their entire entourage of hookers as a reward after they'd finished their night's labors.

Within a few days, Arkoff phoned me and ordered a sequel, upping the budget to an astronomical $475,000. I suggested we act quickly, before everybody connected with the picture decided to raise their fees. The studio already had a release date in mind, which didn't give me very much time to write a screenplay, so I went ahead without one. Arkoff wasn't particularly concerned, but as it turned out, this was a major blunder. *Hell Up in Harlem* is probably my most disjointed and confused film. There are some interesting scenes, but it doesn't hang together at all.

Once again, I tried to give the studio value for their money and ended up giving them too much. Less would have been more. Another problem was that Fred Williamson wasn't actually available to do the film, but with my usual overconfidence, I was certain I could circumvent that obstacle. I'd simply shoot with a double and then cut Williamson in for close-ups. It would be a supreme challenge for a director to make a feature picture with a star who wasn't even there.

I had a general idea of what I wanted to do but left most of it to chance. Meanwhile, Williamson had signed to do a big-budget Universal picture entitled *That Man Bolt*, which would keep him occupied five days a week. I could still work with him on Saturdays and Sundays. Fred was kind enough to borrow his wardrobe from Universal and wear it in our picture. This led to a close call while filming in the American Airlines terminal in New York when Universal Chairman Lew Wasserman walked up to us and inquired what movie we were making. Fred was with us that day, but he was still under contract to Universal for *Bolt*. I quickly changed the subject, asking Mr. Wasserman to be in the picture playing a mob boss. Just a walk-on. That was enough to run him off with no further questions.

Looking at dailies, Fred soon voiced his objections to the double I'd hired, complaining that he had a fat ass. But the substitution of the stand-in remained undetected by the audience.

Back in New York, I'd shot an action sequence at Harlem Hospital where Williamson's character is brought after being wounded. Unfortunately, the two gangsters dragging Fred's double inside walked him straight through a glass door which completely shattered. Being in a hospital, the medical attention for Fred's double was immediate and we were able to continue filming without much delay.

Throughout the New York shoots of both films, my mother provided me with help far beyond the call of duty. What greater sacrifice could Carolyn make than allow us to throw her mink coats off of the 20th floor terrace of her apartment at 57th Street and Second Avenue? But this is exactly what we did. Fred Williamson was supposed to have bought the apartment from the family that had employed his mother as a maid. He purchased everything lock, stock and barrel: the furniture, the clothes and even the furs. Then, to show his disdain, he tossed

LA MAFIA **NERA** SFIDA LA MAFIA BIANCA

FRED WILLIAMSON in

BLACK CÆSAR
IL PADRINO NERO

ART LUND · JULIUS W. HARRIS · GLORIA HENDRY · D'URVILLE MARTIN · VAL AVERY · MINNIE GENTRY

JAMES DIXON · WILLIAM WELLMAN, JR. · DON PEDRO COLLEY · PHILLIP ROYE · PATRICK McALLISTER · MYRNA HANSEN

"DOWN AND OUT IN NEW YORK CITY" di EDDIE GRAINGER · GERRY DE LEON · musica composta e diretta da JAMES BROWN · COLORE DELLA DELUXE · diretto da LARRY COHEN · AMERICAN INTERNATIONAL PICTURES

them off the balcony onto the sidewalks below. I had stationed several production assistants downstairs so that when the coats came floating 20 floors down, they'd be there to retrieve them. I was only concerned that one of them might land on top of a passing taxi and be carried off. The doorman at mom's luxury building didn't seem at all surprised when he saw the fur coats sailing out the window. "This happens all the time. Couples get into fights and somebody tosses the furs out in anger, and I have to gather them up."

We also shot several dramatic scenes in Carolyn's apartment. She took it in her stride, often going to sleep with all the camera equipment and lights surrounding her bed, then being awakened at the crack of dawn when the crew arrived. Mom had always wanted to be in show business. Now she was.

My mother also arranged for us to shoot at the coal yard where she purchased fuel for the buildings she managed. I immediately conceived a massive gunfight during which Williamson was to be picked up by an excavator and buried in a gigantic pile of coal. When I described the stunt to Fred, he responded that his legs would surely be chopped off and, as usual, he insisted I do the stunt first. Showing no fear, I allowed the scooper to bear down on me and threw myself into it just before it struck. I then found myself buried headfirst in the huge coal pile. I dug my way out and we posed for some photographs together, comparing skin tones to see who was darker. I won.

What followed this sequence was a chase to JFK airport with Williamson pursuing his arch enemy, portrayed by Tony King. He arrives too late to prevent King from boarding the TWA flight to Los Angeles. Williamson then races across the airport parking lot on foot to catch an American Airlines jet which is scheduled to touch down in Los Angeles only six minutes after King's flight. The chase continues in Los Angeles, with Williamson catching up with his quarry at the baggage claim, wrestling him onto the baggage conveyor, then pursuing him up the ramp past the tumbling luggage onto the actual field where he finally shoots Tony King to death. Needless to say we stole this entire sequence without permits or permission from either of the airlines. I can only assume the airport authorities thought we had clearance to do it. Who would have the effrontery to stage all this action on private property without authorization?

Even more harrowing was the filming of the sequence in which Williamson was to scale the Sony sign above Times Square carrying a rifle with a telescopic sight. From there, perched precariously high above the city, he is to pick off a gangster who is passing the Palace Theater in the company of a bodyguard.

Again, guerilla-style, we made our way to the rooftop which provided access to the Sony sign, which loomed a full four stories above the roof. We'd have to navigate a rickety metal ladder to reach the narrow platform up top. This would put us about 16 stories above street level.

Once again, Williamson challenged me to make the climb first. Somehow, throughout my experience writing and directing, I've always been required to climb to precipitous heights. When I wrote *Daddy's Gone A-Hunting*, I had to climb to the roof of the Mark Hopkins Hotel, just above the Top of the Mark restaurant, to see if it was feasible to stage a chase there. Eventually the roof was recreated at a studio in Culver City at great expense. For *El Condor*, I had to scale the parapets of the fortress that was under construction in Almeria, Spain. And when I directed *Q*, I had to climb to the very pinnacle of the Chrysler Building, 88 stories up, all the time showing no fear so that my cast and crew would be too ashamed not to follow.

But this particular climb up the Sony sign I would have to make twice. No sooner had I reached the top and then descended than Williamson began his ascent, followed by

James Signorelli with his handheld camera. Half-way up the ladder, Jim began shouting down to me. One of the lenses had slipped out of his grip and to prevent it from falling, he had pressed his body between it and the ladder. All I could think of was the expensive lens crashing down and the thousand-dollar deductible on my insurance policy, so up I went again to the rescue, catching the lens with one hand just as it slipped away.

At the top of the sign, Williamson was aiming the telescopic rifle when one of the crew members below casually mentioned that the police had initiated a helicopter patrol to search for possible snipers. If they saw a black man up there with a rifle, they would certainly open fire. I signaled Williamson to quickly finish the action and get the hell down.

I naturally expected to hire James Brown again to do that score, but I was forbidden to employ him by AIP. I went back to Mr. Bobbitt and told him the only way there was any chance of James getting the job was if he wrote and recorded the music on spec and presented us with the completed tapes. If the studio liked the score, they'd buy it. Otherwise he could do whatever

Hell Up in Harlem.

he pleased with the material. A few days later, Bobbit responded, "The man accepts the challenge."

As unbelievable as it may seem, Brown wrote and recorded all the music for *Hell Up in Harlem* at his own expense. When he sent me the tapes, the AIP executives turned their noses up. They claimed they'd already made a deal with Motown and would not be budged. When I informed Bobbit of the rejection, he took it graciously. The music that James Brown had written for me was subsequently released on an album as *The Payback* and became his most successful in years. AIP blew it, but it was really my fault for not taking a stronger position on James' behalf.

I was in Las Vegas with Janelle on vacation when *Hell Up in Harlem* was given an advance screening in New York. I got an emergency phone call from my mom while I was at Caesar's Palace informing me of the disaster. This time it was my own mother telling me that my movie stinks. "What's the matter with you? You think these audiences are idiots? You show Fred getting on a plane to Los Angeles, then you show the plane landing, then you superimpose the words Los Angeles, and everybody in the theater gets mad 'cause they think you're treating them like idiots! You did this five or six times in the movie."

Once again, I had been warned in the nick of time. I immediately edited those superimpositions out of the picture. I'd been trying to create a visual style but instead I'd offended the sensibility of the audience. They felt we were talking down to them.

The picture turned out to be a hit, but I still wish I had edited about ten minutes more out of it. It would have been twice as good. The problem, of course, is when you go to a great deal of trouble to get a scene, you hate to part with it. I still hadn't learned that faster and shorter is better.

Another problem was that I'd cast so many personal friends who wanted to get killed on camera, including Mario Puzo's son, Anthony, my own son, Bobby, as well as my agent, Peter. I should've been more ruthless and cut them all out of the picture. I have to live with that stupid mistake every time I watch the film.

I suppose no one has the right to complain about success, *Hell Up in Harlem* has been bringing in substantial profits for over 25 years.

Chapter 11
Me and My Baby

While we were finishing filming *Hell Up in Harlem*, I was also making *It's Alive* for Warner Bros. I was shooting five days a week on *It's Alive* and then using much of the same crew to film on the weekend to capture Fred Williamson's sequences. The poor editor, Peter Honess, who had never cut a movie before, was now faced with handling two pictures simultaneously: one at our editing room at Movielab in Hollywood, the other in my guest house in Malibu, which I'd turned into a full-scale editing facility. We worked on each picture on alternate days and sometimes I was certain that the poor fellow wasn't sure which picture he was cutting. Later, he was an Academy Award nominee for *L.A. Confidential.*

It's Alive had been quickly approved by Richard Shepard, Head of Production at Warner Bros. Since I was making a non-union film, this was set up as a negative pick-up deal, but Warners supplied me with all the funding under the table. Most of the picture was shot in my home in Beverly Hills.

It's Alive would tell the story of an average American family whose new baby is a genetic aberration—a jump in evolution—a creature born with the power to defend itself when attempts are made to dispose of it in the delivery room. It is, in essence, a baby that can kill. There had been monster babies in fiction before, memorably in Greek mythology, but not recently. Eventually several other movies about monstrous infants were produced after *It's Alive.* Julie Christie would star in a high-budget MGM dud *Demon Seed* while Joan Collins was seen to poor advantage in *I Don't Want to be Born.*

My concept was to show very little of our monster baby and leave it to the audience's imagination. Even so, I engaged Rick Baker, who would prove one of the biggest makeup artists of the 1980s, winning Oscars for *An American Werewolf in London* and *Harry and the Hendersons*, and who had done on-set make-up for *Bone* and *Black Caesar*, mainly bullet wounds and burns. Now he would be called upon to create a full-fledged creature.

We sat down and sketched out the monster together. I wanted an enlarged head with the veins distended, along with ferocious teeth—kind of a cross between the star child in *2001* and a wolf. Rick drew what I had requested. His initial sketches were right on target and he went off to build the creature.

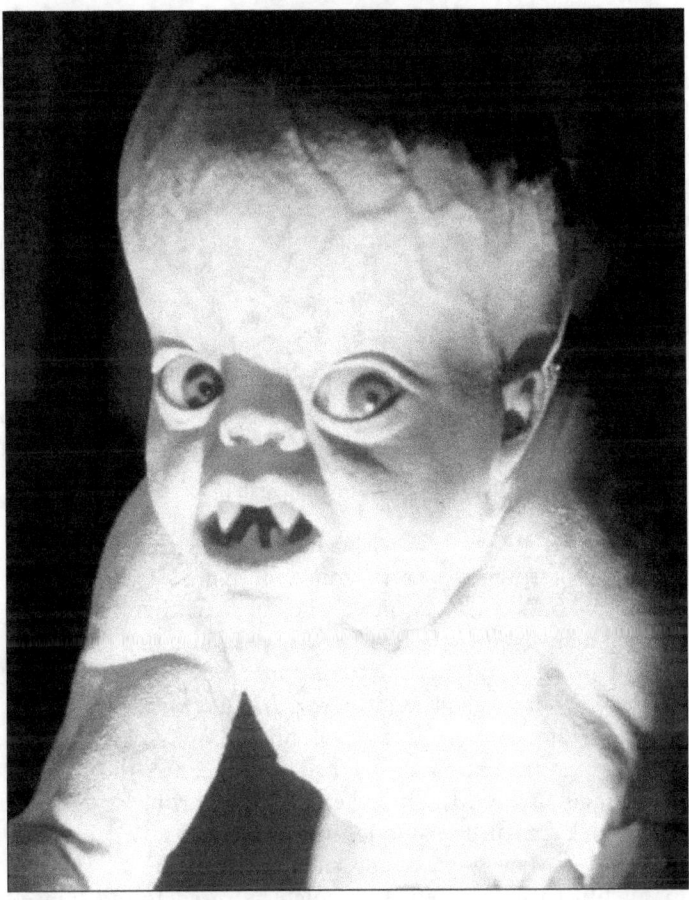

He was designing it so that his wife would fit inside the larger costume. I inquired as to how he could do such a thing to the woman he loved, and he responded that he needed to have someone who was always around. Since his wife was his constant companion, she'd been been given the job.

What would really sell this monster in *It's Alive* would be the performances of John P. Ryan and Sharon Farrell. Once again, my pal Jimmy Dixon would come through for me, this time in the role as the sympathetic detective in charge of the investigation. He also cast most of the supporting players that appeared in the film. Jimmy was an invaluable partner in the

John P. Ryan and Andrew Duggan in *It's Alive.*

making of *It's Alive*, as was Janelle, whose principal achievement was keeping my crew from mutinying. I was working
them 15 hours a day or more and most of them were also
helping make *Hell Up in Harlem* on weekends. And two Larry
Cohen movies at once is one too many.

The 18 days of production on *It's Alive* raced by, with
Fenton Hamilton as director of photography. Fenton had
been the gaffer on *Bone* and had once headed the lighting
department at MGM, where he lit Greta Garbo, Joan Crawford and Lana Turner, among others. He was now an elderly
man and his family was concerned about his health. He did
many films for me, between which he often found himself
back in the hospital on the critical list. But I would call him
and tell him that I needed him, and Fenton would rise to the
occasion, making an instant recovery in time to report to the
set. People often asked me how I could drag this poor old
codger out of his sick bed and make him work a grueling
schedule, but I honestly believe that's what kept him alive.
The one year I went away to Europe and didn't make any
movies, poor Fenton passed away. He reminded me so much
of my Grandpa Moses, and he treated me with similar affection. His presence on the set made my life easier with the
other crew members as well. If an old man like Fenton could

put up with the hours that I required, how could these young guys complain about it?

Fenton must have been pretty close to 80 when he finally fulfilled his dream of becoming a director of photography, and I was pleased to have made that dream come true.

Nothing I'd done previously approached the success of *It's Alive*. But it would take four years from the initial release date for the picture to finally perform. It was a situation without precedent in the motion picture industry and could never happen again.

By the time I'd completed *It's Alive* and presented it to Warner Bros., poor Dick Shepard was long gone. There had been a change in management and now *It's Alive* was held up as an example of the kind of inferior product that the Shepard regime had brought to the studio. All of the current attention at Warner Bros. was focused — and rightly so — on the release of *The Exorcist*.

The advertising division had decided that a movie about a monster baby was taboo, so they concocted an ad campaign which hid the subject matter of the picture from its potential audience. The ad copy simply read: "Whatever it is it's alive and deadly" with a picture of a woman's bloody body sprawled out

Sharon Farrell and Larry Cohen on the set of *It's Alive.*

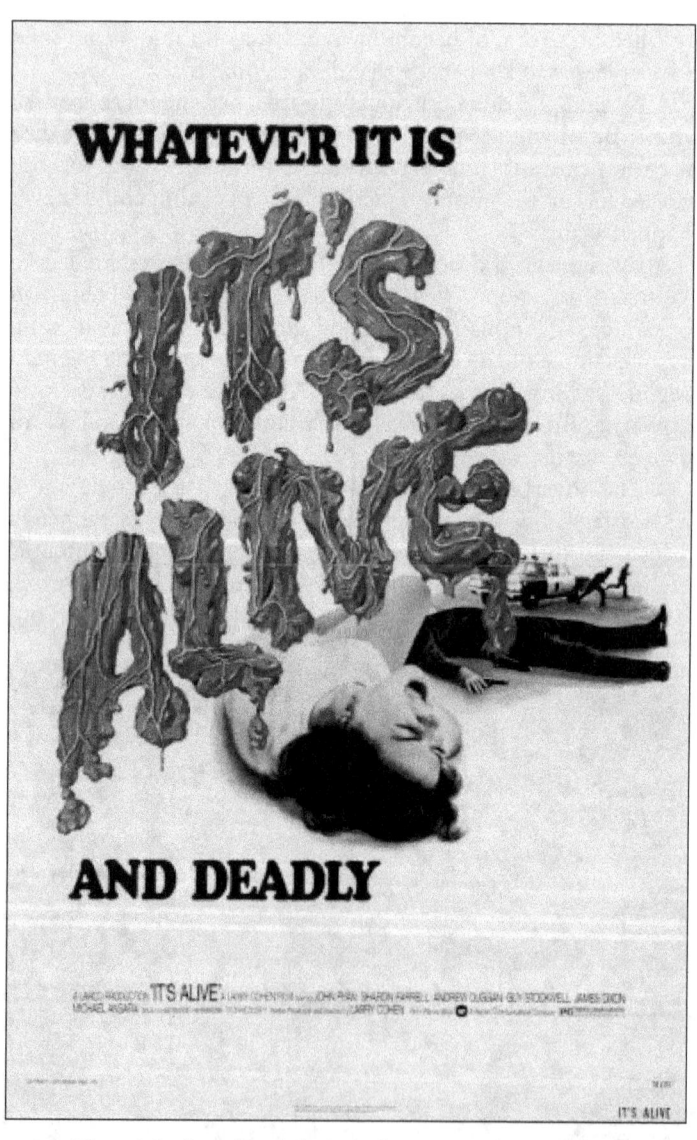

The original, underwhelming ad campaign for *It's Alive.*

and police cars in the background. It was a dreadful campaign, and I knew we were doomed. A horror picture is only as good as its gimmick, and without the monster baby angle, we had nothing to sell.

The results at the box office were not disastrous, but hardly encouraging. Warner Bros. had made only 50 prints of the movie. They were throwing the picture away. Warner Bros.' overseas division saw things differently and gave it a decent chance, even entering it in several festivals. I was surprised to learn that *It's Alive* had won the Special Jury Prize at the Avoriaz International Fantastic Film Festival and that the chairman of the jury was Roman Polanski. Other jurors included novelist Françoise Sagan and Claude Chabrol. This was indeed an honor and it led to an extremely successful engagement for the film in Paris. The picture went on to do strong business in other foreign territories. One morning I was called by Warners foreign division and informed that *It's Alive* was now the second largest-grossing picture in the history of Warner Bros... in Singapore. It sounded ridiculous, but Singapore was actually an important market. Attendance for our picture had only been exceeded by *My Fair Lady*.

Armed with this dubious information, I sought a meeting with Leo Greenfield, Head of Domestic Distribution for Warner Bros., who could not have cared less about my awards or foreign grosses. Leo talked like a carnival pitchman on the midway of some sleazy traveling carnival. "Kid, the heads of the studio have decided your picture is a loser. It's a self-fulfilling prophecy! To them, this piece of crap is an example of the incompetence of Dick Shepard! So go make another picture and forget about this one." On the way out of his office, Leo added, "Hey, but what the fuck do I know? I'm the guy that pegged *Billy Jack* to be a flop!"

I fought hard to salvage *It's Alive* because I knew its potential. When it first debuted at Chicago's Woods Theater in 1974, Janelle and I had flown over from London. Warners was still using the original dumb campaign but the local branch manager was a sweetheart. He authorized me to change the marquee of the theater and pull any stunt I chose to promote the picture.

Pretty soon I had Janelle strolling down the streets of Chicago pushing a baby carriage, from which hideous growls emerged. A sign on the carriage directed audiences to the Woods Theater. The marquee of the theater was altered to read: "It's only three days old, it's killed seven people. Its parents are human. It's alive!" And lo and behold, lines began to form in front of the theater. *It's Alive* actually did twice the business the second week as it'd done the first. And the business held. Over its five-week run, it outgrossed *Thunderbolt and Lightfoot*, the Clint Eastwood picture that had preceded it.

Despite this success, Mr. Greenfield maintained his position—that the picture was a preordained flop. But these results encouraged me to continue my battle.

At one point I'd made myself such a nuisance to Warner Bros. that their legal department had offered to sell the film back to me: "Give us $100,000 in cash, take your movie, go away and leave us alone."

I was certain I could get another releasing company to pony up, going first to Sam Arkoff. Sam and his distribution people enjoyed it, but they told me, "If Warner Bros. couldn't make a hit out of this, what makes you think we can?"

The other studios echoed this remark when I approached them. Nobody wanted to take a Warner Bros. reject. Finally, in New York, I came across a company called Bryanston Films, which had made significant dollars distributing the *The Texas Chain Saw Massacre*. It was rumored that Bryanston was a mob-related company, as later would prove to be the case when the U.S. government filed charges against them. Their management was, however, willing to take on the distribution of *It's Alive* and pledged me the $100,000.

I returned to Warners and accepted their offer. Documents were drawn up, but Bryanston's $100,000 did not materialize and I had to go crawling back to Warners and ask them to let me out of the deal. It turned out to be a godsend that the Bryanston deal fell through since I would never have seen a nickel from them.

Months passed into years and somehow, *It's Alive* always seemed to linger in distribution. It played widely as a second feature in drive-ins and then ended up as the lower part of a triple bill at the World Theater on Hollywood Boulevard. Still I never gave up hope.

Finally the management at Warner Bros. changed once again. The new head of advertising was now Arthur Manson, who'd previously had success at Cinerama Releasing with the Daniel Mann horror film *Willard*. I figured if this guy could make a hit out of a picture about rats, he could do the same with my monster baby. I contacted Arthur and he agreed to take a look, ringing me only a day later to say, "It's one of the scariest movies I ever sat through. I'm going to get Terry Semel to see it."

Semel had just replaced Leo Greenfield as head of Warners distribution, and it took no time at all for him to call. "I really enjoyed the picture. I checked on your earlier distribution and I think Warner Bros. did you a tremendous disservice. I'm going to give this one another shot. I'll order a brand-new ad campaign and see what happens."

I had no inkling that Terry would someday run the entire studio and go on to become Chairman of the Board.

More time passed while Warners devised a clever TV spot that seemed at first like a baby food commercial: gently tinkling bells, then a warm voice explaining that "there's only one thing wrong with the Davis baby   it's alive." The camera had been approaching an infant's crib. As it circled around, we saw a horrific little claw emerging from under the baby blanket. Some chilling music rose up and the spot was over.

The print campaign echoed the TV spot. It was short and simple and effective. Terry told me he was test-marketing the campaign and the picture in the Midwest. I held my breath.

The results were phenomenal. Terry then decided to hold the picture for another four months before going into major release. I said to him, "I hope you're still in the job in four months," to which he replied, "Don't worry. I will be."

This time, Warners made over 800 prints of a picture that had already been in distribution for almost four years and had been playing on triple features for 99 cents. They booked us into Class A theaters and took out sizable ads, spending millions on the television spots alone. It paid off. In May 1977, *It's Alive* became the top grossing movie in America, hitting number one in the *Variety* charts, beating competition like *Rocky* and *Annie Hall*. It played in theaters for months and was again revived to serve as co-feature to *Exorcist II: The Heretic* (which had proved something of a disaster). Audiences everywhere agreed

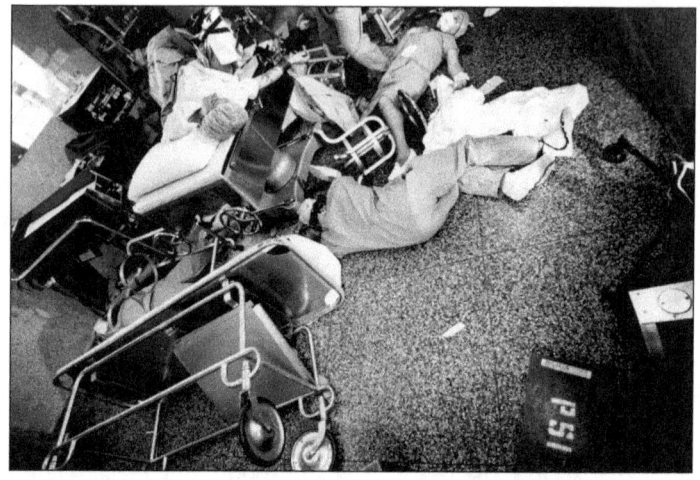

The hospital massacre in *It's Alive*.

The *It's Alive* baby was supposed to be barely seen, but Cohen liked Rick Baker's work so much that he featured it in the film.

Directing John P. Ryan and Sharon Farrell in *It's Alive*.

that *It's Alive* was far more enjoyable than the big budget bomb it was supporting. Eventually, with home video, *It's Alive* would become a cult classic.

With its new campaign, the film eventually grossed $39 million, to which I was entitled to a substantial share. Despite the usual creative bookkeeping that Hollywood was famous for, I was paid and continue to be paid a third of the profits.

Today this reversal of fortune would not have occurred. With video and DVDs coming out only a few months after initial theatrical release, *It's Alive* would've had no chance to be reissued theatrically.

It's Alive made me a millionaire many times over. Its earnings enabled me to buy a sumptuous townhouse in Manhattan just off Park Avenue. It boasted 22 rooms, a full backyard, and had the only private garage on East 79th Street. After our divorce, Janelle would be able to sell the townhouse for five times what we'd paid for it. I owed it all to the little monster baby who would soon star in two sequels, both for Warner Bros.

By that time, Arthur Manson, the kindhearted head of advertising who had started the ball rolling, had been fired by Warners and was now working as a producer's rep. Since I owed so much of my success to him, I called him and told him I was giving him five percent of my profits from *It's Alive* as a gesture of appreciation. And he's gotten a check every year since. He never asked for a penny, but I felt good cutting him in.

I wonder how many other filmmakers have had their picture destroyed by major studios because of internal politics.

Much later I had a similar experience at Warner Bros. under still another administration. I'd been hired to direct two movies for the company's home video division. One was to be a sequel to *Salem's Lot*, a vampire saga by Stephen King which had initially been produced as a four-hour television miniseries. Warners was also allowing me to make a second sequel to *It's Alive*. The films would be shot back-to-back with the same crew and I would have full autonomy. I no sooner had begun than Warners decided to disband the home video division's production arm. The theatrical division didn't want to compete with cheap pictures made by the video department. Why take the risk that one of these video productions might turn out to be more successful at the box office than their expensive blockbusters? When I delivered my two pictures, nobody was remotely interested in seeing them. I felt like a waiter bringing food out of the kitchen and finding new customers at the table who'd complain "I didn't order this." I urged the new distribution chief, Barry Reardon, to give these movies a chance in theaters, and finally went over his head to Terry Semel, who remembered our past experience and gave his approval for a theatrical test run.

Reardon, however, was not to be proved wrong. He deliberately booked the pictures in such a way that they were doomed and also withheld advertising. Despite his negative efforts, *A Return to Salem's Lot* opened to excellent business in New England. We were grossing almost $8,000 per theater, which was an impressive return.

Some at Warners were getting excited, but Reardon insisted that this was a fluke. He would test the picture again elsewhere. This time he opened it in a college town during the first week of the new semester, a totally illogical decision. Failing to generate much business, my movie was quickly diverted to the Siberia of straight-to-video.

Distribution woes are the agony of all filmmakers. Even if you've had hits before, you're usually treated badly. Your contract may include a consultancy clause which simply means that they'll show you the ad campaign after it's already been locked in. You can take it or leave it, but you can't change it. Nowadays, there's no chance to turn a picture around. If it doesn't perform on the first weekend, its failure is announced on *Entertainment Tonight* and the picture is immediately earmarked as a flop. Since nobody wants to pay to see a flop, this damage can never be repaired. Even if you get excellent reviews, the studios will not buy the ad space in the newspapers to run the quotes.

Over the years I entered into many other deals that turned out unfavorably to me. I call it my string of disasters. As usual, I had no one else but myself to blame. One in particular involved Q (which was called Q, *The Winged Serpent* for its foreign release).

For the lifetime of Sam's company, AIP had never been in the red. Then he began turning out more ambitious projects, much of it with tax shelter money. The problem with tax shelters is they made every deal look promising, even when the scripts and casting combinations spelled nothing but disaster. AIP would recover the negative cost of the picture but they would have to eat the enormous advertising and distribution costs when the film did nothing at the box office. Suddenly Sam was looking at a company that was losing money and he panicked. Not foreseeing the future value that media companies would have, he sold out to Filmways but remained in charge of production. Soon after taking over, the new management found an excuse to kick Sam out.

Q offered Sam his chance to get back on the fast track again so he contributed $450,000 to the cost of production at a time when I needed help. He was extremely pleased when I delivered the picture, although he owned only 25 percent of it. I controlled the other 75 percent. We began to show the film to studios for a possible pick-up. Warner Bros. immediately made me an offer of $2.5 million for foreign and domestic rights. Since the film cost only a little over a million dollars to produce, I personally would be walking away with a million-dollar profit. Sam would double his money and there would be a possible back end for both of us if the picture was a hit.

I knew how powerful the Warner Bros. distribution arm could be and I wanted to close the deal, but Sam thought we could do better. Since I was the majority owner, I chose to accept Warners offer, only to learn that Sam had sent them a telegram threatening a lawsuit. He had absolutely no right to interfere, but my attorney, Skip Brittenham, who'd known us both for many years, felt I owed Sam a debt of gratitude and shouldn't pull the rug out from under him. In deference to past favors, I turned Warners down and we continued offering the picture on the open market.

It didn't take long to get a favorable response from MGM to the tune of five million. Clearly, Sam Arkoff's instincts had been correct. We were ready to sign off when, over the weekend, MGM's head of distribution was summarily dismissed. The new management was not interested in Q. The many millions I would've earned fluttered away like birds going south for the winter. All the other markets seemed to have dried up as well.

Finally, with hat in hand, I returned to Warner Bros., willing to accept their initial offer, but now they were only willing to pay $1.5 million. There are no secrets in Hollywood. Each studio knows what the others are doing. Warners knew our back was to the wall, mine more than Sam's. He had only $450,000 in the picture. I had over $600,000 tied up in expenditures and obligations. That's when Sam proposed that he assume all foreign rights in return for his investment.

I think he knew it was a steal and quite unfair since he'd been directly responsible for my losing my million-dollar profit on the original Warner offer. I don't think Arkoff would have done this under other circumstances, but he was still recoiling from the shock of being dismissed from the company that he had built. Poor Sam was running scared and thinking only of himself.

Eventually I would sell the domestic rights for only $650,000 to United Artists Theaters. It was a ridiculously low price and it meant that I would make no profit whatsoever and receive no compensation for my services as writer and director. At least I'd be able to pay off the laboratory and equipment house, plus a deferment to my actors.

Sam went on to prosper from the foreign sales, but never offered me a nickel. I forgave him because I truly cared for this man and enjoyed the many hours we spent together. I didn't want to lose that friendship.

Reminiscing with him years later, I was stunned when Sam categorically denied that the Warner Bros. offer of $2.5 million had ever been made. He couldn't allow himself to remember how badly he'd screwed me on that deal. Instead, he had blotted it out of his mind.

In the movie business, if someone takes advantage of you, you can usually be assured of never working for them again. Your very presence makes them feel like a bad guy. At least with Sam, he developed a case of convenient amnesia, and I made no further attempt to cure him. We continued to go out to dinner, and I was always amused because he habitually ordered an extra main course for the table—which he consumed himself of course. Until his death, Sam and I continued to see each other regularly and I never again brought up the subject of Q. I'd rather remember him as the man who gave me the money to make *The Private Files of J. Edgar Hoover*, despite the fact that I refused to tell him the name of the actor who'd be playing the lead.

I would face similar distribution agonies with Roger Corman's company, New World, which had purchased *God Told Me To*, starring Tony Lo Bianco, Sandy Dennis and Deborah Raffin, back in 1976 for the highest acquisition price they'd ever paid. They immediately floundered trying to figure out how to sell the picture. Some incompetent finally came up with the line, "The leader of every major religion has condemned this film." As if that wasn't the most negative campaign ever devised, they opened the picture in the Texas Bible Belt, of all places.

The film concerns an alien born to a normal woman who grows up with supernatural powers and becomes convinced that he is actually God. He finds himself able to induce others to commit homicides in his name. A detective steeped in his own Catholic faith finally pursues this creature to his destruction and in doing so learns that he too springs from alien ancestry.

Since the initial results were distinctly unsatisfying at the box office, I met with Corman and my two principal backers, Edgar Scherick and Dan Blatt, to come up with a new marketing approach. Roger's solution was to change the title of the movie. I suggested several alternate titles, among then "Alien"—which was immediately dismissed. Roger said, "People will think it's a picture about wetbacks." We eventually retitled the film *The Demon*, which I always thought of as *The Omen* spelled sideways.

The picture opened at my beloved Cinerama Theater, where I'd had so much success with my Blaxploitation films.

This time, however, there was no clever TV spot to promote the picture and the print campaign was bland. Still, *God Told Me To* remains my most requested film at festivals throughout the world. I'm constantly complimented on it by other filmmakers including Oliver Stone, who approached me at Nell's Club in Manhattan many years later, threw his arms around me, and proclaimed it one of his favorite movies.

Demon was the alternate release title for *Gold Told Me To.*

Oddly enough, *God Told Me To* also won me a Special Jury Prize at the Avoriaz International Fantastic Film Festival. This time the president of the jury was Steven Spielberg. I'd like to have been there to receive the award, but I was never invited. Some years later I went to Avoriaz as a judge and presented *The Ambulance* out of competition. When the jurors retired to vote, they wanted to give *The Ambulance* the award but couldn't do so because I was a jury member, and the picture hadn't been officially entered into the competition. Michael Cimino was the chairman of that jury and he refused to vote on any of the pictures because they were all politically irrelevant. Turning his chair to the wall and facing away from everyone, he ignored the proceedings. He then threatened to resign as chairman until he'd intimidated the operators of the festival into buying him a car.

Being on a jury at a European festival can have a lethal effect if you're not a smoker. I was nearly overcome every day. I had to flee outside into the cold mountain air simply to catch a breath.

Although Cimino was decidedly unfriendly at the festival, when I encountered him at Spago's restaurant back in Los Angeles, he behaved like I was his long-lost brother, demanding we have dinner together. I was doubly surprised when he called me up to follow up on the invitation. I let him pick the restaurant of his choice and he selected the Hamburger Hamlet on Sunset. We had a relaxed evening during which he sadly confided that indeed his star had faded. Nobody wanted to make pictures with him anymore.

Listening to Michael, I was grateful I'd never reached a position where one costly failure could put me out of the business forever, as *Heaven's Gate* had for him, despite having made the hugely successful, Oscar-winning *The Deer Hunter*. My movies were low-budget, and nobody could lose on them. Directors have full autonomy only at the very top, when they've got enormous box-office clout, or at the bottom, where nobody cares enough to bother them. Thankfully I still had dozens of ideas for movies and the ability to sit down and write the screenplays to please myself.

One morning, John Landis phoned me to invite me to play a small part in his new movie, *Spies Like Us*. Arriving on location at a drive-in movie in the San Fernando Valley, I found myself

Michael Apted, B. B. King and Larry Cohen
in John Landis' *Spies Like Us.*

surrounded by other film directors, most of them heavy hitters. We spent the entire day hanging out in the trailer waiting for our scene to come up and rapping about the biz. Each of them said they were looking at scripts for future projects. They just hadn't found anything they liked. I foolishly asked, "Don't you have any ideas of your own that you'd like to see made?" To a man they responded that they simply read what their agents submitted and hoped something of interest would come across the desk. I suppose that's the difference between a high-budget director and a low-budget one like myself. We cook up our own stories rather than wait to see what's offered. I also find that low-budget directors who have distinguished themselves and go on to higher-budget films shortly cease writing their own material. They become directors for hire and somehow never achieve the originality that their earlier films promised. Don't get me wrong, I'm not better than anybody else. I've just never even gotten the opportunity to sell out.

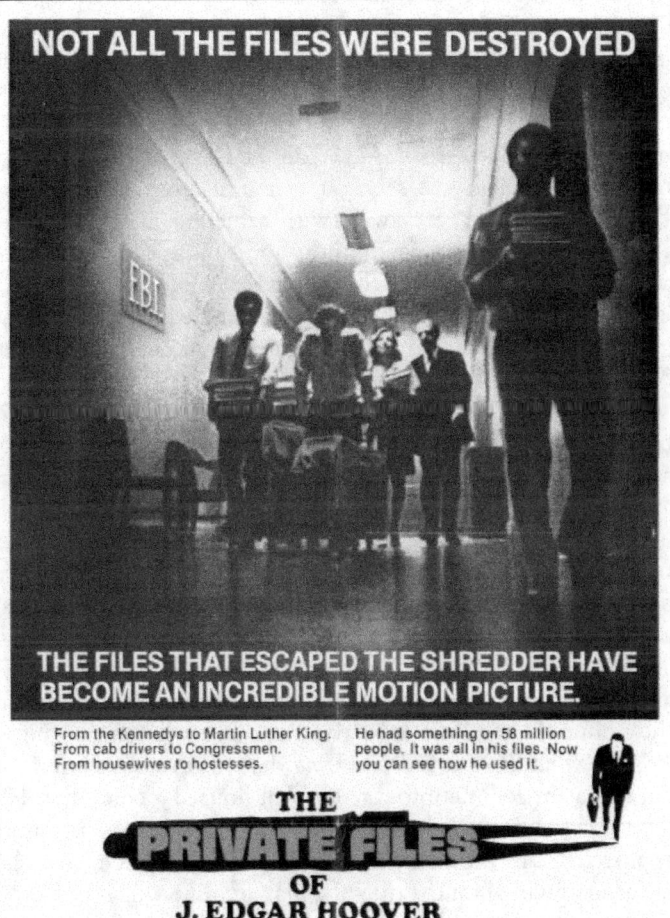

The toughest challenge I ever faced as a director was bringing *The Private Files of J. Edgar Hoover* to the screen. This film bio was to cover 48 years in the life of the notorious FBI director. Critics later called it "an historical horror movie." It required period costumes and locations, antique cars, government co-operation and a huge cast. Everyone warned me such a picture would never be made. No movie or television program critical of the FBI had ever been produced. In fact, at that time it was a federal crime to depict the FBI and its seal without the express permission of the Bureau.

All scripts dealing with the FBI had to be submitted in advance and approved—and an FBI agent was generally required to be on the set as a technical advisor. Somehow, I thought I could get away with violating all these rules. I researched the story for months and sought out a technical advisor, who'd help give the film some validity. Through a literary agent named David Obst, who handled newsmen, I was granted an audience with the celebrated Seymour Hersh of the *New York Times'* Washington Bureau.

I flew to the nation's capital and presented myself at his office. Hersh immediately instructed me to sit down, shut up, and watch him at work. He was phoning a two-star general at the Pentagon whom he explained would attempt to duck his call. He immediately asked the general's secretary if it was true her boss was being demoted to a post at NATO. After a moment the general came on the line to deny this unfounded rumor and Hersh then hit him with the real question he wanted answered—an embarrassing inquiry about a drastic cut in his appropriations. He had tricked the general into picking up the phone. Hersh enjoyed having me as an audience. "Now let's see what *The New York Times* has to say about you," he winked as he led me into a room that housed a computer. He typed my name into it and waited. Pretty soon the printout appeared: "Larry Cohen, alleged drug dealer." I suggested he try again, giving him the title of a play of mine which had been reviewed by Clive Barnes of the *Times*. He punched this in, and the next printout appeared. "Larry Cohen, author, Nature of the Crime, reviewed Barnes, *New York Times*, 1970. Review mixed—alleged drug dealer."

I didn't end up making a deal with Hersh, but fortunately John Crewdson signed on. He was the *New York Times* reporter who actually covered the FBI. And, as it turned out, a far better choice. Crewdson's help was invaluable. Walking into a government building with him carried the aura of America's most respected newspaper. Those who ordinarily would have rejected an interview suddenly agreed, since they assumed any reluctance might be reported in print.

Hoover himself had been dead for only four years but the Bureau was still ruled by his loyal clique. Clarence Kelly had been recently appointed FBI Director after the hasty departure of L. Patrick Gray, who had burned key documents as a favor to President Nixon early in the Watergate upheaval. Among other Hoover cronies, I interviewed Chuck Brennan in person and John P. Mohr by phone. They were usually inaccessible to reporters, but I represented Hollywood, and that interested them.

Along with Crewdson, I flew to Sugarbush, Vermont to visit with William T. Sullivan, who'd been the number three man at the FBI under Hoover. He had betrayed Hoover by removing the Kissinger wiretap authorizations from Hoover's private files and surrendering them to the Nixon White House. He was currying favor, hoping to be appointed as the next Bureau chief once Hoover was forcibly retired. Hoover instantly fired Sullivan, locked him out of the Justice Department building, and survived the attempted coup. Crewdson and I knew that Bill Sullivan would have interesting tales to tell and indeed, what we uncovered soon made headlines in *The New York Times*.

Mr. and Mrs. Sullivan couldn't have been sweeter. She served us a home-cooked dinner and invited us to sleep over in her son's bedroom. Sullivan himself was a small, wiry fellow who only a week before had easily overpowered a belligerent six-foot teenager who'd illegally parked in his driveway. It was difficult to sit across the dinner table from this nice little guy and have him admit he'd personally engineered the sending of a letter to Mrs. Coretta King which contained a tape recording of the Reverend King having sex in a motel room with one of his volunteers. The package had been mailed from Florida to disguise its origins. It was followed up by a note to Dr. King suggesting he commit suicide. Of course, Mr. Sullivan was quick to add the Bureau had pulled the same stunt on Ku Klux Klan leaders who were having affairs with black women—ratting them out to their wives.

That evening, Bill Sullivan also revealed to us the heretofore secret existence of a Security Index listing more than 200 people who'd be immediately taken into custody should hostilities break out between the U.S. and the Soviet Union. These included prominent journalists and celebrities.

I asked Sullivan if Hoover was aware that Nixon had been secretly taping his conversations in the Oval Room of the White House and had my hunch confirmed. A number of the Secret Service men working in the White House were former FBI agents. Once FBI, always FBI. Their loyalties were to Hoover. The FBI director was well aware that these tapes were stored in Room 173½ of the executive office building to which many persons had easy access, including Nixon aides who'd borrowed several of the tapes to play at private parties. I asked if the FBI could've removed certain incriminating tapes and copied them. Sullivan thought this was very possible. He said he wouldn't have been let in on it because he was known to be a Nixon sympathizer. Nixon himself couldn't be sure Hoover hadn't gotten to the tapes and duplicated them. It may have been what finally deterred him from destroying the recordings after their existence became known.

We were treated so kindly by the Sullivans that by the time Crewdson and I departed, we felt like we'd spent the weekend with close relatives. Our Security Index story broke on the front page of the *Times*. I went on to question several other FBI supervisors, many of whom were much freer with information once they learned that I'd visited Bill Sullivan personally. Sadly, Sullivan was shot to death not long afterward in the woods behind his house, apparently by a careless hunter who mistook him for a deer.

Having a newsworthy screenplay and some interesting location footage was not enough. I would still have to find an important actor to portray the complex role of Hoover. My first choice was Rod Steiger. I sent him the material and he responded favorably, but then chose to take on the role of W. C. Fields in a big budget Universal production. I decided to gamble on Broderick Crawford, who had won the Academy Award as Best Actor for his role in *All the King's Men*. Crawford had since become famous for his television series, *Highway Patrol*, but he hadn't been offered an important movie role in years.

I also quickly made a deal with Dan Dailey (who'd been a fabulous song and dance man at 20th Century Fox, usually opposite Betty Grable) to assay the difficult role of Clyde Tolson, Hoover's long-time sidekick confidante and alleged lover.

I pitched the project to producer Frank Yablans, only to have him announce his own Hoover movie in the trade papers a month later. He claimed he had Brando on board to star, which was just hype, but I couldn't afford to wait and find out.

There was still no studio interest, so I decided to start making the film without backing. I had no budget, no shooting schedule, no production manager and no completion bond. Who needed such formalities? I'd simply bring my cast to Washington and begin shooting with a small crew. After the first week I'd have exhausted my funds, but I hoped by then somebody would step up and assume the financial risk.

Broderick Crawford as J. Edgar Hoover

Who else but dear old Sam Arkoff? I had to utilize all my wiles to draw Sam into the deal. After all, I had made a few hits for him. I phoned Sam and announced that I had an Academy Award-winning actor playing J. Edgar Hoover but wouldn't tell him who it was. I suppose my withholding amused him. He assumed it was Steiger and agreed to advance me $100,000. After all, he knew I was already shooting and was in a vulnerable position. His investment would give him a lien on the picture.

Because of Crewdson, I gained access to the Justice Department building for a single day of filming. I used the pretext that I needed to photograph the various rooms and offices so that we could duplicate them in Hollywood on a soundstage. Actually I was shooting scenes for the movie. We shot in the corridors and in Hoover's own private office. The role of the disillusioned FBI agent through whose eyes the story unfolds was being played by Robert Forster, later Oscar nominated for Quentin Tarantino's *Jackie Brown*, but after a few weeks of shooting I had to replace him with Rip Torn. I managed to salvage some of the original footage using jigsaw cutting. When Rip Torn walks into a room, it's actually Robert Forster's feet strolling across the carpet. We also see Forster from the rear and in silhouette in a number of shots. I figured that once I'd gotten inside the Justice Department, I might not be allowed back, so nothing could go to waste.

I noticed key FBI officials kept dropping by while we were filming. They'd been clued in to the fact that we were doing Mr. Hoover's bio. I was certain the Bureau would somehow acquire a copy of my screenplay, but I hoped they'd realize that it wasn't a total hatchet job on Hoover. As with a film like *Patton*, it portrayed both positive and negative aspects of the man.

As filming continued, I managed to bring some other names into the cast: Oscar-winners Celeste Holm and José Ferrer. I also lined up Michael Parks to play Bobby Kennedy.

All these stars were accustomed to working on studio films. The idea of being hustled in limousines and being driven around Washington while I tried to find a suitable location seemed like madness. But they got used to it—mainly because I always came up with some great place to shoot. Often, they

Dan Dailey and Broderick Crawford in
The Privates Files of J. Edgar Hoover.

wouldn't know what scene we were doing next until the location happened to materialize and I'd yell "Pull over, that's it!"

After a few more days of this lunacy, I phoned Arkoff again, informing him that we now had three Academy Award-winning actors in the picture and requesting an additional $100,000 to continue. I still wouldn't tell him who those stars were. And once again he bit. I suppose his curiosity was piqued. Sam always called me a rogue and likened me to Roger Corman, whom he had once caught shooting two pictures at the same time. Roger was making the second one for himself, using the same actors and crew Sam was paying for. When Sam found out, he told Roger "Now we're partners on two movies!"

When I finally needed the third installment of $100,000, Sam flatly demanded to know who the star was. When I announced the name Broderick Crawford, he moaned, "Is he still alive?"

By the time we finally wrapped photography, Sam was in for $400,000 and was not too happy about it. A biopic of J. Edgar Hoover was definitely not the kind of movie that AIP was accustomed to distributing. I assured him this would be the best movie his company had ever produced, one that even his wife, Hilda, would actually sit through. Mrs. Arkoff had a habit of walking out during screenings at Sam's home, almost as soon as the AIP logo came on. I suggested this movie could help him redeem himself in his wife's eyes. Sam laughed heartily at the suggestion—then threw his cigar at me.

June Havoc as Hoover's mother and
James Wainright as young Hoover.

Having Sam's few dollars couldn't overcome the insurmountable obstacles of shooting in Washington. At first, nobody would let us use the interiors we required. They were all reluctant to incur the wrath of the FBI. When we did get permission, it was quickly withdrawn when they learned the subject matter.

I'd originally planned to slip into Washington and shoot without publicity, but the very first day, filming at one of Hoover's favorite watering holes, the Mayflower Hotel, we found ourselves surrounded by reporters and photographers. The hotel's PR man had leaked the story. Pictures of Crawford and Dan Dailey appeared prominently in the next day's newspapers. Fortunately, some of these articles came to the notice of Betty Ford, whose husband was then President of the United States. Mrs. Ford was a former hoofer herself and a big fan of Dan Dailey. We got a surprise call at the Jefferson Hotel inviting Mr. Dailey and Broderick Crawford to lunch at the White House. I tried to wangle an invitation for myself and asked permission to film their entrance into the executive mansion but was turned down. It meant closing down production for a full day, but I realized that if I denied the stars an opportunity to dine with the President and First

Lady, they'd never forgive me, and I'd suffer for it throughout the production. Instead, I tried to make good use of the time to pick up the phone and call every possible location we might conceivably have needed, including the FBI itself.

I announced to the Bureau public relations director that we wished to shoot at Quantico, their training academy, and in the new FBI headquarters that had just been built and was to be known as the J. Edgar Hoover Building. I quickly added, "But we can't shoot tomorrow because the two stars of our film are having lunch with President Ford at the White House."

There was an odd pause. I was then put on hold while my story was verified, and then, minutes later, I was granted virtually unlimited access. Crawford and Dailey had a delightful luncheon with the President and Henry Kissinger. Vice President Rockefeller even offered to let us use his personal limousine in the movie. I must admit I took full advantage of the situation, calling every government agency with the same spiel and locking up all my locations in one day.

We were only granted permission to shoot in the inner courtyard of the Justice Department Building over the Memorial Day weekend when no one was around. We'd been assigned an FBI liaison named T. Carson, a handsome black fellow who moonlighted as a jazz pianist, often sitting in with the Count Basie orchestra. Obviously, Mr. Carson had been placed in a visible position within the Bureau as a PR move. The FBI was not known for employing black people at the time.

Once shooting got under way, any and all restrictions that had been placed upon us gradually fell away and I was soon staging scenes inside the corridors and offices of the Justice Department, shooting within the private sanctums Hoover himself once occupied. We even bluffed our way into the Attorney General's private conference room, which proved to be a great set.

When Attorney General Edward Levi returned after the holiday and discovered that a movie had been shot in his office, he had a fit. He immediately issued a directive forbidding us to use the footage. Then a day or so later he relented and sent a contradictory letter authorizing its use after all. Fortunately, the second letter arrived first.

One of my key contacts in Washington was Terry Lenzner, a volatile young attorney who'd served on the Watergate investigating committee. A rebel himself, Lenzner was most sympathetic to my cause and extremely well connected. When he picked up the telephone, he got results. I credit him with soothing the Attorney General's feelings. Terry went on to become a famous and controversial figure in Washington, founding Investigative Group International, a large investigative agency which sometimes delved into the personal lives of politicians. The Clinton administration apparently hired him to discredit many of its critics. Today, Terry is feared as much as he is admired. To me he was a godsend. All obstacles seemed to fall away and before long, I felt like I owned Washington, D.C.

There was a question of how we could recreate Washington in the 1930s on such a minuscule budget. I discovered there were antique car clubs in Maryland and invited them all to participate in the film. They agreed to show up on Pennsylvania Avenue at an appointed hour in their 1930s vehicles, bringing along their entire families dressed in the wardrobe of the period. All this at zero cost.

Naturally we had to get rid of any modern-day vehicles which would screw up the shots. Since there are endless parades in the nation's capital, wooden police barricades sit idly up on the sidewalk at major intersections. I hit upon the idea of our closing down the streets ourselves. I knew we'd never obtain permission from the District of Columbia. We simply did it—and got away with it. We blocked Pennsylvania Avenue to normal traffic and brought on the vintage cars. We played several dramatic scenes on the sidewalk with the antique cars passing by and also accomplished a number of driving sequences. On some sections of the street, parking meters were visible, so I stood actors in costume in front of the meters to hide them from view. There were also occasional "No Parking" signs which were wrong for the period, so I had our grips tear down the signs, actually pulling the metal poles out of the sidewalk. There was no way to put them back up, so we just left them lying there.

My luck held and I wasn't arrested. The sequence was satisfactorily completed, despite the fact that one of our large equipment trucks turned down a narrow alley and accidentally knocked a fire escape off the side of a local hotel. The driver kept on going.

Broderick Crawford didn't give up his drinking habits during production. Janelle had to bribe him with a few beers each morning when she went in to run lines with him. On camera, however, his performance was always smooth and on target. Late one night, however, José Ferrer brought some vodka onto the set and he's probably to blame for Crawford's going off on a binge. When we finished with Brod, I sent him home in a limo along with my mother, who had come by to watch. I stayed on with Ferrer to complete his coverage. The limo was supposed to come back for us, but it never did. José and I were sitting on the curb like a couple of bums while Crawford cruised whatever bars were still open with my mom helplessly in tow.

Finally, he staggered back into the Jefferson Hotel with his arm around my mother for support, only to find his wife, Mary Alice Moore, waiting angrily in the lobby. Mary Alice was doing a wonderful job of playing Hoover's secretary, Miss Gandy. I don't think she and my mom got along too well after that particular encounter. She had always dreamed of having a romance with some famous movie star, but not a boozed-up Broderick Crawford. To be fair, working for a fly-by-night director like me could drive any actor to drink.

While shooting outside the Old Post Office, I suddenly informed Janelle that we needed additional actors for the scene. I wanted a few middle-aged men that looked like Republicans so I could film them, led by Ferrer, entering the building in order to prevent the shredding of crucial FBI documents after Hoover's death. I suggested Janelle drop by the Palm Restaurant in Washington and round up some likely suspects. Instead, Janelle and my mother prowled the lobby of the Jefferson Hotel. They descended on one gentleman who was checking in with his attorney, asking, "How would you guys like to be in a movie?" I'm sure they thought they were being approached by hookers, but mom explained herself and, in a few minutes, the pair had arrived on set. The short, bald man was H. L. Murphy, President of Murphy Oil. I immediately told him to get a different tie. The make-up woman began powdering Mr.

Murphy's head without any objection. Within a few minutes of shooting, Murphy had begun advising Rip Torn that he was off his mark. He'd already mastered the technicalities of the art of movie acting. Although probably being worth hundreds of millions, Mr. Murphy gladly accepted $25 in remuneration for his performance and cashed the check.

There was a further problem with Rip, who had been sent to the tailor's to have cuffs put on his pants but had refused to allow the fitting to be completed. Naturally the trousers were far too long to be filmed. I sent Janelle out to get a tailor in the middle of the night. Miracle of miracles, she returned with one. We didn't have time to wait so the tailor got down on his hands and knees on the sidewalk and began putting cuffs on Rip's pants while we continued shooting the actor from the waist up.

Rip wore two small hairpieces—one on each side of his forehead. He continually refused to let the hair stylist adjust them. Instead, he would hide them somewhere on location, and sometimes he forgot where he put them. When we shot at Pimlico Racetrack outside Washington, he left them behind at the hotel and we had to send a limo to pick up Rip's hair.

Since my assistants feared Rip, I took it upon myself to issue him his calls, and in New York I personally went to the apartment he shared with wife Geraldine Page and picked him up for work every morning. The sign on their doorbell read "Torn Page."

Early on in the production, I'd had a nasty run-in with Rip, who apparently wanted to test my authority. I told him he was free to quit the job and suggested he vacate his hotel room later that day. He blew up and challenged me to go outside in the street and settle the matter with our fists, to which I immediately agreed. Before we ever reached the exit, Rip grabbed me in a bear hug and said, "Look, Larry, I just want to make the movie!" After that, Rip was as good as gold and even ended up working for free toward the end of the production when I'd run out of money. "All I need is my carfare," he volunteered. He even came back and looped dialogue for free. Years later when we screened *The Private Files of J. Edgar Hoover* at the Museum of Modern Art in New York, I was thrilled to see Geraldine Page in the audience. She'd come to see her husband give one of his best performances.

Rip Torn, who locked horns with Cohen during filming.

Janelle and I subsequently invited Rip to join us for a celebration dinner at Sardi's (New York's most popular theatrical restaurant for decades), only to learn that he'd never been inside the place before. Despite playing on Broadway in dozens of shows, he was a total stranger to Sardi's. He warmed up to it once he saw his own caricature hanging on the wall amongst numerous Broadway stars.

Throughout the production, Rip accused me of working with the FBI. "You're in with them, I know that! How else could you get all this cooperation? All I want is for you to get me my FBI file. You can do it. The FBI has been all over me for years. I need that fucking file." I kept insisting I had no influence with the Bureau, which he couldn't accept. Twenty years down the line I ran into Rip outside a Broadway theater. "Did you ever get your FBI file through the Freedom of Information Act?" I inquired.

Rip replied glumly, "Yeah, I did. There was nothing the fuck there."

He was broken-hearted that the Bureau didn't have a thing on him.

Most of the actors caused me no problem on the Hoover movie, but I can't say as much for the crew. Usually we worked 18-20-hour days, but for once a feeling of generosity swept over me and I gave everybody the night off. Paul Glickman, the director of photography, and seven others decided to spend it at the movies. They chose my own film, *It's Alive*, which was currently playing in Washington and was already a big hit all over the country.

When they got to the theater, they decided not to pay the admission price. After all, why should they shell out to see a Larry Cohen film? One of them would buy a ticket and then open the fire door for the others to sneak in. Once inside, however, they found themselves in the wrong theater and they had to walk across the lobby to get into the theater showing *It's Alive*. En route they were blocked by an usher. Our assistant cameraman, Stefan Czapsky—who later went on to become the director of photography on such films as *Batman Returns* and *Edward Scissorhands*—made the mistake of shoving the usher out of the way. The crew then disappeared into the darkened theater but couldn't find any seats, so they sat in the aisle. Before long, the cops arrived and everyone was placed under arrest. The woman police sergeant in charge gave Czapsky a chance to apologize but he stubbornly refused, and so they were all carted off to jail.

Janelle and I were awakened at our hotel in the middle of the night. At first it seemed like a comedic situation. Glickman, who was an amateur magician, had wiggled out of his handcuffs, much to the amusement of the black cops who ran the lock-up. The crew needed to be bailed out, but the District of

Columbia required a $500 bond for each. That meant $4,000 in cash, and we just didn't have that kind of money on hand.

I tried to get it from the hotel front desk and was able to raise only a thousand. This would be enough to get the two female members of the crew out before they were transferred to the dreaded Women's House of Detention. Then I got a second call from Glickman. The shift had changed, and now white cops were in charge, and they were roughing everybody up. They put Glickman in a choke-hold, and they were already shipping the two girls off to another facility in the company of hookers and petty thieves.

Janelle and I raced down to the jail with our thousand dollars but the girls had already been transferred. It took us until dawn to get them released. We then rushed down to the courthouse where all the crew members were being arraigned and picked up a shabby, down-at-the-heels lawyer who was wandering around the hallways seeking clients. For $50 apiece, he agreed to represent the crew.

After conferring with the assistant district attorney, he returned to announce that the trial would have to be postponed to the following day. The defendants would have to remain in custody. It seemed that the judge's nephew was the owner of the movie theater in which the incident had taken place and he was disqualifying himself from hearing the case.

I was appalled. These kids would be locked up for another 24 hours and I'd lose another day of production. I asked to speak to the D.A. personally and was ushered across the street. He was an intimidating black man who fixed a cold stare upon me as I relayed the story of how the crew had sneaked in to see my own movie, *It's Alive*. The D.A. replied, "Is that the movie about the monster baby? You're the one who ought to be locked up." And then he broke into a broad grin. "I'll arrange it so the judge asks for specific documentation to be placed on his bench and when that material does not appear, he will automatically throw the case out." It was as simple as that. A set-up.

An hour later the crew was back on the streets, but none of them coughed up their $50 to pay for their lawyer or even apologized for losing me an entire production day. One of

With Broderick Crawford.

them even sold the story to the *National Inquirer* for $200. The headline ran: "HOOVER MOVIE CREW ARRESTED IN D.C."

A few days later, Cohen and his ex-cons were privileged to film a key sequence at the home of Nathaniel Davis, the former ambassador to Switzerland. His was a beautiful house filled with original Remington sculptures and a perfect setting for a scene between Broderick Crawford and Celeste Holm. Mr. Davis cautioned we had to be gone by six o'clock because he was throwing a huge party with a celebrity guest list that would include the ambassador from Iran and the editor of the *Washington Star*. That's all I had to hear. "Can't we shoot a scene at the party? I bet your friends would love to be in a movie."

It took me only a few minutes to cook up such a sequence and that night I had a hundred free extras parading around in tuxedos and evening gowns without having spent an additional nickel. Being featured on camera was one of the highlights of the party for the guests.

It was a wildly hot the day we shot in front of the Justice Department. I noticed the windows of the building prominently displayed air conditioners which would've been completely out of place in the Forties. In a moment of absolute arrogance, I instructed one of my assistants to go inside and have the air conditioners removed from all the windows. This was an absurd request, particularly with the unbearable Washington humidity. Who would allow their air conditioner to be ripped out by a total stranger on a stifling day? Much to my amazement I began to see the air conditioners disappearing from sight one after another. It seems people will do anything to cooperate in the making of a movie. Within half an hour the offending air conditioners were gone and we proceeded shooting the sequence.

The climax of my movie involved the removal of certain personal files from the late Hoover's office by Clyde Tolson. I indicated that among the items rescued were copies of tapes that had been secretly recorded inside Richard Nixon's office. Some of these would be the very tapes that proved so crucial to the resolution of the Watergate scandal—the Smoking Gun, as it became known. From my discussion with Bill Sullivan, I felt it fair to speculate that the crucial information leaked to reporters Woodward and Bernstein of the *Washington Post* came from a high FBI source. There were whispers at the time that Mark Felt, a key Bureau official, was actually Deep Throat (he confirmed his identity in 2005). But at the time I believed that Tolson himself was directly behind the leaks. He had long been rumored to be Hoover's lover and, as an inside joke, Woodward and Bernstein might've designated their source Deep Throat as a sarcastic commentary on Tolson's alleged sexual practices. The two award-winning reporters were simply conduits for information that the Hoover faction at the FBI wanted leaked in order to bring Nixon down. The president had attempted to do what the Bureau had been getting away with for over 30 years—black bag jobs, breaking into homes, wiretapping and bugging—often at the request of the executive branch. But when Nixon attempted to set up his own private police force to do these dirty tricks, Hoover turned against him. Although he did not live to see the Watergate break-in, Hoover's instructions were carried out. He took the entire administration down with him.

All this was my educated guess based upon corroborative research. The press, however, generally preferred to believe the fiction that Woodward and Bernstein had unearthed the information themselves, rather than being manipulated as tools of the Bureau.

When my film was finally completed, AIP arranged its premiere engagement at the Kennedy Center in Washington. The *Washington Post* review attempted to discredit the picture but pointedly made no comment on our assertion that the FBI had leaked the information to their star reporters. The *Post* took extreme measures to bury the movie, reviewing it negatively twice in the same edition. That seemed like overkill to me. I think the truth hit too close to home.

Unsure of how to distribute the picture, American International decided to open it just before Christmas 1977 in Washington at a number of first-run theaters, not realizing that D.C. is a totally political town. My movie showed little sympathy for either Democrats or Republicans as it chronicled how both political parties had used Hoover to their own advantage. He had illegally wiretapped for both sides, and none of the presidents depicted in the film came out unscathed. To survive in Washington you have to take one side or another. We had no defenders for the film on either the right or the left. It was only when the picture played in London that audiences fully accepted it. They had no axe to grind politically and they were fascinated with the machinations of government that the film revealed.

The movie did have its champions here at home. The distinguished critic Cleveland Amory called it "The best FBI movie of them all." Robin Wood wrote, "Probably the best film ever made about American politics." The British reviews proved overwhelmingly favorable, selecting it as one of the finest of the year. We had a successful seven-week run at the Screen on the Hill, one of London's leading theaters, followed by two prime-time screenings on BBC TV.

The distribution of *The Private Files of J. Edgar Hoover* in the U.S. had always been problematical. Although he now had $400,000 tied up in the project, Sam graciously gave me the chance to sell the picture to one of the studios. All he wanted was his money back. I began screening the film all over town to generally good response. Universal liked it but eventually declined because MCA was involved in a settlement arrangement with the U.S. government, and they felt that irritating the FBI might prejudice their position.

MGM were extremely enthusiastic at first. When the lights came up after the screening, the only female executive in

Raymond St. Jacques as Dr. Martin Luther King, Jr.

in the room stood up and exclaimed, "I really enjoyed this, and I learned an awful lot." This was Sherry Lansing, later head of Paramount Pictures. I always loved her for being the first one to speak up. She didn't wait to hear what all the other executives thought. I was certain that MGM would buy the picture when MGM CEO Frank Rosenfelt flew out from New York to see it. As usual, I insisted on being present for the screening, and when it was over, Mr. Rosenfeldt took me firmly by the arm and said, "I liked your picture, kid, but we're not in the movie business. We're in the gambling business, and I'm not about to get the FBI pissed off at me when I have those casinos to run."

The other studios seemed equally intimidated. At this time, video cassettes were just becoming popular in the marketplace. The studios were licensing their libraries and were deeply concerned about piracy. You'll notice at the outset of every video you buy or rent the FBI seal appears along with a warning that it is a criminal act to duplicate copyrighted properties. The studios were depending on the FBI to police their product. They were not inclined to rub the Bureau the wrong way by releasing my epic. Some thought it could be a minor success, but hardly worth the risk.

I returned to Sam Arkoff to inform him that he was stuck with the movie. Like the good sport he was, Sam went out and sold the picture to a tax shelter group, getting back his investment plus an extra $100,000 for me. Although *The Private Files of J. Edgar Hoover* was only released in a few domestic markets, it quickly went into profit because of the tax shelter arrangement, and I've been collecting money regularly ever since. Eventually I arranged for the picture to premiere in New York at Joseph Papp's Public Theater, where it received glowing reviews from most of the New York critics.

It had also previously been invited to the London Film Festival and Janelle and I were flown over to attend. Arriving there I was rushed to the National Film Theatre for a luncheon where I was seated next to none other than Elia Kazan, one of my heroes. Kazan was so fascinated with the idea of a J. Edgar Hoover film that he questioned me about the picture throughout the entire meal. Here I was, chatting with Kazan about one of my films, not his.

Kazan had experienced more than his share of trouble with the FBI, and his testimony to the House Un-American Activities Committee remained a permanent blot on his reputation. This subject was of vital interest to him, and he wanted to know all the details. How did I have the nerve to go up against the Bureau, an organization that had destroyed so many Hollywood careers? He seemed to admire me for being so daring. It hadn't dawned on me until then that I could've easily had my life turned ruined at the whim of the FBI. My research had demonstrated that Senator McCarthy was simply a stooge that Hoover set up in the Fifties to stifle dissent, particularly during the Korean War. Together, they destroyed countless lives and reputations. Here I was dealing with Hoover's bad deeds and possible homosexuality, yet I'd been allowed to get away with it.

The following morning I arrived at The Odeon Leicester Square, London's largest movie house, to see lines around the block. I hadn't expected anyone to show up for a 10 am performance on a Sunday, but the huge movie palace was packed and I had to find seats in the upper balcony. The audience loved the film, and I did a half an hour of Q &A afterwards. All this made me glad I'd produced the film and confident that someday it would find its audience.

Prior to the release, I arranged a press conference at the Waldorf Astoria in New York. Press coverage was good and we ended up with a huge article in the Sunday *New York Times* Arts and Leisure section, which led to Broderick being invited to host *Saturday Night Live*. The producers soon summoned me for help. Brod was out of control and was constantly disappearing—usually to be found in Hurley's Bar on the first floor of the RCA Building.

I flew to New York and found the cast members of the show who had been assigned round the clock duties to remain with Brod and keep him sober. Dan Aykroyd had an hour, then John Belushi took over, then Bill Murray came on duty. I told them not to worry, that when showtime came, Brod would be letter-perfect while they'd be falling apart with nerves. Which is what happened. They'd drop lines and Brod would cover for them.

As was often the case, the *Saturday Night Live* sketches lacked an ending. While watching the rehearsal, I came up with finishes and gave them to Jean Doumanian, the producer. The show was all politics, and the regular writers would've been furious to know I'd contributed anything, so Jean presented my ideas as her own—and many were used.

In the big sketch where Brod plays J. Edgar Hoover to Dan Aykroyd's Nixon, the punch comes when Hoover gets into bed with his teddy bear, says "Goodnight, Clyde" to the bear, and switches off the light. I wrote the button the sketch badly needed, and it worked.

Subsequent to the production, Dan Dailey took sick and was diagnosed with terminal cancer. Janelle and I visited him at Cedars-Sinai and showed him AIP's proposed ad campaign for the release of the Hoover film, which Dan didn't like at all. I tended to agree with him. Before we left, Dan asked us for a favor. What he wanted more than anything in the world was a good hamburger. We rushed over to the Palm Restaurant and brought him one. He enjoyed every bite. It was the last time we saw the dear guy.

I suppose *The Private Files of J. Edgar Hoover* is my favorite film because we overcame so many obstacles to get it made and released, and because most people thought I was nuts to try.

Many years later, a book was published in which J. Edgar Hoover was outed as a cross dresser, a claim that was never substantiated. This slander was based solely on the uncorroborated ravings of one alcoholic old woman striving for attention. It was absurd to believe that Hoover, who was obsessive about his privacy, would've attended sex parties in drag. Still, comedians latched on to the allegation and even President Clinton, at a press corps dinner, quipped, "I'm looking for someone to fill J. Edgar Hoover's pumps." That got a huge laugh, but it also perpetuated a blatant falsehood. I'm no great fan of Hoover, but I hate to see the truth distorted. I don't even believe that Hoover and Tolson were practicing homosexuals.

I'd had an opportunity to inspect Mr. Hoover's home in Rock Creek Park and even go through his closets. There was not the slightest feminine touch to anything in the house. Over the years I've been welcome in the homes of many gay friends and acquaintances. There's always some sense of style and decor that was totally absent in Hoover's modest dwelling. His furnishings could've come straight from a thrift shop. If you lifted a doily off a chair, the leather underneath would be cracked and often it would be Naugahyde, not leather. Half of the articles around the house appeared to be gifts sent to Hoover by admirers—a rug with the FBI seal woven in, even FBI bedspreads and towels. There was something sad and quite humble about it all. The ceiling in the basement game room was low and a faded Marilyn Monroe calendar hung on the wall. I could just imagine two old bachelors sitting down here watching ballgames and prize fights together. Drag parties? Forget it!

Frankly, if Mr. Hoover had experienced any kind of meaningful sexual relationship in his life, straight or gay, it might've humanized him. As it was, I believe he was completely asexual. Remember, in those days there was such a thing as a "confirmed bachelor." I'm amused that many of the same people who champion gay causes seem to enjoy perpetuating the gay-bashing jokes about Hoover and Tolson. I was surprised when my movie won London's Gay Critics Award because of its fair treatment of a lifelong gay relationship. If that's the way they interpreted the film, who am I to argue? Or to turn down an award?

I'm sometimes asked how I got permission to use Hoover's own home as a location. That's easy. I'd simply driven up to the house in Rock Creek Park with my cast and crew and rang the doorbell, announcing to Annie, the maid who answered, that we were there to shoot a movie. She recognized the famous actors I'd brought along so she made no objection. Before long the cameras were set up and Dan Dailey and Broderick Crawford were emerging from the house and pausing to look at Hoover's lawn, which he'd actually replaced with astroturf. An elderly neighbor across the street who'd recently been released from the hospital peered out his window and saw two dead men, Hoover and Tolson, having a conversation. It brought on another heart attack and an ambulance rushed over. Indeed, Crawford and Dailey were ringers for the characters they portrayed. In his review, Arthur Schlesinger, Jr., commented that "Crawford even walks like Hoover. He gives a fantastic performance."

The last time I saw *Hoover* co-star Rip Torn was in Musso & Frank having lunch with his son, Tony. I was filming *Wicked Stepmother* directly outside on Hollywood Boulevard. Rip told me that Tony needed a Screen Actors Guild card, so I took him outside, wrote him a few lines, shoved him in front of the camera, and got him into the union. "Larry," exclaimed Rip, "you're the only one in the business who would do anything like that." I pretty much had to agree.

One of my most rewarding collaborations on *The Private Files of J. Edgar Hoover* was with three-time Oscar-winning composer Miklós Rózsa, who'd scored such spectacles as *Ben-Hur*, *Quo Vadis* and *El Cid* and had worked with Hitchcock, Wilder, Wyler and most of the great directors of Hollywood's Golden Age. But there was another side to Rózsa. He'd written the scores for noir classics like *Double Indemnity* and *The Killers*, and ever since college I'd played Rózsa's LPs to put me in the mood while writing screenplays. It was because I'd worked with Bernard Herrmann that I had the courage to approach Rózsa, who I thought would be perfect to compose the music for my Hoover biopic. Mikky, as Rózsa preferred to be called, was the gentlest of men, very much the opposite of the confrontational Benny Herrmann. After viewing my first cut he asked if I'd be willing to accept some criticism. The notes he gave

With Miklós Rózsa.

me were both precise and instructive. Since I was the writer, producer and director, I had no one else to rely on for notes. I enthusiastically followed most of Rózsa's suggestions to the betterment of the film.

I recall one night seated in Cyrano's Restaurant on Sunset with Rózsa and Janelle. We noticed him jotting something down on the inside of a matchbook cover. What had just come to him was the main theme for the movie. We soon traveled to London together to record the score at the Denham Studios with the London Philharmonic Orchestra, which Rózsa conducted.

Denham had once belonged to Alexander Korda, with whom Rózsa had begun his career. Now, sadly, virtually the entire lot had been taken over by Xerox as a massive storage facility. One remaining stage housed the Anvil studio where John Williams had recorded the *Star Wars* soundtrack. Together, Rózsa and I wandered around what was left of his beloved Denham lot. There were tears in his eyes as he saw the fate that had befallen it. Despite his Britishness, Korda was a fellow Hungarian. That's what got Mikky his first job on *Knight Without Armor*, a Marlene Dietrich film, which led to *The Jungle Book* and *The Thief of Baghdad*. Early on, Rózsa picked up the humorous nickname "The Wagnerian Gypsy," which amused him no end.

One day, over lunch, Rózsa told me about a lawsuit he'd settled regarding the theme music from the popular television series *Dragnet*. The famed *dum-dee-dum-dum* signature theme was actually stolen from Rózsa's music for *The Killers*. It was little known that after filing suit, Rózsa ended up receiving half the royalties on the *Dragnet* theme whenever it was played. You could retire on that alone.

Rózsa conducted his score brilliantly, utilizing many of the best classical musicians in London. I remained in London to do the sound mix for a fraction of what it would've cost me back in Hollywood. When I finally ran the answer print for Rózsa, he said that in his entire career at no time had his music ever been featured so prominently. We remained good friends, socializing regularly for years.

Chapter 13
Why I Love Actors

People often say to me "You're so amusing in person, why don't you ever make a comedy?" They seem unaware that I've made a number of comedies, none of which has fared particularly well. Actually, my thrillers with strong comedy overtones seem to work more effectively.

Bone was certainly a black comedy. Years later I made *Full Moon High*, which was again financed by Arkoff and American International. It was a spoof on *I Was a Teenage Werewolf*. We had a wonderful cast with Adam Arkin playing the cursed high school student. It featured Ed McMahon as his father, an ex-CIA operative, and Alan Arkin, Adam's dad, as the psychiatrist who tried to cure Adam of his lycanthropic tendencies.

Prominent among the cast was Elizabeth Hartman, who'd been Oscar-nominated as the blind girl opposite Sidney Poitier in *A Patch of Blue*. She also starred with Clint Eastwood in *The Beguiled* before suffering a nervous breakdown. While I was casting, her agent called and said, "Want to do a good deed? Give Elizabeth Hartman a chance. Everybody seems afraid to use her." Being me, I hired her sight unseen.

She couldn't drive to work so we had her picked up. She was fine in front of the cameras but extremely shy when she was off. I went out of my way to amuse her and make her comfortable on the set. She was such a gentle creature it grieved me deeply to hear that some years after our production she took her own life, leaping from a window.

Adam Arkin had never had the lead role in a picture before and was extremely nervous at the start of shooting. We had the usual argument the very first day and he stormed off—apparently quitting the picture. I told everyone to remain calm and keep shooting. Less than an hour later he was back. He had called his father in New York and had been told to return, apologize, and keep his mouth shut—which is exactly what he did. After the initial row we had no further trouble for the rest of the production.

Adam and Alan Arkin in *Full Moon High.*

I had a similar experience with Eric Bogosian, the noted performance artist who later wrote and starred in Oliver Stone's film *Talk Radio*. On the first day of shooting *Special Effects* (which I consider to be a black comedy), Eric began to freak out almost as soon as we began work. After an unprovoked outburst, he packed up his belongings and quit. I simply continued filming without him. Forty-five minutes later he returned with an honest explanation. "I'm hypoglycemic. If I don't eat every half hour or so, I start to get weird." I asked him for a list of his favorite snacks, and we had them on the set for him every day. We never had another moment's trouble.

When I worked with another Oscar-nominee, Eric Roberts, on the comedy thriller *The Ambulance*, the confrontation occurred during preproduction. Eric had driven to New York from California and was out of touch for over a week, during which time the schedule was revised. It was moved up so that he had fewer days to prepare. This was the producer's idea, not mine. When Eric angrily confronted me in my office, I agreed with his position and said I'd insist we postpone the picture to give him the necessary prep—but Eric wouldn't listen. His tirade

Eric Bogosian and Zoë Tamarlis in *Special Effects.*

continued until finally I told him "Nobody yells at me. Either you're out of this movie or I am."

After he stormed out, I began to empty the contents of my desk. I was certain the producers would choose to keep the star and get rid of the director. Then there was a knock on the door and Eric walked back in. "Let's just make the movie." He was echoing Rip Torn's words in the lobby of the Jefferson Hotel in Washington. After that, Eric showed up on the set promptly every day, gave me a friendly kiss on the cheek, and said, "Okay, boss, what do you want me to do today?" (Thankfully, his kisses weren't as wet as Bette Davis'.)

After the production was wrapped, Eric revealed he'd patterned his character on me, imitating my mannerisms and speech patterns. I loved directing him because he picked up on everything immediately. You only had to say it once. He would reply, "I got it, boss," and then he'd do it.

To demonstrate what direction is all about, let me focus on one particular scene in *The Ambulance*. Eric has been searching all over the city for a missing girl with whom he fell in love at first sight. He's risked his life many times over and finally he's found and saved the lovely Janine Turner. As he leans over her, she whispers, "Would you please call my boyfriend and tell him I'm alright?"

Eric Roberts in *The Ambulance.*

Eric realizes he's gone through this ordeal for a girl who hardly even remembers him and who's in love with somebody else. But he dutifully promises to call the boyfriend on her behalf. In his initial take, Eric showed great disappointment upon being rejected. I took him aside and suggested that he hide his disappointment. "He's such a nice guy he doesn't want her to see it. Instead, he keeps on smiling. We see his heartbreak, but she doesn't." It clicked in immediately, and that's exactly how Eric played the scene.

With every performance, there's a specific note you can give an actor that will affect their entire approach to the part. With Broderick Crawford as J. Edgar Hoover, it came while we were picking out wardrobe. I simply dropped a suggestion that Hoover was so powerful, so omnipotent, that he never needed to raise his voice. Heretofore, Broderick Crawford had always bellowed too much for my liking. He had a powerful voice and he overused it. When he spoke quietly, it took on a richer, mellower tone and allowed for more variation. It also exuded self-confidence. Finally, during a climactic scene in the picture, I whispered, "Now you can play it at full volume, Brod." And it was like a lion roaring. We had waited over an hour and a half to hear him let loose.

I find that with good actors it's important to say very little but be quite specific. Let them know what you want, but don't tell them how to achieve it. I'm not an acting coach. My job is to

Eric Roberts and Red Buttons on the set of *The Ambulance*.

clarify what's needed and allow a talented performer to show me what he's got—by giving him my full confidence.

I also find that being a writer, I hold a particular fascination for actors. They know I made up all their dialogue. As often as not, I try to rewrite a scene during the first or second day of production, and I do it on the set—right before their eyes. There's nothing like giving an actor a hand-written page of dialogue. They seem to learn the lines instantly, after which the actor belongs to you. I tend to add new lines every day just to keep my actors happy and on their toes.

I'm also in the habit of offering my actors a tip when they give an especially good performance. Sometimes it's only a ten- or twenty-dollar bill, but if they get a difficult scene on the first take, I'll slip them fifty or a hundred. They roar with laughter, but they pocket the money. I whisper to them, "Don't tell your agent."

Once they're truly interested in a production, actors give much finer performances. I'm particularly flattered on days when actors who aren't on the call sheet show up just to see what's going on. I ask them, "What are you doing here today?" They reply, "I just thought something interesting might be happening, so I stopped by."

I suppose if I was required to shoot exactly what was on the page, it wouldn't make much sense to show up every day and direct for 18 hours. In some ways, a movie is completed for me when I finish the script. I'm the first one to see the picture. It's been projected in my head. The film is wrapped when I get to the final page.

The kick, then, as a director, is to change things, to make them really come to life. To incorporate some of the actor's true personality into the character. Every day is a discovery process. The performers don't know what to expect and neither does the crew. There's no question that I've made myself the star of the production. On my set the actors aren't the center of attention—I am. I'll sing, dance, do imitations, direct in the personality of John Huston one day, Alfred Hitchcock the next. Anything to attract attention. My aim is to make the actors relax. For many good actors, a thin veil seems to fall when the camera starts rolling. They adopt a pose. I try to get them to forget about themselves and have fun with me and the material.

One reviewer commented, "Cohen's cast seems to be having the time of their lives." I hope so because that's my intent. I remember saying to Yaphet Kotto, "Look at how wonderful the other actors are in this scene. I just want you to watch them and enjoy them and show me how much you're enjoying them." This altered Yaphet's entire performance. He began to twinkle. You could see his pleasure coming to the surface. He was having a ball. Michael Moriarty says the same thing about Q. Hey, I love getting compliments—particularly from talented people.

Whenever Moriarty started to get difficult on the set, I'd simply launch into my Ed Wynn impersonation which would invariably reduce him to helpless laughter. He'd follow almost any direction I gave him if I'd only do Ed Wynn.

Finally, I'd become the stand-up comic I once wanted to be—for my actors.

I loved hanging out with comedians and being a regular at New York's Improv back in late Sixties. I felt accepted in the small private club. A great array of new talent emerged from this little West Side nightery. Often, Bud Friedman would seat me beside a young singer who was playing one of the daughters in the original Zero Mostel production of *Fiddler on the*

Roof. After the curtain, she'd saunter over in 1940s apparel and platform shoes to render Andrews Sisters numbers interspersed with off-color jokes. We'd hang out together and critique the other acts, and more often than not, Bette Midler would invite me to go home with her. I'd always beg off citing the fact that I was already happily married. She'd invariably reply, "Oh, that's so refreshing to hear. It's so nice to find somebody who's actually in love with their wife. Are you sure you don't want to come home with me?"

Once in a while Bud Friedman would invite me to get up and do some of my old comedy bits, but the spark was gone. I was more comfortable performing for my cast and crew. I didn't regain my panache as a performer until many years later when I was asked to emcee the Academy of Science Fiction's Saturn Awards ceremony. I wrote original material for myself and headlined a show which featured Kevin Spacey, director Robert Wise, and a bevy of top stars. I was good enough that night to begin thinking seriously of returning to the stage as a performer. I finally talked myself out of it. I still didn't want to work nights and constantly be away from home. I prefer to surround myself with comedians like my pal Red Buttons, and delight in being reminded that I'm funnier than any of the pros across a dinner table.

The year 1970 brought with it my first stage venture, *Nature of the Crime*, which opened at the Bouwerie Lane Theatre at Third Avenue and Bond Street in Lower Manhattan. It was a first class Off-Broadway production designed by William Ritman, who'd created the sets for *Who's Afraid of Virginia Woolf?* I'd suggested to Ritman the look I hoped to achieve, a feeling of immense depth stretching into infinity. He brought this idea to reality, constructing a set made entirely of white string.

Our director was Lonny Chapman, who had formed the West Coast branch of the Actor's Studio in Los Angeles. A successful character actor in his own right, Lonny was a lackadaisical director. The play only came into focus after opening night when Lonny had left town without saying goodbye to anyone, including the cast. Only then had I been able to step in and pull it all together.

Nature of the Crime at the Bouwerie Lane Theatre.

We cast a young actor named Tony Lo Bianco, who'd recently starred in a cult movie called *The Honeymoon Killers*. Tony originally came to read for the part of an aggressive young attorney, and he was dressed for the part. I told him that role had already been cast but we were still looking for the lead, a quiet, withdrawn young genius, a nuclear physicist who refuses to turn his findings over to the U.S. government. Several hours later, an entirely different person appeared to read for the leading role. Rather nerdy and withdrawn, he seemed the perfect type. It wasn't until after he'd given a fabulous audition that I realized this was the same actor I'd met earlier in the day, only with a strikingly altered persona. Naturally, Lo Bianco got the part.

The actors received a mere $65 a week, which hardly paid for their cab fare and meals. They worked with tremendous dedication, and I was extremely grateful to all of them.

The notices were mixed. Clive Barnes of the *New York Times* had decided to review us three days before we were set to open. It was convenient for him if not for us. We weren't ready, but if we objected, the *Times* would send the second-string critic instead, whose quotes wouldn't carry much weight. Naturally the actors were unnerved by the *Times* showing up early, and it showed. Still, we were able to assemble some excellent quotes for the newspaper ads and the play ran for 50 performances, making it the second longest running dramatic play off-Broadway that season.

The fates were against us, and on Easter Sunday, when we had two shows scheduled, New York was blanketed by a gigantic blizzard. The bums that slept on the steps of the theater were covered with snow. I was amazed that the actors could even reach the theater and I offered to cancel the matinee, but they insisted on going on. That day they were all particularly outstanding and, after the curtain, I was approached in the aisle by one of the few people who had braved the storm to be in our audience. He identified himself as Dr. Mantell and informed me that he represented the Jewish Civil Service Workers of New York and that he was also President of the New York State Teacher's Association. He'd absolutely loved the play and said, "I'm going to see to it that every Jewish civil service worker in this city comes to this show." The theater held

99 seats. According to Dr. Mantell, this play would be running for the next 20 years.

He gave me his card and invited me to come to his offices in Brooklyn the next day. I hoped he wasn't some kind of crackpot as I hopped in a cab and crossed the Brooklyn Bridge to the appointed address, only to find out he was entirely legitimate. As I entered his cluttered office, he was still on the phone, trying to get through to Dore Schary. A former head of MGM Studios, Schary had recently been appointed Commissioner of Cultural Affairs. Unfortunately, it was Easter holiday and Schary was in Florida, along with just about everybody else.

Dr. Mantell informed me that he was sending out a newsletter to all his constituents, extolling the virtues of my play. In about two weeks he would be able to see some results. Once Schary came back from his vacation, Dr. Mantell would work on him. Theater parties would be arranged, and business would pick up in a month or two. I responded, "Doctor, we've been running now for almost seven weeks. We can't hang on much longer. I can't carry this show for two more months waiting for an audience to finally materialize."

After much thought, Dr. Mantell lamented "This just happened at a very bad time. If it wasn't a holiday, my hands wouldn't be tied."

He wrapped his arm around me and walked me back to the elevator, still complimenting me on my skill as a playwright. Just as I was about to step into the elevator, he shook my hand, and I felt him place something in my palm. I hesitated to open my hand until after the elevator door slid shut. When I did and looked down, I was holding a subway token.

Dr. Mantell thought I was so broke that he was offering me subway fare back to Manhattan. All the while the play had been running, I hadn't considered myself a failure. On the contrary, I was very proud of the production. Now, suddenly staring at this subway token, I felt like a complete bust. I had a huge mansion with two acres of property in Beverly Hills, a substantial bank account, numerous television and feature credits—and yet that subway token made it all dissolve into nothingness. I cabbed directly to the theater and posted the closing notice. It was time to get back to Hollywood and sell a few screenplays. As to the subway token, I gave it away. I should've had it framed.

This one venture had taught me many lessons about how things operate both on and off-Broadway. On opening night I'd arranged a party in the Belasco Room upstairs at Sardi's restaurant. It was the major theatrical hangout in midtown, and the traditional place to celebrate a premiere. In those days, Sardi's offered a great deal: only $10 per head for an open bar plus a huge buffet. I packed the party with cast and friends and was particularly thrilled when Harold Clurman, one of the great figures in the American theater, showed up.

Sardi's is located directly next door to the *New York Times*, and somehow the restaurant staff has an inside track on learning whether the *Times* review is good or bad before the paper even hits the streets. Maybe the linotype operator gives them a call. Halfway through the party, I noticed the waiters were beginning to remove the cannelloni and the meatballs and whisk them back into the kitchen. The entire buffet started to vanish before my eyes.

By then the staff knew the *Times* review would not be favorable. The bartender was not pouring the drinks so freely. Insiders recognized this pattern and began to get their coats. As a rule, as soon as negative reviews are broadcast over TV, everyone abandons ship. Experiencing this is definitely a part of your education in the theater.

A few scissor snips and William Ritman's set began to unravel. It took only seconds for it to collapse, quicker even than the departure of our opening night guest eight weeks earlier. Because of its location on the Bowery, I'd hired a watchman to remain inside the theater at night in case vandals broke in. The entire run of the show proved uneventful, but once we wrapped our final performance, the watchman reported that swarms of rats came up from the basement and began to race haphazardly around the stage. The poor guy was terrified out of his mind. He'd never seen a trace of them before. It was as if the rats knew that the show had finally closed and that they could come out of hiding. Still another lesson. The rats are always waiting.

Still, 1970 had been a memorable year. I'd not only gotten to direct a film, *Bone*, but had also taken over the direction of a New York stage production. I found that actors responded to my ideas and that I truly enjoyed the interplay with the cast. Contrary to many directors, I liked actors.

In 1976, with my British production of *Motive*, I would again step in to direct a play. This thriller would have its premiere in Guilford, not far from London, and starred Honor Blackman, George Cole and Ian Hendry, all of them well-established British actors. The director, Val May, had made his reputation staging the classics and had no skill at creating anything new. I've found that those who hide behind the classics often prove totally inept when it comes to developing original material. All I can recall about Val's rehearsal process was that everyone smoked incessantly and I often had to retreat into the hallway to catch a breath of air.

The production was simply thrown together and had a lackluster premiere. Then we went off on tour and, mercifully, May remained behind to administer his theater. With no director around, the cast was more than willing to let me fill the void. By the time we reached the Theatre Royale in Brighton, I'd established some tension between the characters and accentuated the humor. We toured successfully and in 1978 a second touring production was mounted which starred Carroll Baker. *Motive* would be revived again at the Theatre Royal in Windsor in 1999.

There's a wonderful camaraderie between stage performers. Everyone seems to be involved in something they love doing. These same tender feelings may not apply when the same actors are employed on a film project, maybe because moviemaking is so fleeting and disjointed. And the cast is usually denied the privilege of rehearsal. In addition, theater salaries are low. The performers are only doing it because they care.

After having a wonderful experience with Tony Lo Bianco in *Nature of the Crime*, in 1976 I signed him to star in *God Told Me To*. I'd actually begun production with Robert Forster in the lead, but we'd suffered a disagreement over, of all things, chewing gum. Robert insisted on grinding the spearmint incessantly during his scenes. I felt this was an inappropriate habit for a character who's eventually revealed to possess God-like qualities. It turns out his character's actually part alien, so I took the position that Chiclets had not been introduced to other planets. Forster agreed to get rid of the gum but would simply hide it in his mouth and then begin chewing away halfway through a

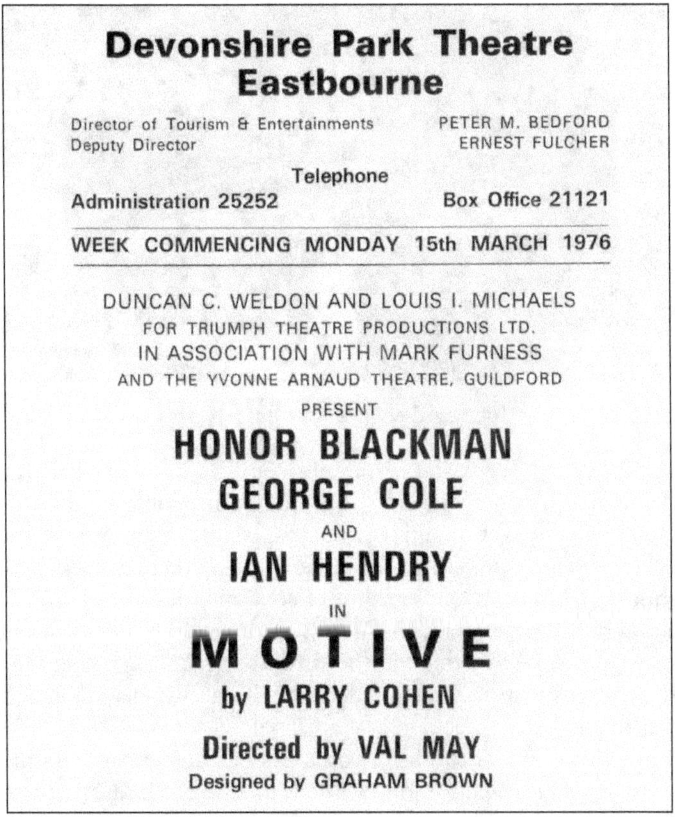

**Devonshire Park Theatre
Eastbourne**

Director of Tourism & Entertainments PETER M. BEDFORD
Deputy Director ERNEST FULCHER

Telephone

Administration 25252 Box Office 21121

WEEK COMMENCING MONDAY 15th MARCH 1976

DUNCAN C. WELDON AND LOUIS I. MICHAELS
FOR TRIUMPH THEATRE PRODUCTIONS LTD.
IN ASSOCIATION WITH MARK FURNESS
AND THE YVONNE ARNAUD THEATRE, GUILDFORD

PRESENT

**HONOR BLACKMAN
GEORGE COLE**

AND

IAN HENDRY

IN

M O T I V E

by **LARRY COHEN**

Directed by VAL MAY
Designed by GRAHAM BROWN

take. Finally I'd had enough, and the next day Lo Bianco was playing the part.

Everything went well until Tony arrived early one morning and excitedly announced that he was leaving for Los Angeles to test for the lead in a Mike Nichols picture. Robert De Niro had been starring in *Bogart Slept Here*, a screenplay by Neil Simon, but Nichols seemed as dissatisfied with De Niro as I'd been with Forster. The picture had been shut down and a replacement was being sought. I realized this was a rare opportunity for Tony and I readily agreed to halt production for a week so he'd have the opportunity to audition. He then informed me that if he got the job he wouldn't be coming back. I'd be left with an uncompleted film and a huge financial loss.

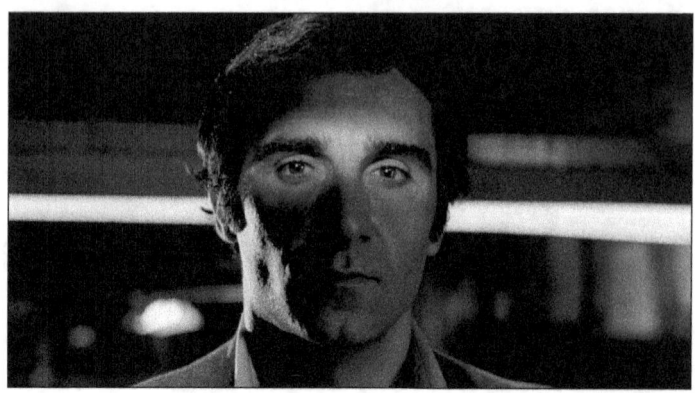

Tony LoBianco in *God Told Me To.*

I advised Tony that he simply couldn't walk out halfway through a picture. The Screen Actors Guild wouldn't allow it. I could easily get an injunction against his appearing in the Mike Nichols film. After all there was only another ten days shooting left. Tony became infuriated and threatened me. "I could hurt you real bad," he hissed, and it sounded like he meant it. I couldn't believe this was the same young actor who behaved so generously during the run of my off-Broadway play. When he was making $65 a week, he was an angel.

Tony went off to Hollywood and did the test, and within a few days returned to my production, with the understanding that if he got the job in Hollywood he would leave immediately. I thought it best to shoot as many of his scenes as possible. If he did quit on me, I'd think of some solution. As fate would have it, he didn't get the part. The script was later rewritten by Neil Simon and retitled *The Goodbye Girl.* It was filmed with Richard Dreyfuss in the lead, a role which won him the Academy Award for Best Actor. I'm afraid that *God Told Me To* marked the pinnacle of Tony Lo Bianco's long career. He never again got a role quite as juicy.

He would have one more curve to throw at me before filming was completed. After losing the *Bogart Slept Here* role, he had immediately accepted the lead in an off-Broadway play. Now he'd have to be finished shooting by 6 pm so he could get to the theater. I was forced to use a double for some of his coverage, which must have worked perfectly because to this day Tony insists that he was present for many of the sequences that I know for a fact he was absent from due to his theater commitment. I tried to convince him to skip a Saturday matinee since we had only one day of shooting left. If I could wrap the picture on Saturday, I'd avoid having to rent equipment for one day the following week. Since a day's rental costs almost as much as a full week's, it'd be a considerable saving. Even though I'd closed down for a week to accommodate him, Tony wouldn't throw me a bone. He insisted on playing his matinee, during the course of which he fell down on the stage and fractured his collarbone. It would take at least a month to mend. I would have to reassemble my crew 30 days later and pick up that one day of coverage. By this time I wished I'd stuck with Robert Forster and his chewing gum.

One of Tony's final scenes when we reconvened involved his escape from a burning basement. Always trying to keep the costs down, I decided to steal the sequence by staging it in the boiler room of my own apartment building on 63rd and York Avenue. Our special effects team spread the walls with a peculiar sort of paste that would burn for only 45 seconds before extinguishing itself. A raging inferno can be created that will quickly go out.

I had placed Tony in the center and ignited the material just as the superintendent of the building emerged from the elevator. It appeared to him that I was burning the place down. We had to virtually restrain the man while shouting, "It's going out! It's going out!" And it quickly did. I was fortunate to get the shot and also not to be evicted.

An even more harrowing experience had occurred earlier. I had placed a sniper on a water tower some 35 stories above the sidewalk. He was supposed to be picking off pedestrians in the street below, and Tony was to scale the tower and try to talk him down. Fearful of falling, Tony insisted that our stuntman wire him to the ladder, but the young actor who played the sniper demonstrated unusual courage. His name was Sammy Williams and he had just won the Tony Award for Best Performance by a Featured Actor in the Broadway production of *A Chorus Line*. I had never seen anyone perform with such courage. Even the stuntpeople expressed open admiration. Either he had no fear of heights, or he overcame them. But we almost didn't get to shoot the scene at all.

Sammy Williams in *God Told Me To.*

The cameras were set and the actors fully rehearsed, but one item was still missing. The rifle with the telescopic sight. Then the production assistant assigned to deliver the rifle showed up and tearfully explained that his friend who had volunteered to supply the weapon had changed his mind. "Why didn't you phone me right away?" I inquired. "Oh, I didn't want to upset you," was the reply. As if I wasn't upset now? At least a call would've given me an hour to secure a replacement. Instead I was standing there like an idiot. I had a sniper sequence but no gun. The situation was totally absurd, as was my solution. I simply turned to the dozen spectators who had gathered on the roof. They were residents of the building who'd come upstairs to watch a movie in progress. "Okay, who's got a rifle with a telescopic sight?" I demanded. Instantly a girl's hand shot up. "My boyfriend's got one."

I asked her to fetch it immediately. Naturally everybody does what you tell them when you're directing a movie. In no time at all we had our prop and were under way. It was another of the many movie miracles that I've experienced. Later in the same production we needed an abandoned tenement which was to collapse in the climactic sequence. So we simply broke into a condemned building and decimated the joint. One of our stuntmen actually punched his way through the walls and began pulling doors off their hinges and throwing them down the staircase as we poured ashcans full of debris over the railing to create the effect of a total collapse.

God Told Me To.

It was that same day in a makeshift dressing room that I got my first look at the body of our co-star Richard Lynch. Years before, under the influence of hallucinogenic drugs, Richard had performed an act of self-immolation. His entire torso now consisted entirely of scar tissue. It had healed in such a way as to create a bizarre pattern of flesh. It was almost as if there was an enormous deep-set eye in the center of his chest. Since he was playing an alien what could be more perfect? Many who've seen the picture believe that the deformity looks more like a huge vagina, and I've done nothing to dispel this interpretation. Richard was a damn good sport to go along with it and allow us to exploit his misfortune, and it certainly was a shocker.

I completed the special effect sequences on a soundstage at Pinewood Studios in England working with some of the same artists who had created the illusions for one of my favorite childhood movies, *The Thief of Baghdad*. Working with this veteran British crew was quite unlike anything I'd experienced as an independent filmmaker back home. There was no over-time unless the crew voted to give the director an additional 30 minutes. You had to put in your request early in the day, and if any single member of the crew found it inconvenient, the director

Richard Lynch in *God Told Me To.*

would not get his half hour. This clearly was not the place for Larry Cohen to continue making films.

Another actor that sadly disappointed me was Jeannie Berlin, the daughter of the celebrated comedienne Elaine May. I'd been casting the role of an eccentric hippy girl for *Bone* and had just about settled on Susan Sarandon when she came to my house for a reading. I thought she was great, but my German Shepherd dog took an instant dislike to her. Mickey was the most placid animal anybody could imagine, and I'd never seen her go after anyone before. I actually had to restrain the dog and lock her in a back bedroom as she continually tried to attack Miss Sarandon every chance she got.

This should hardly be the criteria for casting a role. It certainly cost me the opportunity to work with one of the best actresses around. Instead I settled on Jeannie Berlin, who proved excellent in the part. I'd no sooner finished cutting the film than I received a personal visit from Elaine May herself in the company of her young associate, Eric Preminger (son of Otto Preminger and Gypsy Rose Lee). Elaine was preparing to direct *The Heartbreak Kid* and there was a role for which Jeannie was perfect. Neil Simon, the screenwriter, didn't want Jeannie and the producers considered it nepotism to hand her the role, especially since they'd never seen Jeannie act. I ran *Bone* for Elaine May, and she was all over me with praise. I was an unheralded genius! And by the way, would I mind making a black-and-white dupe of Jeannie's scenes and shipping them to New York? I did so at my own expense, and it clearly did the trick. Jeannie was hired even though Neil Simon allegedly walked off the picture in protest. Jeannie's reviews were extraordinary, and she was nominated for an Academy Award for Best Supporting Actress. Shortly thereafter she was interviewed for *Newsweek*. The reporter mentioned her appearance in *Bone*, to which she responded, "That's something I'd rather not talk about."

I ran into her occasionally and she avoided even saying hello. A few years later she went on to star in a big budget picture for Paramount, *Sheila Levine Is Dead and Living in New York*, which turned out to be a disaster. Jeannie had become a monster on the set and when the picture failed, her career self-destructed.

Years passed and I was at New York's Mayflower Hotel preparing a picture when I met Jeannie in the lobby. She was headed upstairs to read for Scorsese, hoping to get a choice role in *King of Comedy*. A few days later she called to let me know that she'd lost the part. It had gone to an unknown named Sandra Bernhard.

Andrew Duggun and Jeannie Berlin in *Bone*.

I had to laugh. Janelle and I had gotten Sandra started in show business. She'd been Janelle's manicurist, and my mother often described her as the worst manicurist in Hollywood. She was such a lonesome creature that my wife continually invited her to our home for Thanksgiving and Christmas dinners. Always forlorn, she usually sat in the corner and said little, except to express her ambition to someday be a stand-up comic. She seemed the least funny person I'd ever met. Still when my friend Bud Friedman, who owned the Improv comedy club, dropped in for Thanksgiving dinner, I made him promise to give Sandra a chance to perform. Afterwards Bud pulled me aside and moaned, "How could you do this to me, why did you put me on the spot?" I told Bud to showcase Sandra at one o'clock in the morning when no one was around. What was the harm? He agreed but demanded that Janelle and I be present in the club, and so we dutifully accompanied Sandra to all her initial engagements.

She was as awful as I had anticipated, but she finished her act without getting heckled or insulting whatever audience hadn't walked out. A few months later she told us she was playing sets in some gay bathhouses. She'd found her core audience. Her career was taking off.

When Bud and his family came by for holiday dinners, they often brought along a lantern-jawed young comedian who had nowhere else to go. We always welcomed Jay Leno and looked forward to his stopping by. Jay, however, had an aversion to Sandra and kept as far away from her as possible. I never saw them exchange a word. Now when I see Sandra guesting on *The Tonight Show*, I notice that she and Jay never mention where they first got acquainted. Both of them are extremely cordial whenever Janelle and I bump into them, always inquiring whether we still have that same great Spanish mansion off Coldwater Canyon.

Chapter 14
The Art of Getting Fired

I suppose I'm spoiled rotten. I can't direct if I'm not given total control. I've tried working under the close supervision of so-called producers and I've been fired both times!

The first fiasco was my adaptation of Mickey Spillane's *I, the Jury*, one of the biggest selling detective novels ever written. At that point, the character of Mike Hammer hadn't been depicted on film or television for decades, so I was able to take an option on the property for only $5,000 against a purchase price of $50,000.

The book had been filmed, very forgettably, in 3-D back in 1953. My version was mostly Larry Cohen. I subverted the character of Mike Hammer and turned the entire story inside out. Hammer became a violence-prone tool of the CIA, manipulated into killing their enemies. His best buddy, who'd lost an arm saving Mike during the war, was revealed to be a closeted gay and in love with him. No wonder Spillane was appalled at what I'd done to his masterpiece.

I obtained financing through a company called American Cinema. Robert Solo was designated the producer. We cast Armand Assante as Hammer and Paul Sorvino as Detective-Lieutenant Pat Chambers. My girlfriend, Laurene Landon, played Velda, and Barbara Carrera was the villainous psychiatrist.

From the beginning I had problems with Armand's diction, or lack of it. I called his attention to the fact that nobody could understand his dialogue to which he replied, "Yeah, I get that complaint a lot." I didn't seem to have made much of an impression on him because he continued mumbling his lines in take after take. He had all the proper swagger and personality for the part, but my dialogue was lost.

I offered Armand a few days to rehearse, but he was too preoccupied bouncing around New York with an actor friend. I suspected he had also developed a yen for Miss Landon and

Armand Assante and Laurene Landon in *I, The Jury.*

saw me as an obstacle. To fulfill this fantasy, he was looking for some way to get rid of me long before the cameras rolled.

While casting the male heavy, I interviewed a New York actor who supported himself tending bar at Cafe Central. I instinctively asked him to read the Mike Hammer role instead of the villain. This kid knocked me out of my seat. I told him that he was far better than Armand but that it was too late to change leads. The production company would never engage a complete unknown to star in a $7 million dollar film.

Apparently, my compliments gave this young actor a needed boost because years later he approached me at a Golden Globes awards ceremony, tapped me on the shoulder, and asked if I was Larry Cohen. He went on to tell me that I'd given him more encouragement than anyone in New York and that he wanted to thank me for it. He was doing much better now. He'd gotten a TV series and would soon be destined for movie stardom. His name? Bruce Willis.

I guess I was still thinking of Bruce every day when I directed Armand and realized I was getting second best. I continued to utilize the improvisational techniques which had fared so well on my own productions, but the producers didn't understand what I was going for. I didn't like being second guessed and their negativity was causing me to lose the confidence of my cast and crew, who overheard the constant criticism. I retaliated by provoking the producers further.

Soon I was informed that I was no longer welcome on the set and that a television director, Richard T. Heffron, who had worked with Assante before, had been brought in to replace me.

It was assumed by the producers that I'd be vacating my room at the Mayflower Hotel and returning to Hollywood. But I had other ideas. Within a few hours I'd contacted Paul Kurta, a local production manager, and begun hiring a crew. I was launching a film of my own.

Since I had no cast, I decided to begin with second unit photography. I hired Al Cerullo, the finest helicopter pilot in the movie business, and began shooting aerial sequences, sweeping in and around New York's signature skyscrapers and capturing truly breathtaking footage. No rollercoaster ride could equal the thrill of being up there.

The story would concern a giant bird which terrorizes the city of New York and nests at the top of the Chrysler Building. The location of the nest is discovered by a petty crook named Jimmy Quinn, who tries to blackmail the city into paying him a million dollars in return for information as to the bird's whereabouts. I needed somebody terrific to play Quinn, who was the central focus of the picture—which I entitled *Q*.

Once again, I headed to the Improv, where I spotted a young comic named Eddie Murphy, but I wasn't sure if he could act. For the life of me, I don't know why I didn't simply hire Bruce Willis. It was an oversight I'd always regret. The fact was I needed some recognizable names in order to raise money, someone who could guarantee foreign sales.

I had previously tried unsuccessfully to get my old pal, David Carradine, the role of Mike Hammer in *I, the Jury*. Now I wired him in Cannes and asked him to be in my new movie. Without even seeing the script, Carradine agreed and flew back. At least now I had one star.

That same day Laurene and I were having lunch at an outdoor cafe near Lincoln Center. Seated at the next table was

With David Carradine and Michael Moriarty on the set of *Q*.

Michael Moriarty and his wife. I had long admired Moriarty and began to describe to Laurene some of the highlights of his career. He'd won the Emmy award twice, plus the Tony award and the Golden Globe. He surely was one of the finest actors in America. When I looked back at his table, Moriarty was beaming at me. He'd overheard much of the conversation.

I walked over, introduced myself, and told him I had a part in which he might be interested. Later that day I messengered the script of Q to his apartment. The next day the phone rang. It was Michael, expressing complete enthusiasm. This was the kind of role he had always wanted to play. We bonded immediately. I next picked up Candy Clark, from *American Graffiti*, who was playing in an off-Broadway show. *Shaft* star Richard Roundtree was rushed in from Los Angeles to play a sadistic detective.

A week after my dismissal, as the *I, the Jury* cast and crew were assembling in the lobby to leave for location shooting, I was assembling my own actors and production staff only a few feet away. Bob Solo and the American Cinema executives, who had so mistreated me, were astonished. How could I have put an entire movie together in a matter of days? And with a stronger cast than they had!

Richard Roundtree in Q.

"Q" IS HERE!

It's name is Quetzalcoatl... just call it "Q"... that's all you'll have time to say before it tears you apart!

MICHAEL MORIARTY · **CANDY CLARK** · **DAVID CARRADINE** · **RICHARD ROUNDTREE**
AS SHEPARD
IN A LARRY COHEN FILM "Q"
SAMUEL Z. ARKOFF PRESENTS A LARCO PRODUCTION
MUSIC BY ROBERT O. RAGLAND · PRODUCTION EXECUTIVE PETER SABISTON · WRITTEN, PRODUCED and DIRECTED by LARRY COHEN

Released by UNITED FILM DISTRIBUTION COMPANY

R RESTRICTED

I filmed Q in 18 days, finishing before *I, the Jury* wrapped and at a fraction of the cost. The Mike Hammer epic spiraled almost three million over budget after I was fired. American Cinema went belly up. The picture was auctioned at a bankruptcy sale and picked up for domestic distribution by 20th Century Fox. Q grossed three times as much as *I, the Jury*— and we got far better reviews!

I actually had to take American Cinema to arbitration to get paid my directing fee. The company had the temerity to falsify the production reports, destroying the originals and substituting fakes in order to manufacture evidence of my alleged incompetence. Under cross examination, the unit production manager, Marty Hornstein, who had been bullied into falsifying the reports, owned up to his wrongdoing.

It was disgraceful for a member of the Directors Guild to sabotage a fellow member and perhaps destroy a career. But Hornstein had done so under orders from an American Cinema executive. We won the arbitration hands down. More importantly, with Q I had created a Larry Cohen movie that is considered one of my best. I believe I could've made an excellent film of *I, the Jury*, but it never would've truly been my movie.

In 1987 I was to be fired once again from a similar project. This was also a detective thriller which I had originally written as a sequel to *I, the Jury*. Had the initial Mike Hammer film been successful, I hoped to turn it into a franchise. As it was, I was in possession of an intriguing original detective story, and I simply altered the character of the principal player and re-named him "Hamberger." The role was played by Billy Dee Williams and the film was released under the title *Deadly Illusion*. I received co-directing credit on this film with someone called William Tannen, since I'd already completed several weeks work behind the camera before disaster struck. This time I was saddled with producers who couldn't get along with each other, much less with me. I soon discovered that the project was under-financed. I had introduced these producers to local vendors with whom I had done business for years. These included equipment houses and laboratories that had given me exceptionally favorable deals.

A few weeks into production it became apparent that the money was running out. Many of my friends were about to get stiffed unless they began collecting on their bills immediately. They'd only extended credit to the production in the belief that I was the responsible party. I warned them to demand immediate payment or cease providing services. This, of course, did not endear me to our producers, so they watched and waited for a chance to retaliate.

It was just before Christmas when we began filming an action sequence aboard the Staten Island Ferry. Billy Dee learns that the villain has abducted his girlfriend, played by Vanity, and put her on a ferry. He boards the ferry at the last moment and, en route across New York Harbor, spots Vanity and her abductor aboard a different ferry which is passing in the opposite direction. Billy Dee is on the wrong fucking boat! He realizes he must give immediate pursuit, so he makes the only possible choice—to hijack the boat and turn it around. In effect, it's a ferry boat chase past the Statue of Liberty with the city of New York beautifully silhouetted in the background. Sounds like fun? It wasn't.

Directing *Deadly Illusion*, with Billy Dee Williams.

It was two degrees above zero when we began, and by the time the production company had brought aboard portable toilets and dressing rooms and camera trucks, there was hardly any room left to shoot. I could have achieved more with a six-man crew than with the 50 people that were foisted on me.

We were a little more than an hour into production when I felt a sudden lurch and the ferry came to a stand-still in the middle of New York Harbor. A few minutes later, the first mate announced that we'd run up on a sandbar. We were stuck.

"Can this boat sink?" I quickly inquired.

"What do you mean? We're on the bottom now!" came the reply.

Soon tugboats from the Port Authority, which controls the Staten Island Ferry, arrived and attempted to tow us off, but with no luck. Then the Coast Guard showed up. Eventually, word reached the media and helicopters from local television stations began circling overhead. I couldn't pass up this rare opportunity and decided to revise the story.

These choppers and Coast Guard vessels and tugboats would certainly enhance our production values. First, however, I had to call the producers and find out if their insurance policy covered such a calamity at sea. The sequence had not been in my original screenplay and I wasn't certain that the insurance company would pay off. If they would, it might be smarter to wrap and simply collect the coverage. Otherwise, I was ready to improvise a new sequence and not sacrifice the entire production day.

The producers wouldn't give me an immediate response but promised to get back to me within 30 minutes. They hung up and promptly left the office for the day. They chose to make no decision and leave it up to me. Whatever choice I made would probably be the wrong one and I'd be held responsible. When I called back and learned they were ducking me, I shot the scene my way. As it was, we were jammed on that sandbar until nightfall when the tide finally rose and we drifted off on our own. When we arrived back in port, the pier was full of television cameramen and reporters. We made every news program that evening.

The Port Authority made good and we were permitted to re-shoot without charge. Things went slowly that second day.

Billy Dee couldn't seem to remember his dialogue and lost all energy as a performer. Getting a decent acting job out of him required take after take and I couldn't wrap the scene by nightfall. We needed a few more daylight hours on the ferry, which I could have shot in drydock. It would be a minor additional expenditure, but the producers suddenly decided to pull the plug and eliminate the entire sequence. All that work for nothing!

A few days later I received a goodbye note from Vanity. Her contract had run out and she'd been shipped back to Los Angeles without anybody telling me—regardless of the fact that she had several scenes left to complete. The producers claimed they couldn't afford to keep her on salary. I knew I could have gotten her to stay on for nothing.

I had to escape from this nightmare, but I couldn't quit without being sued. Instead, I began provoking all three producers in hope that I'd goad them into firing me. I soon got my wish.

On New Year's Eve we were scheduled to stage a fight scene high above Times Square, utilizing the tens of thousands of people who would gather below to celebrate. A stuntman was to be tossed off a rooftop restaurant down into the huge milling crowd as the clock struck midnight.

Early that morning I was informed that I'd been replaced. My director of photography, Daniel Pearl, who had worked with me on many films, was prepared to walk off and take his crew along with him. But I had no desire to damage the production. I'd engineered my own dismissal—and welcomed it. I simply went back to the hotel and began writing another thriller, which turned out to be *The Ambulance*. It felt wonderful to be alone, creating a movie all by myself.

When it was finally assembled, *Deadly Illusion* was a shambles. Entire sequences were missing and the story made no sense. Still, some of the action sequences were interesting, like the one in which Billy Dee pursues a hitman who has leapt from the window of the RCA Building into the enormous Christmas tree that looms above the Rockefeller Center skating rink. Billy Dee also makes the jump, and the two men struggle while tumbling down through the heavily decorated tree, finally landing on the ice below.

Billy Dee Williams and Vanity in *Deadly Illusion.*

Despite the shortcomings in story and logic, the film got a surprisingly good review from my nemesis, Vincent Canby of *The New York Times,* who began his notice with these words: "Like the devil, Larry Cohen never sleeps." What followed was the best notice Canby had ever given me for the worst picture I'd ever made. I was further amazed when *Deadly Illusion* opened at Grauman's Chinese Theatre in Hollywood. Another movie had been pulled because of poor business and they were desperate to find a substitute. I went down to Hollywood Boulevard and had myself photographed in front of the Chinese Theater—just to prove that the impossible can happen.

I never let these setbacks bother me because I always had my first love to which I could return. My writing.

Chapter 15
It's All in the Casting

I'd tried for a few years to put *The Ambulance* together before finally finding a home at Epic Productions. This was another company which I rightly assumed would shortly be out of business. Though John Travolta was available to play the lead, the enlightened management wouldn't hear of it. Travolta's career was finished as far as they were concerned. He'd had a few recent flops that hadn't even been distributed. They insisted I go with Eric Roberts.

We shot the film in New York with an excellent crew. This time I had a production manager and followed all the orthodox procedures. For a change, I got along with everyone. All went well until the unions closed in on us. The company hadn't used my patented methods of deception to evade them. Pickets surrounded the small warehouse we'd turned into a studio and began spitting on our crew members as they came to work. Our drivers were afraid to unlock the trucks and remove the equipment. I offered to go out and do it myself, but my producers would not allow me to take the chance.

The following day, while we were filming on the banks of the East River, we were besieged by dozens of union members who brought along horns, noisemakers and amplifiers to screw up our sound recording. They arrived early in the afternoon and wore themselves out causing a racket while we were setting up. By the time actual shooting began, they were exhausted, hungry and ready to go home. Earlier in the day I'd excused myself from the set and crossed the street to join the picket line. I told our unit photographer to snap a few pictures of me picketing my own movie. I'd been at it only a few minutes when I was surrounded by several irate members of IATSE who demanded to know what the hell I was doing there. It looked like some punches were about to be thrown, so I quickly explained that my sympathies were with them. As director of the film, I wanted to demonstrate my support by carrying a

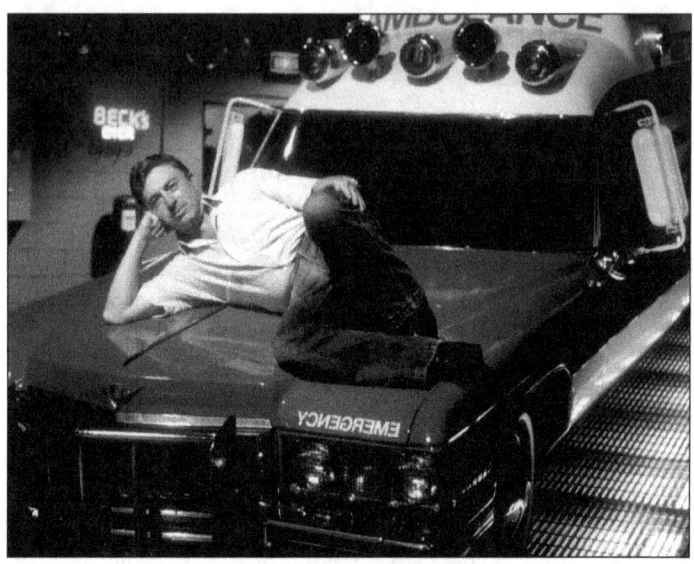

On the set of *The Ambulance.*

picket sign. They began patting me on the back and suddenly I was their hero. A few minutes later, I went back to the set and directed my scene.

When *The Ambulance* was completed and previewed, the owners of Epic Productions confided, "This is far and away the best movie we've ever made—but coming from us that doesn't mean much."

I was far less satisfied. I'd made a stupid mistake. Any suspense thriller is only as good as its villain, and I'd let myself down. The heavy had been played by a fine character actor, Wesley Addy, but he failed to exude sufficient menace. I proposed to the production company that I go back and re-shoot all the scenes in which the villain appeared. I promised them I could do it all in a single day. They thought I was out of my mind, but I'd calculated exactly what angles I needed and how to integrate them into what was already cut. Once again, my mother came up with a good casting idea. One of her favorite daytime soap stars was Eric Braeden from *The Young and the Restless*. I worked out a minimal budget for the re-shoot and finally received permission.

Looking at the movie, you'd assume that Eric Braeden had worked several weeks, but everything was accomplished within 12 hours. I even convinced Red Buttons and Janine Turner to donate an extra day's shooting time.

I recall Janine lying tied to a bed, held helpless by the diabolical physician now played by Eric, who informs her that she will be in perfect health before she dies (he has been kidnapping diabetics to use as Guinea pigs he'd then dispose of in his twisted efforts to find a cure). Janine was supposed to emit a chilling scream at this point, but she just didn't seem to be able to get one out. After I'd tried many takes, I resorted to a director's psychology. I simply told Janine not to worry about it—I'd have another actress loop the scream in post-production. This made Janine absolutely furious at me, and in the next take she emitted a harrowing scream which was more than I'd ever hoped for. I then apologized to her for the provocation.

Substituting a new villain was just what the picture needed. Not only had I made a pretty good movie, but I'd also proved I could work as part of a team and adhere to a normal production schedule. I credit this to a pair of gifted producers, Robert Katz and Moctesuma Esparza, who allowed me the freedom to create and protected me along the way. I wish I'd had them on every picture.

One of my fondest memories of *The Ambulance* was working with James Earl Jones. I'd greatly admired him on Broadway in *The Great White Hope* and more recently in his shattering performance in *Fences*. I found him to be a fabulous collaborator. If I had an idea and proposed it to James, he'd never stand around and discuss it. That booming voice would exclaim, "Well let's try it and see how it works." And then he'd make it work.

He was playing the role of an eccentric police captain who'd just recovered from a nervous breakdown. One of his tics was the incessant chewing of gum (unlike with Robert Forster, I now wanted my actor to chew gum). When it came time for James' death scene, I suggested that he continue to chew his gum vigorously until finally the chewing would slow and then stop, and we'd know he was dead. James immediately got the joke. We put it in and added a bizarre touch of humor to his demise.

Above and right: With James Earl Jones
on the set of *The Ambulance.*

We were shooting in Lower Manhattan on a particularly warm, humid night. James was standing around with a knife jutting out of his chest waiting for the next shot to be lit. He chose not to return to his trailer but, instead, lay down just off the curb on the pavement, informing us that it was "refreshing" down there.

"Move over!" I replied as I sprawled out next to him in the gutter. James commented, "Now we have returned to our true origins." James Earl Jones and I sprawled in the gutter, laughing our heads off. Moments like this make moviemaking an incomparable pleasure.

The film also introduced me to Red Buttons, who became a buddy. I particularly enjoyed Red's comment during a sequence in which his unconscious body was stashed in the rear of the ambulance directly beside the corpse of James Earl Jones, who'd previously been murdered. This was the only moment they appeared on screen together. Once I called cut, Red sat up, turned to James Earl Jones and said "James, it's been great working with you."

Janine Turner soon after became a popular star on the CBS television series *Northern Exposure.* I'd actually spotted her while sitting in the Columbus restaurant, a hangout for show

business personalities. Janine had entered on the arm of Mikhail Baryshnikov, whom she was dating. I took one look at her and exclaimed "That's the girl for *The Ambulance*. She looks just like Veronica in the Archie comics."

The manager of the restaurant called Baryshnikov the next day and got Janine's name and phone number and she was hired. Why is it I always seem to do my best casting in cafes?

Buttons and I became lifelong cronies. He took Cynthia and me along on several Caribbean cruises on which he was appearing, as well as to dozens of events at the Friars Club. I ended up writing jokes for his act and assisted him on his one-man show, *Buttons on Broadway*.

Chapter 16
I Love a Parade

Audiences watching *God Told Me To* are often surprised to discover comedy star Andy Kaufman playing the role of a murderous police officer who runs amok during the New York Saint Patrick's Day parade sequence. Thousands of cops in the march scatter as panic ensues when Andy opens fire.

Naturally, I stole the entire scene which was filmed months before principal photography actually began. I knew if I missed the parade, I'd have to wait a whole year for it to come around again. I decided to grab whatever I could, utilizing three separate camera units. Once the procession began down Fifth Avenue, it wouldn't stop. We had to constantly get ahead of the marchers, which meant running our asses off. I also had cameramen shooting from rooftops along the course of the parade route.

The city would never have given me a permit to run amok wielding weapons in the midst of this celebration, which is highlighted by 5,000 or more cops moving in close formation. I was banking on my hunch that no one would imagine I'd have the nerve to create such chaos without permission. I'd place several phony policemen within the ranks wearing rented uniforms. Everything else would be improvised. There was always the possibility I'd be shut down immediately and even arrested. But getting this scene was worth doing jail time!

A few days before the shoot was to take place, I stopped by Manhattan's Improv club. Budd Friedman told me I'd picked a good night to attend. A new young comic named Andy Kaufman was to appear. Andy soon showed up, a young and very repressed-looking individual who went on stage and immediately alienated the entire audience. Within minutes they were hissing and booing and demanding that he get off the stage. He ignored their jeers and began reading tediously from a Charles Dickens novel. I thought several members of the audience might physically attack him. Then he began to weep as he proclaimed that his career had been ruined by this insensitive crowd. Simultaneously, he began pounding madly on a pair of bongos. Then abruptly, he switched to an uncanny impersonation of Elvis which brought the house down... only to enrage the crowd again a few moments later. Finally he launched into a rendition of "Old MacDonald Had a Farm" accompanied by a children's record and then pantomimed the *Mighty Mouse* theme.

All in all, Andy had been on for an hour and had totally manipulated the audience. As he came off, I stopped him, saying "You're going to be a star and I want to put you in your first movie." He looked terrified, but Bud convinced him I was making a serious offer.

When I explained that he would play a psycho cop going berserk in the midst of the Saint Patrick's Day parade, he went for it instantly. I guess he figured I was as crazy as he was. I'd need a uniform that would fit him, so I asked for his shirt size. He responded that he didn't know. Nor did he know the size of his jacket or even his shoes. I said, "How could you, a grown man, not know your own shirt or jacket size?" He explained, "I wear

On the set of *God Told Me To* with Andy Kaufman.

Andy Kaufman taking his place in the actual Saint Patrick's Day parade.

my father's old clothes." I inquired how he spent his day when he wasn't performing. He told me he slept, then got up, packed his raggedy little suitcase and came to the Improv. Performing was his whole life.

He showed up on Saint Patrick's Day and Jim Dixon took him into the men's room at a nearby coffee shop to change into his policeman's outfit. Andy managed to irritate and enrage the customers and management of the diner by pounding his billy club on the tables until he was chased out into the street. Reporting to me at the start of the parade route, he began making faces at the horde of young Irishmen who were jammed behind the barricades, many of whom were already drunk. He turned his policeman's hat around backwards and openly flirted with some of these tough Irish kids who began trying to jump the barricades and beat the shit out of him. I had to physically fend them off. In the world of lunacy, I had finally met my match.

Mercifully, the parade began, and Andy wedged himself in amongst real police officers. I'd given him a mock .38-caliber revolver.

As our three separate camera units covered the parade, Jim Dixon, playing a police sergeant, led the search for the demented cop who would soon commence a killing spree. Our crew weaved in and out of the ranks of policemen as we struggled to keep pace with the march, and no one ever stopped us or questioned our presence. When Andy pulled his gun, the

surrounding cops could see a camera was focused on him.
I simply shouted "Look, he's got a gun, do something!" And
the cops reacted realistically, proving that everyone wants a
chance to act!

Andy had to kill someone in the reviewing stand, and I
elected to take this part myself. I managed to infiltrate my way
into the ranks of dignitaries. I waited a moment, then reacted as
if shot in the head and threw myself down. Since Andy couldn't
actually fire this prop gun, during the editing I inserted a blank
frame intercut with him pulling the trigger. It looked exactly
like the flash of a gunshot.

Eventually, Jim Dixon and the other actors playing detectives would catch up with Andy and gun him down. As he lies
on the ground dying, he was to speak his only line: "God told
me to." The only problem was that we hadn't brought any
recording equipment or microphones. All the sound elements
would be added in post-production. Andy simply lip-synced
the words. Later on, during the mix, I personally supplied the
voice. Years later when I again met Andy, he took me aside and
questioned me: "You've got to tell me. How did you get my
voice on that movie? I know you didn't have any microphone
there… but I still said the line."

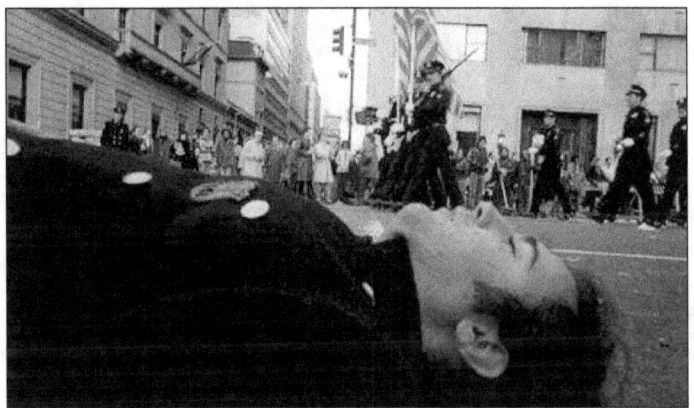

Andy Kaufman lies "dead" as the real parade continues around him.

I explained to Andy that I'd spoken the line on his behalf. This infuriated him. "Oh no, I know my own voice. That was me."

I persisted, "Andy, you agreed there was no microphone. How could it be your voice?" But he wouldn't relent. That debate continued for years, with Andy insisting he'd said the lines, despite all evidence to the contrary.

From time to time we'd meet and have some serious discussions. Because we were fellow lunatics, Andy spoke to me rationally, dropping the act he usually put on.

Janelle didn't have the same luck. When she took him to lunch while we were doing pick-up shots for the parade scene in downtown Los Angeles, he insisted to her that he wasn't Andy at all and demanding that she address him as Tony Clifton, his alter ego. He gave her quite a hard time. By contrast, when I attended his play *Teaneck Tanzi* on Broadway in 1983 during its brief one-week run, I found Andy taking tickets at the door. He invited me backstage and leveled with me about his career problems—most of which he'd created himself. I could identify.

During the last year of his life, Andy and I talked regularly. I'd sent him a screenplay in which I proposed he'd play seven different characters. Andy cheerfully agreed to do the part without ever telling me he was dying of cancer. There was no possibility he could've acted in anybody's movie, and yet every

week I was getting his calls, asking how close we were to a start date. I'd been trying hard to raise the money but sadly there was no great excitement about financing an Andy Kaufman project.

Still, I tried to give Andy encouragement, hoping I'd find a backer. Andy's career had faltered since *Taxi* had gone off the air. This movie would bring him back. And then one day, I heard that he'd died. It was only then that I discovered how terribly ill he'd been for so long. Yes, he'd been putting me on. Or maybe he'd been trying to deceive himself. In any event, I still cherish the one sequence I did film with Andy Kaufman.

Chapter 17
Tricks of the Trade, Part 1

When I'd needed more of the Saint Patrick's Day parade and additional blood squibs and panic, I decided to recreate the havoc in downtown Los Angeles and intercut it with the New York footage. Jim Dixon contacted several Irish-American organizations whose members loved to march in any celebration. Here I was giving them an opportunity to relive their big day for the cameras. They showed up in costume with baton twirlers, brass bands, Irish American flags—everything that was needed.

The combination of the New York shoot and the fake parade footage was seamless. It appears that it's all happening on Fifth Avenue. Again the magic of editing created something which never existed. To me, that's always been the real thrill of filmmaking. Making them see what was never there.

When I filmed *It's Alive*, I convinced the audience that a monster existed while hardly ever showing it. To me this was more of an achievement than hiring ILM to computer-animate some elaborate creature (which the audience tires of after five minutes). Why not exploit the imagination of the audience and have them participate? Let *them* create the monster. What they imagine will be more terrifying than anything we could devise.

Nowadays most directors farm out key portions of their movie to expensive effects houses. The result tends to look homogenized and interchangeable, and such movies don't have any specific look of their own. Rather, they take on the style of the special effects house. I always wanted to make the entire picture myself.

When we shot Q, I didn't lay out any storyboards and I hadn't hired any special effects people in advance. I decided where the monster would appear and precisely where it would move, and shot the footage to accommodate that. When the picture was finally cut, I showed it to several special effects artists, all of whom informed me that I'd done everything wrong. "You're supposed to plan this beforehand in consultation with us."

How could I plan it out? I wasn't even sure what I was going to do until I got there.

A giant bird was supposed to be circling the Chrysler Building, diving and snatching police officers out of these baskets which hung off the pinnacle of the building—tossing the bodies 80 stories into the street below. How could I have guessed I'd capture any such sequence without spending a fortune?

When they got past their initial objections, the special effects team realized that it could all work. I'd always left room for the monster. I'd placed it in proper juxtaposition to the live actors. They could still add the creature to the scene using their traditional methods. At the outset, they insisted all the shots would have to be stationary. We couldn't follow the monster circling wildly around the top of the Chrysler Building as shot from a helicopter. I had the audacity to tell them they were wrong. They tried it and found out it was possible after all.

The giant bird of *Q*.

Granted, the monster in *Q* was not state of the art. But as critic Gene Siskel commented, it perfectly fit the style of the movie, which was funky. I was trying to create a big monster movie in a pseudo-documentary setting. This was a gritty New York cop movie with a gigantic killer bird as a principal character. It was a unique hybrid. Just as *God Told Me To* had mixed the genres of crime melodrama and science fiction, we were attempting to combine cinematic styles—and achieve something that hadn't been done before.

Above, below and over: Additional footage of the Saint Patrick's Day massacre was shot in Los Angeles.

It'd be 20 years until *The X-Files* came along and adopted the same aesthetic that *God Told Me To* had pioneered. I believe I was the first in the science fiction field to rely upon the hand-held documentary style which has now become accepted as the norm, especially in television. *NYPD Blue* and *Law & Order* constantly pan back and forth between characters, shakily simulating real-life coverage of an event. Many other current TV dramas also imitate that look.

Other ideas I initiated have found their way into big-budget productions. Compare the opening flashlight sequence in *It's Alive* with the flashlights moving through the forest in Spielberg's wonderful *E.T. the Extra-Terrestrial*, which also deals with a small alien creature secretly living inside the home of an American family. You'll also notice the similarity to the storyline between *Q* and the big-budget remake of *Godzilla*. Both deal with a huge monster that journeys to New York and builds a nest in which to lay its eggs. Both creatures pick a New York landmark and in both, the thrust of the action is to discover the location of the nest and destroy it. Years before its production, Dean Devlin, who produced *Godzilla*, had told me he was a great fan of *Q*. Well, he certainly proved it.

I went on to create *The Stuff*, a movie which dealt with an ice cream substitute that sweeps the nation—an addictive substance that the public feel compelled to consume, to the exclusion of all other food. The ad campaign read: "Are you eating it or is it eating you?" The film was a satire on consumerism and hype as well as a condemnation of the addictive substances being foisted on the public. Whether it be cigarettes or junk food, these products bring with them the promise of an early death. *The Stuff* was simply an exaggeration of the truth.

New World Pictures gave me the financing to film *The Stuff* and, once again, the loyal Paul Glickman was my D.P. Our opening sequence concerned the initial discovery of a white substance bubbling out of the earth in the vicinity of a mining excavation.

We went to New Jersey to shoot the scene, never expecting to be caught in the midst of a blizzard. We weren't prepared for the heavy snowfall, but it couldn't have been better suited to our needs. Soon our lights were exploding and equipment was short-circuiting. We were knee deep in drifts and there was the

Andrea Marcovicci in *The Stuff*.

risk of someone getting electrocuted. But damn, it looked great on film! We couldn't afford to wrap and blow this sequence, so everybody took their chances.

An equally harrowing experience took place later in the shoot when we were invited to film a sequence at a fur show-room elsewhere in New Jersey. The management had offered to deliver a dozen gorgeous models and a runway on which we could film fake commercials for *The Stuff*. All we had to do was feature the brand name of the furrier.

I admit that the chance to meet a dozen beautiful girls made me immediately keen to accept this offer, so keen that I never scouted the location personally. When we arrived there with cast and crew, we found that there were only two tenants in the building: one was the furrier, the other was the New Jersey office of the Teamsters. We would be shooting a non-union picture inside the Teamster's headquarters. Everybody else wanted to turn tail and run, but I was determined not to blow the day. I staged our fashion show, noticing out of the corner of my eye that a cluster of heavy-set men were slowly surrounding the set. It looked like an open casting call for *The Sopranos*. These wise guys couldn't believe that anybody would have the gall to shoot a non-union picture right under their noses.

Figuring I'd better amuse them, I immediately launched into my rendition of "I Wish I Was a Teamster," a parody of the number from *Fiddler on the Roof*. "All day long I'd sit there in the truck, if I were a Teamster man. Wouldn't have to work

hard, deedle deedle deedle dum…" I followed this up with my
Johnny Friendly routine—a broad satire on *On the Waterfront*.
Pretty soon I had these hard-nosed Teamsters roaring with
laughter. Eventually they split after wishing me well, saying,
"You've got some set of balls coming in here!"

Years earlier I'd had a similar close call while shooting *Full
Moon High* at Burbank High School. I was in the midst of a scene
with Ed McMahon and Adam Arkin when we were descended
upon by the local police and fire marshals who insisted we didn't
have the required permits. I explained that I'd paid a fee to the
school for the use of the facilities and they'd never mentioned
the need for any additional permit. Even so, the belligerent Fire
Marshall was closing us down. I'd lose an entire day's shoot,
and perhaps the next day as well. I was ordered to wrap up and
get out. Naturally I kept stalling in hopes that I'd think of some
way out of this fix. The tension became so great that my production manager suddenly fell to the floor and promptly went into
an epileptic seizure. This was no act. His arms and legs were
thrashing wildly and his eyes rolled up in his head. Fortunately
the firemen were right there with all their emergency gear and
they immediately came to the fellow's aid. His spasms continued
as he was strapped down and removed to an ambulance. We all
stood in abject silence. Then the Fire Marshall patted me on the
shoulder and said, "Go ahead and shoot you movie, kid." For
some reason, people are always calling me "kid."

Robert Frank Telfer and Colette Blonigan in *The Stuff*.

The production manager was embarrassed by the incident and never came back, but I continued to pay him for the rest of the shoot. He'd saved my ass.

Once, while filming *Bone* in Beverly Hills, we were interrupted by a local fire inspector who objected to our having cables stretched across the sidewalk outside. I simply shouted at him, "What's the matter with you? Can't you see we're shooting a movie here?" He backed off, disappeared, and never returned.

The charmed life I live seems confined solely to periods of motion picture production. In normal life, I suffer the same disappointments and setbacks as the rest of us. While directing, I also seem to have a tremendous amount of luck with women. I simply tell them what I want, and they accommodate my every wish. It's some kind of mystique which I can't truly define. Nobody refuses me anything! I continue to take bigger and bigger chances. When I think of all that might've gone wrong and the repercussions, it often makes me tremble.

Chapter 18
The Ones That Got Away

There are always those big projects that never came to fruition.

One of these, *The Hostiles*, was intended to star John Wayne and Clint Eastwood, the two icons of the American western, and, believe me, we came close.

The project came into being because of Mervyn LeRoy, the veteran Hollywood director of *Little Caesar*, *Random Harvest* and the producer of *The Wizard of Oz*. Mr. LeRoy was an old man then, but he had one final dream, to make a picture called *Cowboys and Indians*. My friend Bob Barbash knew him and arranged a meeting.

LeRoy had no story, just a title, and we decided to cook something up. I had the feeling that he was in no condition to direct since his doctor would appear regularly during our meetings and jab him in the ass with a very long needle. We were soon left with a spec script and no director, but almost immediately we were summoned to meet with Clint Eastwood and his producer Jennings Lang at Universal. Clint wanted to star in the film, and he was certain he could get John Wayne to play opposite him. Barbash and I agreed to option the property to Clint, and I admit to being thrilled whenever he'd call me at home. The kids would race through the house yelling, "Dad, dad, Clint Eastwood's on the phone."

After having met with Jennings Lang during the day, I would usually be called by Clint that night and informed not to pay any attention to anything the producer had said. Clint intended to be in control of this project from start to finish. The only problem was that John Wayne didn't like the script.

Clint was not to be dissuaded and when he moved his Malpaso Productions to Warner Bros., he took another option on the material. And again John Wayne passed on it. Duke had won an Oscar for *True Grit*, but since then his choices had become dull and routine. Why wouldn't he do *The Hostiles*, which would team him with his natural successor? Clint was extremely frustrated. There was no one else but Wayne who could play opposite him in this role. Eventually Clint let his option lapse and only a few days later I received a call from Michael Wayne, who was both Duke's son and his producer. I couldn't believe that Wayne's company Batjac now wanted to option a property that the star had constantly rejected. Michael assured me he could talk his father into doing it. Barbash and I quickly agreed to the option and Michael went to work. "Dad and I are going out on his yacht off in Newport for the weekend. I'll bring the script along and make him to read it again."

I waited impatiently for some response and finally I phoned him. "What happened?"

"Well, it's kind of embarrassing. I gave him the script, he looked at it for a few minutes, then said, 'This piece of crap again?' and threw it overboard."

I could see my script afloat in the Pacific and slowly sinking out of sight. Years later when I joined Clint Eastwood at Budd Boetticher's table at a Los Angeles Film Critics Award luncheon, we again discussed the property. "I guess I'd have to play the old guy now, wouldn't I?" Clint mused. Perhaps he finally realized that the younger role was the far better part. Maybe that's why Duke declined so many times.

Bob Barbash has since passed away, but I continually kept this script in circulation, hoping for the day when the phone will ring and someone will holler, "Clint Eastwood's calling," and he'll have found a suitable co-star.

There were significant disappointments in the world of television as well.

During the era of live television, no producer was more creatively daring than Fred Coe, who ran the Goodyear Television Playhouse and then Producers' Showcase, where many of the great writers of their time found their voice. My ambition was to write for Fred. This dream would come true, but unfortunately only at a time when Fred's power and influence in television was at its lowest ebb.

By then, I was scripting TV's most honored series, *The Defenders*, and Fred sought me out to help create a CBS pilot from an idea of his own entitled *The Reporter*. The series was to cover stories of political significance, so Fred suggested that we both hop down to Washington, D.C. and meet with President Kennedy to get his input. Creatively, there was little value to such a meeting. It was simply an excuse for Fred to renew his acquaintance with the President and maybe to impress his young writer.

Fred had produced JFK's official campaign documentary which was telecast the night before the presidential election. He told me that he'd carefully followed his instructions that no footage of Joseph P. Kennedy, the controversial father of the candidate, was to appear anywhere in that film. Wedding footage would have to be blown up to eliminate old Joe Kennedy's presence. JFK would not appear publicly with his dad until the polls were closed on election day.

Fred didn't enjoy flying so we took the train. We were welcomed at the White House and had a lunch with Ted Sorensen, Kennedy's chief speechwriter, in the executive dining room. I chatted at length with Sorensen about the Eisenhower and Dulles policy of massive retaliation and was informed that the Kennedy administration had abandoned that approach and were gearing up for tactical responses. Kennedy's new pet military unit was the Green Berets, which could go into action on a limited basis and would soon be tested in Vietnam. I could see that Sorensen had little respect for Eisenhower, despite the fact that Ike had gotten us out of the Korean War and kept us at peace for both terms of his administration (saving my ass from having to go into combat).

Sorensen seemed to enjoy fielding my questions, so I asked him about the recent speech Kennedy had made, praising Winston Churchill and making him an honorary American citizen. Quoting from the speech, Kennedy had said "When Hitler's forces cast their dark shadow across Europe, Churchill mobilized the English language and sent it into battle." I asked Sorensen, "Did you write that?" To which he replied, with a knowing smile, "I might have had something to do with it."

It wasn't until a year later when reading through some of Edward R. Murrow's collected radio broadcasts that I came upon the identical phrase. Sorensen had lifted it from Murrow—verbatim—and taken full credit for it.

Fred and I never did get our meeting with JFK. Halfway through the lunch, Sorensen was called away and returned with an ashen look. "Something terrible has happened. The Thresher atomic submarine has been lost at sea with all hands. The President has canceled all meetings for the balance of the day." Fred and I returned to New York City by train without ever catching a glimpse of Kennedy. It was one of the great disappointments of my life.

My project with Fred also came to nothing. He was being badly treated at the network, which had no intention of ever going forward with the pilot. Fred finally vented his anger and frustration on me. During a telephone conversation, he exploded, calling me a "young snotnose" and then hanging up. All because I told him the truth—that CBS was never going to greenlight this project. To his credit, a few minutes later he phoned me back and apologized. I could tell he'd been drinking. Word around town was that Fred always had a problem with alcohol. CBS was certainly driving him to drink. The man deserved only the highest respect, being one of the great pioneers in television drama. It was painful to see him in this position of impotence, but it was another lesson that roles change and those in power will soon be out of power and often completely vulnerable.

During my *Defenders* days I'd also created a television series called *The Power*, which dealt with the governor of a state and his youthful staff. In many ways it pre-dated *The West Wing*. To play the role of the governor we zeroed in on Raymond Burr, who was just concluding his long stint in *Perry Mason*. Burr was one of television's most popular stars, and his involvement meant an on-the-air commitment. Burr loved the material and wanted to meet me. A dinner for just the two of us was arranged at the Steak Pit on Melrose. We seemed to get along famously, and at one point Ray wrapped a huge bear-like arm around me and announced that he was taking me with him to Korea to entertain the troops at Christmas. I responded that my wife and kids would probably not take kindly to the suggestion.

I certainly didn't want to offend him and lose a potential star. On the other hand I didn't want to go to Korea, either. Frankly, I was relieved when our candlelight supper was over.

Ray told the producers he was delighted with me and was definitely going forward with the show. Then CBS intervened.

Suddenly they wanted another season of *Perry Mason* in color and they offered Raymond a million-dollar bonus if he would back out of *The Power*. I don't blame him for accepting. That kind of money was unheard of in television in those days. Instead of finding another star, the producers simply caved. I often think of what a memorable series it could have been.

Another disappointment was a half-hour comedy entitled, *Sheriff Who?* which we pitched to NBC. The format was co-created by my friend from page boy days, Curt Sanders, and was produced by Jerry Belson and Gary Marshall. It was their inspiration to cast John Astin as Evil Roy Slade, the meanest man in the west. He's so rotten that each week he either runs off or kills the local sheriff, and a new guest star sheriff appears to take over the job.

The pilot Belson and Marshall wrote based on our idea was deliriously funny. Dick Shawn played an interior decorator who journeyed to the frontier "in order to make the whole west match." At the conclusion of the pilot when Dick left town, Jerry Lewis showed up to become the sheriff—a teaser for what would've been the following week's show.

Sheriff Who? tested brilliantly and NBC immediately locked it into their fall schedule. I'd sold another series! Then astonishingly, Jerry Lewis approached NBC and offered to do an 8 pm weekly show, aimed especially at kids. The network thought Jerry would be as big on TV as he was in movies. *Sheriff Who?* was replaced before it ever got on the air. Incidentally, the Jerry Lewis program was a monumental disaster and was yanked off the air after only a few weeks. Some years later, *Sheriff Who?* was exhumed and made into a two-hour pilot at Universal entitled *Evil Roy Slade*, also starring John Astin and boasting a great lineup of guest comedians, among them Milton Berle, Mickey Rooney and, again, Dick Shawn. Unfortunately, our format that worked well as a 30-minute program was stretched thin over two hours. In 1967, *Life* magazine wrote that *Sheriff Who?* was "falling-out-of-your-seat funny" with an "absolutely original" premise and "the sight gags a delight." But it is otherwise forgotten.

And then there was my own production of *The Heavy*, which I'd written especially for David Carradine. David's father was the noted movie villain John Carradine, and the story was a tribute to all the great bad guys we'd seen in movies over the decades. Their names we may not have known, but their faces were instantly identifiable.

David was to play a small-time actor who had played villains in hundreds of films. While driving across country he's mistakenly identified as a murderer at large. Witnesses swear they've seen his face someplace before. When Carradine is unable to prove that he's simply an obscure movie actor, a mob of locals decides to lynch him. Eventually he escapes and tracks down the real murderer. He finally gets to win a fight and even gets the girl, which he's never been allowed to do in any of his screen roles. At the finale he's acclaimed as a hero and high-powered movie producers come to visit him in the hospital, offering to acquire the rights to his story. It seems Stallone wants to star, to which Carradine replies, "No chance. I play heroes now."

The entire film was to be a labor of love. I obtained low-budget financing and we set off to film in Arizona, where it became a nightmare from the moment of Carradine's arrival. He chose to show up plastered and remain that way for the next four days. Even worse, he was a nasty drunk, heaping abuse on everyone—even my fiancée, Cynthia. Finally I decided to pull the plug. I told the crew to pack up and go home.

The next morning as we were loading up the trucks, David showed up purportedly to apologize. I could smell the liquor on his breath, and I suggested he seek help. I knew alcoholics had to bottom out and perhaps the cancellation of this picture would force David into some kind of recovery program. I realized the decision would cost me hundreds of thousands of dollars, and I agonized over it. If I'd simply completed the picture, I would've fulfilled my contract. Good or bad I'd have earned half a million dollars. Now I would be personally liable for all the production costs so far.

In retrospect, I made a stupid choice closing down the show. Cynthia and I drove back to Tucson, pausing at a gourmet restaurant outside of town. My long-time cameraman, Paul Glickman, who came along with us asked, "What are you going to do now?" Jokingly I replied, "I don't know, I guess I'll just hire the first person I see and star them in the picture." At that precise moment, right on cue, the door of the restaurant opened and Robert Redford stepped out alone and walked to his car.

The fact is we did not hire anyone, nor did we ever resume production. I had one stroke of good luck. A criminal lawyer's convention was in progress at our hotel in Tucson and one of the female attorneys was a childhood friend of Cynthia's. We had dinner with a group of these "mouthpieces" that night during which I got the idea for a screenplay that would be called *Guilty as Sin*. This script netted me a quick $650,000 fee as well as an additional million dollars' worth of work at Disney Pictures the following year. I suppose none of that might've happened had I continued to film *The Heavy*. Life has an odd way of compensating.

In trying to recover some of my losses on *The Heavy*, I filed a claim against the insurance company. Alcoholism had been accepted by the American Medical Association as an illness, and Carradine's erratic behavior, predicated on his drinking, therefore seemed to fall within the coverage of our medical insurance. The insurance company was extremely reluctant to pay, but I challenged them to go to court and set a precedent. If a judge ruled that liability due to alcoholism was actually covered, then the insurance companies would be in big trouble. Every time a drunken or stoned actor showed up on the set, the studio would have the right to terminate production and make a claim. I knew the insurance companies couldn't risk any such verdict.

They eventually settled. I still had to eat some of the losses, but it was worth it. Carradine did undergo treatment for his alcoholism and divorced the wife whom he claimed always shamed him into taking that first drink. In the years that followed we became friends again and he'd often stop by my house unannounced just to say hello. The real loss was that *The Heavy* could've been such an excellent picture, and it might've turned Carradine's career around.

Another project that fell through was *So Help Me God*, a courtroom drama in which a killer pleads not guilty by reason of demonic possession. We had raised Canadian financing and had interested both Christopher Reeve and Raul Julia in starring in the two leads, although Chris was worried that Raul had the better role (which he did). When the Canadian money fell out, the project collapsed. Little could I envision the bad luck which lay ahead for these two fine actors. One would soon die, and the other be confined to a wheelchair for life.

On an earlier occasion, I had come close to directing Peter Sellers in my screenplay, *Ringer*, the story of a man who poses as his own double in order to rob his place of employment—the American Express Company in Paris. Sellers' career was floundering, and he was available even to a low-budget film-maker like me. I negotiated a fabulous deal for his services at a bargain price of only $100,000.

I met with Peter at his agent's offices in London and we seemed to hit it off well. I recall that we had a lengthy chat about Inspector Clouseau, his most popular creation. I observed that Clouseau was a man totally without a sense of humor, a terribly serious person, who was absolutely mortified at his own inept-ness. Sellers agreed that this indeed was the secret of the char-acter and what made him truly funny. Clouseau lived in a state of perpetual embarrassment. Peter Sellers and I seemed to be talking the same language.

Upon signing, I was now responsible for paying Peter $100,000 whether or not the picture was made. I admit I was shocked when all of the Hollywood studios turned up their noses at the idea of a new Peter Sellers comedy. His last few outings had been flops and he had two or three unreleased pictures which no distributor seemed to want. Sid Sheinberg, President of Universal, remarked that he wouldn't hire Sellers for $10,000, much less $100,000.

Eventually I had to return hat in hand to Sellers' agent, Dennis Selinger, and beg him to let me out of the deal. Appar-ently, Peter needed the money badly at the time. "You mean I have to tell this man he's not going to get his $100,000?" Dennis wailed. But he was kind enough to allow me to wiggle out of a firm commitment.

Another lost opportunity with this script came with Donald Sutherland, who happened to lease the same Malibu beach house I usually occupied. (This was the bungalow in which Robert Redford and Barbra Streisand lived in *The Way We Were*.)

After vacating the premises I slipped back inside after the maids had left and before the next tenant took occupancy.

I stuffed a screenplay under the pillow in the master bedroom with a note, to Donald: "This will give you something to read if you can't sleep. Call me if you want to be in the movie."

The very next morning I got a call from Sutherland. He said he'd liked the script and was interested in seeing a sample of my directing. I invited him into town and ran *Bone* for his eyes only. He came out of the screening room beaming. "It was terrific, I'd love to work with you. The only problem is I've got a picture to make with Fellini called *Casanova* and that's going to take a year and a half, and then I've got a picture with Bertolucci called *1900* and that's going to take 18 months, so I'll do your picture in three years."

I figured that in three years' time he'd have forgotten about me entirely, so I took the first good offer to sell the script. In truth, I'd had enough of it. I sold the script for a hefty $300,000 and it was made into a barely-released movie called *The American Success Company* with Jeff Bridges in the role—a case of total miscasting. A few months later Sellers re-teamed with Blake Edwards (who was also down on his luck) to make a sequel to *The Pink Panther*, which became a surprise hit. Sellers was instantly back on top and Sid Sheinberg was soon paying him millions of dollars to star in *The Prisoner of Zenda* at Universal.

Jeff Bridges in *The American Success Company*.

I'd been warned that Sellers was a monster on the set, but I like to believe that we would have gotten on, just as we did that first day. Usually the most difficult actors are the ones I get along with best.

The Apparatus is another of the films I didn't get to make. It had a terrific storyline. A young businessman visits Paris and picks up a beautiful woman. After spending the night with her, he wakes up in the morning and she's gone—and he finds a small device strapped to his chest by a metal band. When he tries to remove it, the box turns red hot. Then the phone rings and a voice informs him that he will die if he attempts to remove this apparatus. He is told to report to a deserted section of a city park, where he encounters a man who wears a similar device. He is told, "You must do everything they demand of you. Only then can you be free." A moment later the man seems to explode, blown to pieces by an identical apparatus. For the balance of the film, the villains attempt to force our hero to become an assassin. How he turns the tables on them and frees himself from the apparatus makes for a compelling thriller.

Cynthia and I spent over four months living in Paris in the lap of luxury while we prepared to make the film, which was to be financed by Guy Job, a successful entrepreneur who controlled the French rights to *Wheel of Fortune* and *Jeopardy*. I was thrilled to be directing my first feature in Europe and Guy was a fantastic host. He took us to only the finest restaurants, places where you'd need a reservation six months in advance. He even spirited us off to the Cannes Film Festival, where he had to pay a thousand-dollar bribe just to get us a room.

We were rapidly gaining weight as we awaited the start of photography. Then disaster struck and a glitch arose in the acquisition of the underlying material. *The Apparatus* was based on a screenplay which I'd sold years before to producer Frank Yablans. The company he'd worked for had gone belly-up and the French producers had acquired the material from the bankruptcy lawyers. At the last minute, it was discovered that the now-bankrupt company had previously sold the video rights to *The Apparatus* to the similarly defunct Vestron Video. In order to clear the rights completely, they'd have to ferret through two bankruptcies, not one. We were too close to production. Guy

Job had already pissed away almost half a million dollars. The entire production crew was on salary while I was scouting the locations with the director of photography.

The plug was pulled, and Cynthia and I were soon on our way home, having been paid a hefty portion of our salary. I would have given it all back for the chance to make the movie. We'd had a beautiful apartment on the Avenue Victor Hugo, a car and a driver at our disposal and all that fabulous food. But we didn't have a movie. And that's what really lasts. You spend the money and it's gone. But the movie is yours forever. It constantly reappears on television or in video stores. It could show up at an arthouse theater or a film festival, but it never entirely vanishes. Some nights you'll switch channels and find it on television.

Producers continually question me about the status of *The Apparatus*. I'd love to be able to make it. As for Guy Job, all my sincere thanks and my apologies. He was a fine fellow and I regret his dream of producing movies didn't come true.

Chapter 19
Happenings and Chance Meetings

One of my life's most bizarre occurrences took place in late November 1963, as my then fiancée Janelle and I were leaving a Beverly Hills restaurant. I thought she was becoming overly alarmed when she realized the necklace she'd been wearing had broken. We immediately found the pieces scattered on the floor, but she gasped, "Something terrible is going to happen."

We returned to the Sunset Tower West where we were staying and late in the evening Janelle began to experience stomach pain. She already had three children from a previous marriage in her teens. Doctors had advised her that she couldn't have any more kids because of tubal blockages. She'd been undergoing treatment to reverse this condition, insisting that she wouldn't marry me if she couldn't give me children. That night she took medication and managed to fall off to sleep. We were both awakened in the morning by a phone call from a friend, informing us that Kennedy had been shot in Dallas.

Since Janelle was from Dallas, Texas, we didn't think that was particularly funny, but we turned on the TV and it remained on for the entire weekend as the nightmare continued to unfold. The president's death was followed by the arrest of Lee Harvey Oswald and his eventual murder at the hands of Jack Ruby—to which Janelle exclaimed, "I know Jack Ruby! I met him twice. I was introduced to him once by the mayor of Dallas."

It had been at a party honoring the Dallas Theater Center and Janelle was terribly afraid that Ruby might recognize her as one of the group of high school girls who'd walked into his strip club pretending to be looking for a job. They just wanted to see what it looked like inside the notorious Carousel Club. Ruby had told Janelle she was too classy to be a dancer and offered her a job as his office manager. Of course, she and her friends never went back. Another coincidence: the Texas judge who swore Lyndon Johnson in as President after the assassination was the same woman who had officiated at Janelle's divorce.

This was only the beginning of the weirdness. Years passed and we were vacationing and just leaving a Honolulu restaurant when once again Janelle's necklace snapped. Once again, she had a feeling of terrible foreboding—I couldn't believe this was happening. Then we stepped outside and got in the taxi. The radio was on, a newscaster was reporting that Robert F. Kennedy had been shot at the Ambassador Hotel in Los Angeles. Janelle was half hysterical.

There is no possible explanation for any of this. I feel hesitant to repeat it because few will believe it could've happened. For many years Janelle did seem to have a sixth sense and the unique ability to read palms with unerring accuracy. She once told a producer of mine that he'd been behind bars, reducing him to tears as he admitted to a stint in a reformatory.

I first met Janelle at a small cafe off Sunset called Chez Paulette that she helped manage. Her name at that time was Janelle Goforth. She was a blonde five-foot-four bundle of energy from Wichita Falls with three adorable kids. When I met the smallest boy, Louie, who was barely three, he took one look at me and exclaimed, "Hello Daddy." I was hooked. On my first date with Janelle she ordered nothing more than a sliced peach and a single scoop of ice cream because she thought I was so poor. After all, if I didn't drive a car, I had to be flat broke—not just a New Yorker.

Despite the doctor's predictions that she couldn't bear more children, we did have two daughters together, Melissa and Jill, and a marriage that endured for 20 years. Today we remain the best of friends, partially the result of sharing the same divorce attorney and trying to be considerate of one another. I still regard her as a close member of my family and my current wife Cynthia loves Janelle as much as I do. She's often a welcome guest in our home which I still consider to be her home in California. Generosity goes a long way, and you always get back far more than you give. Besides, how could I give up all the wonderful shared memories that we can still reminisce about because we remained friends?

For example: the night before the 1968 Presidential election, Janelle and I had been driving through Beverly Hills after dinner, only to see a motorcade turn the corner directly ahead of us. We decided to follow. I was convinced it must be the Richard Nixon party. Both candidates had finished off their campaigns with television appearances in Los Angeles.

The trail led to one of the residential streets close to Sunset Boulevard where I noticed a line of people filtering into one of the more elegant homes. I told Janelle to park, and we strolled casually across the street to join them. Crashing events had always been one of my specialties. Fortunately I spotted Buddy Hackett among the other celebrities and engaged him in conversation until we had strolled past the Secret Service men.

The house belonged to Lloyd Hand, a prominent Democrat. Contrary to my expectations, this was the Hubert Humphrey celebration. Once inside I headed to the bar to get Janelle a glass of white wine. When I returned, she was missing. I searched the party for her and then glanced out on the dance floor. There she was fox-trotting with Hubert Humphrey himself. She later said he had a very strong lead. One number finished and they danced still another before she brought him over and introduced me. The Vice President had no idea we were trespassers. He was simply charmed by Janelle.

Mr. Humphrey turned out to be a lovely guy, much taller, stronger and more authoritative than he appeared on television. I only wished I could have written some of his speeches and communicated the powerful personality which he exuded in person.

The hours swept by and finally after almost everyone else was gone, Janelle and I found ourselves alone in the kitchen with a few Secret Service agents and Muriel and Hubert Humphrey—all of us having coffee and cake together. Then one of his aides rushed in and said that the Vice President had to depart for the airport. He was flying home to vote. We hugged and kissed, and they left—never knowing who the hell we were or how we got there. Of course, Hubert lost the election the next day, much to our disappointment.

Years later I'd have my chance to meet Richard Nixon. I was meandering down Madison Avenue, headed for Kron's to buy a box of chocolate-covered orange slices for Janelle. I noticed a small crowd gathered under the awning of one of the co-op buildings between Madison and Fifth. Wandering over I maneuvered my way past a local television crew and came face to face with none other than Nixon himself. The long deposed ex-President looked straight at me, grabbed my arm, and exclaimed, "What are you doing here? I didn't know you lived in New York."

I wasn't sure who he mistook me for, but I played along. "Oh yes, Mr. President, we've been here for three years now. I bet you must love the city yourself, just walking around and being recognized and welcomed."

Nixon agreed with me that New York was a fabulous city, then he gestured toward the limousine parked at the curb, "There's Pat." I leaned over a bit and saw Pat waving at me from within the limousine. "Hi Pat," I exclaimed and waved back.

Nixon still had me by the hand and had no intention of letting go. He'd also grasped my elbow and was hanging onto that as well. The few newsmen were snapping photographs of us, and the NBC camera was trained on me. All I could think of was, "This is great, I'm going to be on the news with Nixon tonight."

As with Humphrey, Nixon looked much better in person. I noticed none of that five o'clock shadow. He was much taller than he appeared on the tube, and he actually had a very pleasant bright smile. The guy just wasn't photogenic, but in person I had to admit he was a nice-looking man, not at all how I'd imagined him.

The conversation continued on with small talk. Nixon didn't seem in any hurry to terminate it. I couldn't very well tell him I had portrayed him in *The Private Files of J. Edgar Hoover* as one of the villains of the piece. For a moment I felt sorry I'd treated him so harshly. Finally he excused himself and got in the limo. He and Pat were still waving at me as they pulled away. I was left surrounded by spectators and photographers who looked puzzled as to my identity. I rushed home and watched all the nightly news programs, but none of the footage appeared. I hadn't had the good sense to bribe one of the photographers to send me a photo—but I was to encounter Nixon again.

While filming *Deadly Illusion*, I'd set up my cameras to overlook the Rockefeller Center skating rink. Billy Dee Williams and Vanity were supposed to get out of a taxi, stroll past the enormous Christmas tree, and enter the RCA Building. Suddenly one of my crew members came running up yelling, "Look, there's Nixon with his two granddaughters watching the ice skaters."

I peered through the telephoto lens and there he was, bigger than life, Nixon again! What an opportunity to include him in my movie. I immediately got on the walkie-talkie to Billy Dee, instructing him to pass as close to Nixon as possible, glance at him casually and then do a double take before moving on. It would have gotten a tremendous laugh.

The shot came off without a hitch. Nixon wasn't aware he was in the movie but everyone in the audience would surely recognize him. When the producers saw the footage, they exploded. "No way we can keep this in. We'll get sued."

I protested that Nixon wouldn't file any lawsuit. There was nothing derogatory about his appearance in the film. He had a sense of humor and had even appeared on *Rowan & Martin's Laugh-In.* Even if he did issue a complaint, it would be good publicity for the movie and we could always trim the scene out. What was there to lose? Nonetheless the producers decided to excise this priceless shot from the final cut.

After the wonderful lunch I'd had with Elia Kazan at the London Film Festival, I was fated to run into him again years later in Paris. Cynthia and I were en route to still another film festival when I spotted Gadge in the lobby of the Trémoille Hotel. I re-introduced myself and told him I'd just finished his biography, *A Life*, and had actually read it twice. "Why would you do a thing like that?" Kazan demanded suspiciously.

"I don't know, I felt like I was hanging out with you, and I just didn't want it to end"—words spoken from the heart.

"Why, that's the nicest compliment I've gotten on the book yet," he responded with a big grin. And smiling was not a thing Kazan did easily. I then introduced him to Cynthia, and they began chatting fluently in Greek, while I stood by in my ignorance. Kazan finally quipped, "Greek girls are the best." I had to agree with him.

Kazan was in Europe vainly trying to raise money for a sequel to *America America*. With all his monumental credits and awards, he couldn't find anyone to back him. The dream of his life was to complete the story of his family's immigrant experience in America. Much like Orson Welles and Samuel Fuller, he was beloved, emulated and unfinanceable. This was really something to look forward to in my own career. The longer you last, the harder it gets. The more film festivals, the fewer offers of work. That seemed to be the sad equation. It happened to Billy Wilder, to David Lean, and to just about every great director I'd admired. Time was their deadliest enemy.

Chapter 20
More Narrow Escapes

At times, my unorthodox methods put me at odds with technicians who were accustomed to working in a more traditional manner. They expected to see a production board and a shot list. Most had never heard of anyone winging an entire production. Often, I wouldn't hear any direct criticism, but I'd become aware of grumbling behind my back. If this feeling of discontent reached the actors, they would inevitably lose confidence in me. The most important relationship I had on the set was with the cast. Performance came first.

If a crew member tried to undermine my authority, they had to be instantly replaced, no matter how important their position might be. Sad to say, but I found that it was extremely productive to fire somebody during the first or second day of photography. It communicated to everyone that no nonsense would be tolerated. If a person wasn't willing to work on my terms, they were free to go. After all, in these films I was writer, producer, director and chief financial officer. I was my own production manager, my own casting director, and my own location scout. If I'd been technically adept, I would have been my own director of photography, but I wasn't.

Once most crews got used to me, they usually began to enjoy the experience. They, along with the actors, watched in awe as I sat down and wrote entire new sequences while they waited to shoot them. They watched me improvise to accommodate a change in weather or locale. Eventually they got accustomed to the long hours that I demanded. My goal was to get the crew so involved that it wasn't just a job. Hopefully the unpredictability would turn filmmaking into an adventure, not factory labor. There was also the sense of danger because at any moment we could be shut down. The unions were always at our heels, and more often than not we were operating without proper permits.

The majority of the crew must have enjoyed the experience because they came back time after time to work for me when there were plenty of other jobs around. They'd always start out bitching and moaning but would soon get caught up in the momentum which I found it easy to generate. There was chaos, but that's when I'd thrive. Just when it seemed nothing was fixable, I'd concoct a solution that not only solved the problem but seemed to improve the scene.

I certainly didn't see eye to eye with the DP of my *It's Alive* sequel, *It Lives Again*. We were filming in Tucson, Arizona, and the cameraman was continually voicing disrespect. I called him aside and told him he was through. In a fury, he informed me that if he went, he would pull the entire crew off with him. They were all his people, and they would simply walk out. I responded, "In that case, you and your entire crew are fired as of now. Please vacate your hotel rooms. There will be another crew here tomorrow."

Of course, I didn't know what the hell I was talking about. The actors couldn't believe what was happening. They'd be the only ones left. This could have been a disastrous situation since the performers had to be paid whether or not we shot a foot of film. There was also the expense of equipment rental, hotels and location fees. I'd put myself in quite a spot. But again, fate was on my side.

I put in a quick phone call to Daniel Pearl, who'd been the DP on the horror classic *The Texas Chain Saw Massacre*. He knew how to shoot down and dirty.

"I just fired everybody. Can you be in Tucson by tomorrow morning at 8 am with a crew of your own?"

When the actors reported for work the next morning, there were all new faces to greet them. Technicians eager to work, not complain. They all knew what happened to the previous bunch and nobody gave me any problems. Daniel and I got along famously, and he'd end up shooting four of my movies.

The cast of *It Lives Again* was headed by two extremely talented actors, Frederic Forrest and Kathleen Lloyd. Fred was part of Francis Coppola's stock company, starring in the title role of Zoetrope's production of *Hammett*. He was also the lead in Coppola's *One from the Heart* and had a central role in *Apocalypse Now*. He came so close to stardom that it hurt

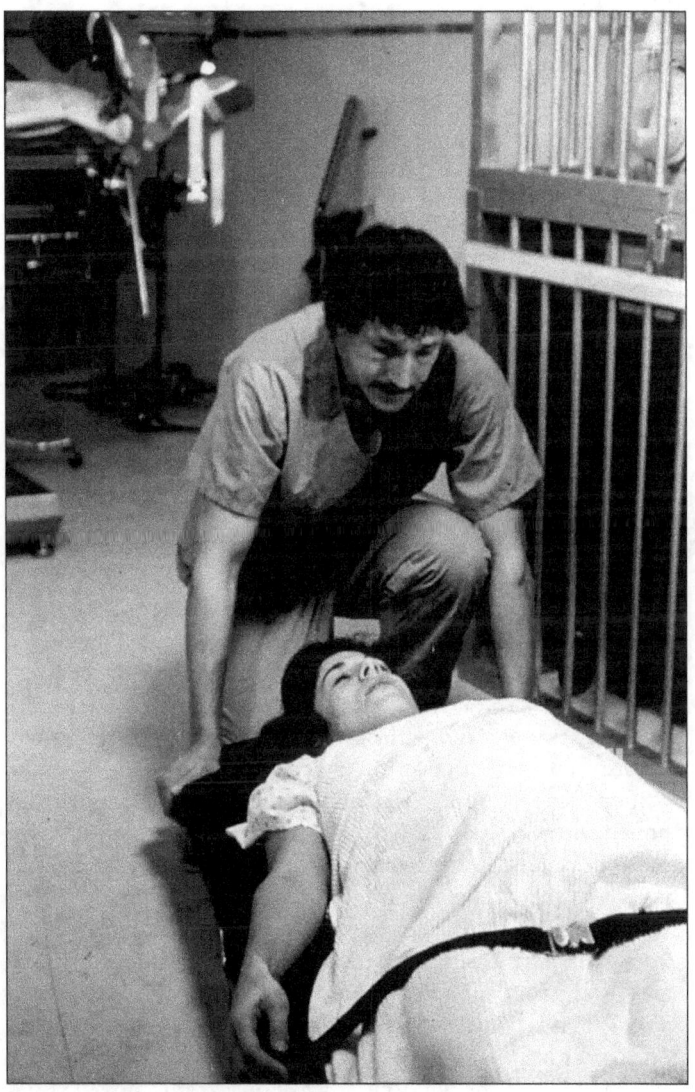

Frederick Forrest and Kathleen Lloyd in *It Lives Again*.

but was never able to cross that line. It's a mystery what makes a movie star click—some undefinable element that eluded Fred.

Similarly, Kathleen Lloyd made her film debut opposite Marlon Brando and Jack Nicholson in *The Missouri Breaks*. Playing the female lead should've rocketed her to fame. She was a young Jane Fonda with tremendous potential. While waiting for *The Missouri Breaks* to open, Kathleen was offered a role in Spielberg's *Close Encounters of the Third Kind*, which she unwisely turned down. When *The Missouri Breaks* turned out to be a total box-office dud, she was unable to regain momentum. Fred and Kathleen were wonderful actors who deserved better than they got.

When we completed filming in Tucson, we all returned to Los Angeles for several more weeks of photography. I had no sooner arrived home than Daniel Pearl appeared at my front door looking grim. "I don't know how to tell you this, Larry, but something terrible has happened."

He finally broke the bad news. The entire soundtrack for the location shoot in Tucson had been lost. The soundman had brought all the original tapes back personally, carrying them safely in his hand luggage along with his microphones. He claimed the bag had been stolen in the airport. We had no duplicates for these tapes. Without them there was no soundtrack whatsoever. With all the ad-libbing and improvisation, there was no chance of looping the dialogue unless I hired lip readers to construct a verbatim script.

For some reason, I remained calm. Daniel departed but phoned me again less than an hour later. "Something's wrong here," he said. "I went over to the soundman's house and discovered that the microphones he claims were stolen were all there. He started to cry and owned up to the truth. Out at the airport when he was loading up the car, he put the box with the tapes on the roof for a minute and then he forgot and left them there. When I drove away, the box must have fallen off with all your tracks in it."

I looked out the window. It was pouring rain now. I could only envision those reels of tape lying on the roadside at the airport being run over by passing vehicles. I simply responded,

The IT'S ALIVE Baby is back...
Only now there are three of them.

"IT
LIVES
AGAIN"

A LARCO PRODUCTION • "IT LIVES AGAIN"

STARRING: FREDERIC FORREST • KATHLEEN LLOYD • JOHN P. RYAN as Frank Davis
JOHN MARLEY • ANDREW DUGGAN • EDDIE CONSTANTINE • JAMES DIXON
MUSIC BY BERNARD HERRMANN • WRITTEN, PRODUCED AND DIRECTED BY LARRY COHEN
A LARRY COHEN FILM • TECHNICOLOR • READ THE BALLANTINE BOOK
Released by Warner Bros. ⓦ a Warner Communications Company

PG PARENTAL GUIDANCE SUGGESTED
SOME MATERIAL MAY NOT BE
SUITABLE FOR PRE-TEENAGERS

©1978 WARNER BROS. INC.

"Okay. Send somebody out to the airport and pick them up. They're still there."

Daniel thought that was crazy. Hours had passed by now and the rain was torrential. Besides, Los Angeles airport was large and complex. They'd never find anything. But I was adamant. "You'll find them. They'll be there. Just do it!" I guess Daniel thought it was the least he could do, so he dispatched several of the crew to LAX on a fool's errand.

If only the soundman had admitted his blunder, they could have gotten there three hours earlier. I felt like strangling him. Only the fact that he was the son of the celebrated film composer, Jerry Goldsmith, saved his life. I figured some day in the future I might want Jerry to score one of my films. When I actually met Jerry Goldsmith years later, he seemed to know the entire story and we had a good laugh over it. To Jerry it seemed typical of something his son might do.

The rain continued all of that afternoon. It was after dark when my doorbell rang. I answered it to find Daniel and his crew sheepishly holding large cardboard boxes filled with what looked like wet spaghetti. It was what was left of my soundtracks. They had been run over numerous times by airport traffic and they'd been soaked in the punishing storm. The situation looked hopeless. But somehow, I knew it wasn't. "Don't worry about it," I assured Daniel. "I'll hire an assistant editor to unravel the tapes and put them on spools and we'll see what we've got."

As if by a miracle, we seemed to have one decent sound take of each sequence, enough to piece together a usable track for every scene we shot in Tucson. The absurdity of it all does not escape me, even after all these years. That the crew members were able to find the tapes in the massive LAX complex boggles the mind. Thereafter, the crew regarded me with a sense of awe. I seemed infallible—which, of course, I was.

Still, the casting of Eddie Constantine in a pivotal supporting role in this film may still qualify as a colossal blunder on my part. What could I do? Eddie was my brother-in-law at the time. He'd met and married Janelle's sister. I was to blame since I made the introduction.

Eddie had been one of France's most popular movie stars. He appeared in the French B pictures, usually playing

Eddie Constantine in *It Lives Again.*

the same role of Lemmy Caution, an American private eye working in Paris. At this point he's best known for playing the part in Jean-Luc Godard's take on the character, *Alphaville.*

Eddie was an ex-G.I. visiting France when he met Edith Piaf and became one of her many lovers. She turned him into a singing star and eventually an actor. When Eddie's first film appeared in the U.S., the *Herald Tribune* review read: "Fifty million Frenchmen can be wrong." Eddie never caught on in this country but because of his resemblance to Humphrey Bogart, he became a French icon in numerous tough guy roles.

When we visited Paris with him, we could hardly walk down the streets without being mobbed. Frenchmen loved him, but the studios stopped making his type of picture and he had lost all of his money due to a massive tax audit. The rest of his savings went on racehorses that never seemed to finish as winners.

When we visited the Louis Vuitton store off the Champs-Élysées, a huge line stretched around the block. Eddie simply jumped the line, walking straight in, and the crowd began to jeer. Eddie turned to them and shouted in French, "If you want to get to the head of the line, become a movie star!!"

The crowd of Frenchmen roared with laughter and began to applaud. This was the Eddie Constantine they loved in the movies—the tough guy. Though he loved playing the part, in life he was actually a kind and gentle soul.

The sad fact was that Eddie was broke, and he probably married Janelle's sister simply to put a roof over his head. I actually felt privileged to have him in a picture, but Eddie's problem was that he thought in French, and by the time his mind translated his lines into English, they came out backwards. In one take he was supposed to say, "I'm here to protect the infant." Instead the line came out, "I'm here to prevent the vermin!" And, as the *New York Times* review later pointed out, he walked like a man wearing a concrete vest.

It wasn't long after the production that Eddie got a divorce and moved back to Europe, marrying a German woman and resuming his career, this time as a supporting player.

Nothing I'd experienced previously could prepare me for the disasters that awaited us on the island of Kauai, where we shot a portion of *It's Alive III: Island of the Alive* in 1986.

In this sequel, the mutant babies have been left on a deserted island to mature and scientists are now returning to have a look at them. We rented a sailing vessel called *The Discovery* which seemed perfect for our needs. The scientists were to arrive at the island aboard this two-masted schooner, and much of the action took place at sea.

I knew nothing about boats, so I was surprised to learn that this one had a concrete hull. Once we got aboard and heavy seas rolled in, we learned that being passengers was like riding a bull. The bucking and pitching was unimaginable. Actors and crew were turning pale, and soon leaning over the side. Only Daniel Pearl, Michael Moriarty (who was playing the lead role) and I seemed to be immune to seasickness. The others were all begging me to head for shore. Even stuntman Paul Stader, who had supervised the action in *Moby Dick* and other seagoing dramas, was suffering visibly. But I couldn't give in to their pleas for mercy. I was paying for the boat whether we used it or not and I'd also engaged a helicopter for aerial coverage of the boat plowing through open seas. I knew these rough waters would look great on film. The misery the crew was experiencing would be compensated for by production value.

It Lives Again.

The problem was that Moriarty had to appear to be alone on deck, which meant no one else could be visible to the helicopter camera. Everybody else would have to descend below and remain out of sight. If the mal de mer wasn't bad enough already, it would be worse experienced from below deck. I managed to herd most of them down there and hide the rest of them under tarpaulins on the deck. We got the scene, and it was more spectacular than I'd ever expected as huge waves splashed over the bow.

Shortly after we finished filming, *The Discovery* was seized and impounded. The government charged that it was being used for the transport of marijuana.

Our troubles on the island were just beginning. Although the mayor of Kuai and a local Priestess had arrived our first day to bless the production, the Gods obviously were not listening.

I'd engaged my friend, Neal Israel, a talented writer and director (*Bachelor Party* with Tom Hanks) to play the part of one of the scientists. In one sequence, Neal was supposed to be bathing alone in an idyllic pond at the foot of a small waterfall when one of the full-grown monsters appears behind him and drags him under to his death. The actor playing the monster was outfitted in a rubberized suit and looked fairly convincing with his huge head and fake claws. When I called "action," the monster was instructed to submerge, wait for five seconds, and then rise up behind Neal, seizing him.

The babies have grown in *It's Alive III: Island of the Alive.*

The actor went under but never came up. Neal continued soaping himself up waiting to be grabbed, but nothing happened. After about 30 seconds of waiting, we realized something was wrong. The monster's rubberized suit had filled up with water. The poor guy was drowning. I shouted to Neal, and he dived down and took hold of the monster suit, finally pulling the actor to the surface. Weighted down with water, he was heavy, and it took all his strength, but Neal Israel single-handedly rescued the monster. He was the hero of the day.

But the day wasn't finished. Only an hour later, we all heard a sound similar to a log cracking open in a fireplace, but magnified hundreds of times. And then, almost instantly, the small waterfall beneath which we were shooting turned into a veritable Niagara. There must have been a log jam upriver that had suddenly broken, unleashing a flood. Everyone was fleeing the deluge, grabbing the cameras, sound equipment and lights in an attempt to save them. Some of the crew were already waist-deep.

The torrential flow wouldn't stop. The camera operator and the gaffers were trying to scramble up the steep incline, stumbling and falling backward into the water. Fortunately, no serious injuries occurred. The entire area where we'd been shooting was completely submerged. Then I realized one of our cast members, Art Lund, was still down there. In the sequence, his dead body was seen dangling from a tree. We'd wired Art onto the branches and he couldn't get loose.

"Don't worry," he hollered in his booming baritone, "I got a great view from up here." It took us quite a while to finally come to his rescue.

We moved to another location and began shooting another sequence in which Michael Moriarty pauses in the jungle and calls to the monsters, assuring them they have nothing to fear. Michael was shouting into the bushes when he got a sudden response. A wild boar came darting out right on cue. Michael leaped out of the way just in time. The boar panicked and began circling madly, racing back and forth amongst the crew and the equipment, finally disappearing into a thicket. I kept prodding Daniel to grab a shot of the animal, but he was too busy getting out of its way.

The capper to the day was when our huge equipment truck rolled into a swamp by mistake and nearly capsized. By that time the crew and cast were ready for a few drinks. Their only compensation was knowing they wouldn't have to go back on the boat again.

Chapter 21
Winging the Serpent

My most hazardous tour of duty came with Q, high atop New York's Chrysler Building. After four attempts, we finally gained permission to film on the level just below the tower that leads up to the pinnacle of the skyscraper. Naturally I wasn't content to remain where I belonged. The only access to the area above was via a narrow metal ladder which I immediately set out to climb. This took me to a platform which was totally exposed to the elements. There were no windows, just triangular arches large enough for a man to step through and plunge 87 stories to a certain death. These openings surrounded the platform on all sides.

There was still another skinny ladder which I scaled, leading to an even narrower platform, and then above that was the final climb into the very needle. I immediately descended and told the crew members to begin hauling their equipment up by rope and without hesitation they obeyed. I don't know what made them follow me up there without any question or dissent.

The cameras, the lights, the sound equipment all had to be lifted into position and rigged. I wanted pigeons in the scene and there weren't any, so we phoned around town and located a pigeon wrangler who soon showed up with a cage full of birds. They too were hoisted to the upper platform.

The special effects make-up people arrived with several human skeletons which were supposed to be the remains of the flying serpent's most recent victims. I could see everyone was scared but also turned on. I suppose we were all caught up in the spirit of adventure.

The pinnacle of the Chrysler Building was never meant to be visited by the general public. It was a maze of wires and cables in which one could easily become entangled. At times the wind whipped through with brutal force. I instructed one of the stuntmen to cease all other duties and stick by me. His only job was to keep me from falling. I knew I'd be totally

distracted as I set up the blocking for the scenes. All I needed to do was to take one wrong step backwards and I'd have found myself plummeting through space. The stuntman kept his hand securely on my belt at all times.

I realized we'd be thrown out if the management of the building realized we had exceeded our authority and ascended into this no-man's land. That meant I had to shoot as much footage as possible the first day. I couldn't be sure we'd be allowed back.

We shot late into the day. Suddenly, darkness closed in. It was a beautiful sight to behold, all of New York stretched out before us with the city lights slowly going on. Our own electrical equipment kept the platform illuminated. Then abruptly, before we could descend, everything went black. Somewhere along the line we'd experienced a power failure.

I shouted, "Hold your positions. Stay put where you are until the lights come on again."

I was assuming the lights would come on. For all I knew we might well have been there all night. It took only ten minutes for the problem to be corrected. I've never held my breath for so long.

I'd noticed huge baskets suspended around the outside of the tower. These were being used by steeplejacks who were currently completing repairs. I immediately invited them to act in the movie. They'd dress as police officers and get to handle automatic weapons. They all welcomed the opportunity to be stationed in the baskets, firing at the imaginary serpent that would be circling the tower.

I also hired a dozen off-duty police officers to portray cops in the sequence. A great many patrolmen are members of the Screen Actors Guild. Producers prefer to hire them because they arrive for work wearing their own uniforms. You not only get an actor, you get a costume as well. Actually, renting a policeman's uniform along with all the accoutrements like gun belts, caps and badges would cost more than the salary you'd be paying the extra.

So with my policemen and steeplejacks in place and with a helicopter and cameraman buzzing the pinnacle, I commenced fire. Machine guns were blazing on all sides of the Chrysler Building. I had coverage of the action from both inside the building as well as from the chopper. I even sent a second unit down to the street level to capture the reactions of passersby to the small war that was waging overhead.

What I hadn't counted on was the shell casings that are expelled when an automatic weapon is fired. They showered down to the street. Once again, I was saved from calamity. There was reconstruction work being done on the lower floors and protective canopies had been erected upon which the shell casings landed. No one was hurt or even endangered.

The barrage of gunfire was heard in the nearby offices of WPIX, a local television station, and they immediately dispatched a camera crew. Other news agencies hastened to follow suit. Soon local TV commentators were proclaiming that a Hollywood movie company had caused a panic in the streets.

The following day, the *New York Post* would run a head-line on Page 1: "MOVIE CREW TERRORIZES CITY." The New York *Daily News* would carry a similar front page story. None of it was true. My cameramen stationed on the sidewalk couldn't get any coverage of interest because the pedestrians passing by simply glanced upward for a moment and then went on their way. There were other erroneous reports that police officials had feared an attack on the United Nations building, which was located just east of the Chrysler Building.

I love nothing more than publicity, so I took out a full-page ad in *Variety* headlined: "DEAR NEW YORK, SORRY WE SCARED YOU."

Meanwhile the New York Film Commission was trying to cover their own asses. They issued a statement that we were filming without their knowledge even though we actually did have permits for a change. They failed to mention that the people manning the weapons were mainly their own off-duty cops and that everything had been cleared in advance with the local police precinct. Some irate editorials appeared in the newspapers and Mayor Koch raked the Film Commission over the coals. The Mayor and the Film Commission quickly issued public apologies. Larry Cohen was suddenly persona non grata. It seemed I might even be denied permission to continue filming in the city.

As a compromise, a police sergeant was assigned to our crew with instructions that no further gunshots would be permitted for the duration of our production.

In the story, a huge nest is found in which the serpent had laid its egg. It was far too cumbersome to construct this nest in the actual pinnacle of the Chrysler Building. As a substitute loca-tion, I used the circular dome which stood atop the abandoned Police Headquarters Building in Little Italy. This structure was completely uninhabited except for hordes of rats and a number of vicious guard dogs that were constantly on patrol. We got them to lock up the dogs. The rats were our problem.

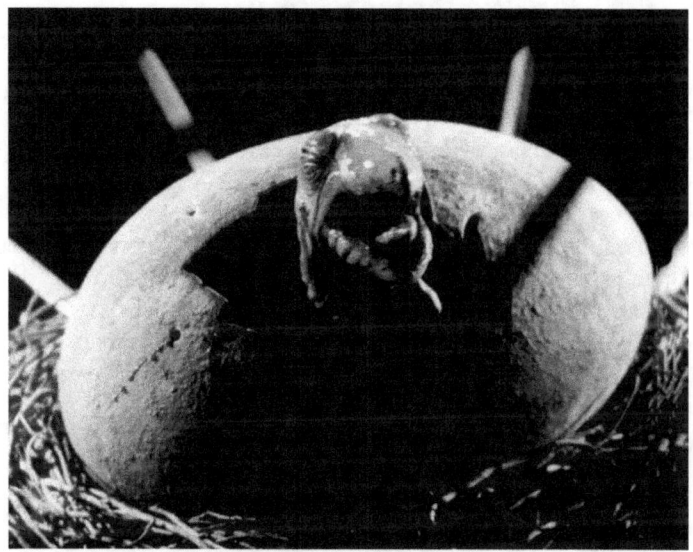

A Quetzalcoatl hatches in *Q*.

Our art director and his staff built the nest out of twigs and branches gathered from the parks of the city. In the sequence, the egg cracks open and a junior serpent emerges, only to be destroyed by the SWAT team.

For a change, we completed the sequence without any trouble. (But with plenty of gunfire. Our bird-dogging sergeant had been transferred to other duties by then.) When I ordered the crew to wrap, they removed the lights and camera equipment, and I went home. I had no idea that the scenic grips decided to remove only the egg, leaving the giant nest behind. That way they'd save themselves hours of hard labor.

Nothing more was heard of that nest for months. Then I received a phone call informing me that a small article on the front page of the *New York Times* noted that anthropologists were flying into New York from all over the country to examine a strange nest that had been found in the turret of the old police headquarters building. It seems the place was to be converted into condominiums and on an architectural survey, our nest was finally discovered.

Nobody seemed to recall that a movie had been shot there. It appeared some huge creature had actually inhabited the turret—hence the scientific investigation. For a change, I thought it better to keep my mouth shut.

Nothing will equal the thrill of flying over New York in a chopper piloted by Al Cerullo, who'd handled the aerial footage on such movies as *Superman*. He knew the canyons of the city by heart. He not only circled the buildings, he flew in between them. When night fell, navigation became even more challenging. Many of the skyscrapers had antennae rising above them that were virtually invisible to the naked eye after dark, but Al knew all the danger spots.

During another daylight run, I spotted a runaway balloon rising from Central Park and floating over the city, carried by strong gusts of wind. "Let's chase the balloon," I told Al, already improvising a sequence in my head. So wherever the red balloon went, we followed. Eventually I would animate the flying monster into the shot. Then, below, I noticed what looked like a scale model of the Statue of Liberty on a rooftop across from Lincoln Center. It was large enough for a chase to be staged inside, and so I immediately wrote such a sequence into the script. The wonderful thing about filming in New York is that you're limited only by your own imagination. I've always called the city the world's greatest backlot.

Today, as I walk around Manhattan, there's hardly a corner I pass where I haven't filmed some scene. I've covered almost every landmark and quite a few places off the beaten track. And I must admit that while I was filming, I felt like I owned New York.

Another close call took place while completing the climactic scene for *The Ambulance*. Eric Roberts was being pursued on foot by the vehicle with its siren blasting. Trapped at the foot of a high fence, Roberts scales it to see a huge excavation about 20 stories deep on the other side. The villain inside the ambulance has no idea what's beyond that fence. Eric goads him and the villain steps on the gas crashing into the fence with Eric still atop it. The ambulance then plunges down into the excavation and explodes in a huge ball of fire. Above, Eric clings to a jagged section of the fence and dangles back and forth above the explosion.

With Eric Roberts on the set of *The Ambulance*.

The New York Film Commission refused us permission to shoot the sequence anywhere in the city because it was considered too dangerous. After we wrapped the picture in New York we reconvened in downtown Los Angeles where a proper excavation had been found and leased. For a change I would have all the necessary permits, but things would still go wrong.

Our stunt coordinator was Spiro Razatos, a capable and affable fellow whom I would later help start a directing career of his own. A catapult had been built to help propel the ambulance further into the excavation. The rigging of this device was taking an inordinate amount of time. I kept myself busy shooting inserts to the chase sequence, but as the hours passed, I was growing concerned. We had only this one night to shoot the scene. If we didn't get it, we wouldn't have an ending and there would be hell to pay. Spiro was having trouble with the crew who were taking their orders from the special effects coordinator rather than him. I had to step in and mediate, but already the glow of morning was approaching. "We're losing the dark," I shouted. "We've got to shoot this now."

The Ambulance.

Spiro was ready, doubling for Eric Roberts. He climbed the fence and waited, and as I called action, the ambulance burst forward, smashing through the fence and tumbling into the vast pit beyond. Spiro was wired into position so he couldn't fall and swung out over the expected blast area as if hanging on by his bare hands. The ambulance hit bottom but did not explode. It had been armed to detonate on impact, but nothing happened. Our cameras kept rolling until it was apparent no explosion would materialize. Of course, it could still go off without warning. Anybody who went down there to find out what went wrong could be killed by a sudden detonation.

Dawn was breaking. A crew member came up with the solution: a solitary gasoline can rigged with a length of electrical wire. He would scoot down the incline and slide the gas can so that it would skitter beneath the overturned ambulance. We'd then ignite it from up top. I didn't like the idea of anybody venturing down there but he didn't wait for me to think it over.

We all held our breath as he descended, tossed the can, and with unerring accuracy it disappeared underneath the ambulance. The wire was hardly visible. As he reached the top and signaled me, I called action. An electrical charge set the gas can off. All the previously rigged explosives ignited too, while

Spiro still dangled overhead surrounded by billows of smoke and flame.

Several minutes later we were staring at each other in daylight, but the sequence was finished. I'd covered it with four cameras which was lucky since one of them malfunctioned. Once again, I had lucked out at the last possible moment. I wondered why my movies always had to be akin to skydiving or riding the rapids. Why was there always so much risk involved, the hair-breadth escapes, the last-minute rescues? I was not the kind of person who sought out high-risk sports. You'd never find me climbing a mountain, but my moviemaking seemed to be fraught with peril. My life resembled a 15-chapter serial with cliffhangers at the conclusion of each segment.

When I read the biographies of other directors, they seem tame by comparison. For me it's always been exciting work, carried out in circumstances that always seemed both bizarre and hazardous. How long could my luck last? When would it run out?

It was with great sadness that I read of the tragic *Twilight Zone* incident which involved my friends John Landis and George Folsey, Jr. They had applied for permits to have two children involved in a Vietnam War sequence and had been turned down. Anxious not to abandon the scene, George went out and

Directing *The Ambulance*.

found two youngsters and hired them off the books. When they were killed along with actor Vic Morrow, the director and producer were both indicted and brought to trial. George might well have thought, "What would my friend Larry Cohen do in this situation? He'd just go get the kids and wing it." How could anyone predict that an explosion would knock a helicopter out of the sky, resulting in three fatalities?

All were acquitted but the proceedings took their toll on George. He seemed shrunken and older, and he soon dissolved his long association with Landis. John never recaptured the momentum of his career either. Although I had nothing whatsoever to do with it, I somehow felt guilty.

I was obviously setting a terrible example for others who might not be as lucky as I. Maybe it was time to stop stealing movies. Maybe it was time to grow up.

Chapter 22
Beware of Compliments

I've discovered that when fans confront you and begin to rave about your films, it's best to cut it short and make your escape. If you linger too long, the compliment will invariably turn into an insult. For example, a fan will say, "I saw your movie and I just loved it. My boyfriend and I both thought it was one of the best pictures of the year." And then they will continue, "We saw it in Westwood the other night. We were the only ones in the theater. I don't know why nobody else came to see it, but we liked it."

Another favorite goes like this: "That film of yours was really good... I don't know why the reviews were so dreadful." You're always pushing your luck if you hang around too long.

In 1975, Janelle and I were invited to Deauville American Film Festival in France, where I presented *Bone*. The screening was early one morning and the attendance was sparse. Seated directly behind me, however, was the famed character actor Burgess Meredith, for whom I had great admiration. If he had been a British star, he certainly would have been Sir Burgess Meredith by now, for he had an auspicious career on both stage and screen.

During the showing, I glanced back over my shoulder several times and Buzz, as he was affectionately known, was on the edge of his seat, leaning forward, totally captivated by the film. When it was over, he deluged me with compliments. "Why don't you write a part like that for me sometime?" he exclaimed. In the days that followed, each time he saw me, Burgess lavished additional praise. People came to me saying, "We had dinner with Buzz Meredith last night and all he talked about was your film. When can we see it?" I had the unfortunate duty to inform them that the screening was already over.

One evening, Janelle and I were in a Deauville restaurant when Buzz entered, slightly inebriated. He crossed to my table and bellowed, "You aren't even aware of the genius you have

achieved." Before the Festival had ended, Buzz had introduced us to writer James Baldwin, who was particularly interested in my film since it dealt with race in America. Back in the Sixties, Buzz had directed Baldwin's play *Blues for Mr. Charlie* on Broadway, which had long been one of my favorites. It felt great to be in the company of talents of the caliber of James Baldwin and Burgess Meredith, and to be treated as an equal. Before we left, Buzz gave us his phone number in Malibu and invited us to join him for dinner when we returned.

Naturally I wasn't going to pass up this invitation. I called Buzz and he set a date for later that week. He had his maid cook a turkey, and when we arrived, we found out he had a date for the evening—the statuesque beauty Edie Williams, former wife of softcore porn director Russ Meyer. Edie had been one of his Supervixens and she was considered a bit of a joke around Hollywood, appearing in various stages of undress at Oscar presentations and other events. She was the least likely date for an intellectual like Burgess. Yet we had a very pleasant evening together and polished off several bottles of wine.

As the evening drew to a close, I made the mistake of saying, "You know, Buzz, the fact that you liked my film so much made the whole festival worthwhile. Your enthusiasm meant so much to me." To which Burgess Meredith replied blankly, "What film was that?"

He'd forgotten all about it.

I should've given up then instead of trying to remind him of the story—to which there was no response whatsoever. This masterpiece had somehow been erased from his memory.

Janelle and I returned home in abject defeat. If only we had not seen Burgess Meredith again after the festival. But we pushed our luck too far.

Incidentally, Russ Meyer and I became buddies when I attended the Madrid Film Festival at which we were both being honored. Russ was a great down-to-earth guy and we ended up taking all of our meals together. Upon returning to Los Angeles, I invited Russ to a party at my Coldwater Canyon house and he showed up with his date of the evening, none other than John Waters. What a combination: Russ Meyer and John Waters! They couldn't come from more opposite ends of the spectrum, yet they were pals.

The most frightening words I've ever heard are, "This is one of the best scripts I've ever read." I know for certain that shortly thereafter it will require a massive rewrite and enormous changes, many of which will make no sense at all.

I liken a screenplay to a piece of fruit. At the time of purchase, it's fresh and juicy and extremely appetizing. Then a few days later, after it's been left out, it begins to acquire a few spots. By the end of the week, it's already grown mooshy. And 24 hours later, it's a piece of garbage ready for the refuse heap.

I believe someone's first reaction to a script is the most accurate. Movies are made to be seen once. If you sit through any film a dozen times and try to pick it apart, you won't have any trouble doing so.

In the Hollywood system, scripts are there for everyone to meddle with. After all, executives have to come up with some criticism to justify their job. My motto is: "If someone says anything nice about your script, accept the compliment, then flee for the hills. And hope that you don't run into them again. They will surely have changed their mind."

Chapter 23
The Greats (and Near Greats), Part 1

Over the course of my career I've had the good fortune to be associated with a few authentic geniuses. Among them was Joshua Logan, the gifted Broadway director of such smash hits as *Mr. Roberts*, *South Pacific* and *Annie Get Your Gun*. Logan's career extended to motion pictures, including *Picnic*, *Sayonara* and *Bus Stop*.

My stage play *Trick* had been submitted to Josh's production company and had been favorably received by his wife Nedda Harrigan Logan, a respected stage actress and one of New York's prominent socialites.

I was summoned to Josh's elegant co-op in the River House just off Sutton Place, one of the city's most prestigious residences. The lush carpets and draperies were deep red and the sprawling living room was populated by automatons—19th-century mechanical figures capable of playing exotic musical instruments. Operated by intricate sets of springs, these creatures, when activated, could launch into an extensive performance which Josh was always generous enough to demonstrate.

Visiting his home was like attending some fabulous party, and he was a gracious host. A tall man who'd put on considerable weight, he spoke with a lilting southern drawl that was immediately soothing. He'd enjoyed reading my play and was willing to work on making it better, which is exactly what I wanted to hear. Convening there three or four times a week, we seemed to spark each other's creativity. Josh liked to jingle the loose change in his pocket as he wandered in circles picking dialogue out of the air. I'd revise the line and he'd polish it some more before we recorded it on his old-fashioned Dictaphone. After each of the blue floppy discs was completed, Josh would simply toss it on the carpet and, in short order, it would be retrieved by his long-time assistant, Joe Curtis, who'd disappear with it into an adjoining office. After about three hours

Joshua Logan.

we'd quit and Josh would offer me a martini, over which he'd regale me with tales of his exploits on Broadway and in Hollywood.

Coincidental with his early successes on Broadway, Josh had experienced an enormous surge of nervous energy. He could work for 26 hours straight, exhausting all his collaborators. Ideas came flooding out of him and he seemed to have no fear of failure. It sounded much like the way I felt making my independent movies.

As a youth, Josh had been terrified of heights, but now suddenly he found he could walk on his hands, which he occasionally did for hours at a time—even onstage during rehearsals—to the confusion of the cast. Eventually he felt the urge to climb out on a high window ledge to demonstrate this complete lack of fear. His wife and other loved ones were forced to have him institutionalized for his own safety. Yet Josh came back and had some of his greatest successes following his illness, but he would be dependent on Lithium for the rest of his life. Some days he would tell me that he'd had a little too much or too little of what he called his wonder drug.

The play we were working on was 200 percent better because of Josh's involvement. His mind worked in devious ways and often I'd have to struggle to follow his line of thought, but eventually he would circle back and I'd make the connection. It was always the correct choice.

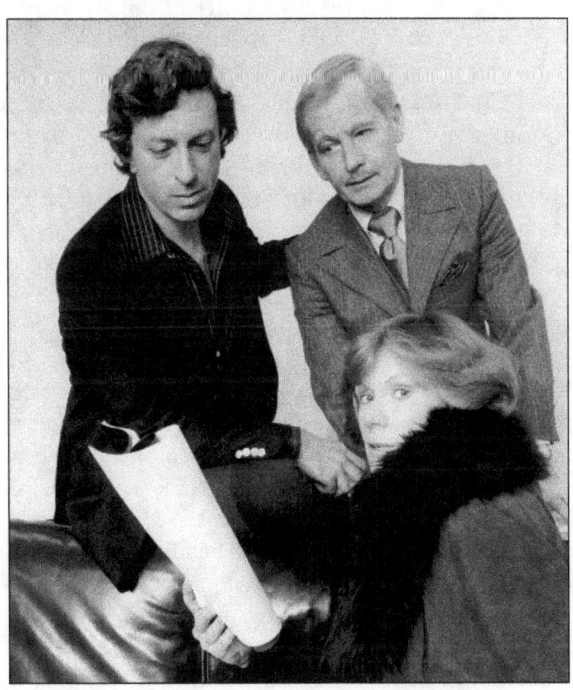

Directing Tammy Grimes and Donald Madden
in *Trick*, produced by Joshua Logan.

Each afternoon during our cocktail break we'd be interrupted by Joe Curtis, who'd enter with over 30 typewritten pages, the product of our previous day's efforts on the Dictaphone. I couldn't believe we were turning out such an immense volume of material. We'd read it over quickly and then I'd head home to my little York Avenue apartment a few blocks away and simply collapse. I was so worn out I had to go to sleep. Just keeping up with Josh was a feat worthy of the Olympics.

Actually Josh was perfect casting to produce this comedy thriller. He'd once optioned what later became *Rear Window* years before Hitchcock finally bought the Cornell Woolrich story. Josh sought to develop it for the screen, writing a treatment himself. This play of mine had many of the same elements, including an apartment facing a courtyard which looked out onto hundreds of neighbors' windows. No wonder Josh was attracted to the project.

Although I maintained a close friendship with Josh and Nedda, nothing immediately happened with the play. Josh hadn't had a recent success on Broadway and found it difficult to obtain backing. It seems a common phenomenon in show business that while people won't give you a job, they will certainly lavish you with honors. A tribute to Josh Logan was held at the Imperial Theatre on Broadway in 1975 with Henry Fonda performing a scene from *Mister Roberts*, Jimmy Stewart doing a monologue from *Harvey*, and Ethel Merman reprising some numbers from *Annie, Get Your Gun*, then staying on forever to do her entire repertoire.

Josh and Nedda were completely down-to-earth. Years later when I directed Nedda Logan in a television pilot that ultimately aired as a standalone movie, *See China and Die*, we were shooting on location on the west side of Central Park. There were some problems with the toilets in the trailers and the younger actors were bitching and moaning. But Nedda simply ambled off into the park and relieved herself behind one of the bushes. She returned to the set with a smile, commenting, "I guess these young actors have never worked in summer stock."

Eventually *Trick* did get its chance on Broadway in 1979 with Josh Logan as its producer. I was to direct and Tammy Grimes would star.

Tammy was a Tony Award winner and notoriously difficult with directors. I had never directed a stage play, not even a high school production, and Josh was not about to help me out. "If I come around everyone will think I'm directing the play, and that won't be good for you. So I intend to disappear until after the first preview." He was as good as his word. Josh went down south to supervise a student revival of one of his old classics, leaving the entire production on my shoulders.

I went out and bought a textbook on how to direct plays, but fortunately I never had time to open it. I simply followed the same approach I had applied to my films. We had a first reading, answered all of the questions the actors might have, then put the play up on its feet as quickly as possible. I found that directing for the stage was a holiday compared to making a movie.

The most miserable day in the theater is what's called the tech rehearsal. This is the first time the actors go through the entire show from start to finish, including all the lighting cues and set changes. A two-hour play will take ten or twelve hours from start to finish with all the mistakes and delays. It's exhausting, irritating, and absolutely necessary. Making a movie is like 30 days of continuous tech rehearsals. There is seldom any sense of a full performance. That happens in the editing room later on. Having suffered the agonies of filmmaking, I could easily endure one tech rehearsal and go on to enjoy all of the other days when I'd get to improvise with my cast with no distractions. I didn't have to be concerned about an airplane flying overhead while the camera is rolling or a microphone shadow killing the best take. I didn't have to worry about being kicked off of a location or about the film running out. I absolutely loved directing theater.

As anticipated, the first day was a difficult one because Tammy Grimes was testing me. Every time she was called upon to read a line, she'd pause and question its meaning or relevance. And each time she asked a question, I very calmly gave her an answer. If I didn't have one, I simply made something up. I never showed any irritation or impatience. I welcomed her questions and some of them were good ones. At the end of the day Tammy gave me a huge hug, and throughout the balance of the rehearsal period she never once questioned my direction. No matter how outlandish my suggestions might be, she tried them out. We had a fabulous relationship and one week during the run she asked me if I'd buy her a mink coat instead of paying her salary—which I was only too happy to do. The play's long gone, but the coat still keeps her warm in the winter.

Nedda came to a few run-throughs, but Josh didn't appear until well into the previews. Before seeing the show, he strolled backstage to Tammy's dressing room. I accompanied him, interested to see what a great director like Logan would say to a star before curtain time. I was shocked when he confided to her, "I went to a party the other night and a woman I met told me 'I never liked Tammy Grimes. I've seen her in half a dozen shows and I really never cared for her. But when I saw her in a preview of *Trick*, it changed my entire opinion. She was wonderful in that play.'"

Tammy couldn't believe it either. She shot back, "So my whole career is shit except for this play?"

It was all I could do to get Josh out of the dressing room. A few minutes later the curtain went up and Tammy Grimes gave the best performance she had ever given since rehearsals began. Josh had gotten under her skin and provoked her. She was going to show him just how good she could be. And she was.

The play opened to mixed reviews, but there were enough great quotes to make it sound like a hit. We were filling up the theater every night, thanks to the half-price TKTS booth at 47th and Broadway. But winter was rapidly approaching. Legendary agent Swifty Lazar called me one day telling me if we could run the show for four more weeks he could make a movie deal on our behalf. I told him I didn't know if we could hold out that long. Snow was already falling and it was getting harder to get people in. We did have every seat full on one fateful night when co-star Lee Richardson fell ill with stomach flu. Tammy came to me. "We don't want to give back all of that money, do we? Why don't you go out and play the part?"

The understudy had panicked and was afraid to go on. Since I had written and directed the piece, Tammy was sure that I could do it. The third member of our cast, Donald Madden, was game but suggested that I carry a copy of the script in my hand as insurance. At curtain time, it was announced that the author was playing one of the three roles, and nobody asked for their money back. I actually got a few more laughs than Lee usually did, and only had to resort to the book two or three times. If I'd let myself think about it, I might've panicked, and if my wife and two daughters had been seated up front, their presence might've thrown me completely. As it was, they sat in the last row cheering me on. My appearance was a stunt that the audience seemed to enjoy, particularly in the final scene when Donald Madden kills and hides my corpse behind the sofa. Remember, I'd been carrying a copy of the play in my hand all through the performance. When Donald struck me over the head and dragged me to the hiding place, I whispered to him, "Now go back and get the script," which had been left lying center stage. Donald quickly raced back, picked the script up, and tossed it behind the sofa where he'd previously hidden my body. The audience broke into gales of laughter and spontaneous applause.

It seemed that moment would be the highlight of my day, but after the curtain fell, Janelle and I headed over to a small, prearranged dinner party at the home of Janet Villela, the former wife of the ballet star Edward Villela. There were only six of us at the table, two of whom were Robert De Niro and Al Pacino. And what was the topic of discussion over dinner? Larry Cohen's Broadway debut! The two most important actors in America demanded to know how I'd had the guts to get up there and what it felt like. A capper to a perfect evening.

After about seven weeks of performances, *Trick* closed, but it had been such a rewarding experience that I would gladly have done it again. The show didn't lose any money and it gave me so much pleasure. Reginald Rose, creator of *The Defenders*, showed up in the audience one night, as did Dr. Sam Sumberg, my old City College mentor who had served as faculty advisor for Dram-Soc, the acting group where I'd gotten my first taste of theater. Seeing him there actually brought tears to my eyes.

Over the years Josh Logan often complained to me that his contemporaries like John Houseman, John Huston and Lee Strasberg were offered acting roles while he was overlooked. I promised that someday I'd find him a part in one of my movies. When eventually I did call it was too late. Josh laid out the ground rules under which he and Nedda could appear. "First of all I have to be either standing or seated for the entire scene. I cannot rise or sit down on camera. And Nedda has a problem with her right eye and can only be photographed from the left side."

He wasn't surprised when I begged off.

As a collaborator, Josh could be tough at times. When he felt I was taking the wrong course, he'd simply threaten to remove his name from the production if I didn't do things his way. I must admit he was usually right.

Chapter 24
The Greats (and Near Greats), Part 2

Josh Logan's working procedure was not that much different from that of Bernard Herrmann, the noted film composer who created the scores for such films as *Citizen Kane*, *Psycho*, *North by Northwest* and *Vertigo*. Benny was to become another great and loving friend, but it all started off as a job. When I filmed *It's Alive* for Warner Bros., my dream composer was Bernard Herrmann, and the studio attempted to contact him on my behalf. At that time he was unavailable since he'd been engaged to score William Friedkin's production of *The Exorcist*. Benny flew to New York to view the picture and took an immediate dislike to Friedkin. After the initial screening, Friedkin reportedly told Benny, "I want you to write me a better score than you did for *Citizen Kane*. To which Benny replied, "Then why didn't you make a better movie than *Citizen Kane*?" A few days later I was informed that he was suddenly available.

Working with Bernard Herrmann on the score for *It's Alive*.

A phone conversation was arranged between me and Benny, who was already back home in London. (Those who really knew him well called him Benny. Those who pretended to know him called him Bernie, and it was a dead giveaway that they were not intimate friends.)

Our initial conversation was brief. I told him I'd be honored if he'd score my picture and that I'd send him a black-and-white dupe of the picture and soundtrack. "See if you like it," I suggested. About two weeks later he responded favorably and inquired how I wanted to work.

"I'm not going to tell you what to do. That's all up to you. When you're ready to record the music, I'll come over if you want me."

This was exactly the right approach to take with someone like Benny, but a few weeks later we did have a major blow-up over a sequence in which a cartoon is seen playing on TV. I inquired if he could possibly write a cue to accompany the animation. Benny exploded, "I don't write music for cartoons. Go hire yourself another composer!"

Before he could hang up, I immediately withdrew the request. I'd use sound effects instead. So ended our only dispute. Sometime later he rang me to inquire if I'd be in London for the recording session, which was to occur during Christmas week. He wanted to make sure I had a place to be on New Year's Eve. He'd arrange all that.

I flew to England with Janelle, both of us looking forward to finally meeting this ogre, as he'd been constantly described. Benny had earned the reputation of being one of the most vitriolic men in Hollywood, with an unkind word for everyone. He was fearless and acerbic, and producers and directors fled his presence. He'd even had a blow-up with Alfred Hitchcock and the two men were no longer on speaking terms.

Janelle and I checked into the Savoy Hotel and arranged for a Daimler limo. We'd pick Benny up at his home in Chester Close near Regent's Park and drive him to the recording session at St Giles Cripplegate Church, which Benny had chosen because of its enormous pipe organ. The weather outside was freezing and London was suffering from a power cut because of the OPEC fuel embargo.

We arrived in front of Benny's townhouse, and he came down to greet us in the company of his wife, Norma, who was at least 40 years his junior. A very pretty brunette who reported for the BBC, Norma bundled Benny into his overcoat and sent him off to work. As he stepped into the back seat of the limo he tripped and fell face down on Janelle's lap. There was a long silence. Then, as the limo pulled away, Janelle tried to break the ice by commenting on what a pretty daughter Benny had. Knowing it was his wife, I cringed and was surprised to see Benny's face light up in a broad grin. He began giggling like a child.

"That's me! The world's oldest composer with the world's youngest wife," he cracked. From that moment on he adored Janelle.

To me it seemed that Benny's insulting remarks were usually made in jest. If someone insulted him back, they became his lifelong pal, but if they fled, he never forgave them.

When we got to the church, we found 50 musicians still wearing their gloves and overcoats. It was like stepping into a deep freeze. Benny himself would conduct in topcoat and muffler. The first cue he recorded that day was the opening title music. He'd asked me for 90 seconds to prepare the audience for the movie that was to follow. My job was to create some kind of visual to accompany this overture. I hadn't heard any of it, nor had he seen my title treatment, which consisted of multiple flashlights coming on in the pitch dark. First there were only two or three beams, then ten or 20, then 30 or 40 narrow streams of light. When Benny had completed recording the cue, we ran the music along with the footage which I'd brought along. The combined effect amazed us both. All of the musical beats seemed to coincide with flashlights popping on. It couldn't have been more perfect.

Benny and I exchanged a look. The impossible had happened—each of us working independently had created something that synchronized completely. Our friendship was cemented forever. It was like we'd known Benny all of our lives. I even had the nerve to make a couple of suggestions that Benny actually liked and incorporated into the score.

We spent that New Year's with Benny and Norma at the home of Laurie Johnson, a noted composer in his own right.

Bernard Herrmann.

The warmth of the fireplace in their country home was only exceeded by the warmth of the Johnson family as they encouraged Janelle and me to move to London and become part of their lives. Benny was especially enthusiastic about that prospect—he'd already decided to adopt us as his own. Apparently, Benny had little to do with his own grown-up children since his marriage to a much younger woman. We were to be his new-found family. He loved taking us to his favorite London hangout, Goodies, a kosher restaurant which had the best whitefish in the city. We often reciprocated by inviting Benny and Norma to some of the fancier eateries which we wanted to see for ourselves.

One night at the swanky Les Ambassadeurs Club, Benny flew into a rage. A quartet of musicians were playing—and poorly. Benny couldn't abide bad musicians and he began bellowing for them to stop. Soon he was pounding his cane loudly on the floor. I got the check and we headed for Goodies. I'd learned not to take Benny to restaurants which featured live music.

I returned to Los Angeles to complete the mix of the picture and took the chance of reusing one of Benny's cues for a second time in a place he hadn't intended. When he found out, he shrugged it off with an "It's okay." Anyone else would've suffered Benny's rage for such an affront.

Not long afterward, Janelle and I made the move to London, along with our five kids. We found a beautiful townhouse in Belgravia at 9 Chapel Street, not far from Buckingham Palace. The rent seemed unbelievably reasonable. It wasn't until after we moved in that we realized our next-door neighbor was the Irish Embassy, which not long before had been the target of a terrorist attack. We often brought him tea and snacks to the bobby stationed in front of our door. I noted that on one wall of the Embassy, the bricks were of a slightly different tone. The bobby explained, "Oh, that's where the explosion blew the original wall away." Fortunately there were no further incidents during our stay.

Benny and I found we had one thing in common. As a teenager, he'd sneaked into Carnegie Hall to watch the great conductors rehearse, much as I had slipped into the NBC studios to watch the rehearsals of live television programs. Benny knew a circuitous route which would lead him to a broken door through which he could gain balcony access. From there he watched Stokowski, among others, as they ran their rehearsals with iron discipline.

Although Norma loved Benny dearly, she certainly didn't fuss over his appearance. Often there were gravy stains on his necktie, and I noticed little laundry tags were always still attached to his socks. Norma never saw fit to remove them. Yet she was always patient with him, and quite loving.

I recall one day in particular when she took us for a stroll around Regent's Park and confided that she'd been advised by Benny's doctor that he suffered from a degenerative heart disease, which was untreatable. She was telling us that Benny did not have long to live. For a moment she seemed almost childlike in her fear of losing him. I never saw him be cruel or critical of her in our presence. There was a calmness in their relationship that was absent in most of Benny's encounters with others.

Bernard Herrmann was one of the few notable film composers to do his own orchestrations. He was a meticulous craftsman who had little respect for most of his contemporaries. One day I was hanging out at his home when he got a call from Elmer Bernstein, who was passing through London on a brief visit. He wanted to know if Benny would have lunch with him. Benny's reply was terse. "Listen, I wouldn't eat with you in Hollywood, why would I eat with you here?" and he hung up. Then he began chuckling.

"Why would you say such a terrible thing to the man?" I demanded. Benny's response, "He deserved it. His whole *Magnificent Seven* theme was stolen from Aaron Copland's *Rodeo*. Did he think he could get away with that?"

One of Benny's great disappointments was that his original opera, *Wuthering Heights*, had never been produced, and one afternoon he decided to play the entire recording of it for me. Halfway through I fell asleep, but he was completely forgiving. If he liked you, he made allowances for everything. If he didn't like you, there was no pleasing him.

He knew I was interested in both Hitchcock and Orson Welles, whom he regarded as authentic geniuses, and he entertained me by recounting stories of his long association with both. Describing Welles as star and director of radio's Mercury Theatre on the Air, Benny recounted how during a production of *The Barrett's of Wimpole Street* (in which Welles was starring opposite Cornelia Otis Skinner), the unthinkable occurred. While they were performing on the air live, Miss Skinner dropped her script and all the pages fluttered to the floor, scattering across the studio. Standing opposite her Welles responded by simply dropping his script as well and the two actors improvised the rest of the play from memory, making up what they couldn't remember. Welles had that kind of audacity. Though Welles told everybody else what to do, he never intruded into Benny's domain.

Benny had written the music for Welles' radio broadcasts before he was brought to Hollywood to score *Citizen Kane*, and eventually *The Magnificent Ambersons*. Later, at Welles' suggestion, Benny was engaged to score *Jane Eyre*, in which Welles starred. Welles has been quoted as saying that half of the success of *Kane* should be credited to the music.

Benny's experiences with Hitchcock came to a sadder conclusion. In his opinion the executives at Universal were to blame. MCA had made Hitchcock a very rich man by allowing him to acquire huge blocks of stock in the company. Hitch was soon spending all of his time in the company of studio execs Lew Wasserman, Taft Schreiber and Edd Henry, who poisoned his mind against Benny. They urged him to find some new guy who could write him pop songs. This was an era when every movie had a title song, usually performed by Johnny Mathis. The Universal hierarchy tried to convince Hitch that Bernard Herrmann was old hat, and that orchestral scores were passé. Henry Mancini was then the flavor of the month.

Finally, feeling cornered, Hitchcock made Benny promise that the score for *Torn Curtain*, to star Paul Newman and Julie Andrews, would be something radically different. At the recording session Hitchcock became incensed when he heard what he thought was typical Bernard Herrmann music. Instead of allowing the session to continue, Hitchcock cut it short and, in an uncharacteristic fit of anger, dismissed his longtime friend in front of the entire orchestra and stalked off the soundstage, thereby burning his bridges. Actually Benny's music was far superior to the score that was eventually used on the picture, which was a great failure both critically and at the box office. *Torn Curtain* desperately needed Benny's help.

Benny was willing to forgive Hitch and actually visited his bungalow on the Universal lot to try to heal old wounds. Apparently, Hitchcock hid in his office and pretended he wasn't there. Hitch hated confrontations of any kind, yet some years later when he was in London filming *Frenzy* he had a representative of Universal contact Benny and inquire if he might like to score this latest Hitchcock thriller. Benny's belligerent response was, "If Hitch wants me, why doesn't Hitch call me himself?" Thus ended the possibility of a reunion between these two very talented men. Many years later when John Williams was hired to score Hitchcock's final film *Family Plot*, he pointedly asked the director, "Why don't you just get Bernard Herrmann to do this?" Hitchcock's response was brief: "That's all over."

I have a strong belief that the break-up between Hitchcock and Benny was about more than just music. While there's no question that Universal executives lobbied against Benny's continued participation, it may have been something deeper and more personal that finally tore them apart. Benny and Hitch were both physically unattractive men. The difference was that Benny was a great ladies man. He unashamedly pursued women and was surprisingly successful with them. He once told me that Hitch often lamented to him about his desire for women other than his wife. Hitch would moan, "Even if Alma wasn't around, who would want me?" To which Benny would reply, "Hitch, fame is the greatest aphrodisiac of all. You can have any woman you want because you're Hitchcock."

Hitch was reluctant to try. He claimed Alma was the only woman with whom he'd ever been intimate. He stood by and watched Benny achieve conquest after conquest. Benny had once been married to the famed radio writer Lucille Fletcher who penned *Sorry, Wrong Number*. After he divorced Lucille he married her cousin, also named Lucy. After this marriage failed there were numerous other liaisons, and finally this lovely fiancée some 40 years his junior. It was only after Norma appeared that the relationship with Hitchcock totally deteriorated. Perhaps Hitch subconsciously resented constantly seeing Benny with a beautiful young woman. It brought his own frustration to the surface. He'd suffered a deep humiliation not long before when his protégée, Tippi Hedren, had rejected his advances.

Heretofore Hitch and Benny had dined together regularly and been the closest of friends. Now the great director felt the need to break away. The studio's opposition to Benny gave Hitch the excuse he needed to discard his old friend and banish him from his company forever. After the debacle with Hitch, Bernard Herrmann elected to abandon Hollywood for his beloved England.

Herrmann and Orson Welles.

It was not long after settling in London that Benny began to receive calls from a new breed of director like Brian de Palma and Martin Scorsese, who wanted him to score their pictures. At lunch one time with Benny I was introduced to Scorsese, who'd brought along his screenplay *Taxi Driver* to recruit Benny's participation. He sat in the restaurant and tried to explain to us what the picture was about. That wasn't easy. But Benny understood it immediately. Later Janelle and I took Scorsese and his girlfriend to Harrods for a tour. Somehow, we got separated and I didn't see Marty again until I visited *Taxi Driver*'s Columbus Circle set.

Perhaps only Norma realized that *Taxi Driver* would mark the end of Benny's career and his life. I had spent some time with him in New York when he came over to supervise the final mix of De Palma's *Obsession*. He invited me to view the answer print with him in a small Manhattan screening room. As I sat beside him, I could hear him sobbing, and when the lights came up the tears were streaming down the face of this tough old bird. This would be the last time Benny would ever see one of his films completed. Perhaps, somehow, he sensed it. He'd written a compelling score for *Obsession*, a movie that was clearly influenced by *Vertigo*.

I'll always enjoy the memories of our trip to Paris with Benny and Norma. I'd been invited to screen *It's Alive* at the

Cinémathèque française. I'd asked Henri Langlois if he'd like me to bring Bernard Herrmann along. Langlois jumped at the opportunity and arranged a cocktail reception in our honor inside the Musée de Cinéma.

We'd dined earlier that night with Langlois and his companion Mary Meerson, who were both close to obese, although they proclaimed themselves to be vegetarians. Janelle and I soon realized what accounted for their enormous weight. Their dinner that night consisted only of fried potatoes and flageolets in immense quantities. They both proved to be endearing personalities, who adored film and filmmakers. Through their efforts, hundreds of films were rescued from oblivion. Following the meal, we adjourned to the Cinémathèque for the screening of *It's Alive*. I hadn't been informed that there was a double feature booked that night. In honor of Bernard Herrmann they were showing *Citizen Kane* first. We had to follow the greatest movie of all time. When Benny heard that *Citizen Kane* was running, he refused to step inside the theater and look at it. He grumbled that he'd seen it too many times. Finally, after a few minutes, I noticed him peeking through the doors into the theater. He came back grumbling, "They're not playing it loud enough!"

The Cinémathèque had put us up at the Plaza Athénée, where our room was located directly across the courtyard from Benny and Norma's. Since Paris is the city of romance, Janelle and I had hopped into the sack early in the afternoon and had asked the hotel to hold all calls. The shutters on our window remained partially open and I could catch a glimpse of Benny's room. I saw someone walking around in there that looked very much like François Truffaut. Finally I had the sense to call Benny, who shouted, "Where have you been all day? Truffaut is over here, and he wants to meet you. He's been waiting for hours." We quickly got dressed and ran over, but by then Truffaut only had about 15 minutes left before his next appointment. Norma translated for us, and we exchanged pleasantries. Then he was gone. What a wasted opportunity. I would meet him again at Bernard Herrmann's funeral in Los Angeles.

Benny finally returned to Los Angeles to supervise the scoring of *Taxi Driver*. For years he vowed he would never come back to Hollywood, much less to the Universal lot. But there he was ensconced at the Universal Sheraton situated above the backlot of the studio that he had grown to hate. From the window of his room he could even see Hitchcock's bungalow in the distance. Why he had agreed to be put up in this hotel is a question that's never been fully answered. It was just two days before Christmas when he completed the scoring session. There were a few cues that were intended to be carried over to the following day, but for some reason Benny insisted that they wrap up that evening. He and Norma had an appointment to join me at Samuel Goldwyn Studios where I was going to run *God Told Me To* in hopes he'd score it for me.

Janelle picked them up and en route to the screening, Benny decided he'd love to stop for an Orange Julius. He hadn't had one in years. That's the kind of unpretentious person Benny was.

That night I ran them the picture, which they enjoyed. Benny made a number of useful suggestions, then we drove to a West Hollywood restaurant where he bought us dinner. It was a miserable meal. Earlier that evening, there'd been a fire in the kitchen and there were very few items available. Benny felt disappointed that he hadn't taken us to a better place. Later, Janelle and I took Norma and Benny back to the Universal Hotel. It was ten o'clock and he seemed in excellent spirits when we hugged and drove off.

The next morning we received a phone call around eight in the morning. It was from Martin Scorsese's girlfriend, Julia Cameron. She and Marty had gone to the hotel to have breakfast with Benny, only to discover that he'd died in his sleep. We rushed over to the hotel, arriving only a few moments before John Williams got there. He too had been a close friend of Benny and Norma. He also understood the pain of losing one's mate. His wife, actress and singer Barbara Ruick, had passed away a few years before.

I stepped into Benny's room and found him lying peacefully in his bed, his two hands folded under his cheek like some cherub. I've never seen a more beatific pose. There was no evidence of stress. He had slipped away during the night without pain or fear. We decided to bring Norma back to our Coldwater Canyon house. After all, it was the day before Christmas, and we had plenty of room. Only several days earlier, while Benny was visiting my home, he had expressed disappointment that he'd forgotten to bring me a copy of his latest album—the newly recorded score from *Psycho*. A few minutes later I noticed Benny was gone. He'd gotten my son Bob to drive him all the way back to the hotel to pick up the album.

Now he was gone—at the time of one of his great triumphs. *Taxi Driver* would bring him back to the forefront of movie composers. He would be nominated for two Academy Awards that coming year for both *Obsession* and *Taxi Driver*. Unfortunately, splitting the vote cost him the award.

On Christmas day at our home, Norma took out a sketchpad and drew a picture which depicted all of the members of our family seated together having our turkey dinner. She added the figure of Benny to the group and gave it to me as a gift. I'll cherish it always.

In the week following Benny's passing, our house was crowded with visitors. Marty Scorsese came every day as did Brian De Palma, and John Williams stopped by regularly. After the funeral, a reception would be held at my home. Late in the afternoon the rabbi decided he would like to hold a minyan in the living room, a ceremony which would require the participation of ten Jewish men. There weren't ten Jews in the house so we did the best we could under the circumstances. De Palma, Robert De Niro, and Scorsese all donned yarmulkes. De Niro asked me what he should do, and I told him to keep nodding his head up and down throughout the ceremony. I wish I had a photograph to commemorate the moment, as these famous Italians formed a circle filling in for the absent Jews.

Hours earlier, a service had been held at a cemetery in Hollywood. A stereo was set up to play some of Benny's music, but it was a miserable system and I know he surely would have smashed it with his cane had he been around to do so. Many friends got up and made speeches, always emphasizing what a difficult man Benny was, how irascible, insulting and abrasive. He was none of these things to us. It sounded like they were talking about a complete stranger. In retrospect, nobody said anything nice about him. I should've jumped up and told them how lovely he was, but I was too busy crying.

Peggy Robertson, Hitchcock's assistant, made an appearance at the funeral, claiming that Hitch was in Switzerland but sent his condolences. She mentioned that she and Hitch had watched *It's Alive* together in his private screening room and how charmed he was by the little monster running around attacking its victims. I'm sure Hitch only ran it because Benny had done the music, but the very fact that Hitchcock had even looked at my picture brought me a great deal of satisfaction.

Then, glancing at the last row of the chapel, I caught a glimpse of a familiar face. It was Truffaut. I informed Norma and we both went back to greet him. He didn't speak much English, but Norma translated as usual. He declined to come to our house for the reception, saying that he had to board a plane back to Paris immediately. He had flown over just for the funeral service. I was deeply moved by his love for Benny and that he'd journeyed all the way across the Atlantic for this brief farewell. Clearly, he held Benny in his highest regard.

Shortly after Benny's body had been removed from the Sheraton, I'd noticed that his cane stood abandoned in a corner of the room. Norma intended to leave it behind and I asked if I might have it as a personal remembrance. It's still one of my cherished possessions. Benny's cane, which he'd tap so violently on the floor if ever displeased. It was like keeping part of him.

Soon after Norma moved in with us, she came to me with a personal request. Benny had only come over for a few days to record *Taxi Driver* and hadn't brought much in the way of clothing. There was nothing appropriate for him to be buried in. She asked if I might have something, so I located a dark jacket and slacks, a shirt and tie. So it is that my dear friend Benny was buried in my clothing. I guess you can't get too much closer than that. Since Benny's estate was to be tied up for some time, I sent Norma back to London with $10,000 in cash. It's the only loan I've ever made that was paid back promptly and with gratitude.

Years later, when I filmed the sequel to *It Lives*, I wanted Benny's music to be part of the film. I asked Laurie Johnson if he would score the picture based on Benny's original themes. Laurie decided to contribute his services so that the entire fee could go to Norma. It was a gesture of true generosity. Laurie also returned to score the third *It's Alive* film using variations on Benny's original themes. But this time I insisted he be paid.

I can only imagine Benny's first encounter with God upon arriving in heaven. "So you're the big shot!" I hope the Lord had the good sense to insult him right back so that he and Benny could become the greatest of friends for all eternity. And I hope that somehow Benny and Hitchcock have managed to renew their friendship as well.

Chapter 25
The Greats (and Near Greats), Part 3

I was fortunate enough to have a number of pleasurable encounters with Mr. Hitchcock. The first was courtesy of the Universal story department. I had pitched them an idea for a thriller that they felt was up Hitchcock's alley, and they arranged for me to meet the master of suspense while we were both in New York.

Hitch always stayed at the St. Regis Hotel in the exact same suite which he recreated for a scene in his movie *Topaz*. I was met in the lobby by a representative of Universal who ushered me upstairs, the door opened and there he was, larger than life. Hitchcock was quite jovial and anxious to amuse. We'd be together for an unbelievable three and a half hours, and during most of it Hitchcock did the talking. He seemed to feel he was required to perform, and he put on quite a show. The first thing I noticed about him was his enormous hands and how expressively he used them. Contrary to what one might expect, he had a very powerful handshake, and he moved gracefully around the room once he got caught up in telling a story. He expressed himself in visual terms and exuded a marvelous enthusiasm. Before he heard my story, he had to tell me a number of his own.

I never mentioned that I'd shadowed him around New York when he was shooting *North by Northwest*. I was at the Plaza Hotel watching while Cary Grant was being kidnapped. I was also at Grand Central Station during the sequence when Grant made his escape from the city. My friend Merv Bloch and I spent the day inside the terminal constantly trying to attract Hitchcock's attention by paging some of the characters from his most notable films over the public address system. We kept paging John Robie, the character Cary Grant played in *To Catch a Thief* and Scottie Ferguson from *Vertigo*, yet there was never a flicker of recognition from Hitchcock. Having directed films myself I realize now that Hitch was so totally immersed in his work that he screened out anything extraneous. He didn't even hear the names of those characters blaring over the PA system.

But seated now in his suite at the St. Regis, Hitch's full attention was focused on me as he laid out the entire plot, scene by scene, of a project in development which he called *Frenzy*. What he related bore no resemblance to the movie that was later released bearing that title, which was based on a British novel. The tale he unfolded to me was completely original.

It concerned a famous stage actress and her handsome young son who had a secret life as a psychopathic serial killer. I assumed that he had Ingrid Bergman in mind for the role of the mother since he had long expressed interest in working with her again. Hitch took special pleasure in detailing the young psychopath's modus operandi. Being impotent, he utilized his riding crop as the implement of his sexuality. Hitch based all of this on some actual case history in England. He was graphic in his descriptions of the rape sequences, but the expression on his face was that of a man telling an elaborate shaggy dog joke. It was pure Hitchcock—murder spiced with merriment.

As the story unfolds, the Broadway actress has hired a very plain looking young woman as an assistant and sets out to make her over into someone desirable to men. As the girl's sexuality emerges, she became suddenly attractive to the son as a possible victim. "You see, he must be aroused in order to kill," said Hitch.

One of the most graphic sequences Hitch outlined was to be photographed aboard what was commonly known as the Mothball Fleet. At the end of World War II, scores of warships and transport vessels had been moored in a secluded harbor in upstate New York and left there to rot. By now they had rusted over. The only inhabitants were rats. It was here that the young killer was to bring his hapless victim and imprison her aboard one of the ships in preparation for her demise.

It was to be freezing cold aboard so the murderer would light a small fire in one of the furnaces. A tell-tale wisp of smoke rising above the phantom fleet was to be spotted by a watchman who would row out to the ship in search of a trespasser. While the watchman was being liquidated, the girl attempted to make her escape. She'd been stripped of her clothing and so she dashed naked through the bowels of the ship finally finding her way to the deck. The killer was in pursuit and so the girl was forced to climb one of the huge smokestacks, a phallic symbol if ever there was one.

Hitchcock then described shot by shot how the killer would pursue the naked girl up the smokestack until eventually she'd tumble to her death. The grand finale would occur back in the Broadway theater where the killer's mother was appearing in a successful comedy hit. She'd come to suspect that her son might be a murderer. She'd be on stage playing a role which required her to dissolve into gales of laughter. When she sees her son appear in the wings of the theater brandishing his riding crop, she realizes he is indeed the homicidal maniac. Her laughter becomes a hysterical scream as she loses control of herself in front of the confused theater audience.

Hitch enjoyed making movies that climaxed in theaters. He had done it many times in his British productions, and he planned still another variation in this new film. However, after acting out the story so vividly, he finally admitted that Universal didn't care for it at all and that was why he was looking for another subject to develop. I would've thought Hitch had the autonomy to choose his own projects, but he seemed to have surrendered his control to Lew Wasserman and his minions.

I still didn't have the opportunity to make my pitch because Hitchcock then launched into a dissertation on famous serial killers, most interestingly Jack the Ripper. "You know who Jack the Ripper was, don't ya?" he queried. I wanted to hear Hitchcock's solution to one of the great unsolved mysteries of all time. "He was an orthodox Jew who worked in a kosher slaughterhouse in the Whitechapel district of London. He had all the skills of a surgeon and possessed the necessary implements. The police discovered his identity but feared to make it public lest it create a surge of anti-Jewish sentiment. They left it up to the local Jewish community to hunt the killer down themselves and dispose of him. These Jews caught the Ripper and executed him—and all the details remained secret. And that's the truth of it."

Whether this was factual or not, it was certainly entertaining to hear. "Of course, the censors would never let that story get by," he added.

This led to another anecdote about his early dealings with the British censors.

Alfred Hitchcock.

London's chief censor happened to be blind in his left eye. Hitchcock would always sit to his right during the screenings. A moment before an offending scene was about to appear, Hitchcock would suddenly engage the man's attention, causing him to turn his blind eye towards the screen. He'd keep the fellow preoccupied until the questionable frames had flickered past. In this way, he managed to get several questionable scenes approved without making any cuts.

Telling me about the writers with whom he enjoyed working, Hitch singled out Ben Hecht, who wrote the screenplay for *Notorious*.

"Hecht was a very odd person when it came to money," he explained. "He was so distrustful that he insisted on being paid $,1000 a day in cash. Otherwise he would not report for work the following morning. I'd have my secretary run out to the bank before closing each day and bring back a thousand dollars in an envelope, which I'd present to Mr. Hecht upon his departure. I had to be sure he'd show up again, didn't I?"

I told Hitch there'd be no such problem with me. I was perfectly willing to accept the studio's check. Finally, after hours of fascinating chatter, Hitch said, "Now let's hear what you've come to tell me about."

I then related my story, which was called *Daddy's Gone A-Hunting*, about a lovely young commercial artist who arrives in New York and falls in love with a handsome photographer — only to discover that he's mentally unbalanced. She decided to break off the relationship when she discovers she's pregnant. Without informing her boyfriend she has an abortion. When the boyfriend learns about this, he accuses her of murdering his child. Years pass and the girl now has a wonderful husband and is once again expecting. The former boyfriend shows up and quite calmly tells her, "We've got to be absolutely fair about this. You killed my baby, now you have to kill his." He then attempts to trick and intimidate her into murdering her own child.

When I'd finished, Hitch had a gleam in his eye. "That's a damn good story and it certainly is full of suspense." Quite a compliment coming from the master himself. "Do you want to do an outline, or shall we simply jump into first draft?"

I couldn't believe it — I'd be working with Hitchcock! He was flying back to Los Angeles the following day and I agreed to cut my New York visit short and join him there in two days. I knew there would be no problem in making the deal because I'd be willing to work for scale if necessary. This was clearly a career-making opportunity.

Hitchcock was already thinking of casting. He wanted Sandy Dennis (who'd later star in *God Told Me To* for me) for the girl, and mentioned an actor named John Philip Law for the male lead. I left the St. Regis dancing on air. About an hour later I phoned Hitchcock, and he took the call immediately. I just wanted to convince myself that it'd really happened. I told him I agreed with his suggestion that we go straight into first draft. In the back of my mind I knew how troublesome the Universal executives could be. I didn't want to risk being cut off after an outline without having the chance to write an entire script. Our phone call ended on a highly optimistic note and a few days later I was back in Hollywood waiting for the deal to be locked up.

That's when I got a call from the Universal story department telling me that Hitchcock had passed. Apparently, Edd Henry had talked him out of it. Henry was known around the studio as Doctor No because he felt it was his duty to kill every project. When I informed the story editor of how enthusiastic Hitch had been, I was advised that he always told writers something positive. He never liked to let anyone down. That's exactly why the studio tried to avoid having Hitchcock meet with writers. He'd say yes and then just as quickly change his mind.

My guess was Universal was worried about making any movie that hinged on abortion as a major plot device. They shied away from controversy. I was determined to see Hitchcock personally and find out exactly what had happened. Despite the protestations of my agent, I went to Universal and appeared at Hitchcock's bungalow. A tiny British woman with thick glasses informed me that Mr. Hitchcock was out of town.

I left the bungalow, and as I looked back over my shoulder I noticed the actor Farley Granger, star of Hitchcock's *Strangers on a Train*, approaching from the opposite side. He walked up a few short steps and knocked on a back door, which was immediately opened by Hitchcock himself. "Why Farley! What are you doing here?" he exclaimed. They had a brief conversation and made plans to have lunch later in the week, since Farley was working on the lot. Immediately upon Farley's departure, I hurried to the same door and knocked. It was opened again, this time by that same small woman with glasses. "Didn't I tell you Mr. Hitchcock was away on vacation?" Then she slammed the door. Naturally I was depressed. I'd told everyone that I'd be working with Hitchcock, and now I felt like a fool.

In an effort to cheer me up, my friend and fellow screenwriter Lorenzo Semple, Jr. suggested that we team up and write the script on spec. Together we could knock out a first draft in a week and bring it back to Hitchcock. When Hitch saw it all on paper, he'd surely love it. He showed up at my house early each morning and we'd feverishly hammer out some 20 pages. It was an enjoyable collaboration, and the screenplay was even better than we'd expected. We shipped it back to Hitchcock, and his response was gratifying in part: "It's excellent, but you haven't left me anything to do."

In working out every scene we had defeated our own purpose. Hitch liked to develop material himself and we'd done it all without him. He must have liked it quite a bit because a few days later I got a call from Joan Harrison, who'd collaborated on many of the best Hitchcock films and had produced the *Alfred Hitchcock Presents* TV series since its inception. She also happened to be the wife of Eric Ambler, a renowned author of thrillers. I had lunch with Joan at the Beverly Hills Brown Derby, and she said she'd love to produce our screenplay. She was just as disappointed as I that Hitchcock had declined it, and agreed that he needed a story as good as this one. *Torn Curtain* had been such a disappointing experience for him that he was deeply depressed.

He'd passed our script on to her, but unfortunately Joan had no funding and would have to beat the bushes in order to find some.

I was inclined to give her that chance, but almost immediately we got a firm offer on the property. A top director, Mark Robson, had been attracted to the script and National General Films wanted to purchase it for him. Robson had directed some great films in his time, including *Von Ryan's Express*, *The Bridges at Toko-Ri* and *Peyton Place*. He had just scored a huge hit with *Valley of the Dolls*. The purchase price for our screenplay was $200,000, which was a great deal of money at the time. In retrospect it was a mistake not sticking with Joan Harrison, who would've given us a much better picture.

Mark Robson's initial mistake was in the casting. He should've gone for stars rather than unknowns. Much like Hitchcock, Robson had far more success when stars toplined his films. Our movie never recovered from its initial casting deficiencies. Robson was a gentle soul and was considerate enough to ask me to stick around during production. I visited the set and viewed the dailies, but after a few days I was so disappointed I couldn't bear to come back.

I thought he might be the ideal person to shepherd a tight little thriller, but he'd grown soft over the years thanks to his success. Now a Hollywood fat cat, Mark spent an inordinate amount of time absorbed in the details of the ladies' wardrobe.

Mark Robson (right) with Scott Hylands
on the set of *Daddy's Gone A-Hunting*.

In the nude love scene, the leading man was clearly wearing a G-string, which the audience couldn't help but notice. It always got an unwanted laugh. Mark never seemed to transmit much energy to the players, but did carry around his two-million-dollar profit check from *Valley of the Dolls*, which he enjoyed showing off.

Although it got some good reviews and did respectable business, *Daddy's Gone A-Hunting* left me totally unfulfilled. I'd blown the chance to work with Hitchcock and ended up with a lousy movie. All I had to show for the experience was the money, which was quickly spent. This was a turning point in my career because I decided that next time, I'd have to make the movie myself.

I wouldn't see Hitchcock again for quite a few years. During that period I'd direct several films of my own.

I'd written Hitchcock a note hoping that he might take a meeting. I still hadn't given up hope of someday collaborating with the master. One morning I got an early call from Hitch's office. Would I be available for lunch that very day at his bungalow at Universal? And would a steak and French fries be alright?

Carol White in *Daddy's Gone A-Hunting.*

Naturally I jumped at the opportunity and arrived at his office just as the waiter who was delivering the meal from the commissary. It was more or less the same menu that Hitch always ordered.

Again, this would be an enjoyable three-hour meeting during which Hitch seemed in no hurry to be rid of me. I inquired about the original *Frenzy* that he'd acted out for me at the St. Regis and was told the project had been totally abandoned.

Hitch actually seemed to be a prisoner at the studio. The previous year, Universal had induced him to take on *Topaz*, a bestseller in which he had very little interest. He was bored with it even before it went on the soundstage, and for the first time he found himself stuck for an ending. He managed to create a rather slipshod finale by piecing together snippets culled from elsewhere in the movie. An unidentifiable figure goes through a doorway. The door closes and there's a gunshot from inside indicating that the villain has committed suicide. It was totally disappointing, but by that time, Hitch didn't much care. He just wanted to get it over with. He hadn't enjoyed *Torn Curtain* either. He kept murmuring, "Never again Julie Andrews... never again." Apparently, he blamed her for the failure of the film, which I felt was unfair, though I didn't say so.

Hitchcock had become a very wealthy man thanks to MCA, but the creative juices were no longer flowing. He was bored, and I suppose that's why he invited people to lunch to fill up the day. That's why I was there, so he'd have someone to talk to. The studio was not giving him decent projects and he'd allowed them to pressure him into doing inferior ones.

I brought along a little gift for Hitch, an 8x10 black-and-white photograph snapped on the set of *The Paradine Case*, in which Gregory Peck and Ann Todd are locked in a passionate embrace while directly behind them, Hitchcock is caught in the act of sneezing. He'd never seen the photo before and it gave him a bit of a laugh, although anything that reminded him of that particular movie also depressed him. It was his last picture under his "slave contract" to Selznick, and all he wanted out of it was his freedom.

After lunch I felt comfortable enough to tell Hitch that after viewing *Strangers on a Train* dozens of times, it had finally occurred to me that the premise for the climax is contrary to all logic. Farley Granger desperately needs to wrap up his championship tennis match so he can rush to an amusement park and prevent the killer, Robert Walker, from framing him. But instead of simply losing the game, Farley seems compelled to win every set. I said, "Wouldn't it have been more sensible to lose if your life depended on it?"

Hitch instantly responded, "Yes, but that wouldn't have been a very interesting scene, would it?"

I again met Hitchcock after the initial screening of his new version of *Frenzy*. This was unquestionably a huge comeback for Hitch. He'd returned to London to film it and that homecoming had clearly invigorated him.

It was at the party at the Century Plaza following the movie that he introduced me to his wife. "Alma, this is Mr. Cohen." She was a small, highly intelligent woman whose opinions were critical to Hitchcock's success. In fact I don't think he made a move without her. It's said that he planned everything out in advance and completed the movie in his head before setting foot on the soundstage, and he seldom made any alterations during production. I'm sure Alma contributed tremendously to this period of preparation. Their daughter, Patricia Hitchcock, indicated as much in a recent appearance at the Directors Guild of America in which she paid tribute to her mother's contribution to all of Hitchcock films. It seems Mr. and Mrs. Hitchcock were truly collaborators. Alma did accept credit as screenwriter on some of his films, but was later content to allow Hitch to receive all the glory. Like Agatha Christie, I suspect that Alma Hitchcock had a brilliant mind for thrillers and that Hitch constantly deferred to her judgment.

Miklós Rózsa, who wrote the exquisite score for Hitch's classic film *Spellbound*, once offered insight into how Hitchcock related to other colleagues. Rózsa had little to do with Hitchcock during the planning of the score, and the director didn't even show up for the recording session. Rózsa won the Academy Award for his score that year but never received a phone call or any form of congratulations from Hitchcock. Even David Selznick, the producer, sent Mikky a telegram. But from Hitchcock there was nothing. Rózsa later learned that Hitchcock resented all the attention his music had gotten and he never invited Rózsa to write another score for him again.

I don't doubt the veracity of this story, but it's in direct contradiction to the Hitchcock that I knew, who was always so generous with his time.

The last time I saw Hitchcock was in the commissary at Universal Studios. I'd wandered in late one afternoon after noticing a small crowd gathered outside. I couldn't believe my eyes as I suddenly came face to face with Brezhnev and Kosygin, the two leaders of the Soviet Union, who were visiting the lot as guests of Lew Wasserman, the head of Universal. Accompanying them was Hitchcock. For a moment I caught his eye and whispered to him the quote from the TV commercial in which he was then appearing to promote the Universal Studio Tour. Imitating his voice I said, "You do meet the strangest people on the tour." He chuckled and then went over to repeat the joke to Wasserman. This was the closest I ever got to writing for Hitchcock.

The unproduced *The Man Who Loved Hitchcock*.

Since I identified so much with Hitchcock and was such a dear friend of Bernard Herrmann, a few years after Hitchcock's death I decided to write a screenplay, on spec, which would deal with both of them. It would be called *The Man Who Loved Hitchcock* and was entirely fictional. In this story, Bennie and Hitch would meet again long after their estrangement and be forced to work side by side in order to trap a real-life killer who had stolen some of Hitchcock's ideas for murders. The two elderly gentlemen would be aided in their adventure by an aspiring young director, clearly inspired by Steven Spielberg. This wannabe filmmaker had sneaked onto the Universal lot and set himself up in a vacant office. By trying to create the illusion that he was a movie director, he's attempting to make his dream come true.

The script I conceived was one of my favorites. Robert Morley originally agreed to play Hitchcock, but when I met with him in a London restaurant, his opening words were, "Where's the money?" Of Hitchcock, Mr. Morley said, "I met him only once. Didn't care for him." I had better luck with Peter Ustinov. He had achieved great success playing Hercule Poirot in two Agatha Christie mysteries, *Death on the Nile* and *Evil Under the Sun,* and I thought I could find backers based on his involvement.

I got my Hitchcock script to Ustinov and was invited to meet him in his suite in the Beverly Hills Hotel. Ustinov generally hated reading screenplays and could barely get through them, but he'd read mine from start to finish without ever putting it down. Naturally he wanted to play the lead, and I couldn't have been happier.

Ustinov was cooperative enough to agree to a photo session which would enable us to produce a trade ad featuring him as Hitchcock that ran in *Screen International*. Ustinov further agreed to appear at the Cannes Film Festival to help raise funding for the picture. The foreign sales agents threw quite a shindig, which was widely attended as Ustinov talked up the movie.

Unfortunately, not enough offers materialized. It was a major disappointment for both of us. We thought it was a sure thing. I learned that the movies you're dying to do are always the hardest to put together.

For years I tried to raise funding for the Hitchcock project, with little success. It's strange, but people with absolutely no talent who make the most unbelievably awful films seem to have constant access to investment capital. The worst picture-makers always seem able to find the money. Maybe that's their skill. I was never very good at it.

Despite the fact that many of my films performed well at the box office and others received excellent reviews, I still have a hard time coming up with the dough to finance a production. That's why I've often had to start shooting without the money. It always seemed to come in later... just when I was most desperate. I suppose I should have just started shooting the Hitchcock movie and taken the chance. What stopped me was the belief that somebody would step forward with a more than adequate budget and allow us to make the picture in a first-class manner.

Chapter 26
Going West

Producer Walter Mirisch had seen some of my television work and proposed I write a pilot for a TV series based on *The Magnificent Seven*. I told Walter that he should make a theatrical sequel instead, and eventually United Artists gave him permission to hire me to do just that.

When the time came to film *The Return of the Seven*, Walter brought me to a bungalow at the Beverly Hills Hotel to meet Yul Brynner. No matter what role he played, Yul was without question the King of Siam—both on and off screen. He had some notes for me on the script, but before we got to them, he poured me a drink. It was a water glass filled to the brim with vodka. By the time we got around to the script changes I was so plastered I would've agreed to anything. The next morning I couldn't recall any of the details of the meeting, so I just rewrote what I wanted. No one ever complained.

When question of the music for *The Return of the Seven* came up, Walter explained that he couldn't re-use Elmer Bernstein's score from the original film because over the years it had become associated with a Marlboro commercial. I exploded with, "Don't make the picture if you can't use the music. There is no *Magnificent Seven* without that score."

Walter listened to my advice and oddly enough the score for my sequel received an Academy Award nomination. Bernstein's score for the original picture had been overlooked completely by the Academy. Unfortunately, Elmer did not win.

My sequel went on to be a box-office hit, and Walter went on to make two additional sequels without either Yul Brynner or me. They were undeniably awful and destroyed a valuable franchise.

My experience in writing westerns for the big screen would continue with a movie called *El Condor*, which was to star Jim Brown and Lee Van Cleef. National General had financed the movie and had authorized the building of massive sets in

The Return of the Seven, written by Larry Cohen.

Almería, on the Costa del Sol in Spain. Construction was almost completed when the studio executives suddenly decided that they hated the script. Janelle and I were hastily flown to Spain to look at the scenery and concoct a new screenplay which could utilize what had already been built. If I could come up with a viable screenplay, the picture would be made. If not, the entire project would be scrapped. The producer was the legendary André De Toth, who'd also had a distinguished career as a director. John Guillermin had been hired to direct and these two strong personalities were already clashing. Guillermin was rightly convinced that De Toth wanted to get him fired so that he could direct it himself, a tactic André had used successfully to gain control of a Michael Caine war film called *Play Dirty*, on which he'd replaced René Clément.

André and John both did their best to court our favor, taking Janelle and me for lavish dinners and even buying us expensive gifts. De Toth was a national hero in Almería since he'd virtually put the place on the movie map when he staged the second unit action sequences for *Lawrence of Arabia* in the nearby desert.

The sets that were built there for *El Condor* included a massive fortress that remains standing some 35 years later and is still used in motion picture production today.

Jim Brown in John Guillermin's *El Condor,* written by Larry Cohen.

Janelle was given horseback riding lessons by the stuntmen while I toiled in my hotel room. If I paused to go down to the beach for a swim, I'd find myself surrounded by crew members, desperate to keep their jobs, begging me to go back upstairs and write.

I recall one characteristic dispute between Guillermin and De Toth over which uniforms should be brought from London to clothe the fortress garrison troops. Guillermin favored red uniforms, while De Toth insisted blue uniforms would be more appropriate. Finally Guillermin exploded, "André, I'm directing this film, and I want red uniforms!" De Toth softened, replying, "John, you're absolutely right. You are the director, and you shall have red uniforms." Guillermin left the room, at which point André picked up the phone and called the London costumer. "Send blue uniforms!" he barked. When the uniforms arrived there wasn't much Guillermin could do about it. He would eventually learn that André was sneaking off with a second unit crew and shooting scenes behind his back. The hostility between them finally erupted into a fist fight after Guillermin wrecked André's office in a moment of frustration. André had suffered a severe back injury in a ski accident years before and now his arms locked, preventing him from throwing a punch. Fortunately, the staff saved him from a beating. By that time Janelle and I had departed for the U.S. Since I'd "saved the movie," a lavish party was thrown to see us off and I was presented with a statue of a knight in armor bearing the inscription, "To Larry Cohen, the liberator of El Condor." As our boat pulled out of the harbor bound for Morocco, a huge fireworks display bid us farewell. If only all the movies had treated me so kindly.

On arriving back home I got an emergency phone call from National General. Lee Van Cleef had refused to get on the airplane. He was an international star of spaghetti westerns ever since appearing opposite Clint Eastwood in *For a Few Dollars More*. Now his Italian producer Roberto Grimaldi advised him that playing the role I had written for him in *El Condor* would ruin his career. He was pulling out of the picture unless I could change his mind. I joined Van Cleef at a local restaurant and found him immediately hostile. He was certain he would look like a fool playing this part. He'd be laughed at.

"That's exactly what I intended," I said. "For the first time in your career you're getting to play comedy. This is a role like Bogart's in *The African Queen*—a broken-down drunk who becomes a hero. It's a terrific acting challenge."

All at once Van Cleef's attitude mellowed. "You mean it's supposed to be funny?" Within a few minutes he was dying to do the part. "I'll even play it without my hair piece," he volunteered.

This was one of the first times I'd been called upon to deal directly with a star, and I realized I had certain skills in that department. Van Cleef boarded the plane the very next day and never gave anyone a bit of trouble.

I didn't want *El Condor* to be a routine western so I proposed to National General that they shoot an X-rated version. I thought audiences would rush out to see Jim Brown totally in the raw making love to the beautiful leading lady, Marianna Hill—both of them in full frontal nudity. I was surprised when the actors readily agreed to shoot it that way. This was in an era when major studio films like *Midnight Cowboy* were being released with an X rating. The scenes were actually shot as I suggested, but National General chickened out at the last minute and trimmed the sequence down. The night of our sneak preview at the Paramount Theater in Hollywood

Lee Van Cleef in *El Condor*.

I noticed National General executives filling out audience response cards themselves. Later on in the evening I watched in amazement as they quoted from their own cards. Unlike them, I recognized many of the deficiencies of the film. I gave De Toth a detailed list of changes and was surprised when he followed my suggestions to the letter, knocking six minutes out of the picture in all the right places. I was starting to believe that I knew more about movies than just how to write a script. I was also a skilled editor.

I'd studied editing at CCNY in the days when the cutter had to scrape the emulsion off the film with a razor blade before making a splice and join the pieces using liquid cement, which always accumulated under your nails. Today, with electronic editing, I can cut a film in ten days, not ten weeks. But I do miss the tactile experience of having the celluloid run through my fingers. Maybe that's why I've gone back to writing my scripts in pen and ink. I like the feel of creating something with my own hands.

Chapter 27
Chance Encounters

Why was it, I wondered, that every time I latched onto a beautiful woman, I'd learn she had a boyfriend on the side? Or maybe I was the boyfriend on the side? And inevitably the other guy was far more important than me.

Early in my twenties, new to Hollywood and still unmarried, I became involved with a girl whom I will call Barbara. An extremely intelligent and well-read young woman, she also had a powerful sexual appetite. She was always ready. In fact, she was usually impatient to finish with dinner and get on to the bedroom. We usually didn't bother going to a movie or a play—why waste the better part of the evening? She was certainly a welcome change from many of the other girls, who had to be entertained first.

Barbara's principal lover, however, turned out to be the distinguished playwright, Clifford Odets, who'd come to Hollywood to write and produce *The Richard Boone Show*, an NBC series which would introduce the television to its first repertory company. NBC had given Odets carte blanche. He was perhaps the most renowned writer ever to enter into a television deal at that time, having gained fame on Broadway with such plays as *Country Girl*, *Golden Boy* and *Awake and Sing!* Among the movies he'd written was *Sweet Smell of Success*. I was in awe of Odets, but I wished Barbara hadn't confessed her relationship with him. Apparently, she told him about me as well and convinced him to watch one of my episodes of *The Defenders*. He was impressed and wanted to meet me. What did I need an agent for when I had Barbara?

Eventually a get-together was arranged at Odets' office on the MGM lot. I arrived on Friday afternoon for what I expected would be a half-hour session. Odets took to me immediately, perhaps because we were sharing the favors of the same young woman, and it amused him. After all, he had to be at least 35 years older than me.

Clifford Odets.

As I recall, he seemed a bit lost in the world of television. He could have used a better hairstylist and someone to pick out his wardrobe. He looked like he'd just gotten out of bed after having slept in his clothes. Years later, Bernard Herrmann would tell me a story about Odets and his wife, the sophisticated two-time Oscar-winning actress Luise Rainer. Apparently, Luise was always criticizing Odets' manners and appearance. He took this criticism in his stride until one day in a restaurant she began instructing him on how to eat whitefish. This time Luise had gone too far. In a rage, Clifford threw down his knife and fork and shouted, "You can tell me anything, but my ancestors have been eating whitefish for two thousand years. Don't ever tell me how to eat whitefish!" With that he got up and walked out of the restaurant and never spoke to her again.

Here I was enjoying the company of this famous theatrical figure who'd romanced Frances Farmer among other great ladies of the stage and screen. Time raced by and we'd been together for hours just shmoozing. The secretary came in to say she was going home for the weekend, but we continued on. Finally it was after seven and Odets suggested that we adjourn until Monday morning. I phoned on Monday to reconfirm only to be told that Clifford was ill and wasn't coming in. I received similar news on Tuesday and Wednesday. On Thursday the newspapers announced that Odets had died. Mine was probably the last professional meeting of his life. *The Richard Boone Show* was quickly canceled and goes unremembered. Sadly, Barbara herself was killed in an automobile accident only a few years later. I've always appreciated her honesty, her affection and her efforts to get me a job when I needed one—and with somebody as likable as Clifford Odets turned out to be.

Another memorable encounter took place purely by chance in New York. It happened across the street from Loew's State Theater where the movie *Lolita* was in its second day of release. I was passing the out-of-town newspaper stand on Times Square when I noticed a shabbily dressed fellow doubled over a garbage can, digging inside. I immediately recognized him as Stanley Kubrick. I, along with many others, had discovered Kubrick early on after seeing *Killer's Kiss*, when it played on the second half of a double feature at Loew's. I was the first one at the box office on the opening day of the release of *The Killing*, and I had the opportunity to sneak onto the set of *Spartacus*, which Kubrick was directing at Universal.

At this particular sighting, Kubrick was focused on scouring the trash receptacles where yesterday's out-of-town papers had been dumped. I walked up to him and calmly said, "Looking for your reviews?" Without even glancing up, Kubrick responded as if we'd been together all day. "Yeah, I got the *Chicago Tribune* but I'm looking for the *Philadel-

phia Inquirer." That's exactly what he was up to—collecting the notices on *Lolita*.

I hung around, helping him out. Finally he suggested we walk over to the front of Loew's State and watch the customers buy tickets. He seemed to enjoy that immensely. We chatted together about movies for about 20 minutes more before we went our separate ways. I never saw him again, but I did have the occasion to discuss Kubrick with Kirk Douglas over dinner one night at the home of Frank Yablans. Kirk described Kubrick as "a talented shit." The screenplay for *Spartacus* had been written by Dalton Trumbo, a blacklisted writer. There was a question over whose name should be put on the screen since Trumbo's identity had to be kept secret. Kubrick immediately volunteered to take the credit himself, which enraged Kirk. Things were never the same between them after that. Kirk finally saw to it that Trumbo's name appeared in the credits and effectively broke the blacklist.

One of the great pleasures of being in the movie business is that you do get to meet some of the famous people you admire. Through the years we had several run-ins with Groucho Marx, who could be regularly spotted roaming the wilds of Beverly Hills. Once while shooting a scene for *Bone* on Beverly Drive, Groucho actually walked into a shot. He looked around, confused for a moment, and then realized he was in somebody else's movie. I would have loved to have included his footage in the finished film but didn't dare.

Years before in New York, Janelle and I went to see Carol Burnett in the musical *Fade Out–Fade In*. It was a hot show and seats were hard to come by, so we had to sit separately. She found herself sat directly next to Groucho, who as it turned out was hard of hearing. Throughout the show he kept leaning on Janelle's shoulder, inquiring, "What did he say? What did she say?" The smell of stale cigars on his breath almost knocked her out. During the intermission, Janelle introduced me to Groucho as her husband. "So you're the bounder?" Groucho snarled.

A few weeks later, while shopping in Beverly Hills, Groucho approached her, gave her a big hello, and invited her to lunch. It wasn't until well into the meal that she realized he didn't remember her at all from the encounter in New York.

She was simply some girl he'd picked up on the street. The following month he picked her up again on Rodeo Drive and she got a lunch out of it—and he still thought this was their first meeting.

When Bobby Darin invited us to Vegas for his opening, we flew in on a private aircraft, where we found ourselves once again in the company of Groucho Marx. Bobby knew I did an impersonation of Groucho and he requested a command performance. Naturally I obliged. He wiggled his eyebrows, flicked his cigar ash at me, and responded, "Sonny, every Jewish man over the age of 30 can do an impression of me."

Although I'd lived in England for a year, I never caught sight of Laurence Olivier except on stage. Now on a fateful afternoon just off the Sunset Strip in the late Seventies, I'd just screened *The Private Files of J. Edgar Hoover* for a team of legal experts. We had overstayed our time in the screening room when the door opened, and a gentleman poked his head in apologetically. "Oh no," I exclaimed, "the screening room is yours," and we quickly left. Out in the parking lot I turned to Janelle and said, "Maybe I'm out of my mind but I could've sworn that man who walked in was Laurence Olivier."

We remained in the parking lot with the lawyers talking about the changes they requested before the picture could be released. Not long afterward Olivier emerged from the screening room in the company of his director, Daniel Petrie, whom I knew from live TV days. I ran over and asked to be introduced. They'd been watching dailies for *The Betsy*, in which Olivier was starring. I asked him how it looked, and he immediately held his nose with one hand and gestured thumbs down with the other, breaking us all up. Then he proceeded to tear the picture to shreds. I couldn't tell if he meant it or if he was kidding. Even poor Dan Petrie wasn't sure. Olivier seemed extremely robust considering the many reports of his illness at the time. I do remember that he was wearing blue jeans and a plaid shirt—hardly Olivier attire. He soon climbed into a station wagon with his associates and was gone.

Like every young filmmaker I idolized Orson Welles, and so when I learned he'd returned to Hollywood and lunched every day at Ma Maison on Melrose, I immediately made reservations. Though the majority of the celebrities that frequented this bistro preferred the patio, Welles was always ensconced at the same corner table inside, and I requested a spot close by in order to eavesdrop. I wanted to hear everything Welles said, which turned out to be not in the least bit encouraging to anyone interested in a career in filmmaking.

The great director had been reduced to making appearances in wine commercials and on Dean Martin Celebrity Roasts. Now, with my own ears, I could hear him lamenting his situation. Everyone he was counting on seemed to have disappointed him. He'd visited with Spielberg, expecting to be complimented but also hopeful that he might be offered an opportunity to direct again. The young director had the power to give Welles a job, but nothing was forthcoming and he left heavy hearted.

Many financiers approached Welles but always seemed to back out at the last moment. He had a project for Robert Redford but was reluctant to phone the actor for fear that Redford wouldn't accept the call. "Suppose he doesn't pick up the phone?" Welles asked of his constant lunch partner, director Henry Jaglom. "Don't be foolish, you're Orson Welles. He's got to take the call."

"But suppose he doesn't," Welles groaned, unwilling to take the gamble.

I couldn't figure out why I could raise money to make pictures and this great director couldn't. The business made no sense to me.

A producer friend related how he'd gone to Welles with an offer to direct a film. Welles was then staying in a suite in the Beverly Hills Hotel, where the producer appeared hat in hand. He spent half an hour relating the plot of the movie he had planned. Once he was finished there was a long silence, then Welles leaned forward and said, "Look, I need $15,000 right away to get out of this fucking hotel." Needless to say the project never materialized.

Another story going around had it that producer Ray Stark, a longtime friend, had called Welles and offered him a chance to direct anything he chose for a budget of four million dollars. He had put Welles on the spot. After pondering it a while, Welles' response was, "Listen, I just can't get up at six o'clock in the morning anymore."

I was in New York when my friend Merv Bloch informed me that he'd hired Welles to do radio and TV spots for *Conan the Barbarian*. Welles could command $25,000 for a few minutes of his time doing the voiceover for these trailers. He'd already done one for Merv for *Star Trek—The Motion Picture*. During the recording sessions he had proved extremely difficult, refusing to say "motion picture." He complained, "What the hell do they think it is, a tube of toothpaste? I won't say that. It's a movie! Every idiot knows it's a movie."

Merv was anticipating another memorable recording session, to which he invited me. Welles arrived at the studio alone, carrying a small paper bag in his hand. He was shaking with anger. He'd been informed that there were no steps to be climbed, but in fact there were five steps in the lobby leading to the elevators. He bellowed that he was now physically exhausted and couldn't go through with the session. Yet instead of going home, he'd come all the way upstairs to inform Merv of his decision. This was all bluster. We knew he wasn't going to blow that 25 grand.

The paper bag contained a can of 7 Up, which Welles liked to drink just before recording. He said it coated his vocal cords and gave his voice a moist sound. When he'd finished thundering about the deception that had been perpetrated upon him—those five steps he'd been forced to climb—Orson finally read over the copy and agreed to most of it. However, he would not say, "Opening at a theater near you." "That's for a lower-priced announcer to say," he declared.

After bantering back and forth with Welles for a few minutes, Merv gave in. After Welles left, he imitated his voice and added the disputed words to the track. No one would ever notice the difference. Throughout the session, Welles had grown more affable and finally signed autographs for Merv and me. Since the commercial was for *Conan the Barbarian*, he inscribed my photograph with the words, "To Larry Cohen, the barbarian."

For years I'd been visiting Welles' longtime associate Richard Wilson and his wife at their Santa Monica beach house. Dick had turned his garage into a warehouse of Welles memorabilia. Welles was waiting for the tax laws to change so he could donate these materials and take a large deduction. Meanwhile they remained there for all to see—the sketches for the unmade *Heart of Darkness* adaptation and a wealth of material from the preparation of *Citizen Kane*. I'd been privileged to sift through it all. The experience reminded me of the sequence in *Citizen Kane* where the worldly possessions of Charles Foster Kane are examined in an attempt to discover the identity of Rosebud. Here amongst all these old scripts, sketches and photographs lie the heart and soul of Orson Welles. This was the true Welles, not the fat man holding court in Ma Maison every day but the great storyteller overflowing with ideas, so cocksure of his success. He thought his great talent made him invulnerable. Hollywood taught him he was wrong.

Chapter 28
A Kindred Spirit

One of my great friendships was with Sam Fuller, with whom I've often been compared. Sam was the volatile director of such low-budget classics as *I Shot Jesse James* and *The Baron of Arizona.* He later went on to make such film noir hits as *Shock Corridor* and *The Naked Kiss.* As a kid I'd taken notice of these fast-moving black-and-white thrillers, which I much preferred to the big-budget glossy studio productions. I even borrowed elements from *I Shot Jessie James* in creating my series *Branded.* Both stories were about men trying to outrun their reputations. In Sam's film, Bob Ford struggled to live down having shot Jesse in the back. A song was featured proclaiming "Bob Ford was the dirty little coward." *Branded* had a theme song, as sung by Tex Ritter, with the line "marked with a coward's shame."

I met Sam because of the mansion I bought off Coldwater Canyon. After moving in I went through the basement and found a large wooden packing case with the name Samuel Fuller stenciled on it. Sometime later John Ireland came to the house to read for a part in *Black Caesar.* "I've been here before, you know," he commented. "This was Sam Fuller's house."

As far as I knew Sam was living in Paris and it wasn't until I attended a party thrown by the French Film Council at the Beverly Hills Hotel that I had a chance to meet him. I immediately mentioned the house and he seemed excited to hear I owned it. He'd lost it in a divorce settlement, but he wanted his second wife, Christa, to see the place. I invited them to come up for dinner and found we had much in common. Sam and I were both fierce independents and getting pictures made was always a battle. We'd had our hits and our flops and our problems with distribution.

At that time Sam was at a low point in his career. His great war film *The Big Red One* had been taken away from him and re-edited. His Paramount picture, *White Dog*, was barely released because of claims that it was racist in content (which was, of course, nonsense). There was no work for Sam Fuller and he was spending most of his time traveling to film festivals all over the world to receive honors, but the accolades were not leading to gainful employment. Still, Sam kept writing, and he respected me because I created my own material. He'd seen my movie about J. Edgar Hoover, which was a subject he'd always wanted to tackle. He thought I'd been too kind to Hoover in my treatment of the character.

I had a standing invitation to visit Sam in Paris, and I took advantage of it. He had a huge apartment not far off the Champs-Elysées, and we'd often go walking together arm in arm, which was perfectly acceptable behavior for two guys in Paris, if not in Los Angeles. The days we spent together were never long enough. There was so much to talk about. Neither of us wanted the time to end. When my daughter Jill stayed in Paris for a year, the Fullers looked after her like godparents.

I particularly wanted to do something for Sam, so I thought the best idea was to write him in as a character in one of my films. Sam had done some acting for Godard and Wenders, but these were only cameo roles, a few days' work at most. I wrote Sam a principal part, one that would take him at least four weeks to film. I got Warner Bros. to approve him for a fee of $40,000 and offered him the job. Sam's daughter Samantha was ill at the time, but I suppose he couldn't afford to turn down the money. Besides, he liked the part. He was to play a feisty old Nazi hunter tracking down a war criminal somewhere in New England. He would stumble into the small town of Salem's Lot where instead of Nazis he would find vampires. The picture was the sequel to Stephen King's novel which had been made as a four-hour television miniseries in 1979.

A Return to Salem's Lot was filmed in Vermont, mainly in the town of Peacham, Vermont. At first Sam was a bit frightened of the role, as there was so much dialogue. I quickly convinced him that he'd have no problem with it. If he forgot his lines he could improvise, which was standard Larry Cohen procedure.

Sam proved an exemplary performer, even though we were shooting almost 24 hours a day. Since vampires only come out at night, the majority of the shooting was at night. We would call the cast and crew in around 5 pm and film until sunrise,

The French poster for *A Return to Salem's Lot.*

then we'd go on to do some day sequences. A few times we shot 26 hours straight. Everyone was on the verge of collapse except Sam and me.

The other actors couldn't very well complain, since Sam was an old man (78) and was performing with vigor and constant enthusiasm. I knew his secret. Every time he got a break he'd return to his motel room, take a shower, shave, and then come back looking totally refreshed. Although he had directed 22 movies Sam wasn't particularly good at cheating to the right or left or clearing his shadow off another actor's face. Nor was he accurate at hitting his marks. Often, I'd be lying out of camera range on the ground next to Sam grabbing his legs and turning him to the right or the left or moving him a step backwards. Sam didn't seem to mind. He never tried to give me any hints at directing—except once, and it was an excellent suggestion which I immediately followed. His presence energized the entire cast, even 10-year-old Tara Reid, who played a child vampire and later went on to stardom in the *American Pie* series.

The only problem that arose with Sam involved the static on his wireless radio mic. At first we thought it was defective equipment and I berated the sound man. He changed microphones but the crackling remained. I sent back to New York for a substitute sound recordist—only to have the same problem re-occur. Static and more static. Finally, after several days of this, I had the good sense to ask Sam, "Do you have anything in your pockets?" Sam pulled his jacket open wide. "Only my cigars." He had three cigars wrapped in cellophane in each of his inside pockets. "I can't leave them in the motel room. The maids will steal them."

Every time Sam moved, the cellophane crunched. On the track, it sounded like static. Sam had been a party to all of the discussions, but it had never occurred to him that his cigars might be the culprits. I felt so badly about the other sound man that I sent him a week's salary and a note of apology.

Some months after we completed the film I brought it to the Avignon Film Festival in France, where Sam saw it for the first time. His opinion meant more to me than anything else, and I was relieved when he gave me a hug and laughed, "Damn good, very well put together."

I suppose from the lunatic way the picture was made he might've expected a shambles. We'd recruited the children of the town to be child vampires and had them camped out in an abandoned church in sleeping bags on the floor, ready to be called to the set at any time. The parents put up with this because many of them were cast in the film, but one of them finally confided, "We were very happy when you came, and we'll be even more happy when you leave."

Director Samuel Fuller as a Nazi Hunter/Vampire Killer
in *A Return to Salem's Lot*

One of the adult vampires was played by the celebrated film actress Evelyn Keyes, who'd been in everything from *Gone with the Wind* to *The Jolson Story*. She'd also been married to such directors as John Huston and Charles Vidor, as well as bandleader Artie Shaw.

With these credentials I was clearly flattered when she told me how much she enjoyed the shoot. Later she would play a supporting role in *Wicked Stepmother*. She'd become a Larry Cohen fan, and she wrote an article about me which I'm reproducing in this volume (with her permission). I've never gotten a better testimonial from an actor.

You say you wanna make a movie?

Well, lemme tell you how to make a movie. What you do is follow Larry Cohen around for about a year or two, do every single thing Larry Cohen does, and at the end of that time, you'll have yourself a movie. Maybe even two.

So who, you ask, is Larry Cohen?

My Dears, if you don't know yet, you will. You will.

Larry Cohen is this guy who leaves no stone unturned to accomplish what he wants, this one-person whirlwind who writes the scripts, hustles up the money (as hard to do as write the script, I might add), after which he produces and directs, himself. I don't know how many movies Larry has made. I do know he started making 8mm ones when he was a mere lad (he's in his forties now), and while I was in New York a couple of weeks ago, a retrospective of eleven of his grown-up ones were showing down at Joseph Papp's Public Theater. They are of the horror-fantasy-comedy genre with a dash of biting social critique thrown in for good measure, and he's got quite a nifty following for them.

One thing Larry seems allergic to, however, is making his flicks in a studio. He much prefers to make them… out there, somewhere. Out where it's hard to do. Studios, Larry says, where everything is ready and waiting for you, easy to come by, takes the fun out of picture-making. To face the challenge of the unexpected, to deal with surprise and have to invent, have to create something out of nothing, that's what's the fun. That's the thrill of making a film.

Well, who could resist going to work for somebody like that, especially somebody like me who had grown up within the hallowed walls of the old studio system where every single detail from buttons on a shirt to the wallpaper on a set was carefully and meticulously orchestrated. I wanted to see for myself how a free-wheeling, free-spirited, whirlwind operation worked.

And I have to tell you, I wasn't disappointed.

"Don't worry about your (non-existent) part," Larry said to me. "I'll fix it as we go along," And so I didn't worry. Once you've taken a course, I've always believed, you gotta have faith. And sure enough, true to his word, every so often, he'd hand me some new dialogue to say. "You learn lines fast," said he.

Andrew Duggan and Evelyn Keyes in *A Return to Salem's Lot*.

"Because you write them right," said I. Kiss, kiss. Hug, hug. We got along smashingly. Of course, I might be doing a scene in an ancient Georgian mansion up in Harlem (New York City) that was built in 1765 and therefore devoid of any air-conditioning on a stifling, muggy August day or plunked down in the middle of a grassy pasture up in rural Vermont with a zonked-out cow in the middle of the night when he did it. Like he said, I wouldn't want to miss the excitement of the unknown, the improvisation of the moment. Besides, I had never acted with a cow, before. Dogs, yes, horses, children, a monkey once, even an elephant. But a cow? Never. (They are very big and not too chatty.)

The fact that it started to rain didn't stop anybody, they simply put umbrellas over the camera and sound equipment and left the cow and me to our own devices.

It did remind me of something a then father-in-law, actor Walter Huston, once said to me many years ago as he and I sat side by side in directors' chairs in a similar such field, this one south of the border, down Mexico way, and this time in midday with a ferocious sun pounding the top of our heads and dust swirling up our noses—Walter was the one working (in *The Treasure of the Sierra Madre*, directed by his son), I merely a camp follower. Said he, after a deep and heart-felt sigh. "Acting... is just... not... supposed to be done... outdoors..."

I quite agreed with him, then, but, of course, in those days I was playing "the love interest" and having to "look good," having to be concerned about hair and makeup and things like that. But now? Who cares? I certainly don't. I'll act anywhere, oh I tell you, there are so many marvelous advantages to getting older, and not having to worry anymore about your damned looks is one of them! I am playing a vampire (vampire... ess?) in Larry Cohen's cinema, that's what I was doing out in the pasture with the zonked-out cow—uh... if none of this is making sense to you, I guess you'll just have to go see the movie, won't you...

Another thing I couldn't help but notice in this post-studio world of filmmaking is how all the equipment has so vastly improved. Much smaller cameras, easier to lug about, lights don't have to be so all-fired glaring, sound can pick up the dropping of a pin at a hundred paces. It's only the actors whose lots haven't ameliorated one whit that I can see. They (we) still have those frightfully long hours—in Larry Cohen's epic sometimes from, say, three of an afternoon to six or seven the following morning (vampires, as everyone knows, only come out at night!), still have to memorize lines in the same old way, find marks and key lights on the set (even if it's a cow pasture) in exactly the same old way...

Mmmmmmm...

It does occur to me as I put these words down that perhaps it would be a splendid idea to heed my own advice...? That I, myself, should start following Larry Cohen around and doing everything he does...?

It would mean being on the other side of that camera, wouldn't it?... and under that umbrella...

Well, hey, that could sure be one way of getting in out of the rain...

                                        Evelyn Keyes

Michael Moriarty and Andrew Duggan in *A Return to Salem's Lot.*

Eventually Sam returned to the U.S. and to his home on Woodrow Wilson Drive off Laurel Canyon, where he spent the final years of his life. He was idolized by young filmmakers like Quentin Tarantino, who spent much time in Sam's garage which was full of memorabilia as well as stacked with hundreds of unproduced scripts.

The last time I saw Sam was at a tribute the American Cinematheque arranged at Raleigh Studios in Hollywood. Sam had suffered a stroke that impaired his speech, but he still chatted amiably away, holding court for old friends like Angie Dickinson, who had dubbed the voice of the leading lady in Sam's *Run of the Arrow*. He then gave her the starring role as Lucky Legs in *China Gate*.

None of the friends gathered around Sam could understand a word he was saying but they all basked in his enthusiasm. Whenever he told you a story, Sam would grab you by the wrist and hold on tight until his story was done. Then finally you would be released from his iron grip.

Even though he's gone, I still feel that grasp occasionally and the whisper of his indomitable spirit urging me not to give up. Both Sam and I willed our pictures into being against all obstacles. Even if they were ignored, we went on to our next project knowing that someday the previous film would be discovered and given the respect that was its due. Time and time again this has happened to both of us. I think we both believed that although we fathered our films, they had a life of their own. We knew that somewhere in the world, fans were watching our pictures and sometimes writing about them. Sam's pictures outlived him, and his reputation continues to grow. He stands as an example to all independent filmmakers.

I suppose Sam's greatest hit was his 1950s Korean War film *The Steel Helmet*, which was highly profitable. He was never able to equal that financial success again, just as I've been chasing the box-office success of *It's Alive*. Despite disappointments, he continued on much as he had as a dogged combat soldier in World War II, fighting battles, never retreating, never accepting the possibility of failure. He knew the system was against him, but he probably liked it that way. He's my hero.

Chapter 29
With Friends Like These...

Richard Levinson and William Link were two of my oldest friends in Hollywood. We first met in a hallway at the William Morris Agency, and we had plenty to talk about. We were all struggling writers. They were a curious Mutt and Jeff combination—the tall one and the short one. Everyone might have suspected that the little Jewish guy was Levinson and the tall, waspish-looking fellow was Link. But the reverse was true. You'd also have assumed that the very verbally skilled Levinson did the dictating while the quietly repressed Link typed away, trying to keep up with him. But actually it was Link who paced and dictated while Levinson banged it out on the keys.

When I began to have my teleplays produced on *The Defenders*, I could always expect a telephone call from them as soon as the program went off the air, ringing up to critique the show. That call was very important to me as I valued their opinion the most. I also followed their career with tremendous interest. They usually wrote detective dramas, one of the best of which was a *Chevy Mystery Show* production entitled "Prescription Murder." The story featured a plodding detective named Columbo who was played by character actor Bert Freed. I encouraged them to do something more with this script and they eventually turned it into a stage play which was optioned by producer Paul Gregory. It went on tour and starred Joseph Cotten, Agnes Moorehead, Patricia Medina (Mrs. Cotten) and the veteran character actor Thomas Mitchell playing Columbo.

While I was in the army, I went to Philadelphia to see an out-of-town tryout but sadly the play never made it to New York and was soon forgotten. But some years later Universal purchased the rights and filmed it as a Movie of the Week. The role of Columbo was originally offered to Bing Crosby, who turned it down. The studio then went after my old buddy, Peter Falk.

Here's where I came back into the story. By coincidence Peter and I were both represented by the same business managers. Their job was to do our taxes and advise on investments. One afternoon they invited us to a luncheon at the Kings Four in Hand restaurant on Beverly Boulevard. Both of us sat there in shock as we were informed that all the money we'd put into the construction of modular schoolhouses had been lost. The builder had absconded with the funds. I had $100,000 at risk, but Peter had invested four times as much—the majority of his savings. Peter's screams echoed through the restaurant, "Julie—where's my money? I want my money back. Julie, what did you do to me? I need that fucking money!" Everybody in the joint was staring at us. I pulled Peter aside and told him I knew a good lawyer who might help us. Bert Fields immediately rushed over to the restaurant and calmed Peter down. (He was to remain Peter's lawyer and would later negotiate fabulous deals for him at the network.)

This financial disaster had overtaken him at a time when he'd just been offered the *Columbo* series. He'd already played the role twice in TV movies but was reluctant to commit to a regular monthly show. Peter had his mind set on a career as a movie star. Someone had convinced him that he was another John Garfield and could play romantic leads. Being identified as a sloppy TV detective did not fit into his long-term career plan, but now that he had money problems, he quickly latched onto the security of having a 90-minute series on the small screen.

It would be the best decision of his life, and it gave him the role with which he will always be identified.

Some six months later, Bert Fields got us our dough back. The business management firm had been insured and the company finally paid out. By then, Peter Falk was on his way to immortality in that rumpled trench coat.

Link and Levinson had been brought aboard to produce and write the series, but coming up with the intricate mystery plots that the format required was no easy matter. They asked me to write an episode, but I declined. I wanted to create my own series or else write features. One afternoon I was lunching with Janelle in the Universal commissary while Levinson and Link were seated in the booth directly opposite us. They began to speak loudly so we couldn't miss what was being said. "Here we are in desperate trouble and our good friend Larry Cohen won't lift a finger to help us. We're drowning and he won't even throw us a life preserver..."

This went on for about 15 minutes before I finally got up and crossed to their table. "Okay, I'm going to give you a story as a gift because I love you. I don't want anything for it. Levinson murders Link. They're mystery writers, but Levinson hasn't got any talent, Link does all the writing." Mercilessly I laid out an elaborate scenario describing how Levinson tricks Link into making a telephone call and telling his wife that he's working late at his office in Los Angeles—when actually he's gone up to a cabin in Santa Barbara to collaborate with Levinson on a new storyline. In the midst of the phone conversation Levinson shoots Link and his wife hears it over the phone. She panics and calls the police—then immediately calls Levinson in Santa Barbara to tell him what she's heard. Of course, he's there to take the call and this provides him with a perfect alibi since the wife can testify that her husband was murdered back at his office in Los Angeles. Levinson then tosses Link's body in the trunk and drives it back, dumping it somewhere near the office.

I don't know where the idea came from. I just made it up while I was standing there at their table. They didn't understand that I was needling them and insisted that I return to their bungalow on the lot and jot down an outline on paper. Janelle and I followed them to their office, and I spent a half an hour during which their young story editor showed up and tried to pick holes in my plot. I ran him off saying, "I'm not here looking for a job, this is a gift to my friends so please keep out of it." The story editor fled, and I finished outlining the yarn and went home.

Several days later Levinson phoned me. "Universal loves the story. We're going right ahead with it, but Bill and I aren't going to write it. We promised to give an assignment to our story editor and since this is so well worked out, we think he can handle it." I was astonished. I replied, "I gave the story to you two as a gift. You can't simply give it to somebody else to put their name on." Levinson seemed genuinely peeved. "Larry, when you give a gift to someone, they have the right to

Peter Falk as *Columbo.*

dispose of it in any way they see fit." I was getting upset now. "Dick, this is the same guy that didn't even like the story. He tried to punch holes in it, I had to chase him out. Now you're giving him authorship to my story?"

I was about to tell Levinson to forget about it, that he couldn't have the story at all, when Janelle chimed in. "Dick is right. I was there and you did give him the story as a gift. He has the right to do anything he wants with it—and you have the right never to speak to him again."!

Now I had Janelle on my back as well. "Okay!" I shouted at Levinson. "Take the goddamn story, who the fuck cares. I made it up in five minutes as a joke anyhow and I don't want to hear any more about it." I hung up the phone.

A few days later Levinson called again. "Universal says we have to give you something in exchange for the story so I'm sending you a catalogue of RCA television sets. You can pick out any one you please." I picked the most expensive set available, which Levinson did not fail to point out at our next meeting.

That is how the teleplay "Murder by the Book" came to be written and credited to Steven Bochco, who later created *Hill Street Blues*. The night it was televised, Levinson and Link came to my home to watch it with me. I thought some surprise awaited me as the show unfolded—perhaps the name Larry Cohen would be used as one of the characters. Or perhaps there would be a note of appreciation in the final credits. Nothing materialized. The boys ate their dinner, watched the show and went home. They didn't even bring flowers. To make matters worse, the teleplay was nominated for an Emmy. I swear if Bochco had won, I would have run up on stage along with him. The final agony of it all is that the teleplay was directed by the very gifted young Steven Spielberg.

As the months passed into years I grew to hate that color television set in the center of my living room. Many people at the studio knew the true authorship of the show, among them Peter Falk, who eventually insisted that I be hired on as a regular "murder consultant" on the series. By then Peter was running the show and the network had no choice but to accommodate his demands. I ended up contributing three more stories that were produced as *Columbo* episodes. This time I was credited and properly paid.

In 1979, Levinson and Link were visiting New York and asked to be invited over to my new townhouse on East 79th Street between Park and Lexington. I had a feeling they had some other motive, and finally after dinner, as we all settled down in front of the fireplace, they sprung it on me. "We just sold a new series called *Mrs. Columbo*. It's about Columbo's wife who goes off and solves mysteries on her own, but we have a problem. She has no authority to be investigating these crimes. Can you figure out how we can get a housewife mixed up in all these murders?"

I couldn't believe they'd come to me for help again. "Guys, if I work this out for you—what do I get out of it?"

"You want another color television set?" said Levinson.

I hadn't had the heart to break up the friendship and I still continued to see both of them in the years that followed. Janelle had even introduced them to a novel that she thought might make a good television movie. I hadn't any interest in adapting it, so she pestered Bill into reading it. The book was called *My Sweet Charlie* by David Westheimer, and the resulting TV movie won an Emmy for Levinson and Link and for Patty Duke as its star in 1970.

They invited us to join them at the ceremonies and at the party afterwards. Levinson even had us to his home in order to introduce us to David Westheimer, who thanked Janelle for discovering the book and getting it adapted for television.

Therefore it was with some degree of amazement that years later when we leafed through Levinson and Link's published memoirs, we came to a paragraph that read, "Somehow we came across the book *My Sweet Charlie*…" The next time we met I made a point of reminding them that it was Janelle who'd found the book for them. Link barked, "That's not true." Levinson quickly added, "That never happened." I called up the Westheimers and asked them for their recollection, which coincided with our own. Why then had Levinson and Link completely erased the truth? What would it have cost them to acknowledge Janelle's small contribution to their success?

Still, we liked these two guys so much that, again, we let it pass. They were simply guilty of selective memory, a malady which afflicts so many people in Hollywood. Let's face it, this is a city where you'd best beware of your friends more than your enemies.

It might give some insight into Link's personality to know that he eventually purchased and lived in the Menendez home in Beverly Hills. He got it at a very attractive price. After all, not too many people would be comfortable sleeping in a house where a double murder had taken place. How could Link ever relax in a living room where Mr. and Mrs. Menendez were shot-gunned to death by their own sons? I suppose it just takes a certain type of person.

We sincerely grieved for Dick Levinson when he died prematurely of a heart attack in 1987. Bill Link was never the same without him. The magic was gone. He wrote nothing significant afterwards. Levinson was gone but Bill Link wasn't finished with me. He still had to produce two more seasons of *Columbo* alone and needed writers. He called me lamenting the position he was in, and I agreed to help. I proposed a storyline that was quickly approved, but before I could begin the first draft a writers strike was called. Link took me to lunch and implored me to write the two-hour teleplay anyway and keep it in a drawer. Once the strike was over, I could wait a few days and then deliver it, and he'd have an episode to produce.

I should have known I was courting disaster, but I actually enjoyed writing the piece. Many months later, when the strike was settled, I called Link to inform him I'd be sending in the draft as suggested. He replied: "Oh, we don't want that script anymore. You know all existing deals were canceled when the strike was called." I tried to remind him of his fervent request, but once again amnesia had set in. "Even if I did ask you to do that, I had no right to."

Even then I didn't stop speaking to Link. He stopped speaking to me. When we both appeared at an Edgar Allan Poe Awards ceremony where I'd been nominated for best screen-play, he simply ignored me—walking directly past as if I didn't exist. I came over to his table but he refused to acknowledge me. I was reminded of one of Hollywood's cardinal rules, that when you screw someone over, you never want to see them again. It just makes you feel too guilty. I went home and took it out on the color television set, which moved down into the basement.

Then I sat down and began recalling all the lunches and dinners we had together and the conversations about ideas I'd had for movies and television. What about my idea *The Adven-tures of Agatha Christie*, about an elderly female mystery writer who solves real murders? Not dissimilar to *Murder, She Wrote*, which Levinson and Link created in 1984. And how about my story tracing the life of a firearm from its time of manufacture

With Paul Bartel.

through its theft and use in a number of crimes? Levinson and Link later wrote and produced a two-hour TV movie entitled, *The Gun*. Then there was my story, *Queens Blood*, about a teenage boy who discovers that his father is gay. Didn't that bear a striking similarity to Levinson and Link's Emmy Award-winning *That Certain Summer*?

What was it about me that allowed them to do this time and time again? I sought them out and opened my big mouth, then looked the other way while they borrowed my ideas without any sense of shame. But they weren't to blame. I was!

It was an act of colossal ego to walk to their table in the Universal commissary and spout off, "Levinson kills Link, etc." For some reason I was trying to prove my superiority to them, and they simply took advantage of it. I deserved what I got. Incidentally, Steven Bochco never thought to say thank you for the storyline I gave him, or for his Emmy nomination. He went on to become one of television's top producers. And when I happened to write an episode of his series *NYPD Blue* in 1995, Bochco never thought to give me a call or drop me a note. For all the success he'd had, one might imagine he'd be big enough to finally show some appreciation for the gift of a very important credit—not to mention the many thousands of dollars in residuals which should've gone to me for the story.

I've learned that you can't expect much back from people in the world of show business. If you befriend them on the way up, don't expect them to repay that friendship once they reach the top. They will have acquired a new circle of friends and usually become embarrassed if they accidentally encounter you at some event. They'll avert their eyes nervously, but if there's no way of avoiding you, they'll eventually shake your hand, avoiding eye contact whenever possible. It's amusing to witness this ritual, and I often go out of my way to circulate at Oscar parties simply to corner a reluctant "old friend." I know it's sadistic, but I can't help it.

More often than not when someone's career hits a snag and they begin to descend back into the real world, you will invariably hear from them again. And you know what? I usually take them back into the fold.

The last time I saw Bill Link, he generously agreed to speak to me again—if only to complain about his situation in Holly-wood. The studios and the networks were not returning his phone calls. The people he had helped get started were ignoring him. He was a self-proclaimed forgotten man, and he was terribly bitter. I'm sure he had plenty of money saved and I knew he had an extensive art collection, but what Link wanted more than anything was to work again. And that did not seem a likely prospect.

Chapter 30
Trials and Tribulations

In 1981, the opportunity arose to return to television with a television pilot of my own. This time I'd also direct. The star of the show was to be the wonderful black actress Esther Rolle. I didn't realize how popular she was until we met for lunch in the Oak Room of the Plaza Hotel. On the way out the Plaza doorman asked for her autograph—this from a guy who must see every star in the world.

Momma, the Detective was to be a mystery series recounting the adventures of a housekeeper whose son works on the homicide squad. Yet it's the mother who has the brilliant knack for solving crimes. She works in the finest homes in Manhattan and usually comes upon a homicide which she alone unravels.

NBC ordered a one-hour pilot, but I decided to film a feature-length version for the same money. The network could have their choice. An unsold one-hour pilot is useless. At least a feature length pilot could be sold into syndication as a TV movie.

The project was doomed before it began. Almost as soon as it was announced, a handful of letters arrived at NBC objecting to a black woman portraying the role of a maid. Even though Momma was a brilliant woman and a lot smarter than all the white people that she encountered, her choice of employment was politically incorrect. I tried to switch her to being a cook rather than a housekeeper but that still appeared to be too servile a position. NBC caved in immediately and the fate of our pilot was a foregone conclusion.

We went through the motions of filming the show, an experience which I thoroughly enjoyed. One of the supporting roles was portrayed by Miguel Piñero, an award-winning author, who had written his play, *Short Eyes*, while he was in prison. He was now regarded as the poet laureate of the Puerto Rican community.

Miguel and I hit it off well. He was a gifted actor, and we enjoyed improvising together. He was a wiry little guy, very hyper with a keen sense of humor. At least with me. He even invited me to join him at his poetry reading sessions. My only reluctance stemmed from the fact that Miguel was deeply involved in drugs, for which I had no weakness whatsoever. Janelle had once given me half a Valium en route to Europe and I slept through the entire flight. I'd smoked a few joints at parties when they were passed around. You couldn't very well refuse to take a toke that was handed to you, even if it was dripping with everyone else's saliva. Not unless you wanted to be excluded as a square.

Because it was a union production, I had to carry a full crew, which sometimes cramped my style. When we were scheduled to film a chase through Manhattan's diamond district, I knew it would be impossible if we arrived with trailers and portable toilets—we'd clog up the street and attract undue attention. I would have to steal the sequence and that meant ditching the crew.

I slipped away with the actors and cameraman, diverting the rest of the crew to a phony location beneath the West Side Highway where they waited all afternoon for us to show up. Meanwhile, I was successfully shooting the sequence while we raced with handheld camera along 47th Street and up Sixth Avenue. Once I wrapped the scene I rejoined the rest of the crew, keeping what we'd done a secret.

Although NBC didn't pick up the series, I still had a saleable movie on my hands. By turning the one-hour pilot into a full-length feature called *See China and Die*, I'd again managed to turn a total failure into a minor success.

Perhaps the most difficult problem faced by any creative person is dealing with industry executives. It is usually inadvisable to confront them with their own incompetence. Should you be pitching a movie or television series and refer to some prior classic film for comparison, you will inevitably be met with a blank stare because the executive will have never heard of the movie. By making him feel stupid, you'll alienate him and probably cause your project to self-destruct.

Often executives come to meetings unprepared. One such a circumstance occurred in the 1970s at the Bel Air Hotel where I'd been summoned to confer with key members of the ABC programming staff to discuss a television pilot I'd written for them. These two gentlemen kept me waiting in the lobby for 45 minutes. Usually I'd be prepared to wait 15 or 20 minutes before feeling badly treated. In this case, when I was finally granted an audience with the executives, they launched into a detailed critique of my pilot but continued getting the details of the story ass-backwards. It soon became clear that they hadn't actually read the script. An underling had been assigned that chore and had given them the gist of the story. They were winging it. When I'd finally had enough, I called them on it. "Tell the truth… you never read the script!" By now their analysis had become so hopelessly confused that they had to own up. "We read coverage."

I told them I didn't mind waiting 45 minutes for a meeting if the executives were prepared, but I didn't intend to sit there anymore. "Why don't you read the script, and I'll come back and we can have our meeting."

I should've known I was sealing my own doom. I flew to New York several days later. Janelle and I were dining in the La Caravelle when Leonard Goldberg, the head of ABC, walked in with his girlfriend, Marlo Thomas. He spotted me and crossed to my table. "I hear you roughed up my boys out in Hollywood," he remarked with a sly grin. To which I responded, "They came to the meeting unprepared." To his credit Leonard answered, "You did the right thing" and he shook my hand. Nonetheless there was never a second meeting. I never received any further notes. I was paid in full, and my television pilot was never heard of again.

The two executives were Martin Starger (who was later to become head of the network) and Barry Diller, who would eventually top Paramount Pictures and go on to create the Fox network. It seems to be a rule that if I offend anyone, they'll go on to great success in the industry.

Later I sat in front of Barry Diller at Lincoln Center during a screening of Visconti's *The Leopard*. He arrived with Diane von Fürstenberg. Just as the lights dimmed, I turned around and said, "Barry, no phone calls," which got the expected laugh.

A few minutes into the picture, hearing noises, I sneaked a look and caught sight of Barry and Diane locked in a furious embrace. I quickly looked away. About five minutes later I glanced back again. The two seats were vacant. It took almost 20 more years for Barry and Diane to become husband and wife, but it was clearly ordained.

Barry has always been polite to me when we've met in public, but I believe he hasn't forgotten that early slight. It took me many years to get an ABC Movie of the Week when Barry controlled its development. But finally I sold them a pretty good thriller called *In Broad Daylight*, in which Richard Boone played a blind man who commits a murder.

Richard Boone in *In Broad Daylight*.

When I created a World War II series for Universal, Sid Sheinberg, the President of MCA, thought it would be an excellent project for the Fox network. Sid was so enthusiastic that he decided to pitch the concept himself to Barry Diller. Such a meeting of the giants was virtually unheard of—and I was invited along.

I don't think Sid had pitched a series anywhere for over a decade. He was above all that. Diller greeted us graciously from the end of a long conference table with a half dozen of his underlings lining both sides. Sid began his pitch with a compliment. "If I'd read this idea without anyone's name on it... it's so inventive... so clever that I would've known it had to be written by Larry Cohen."

He then went on to detail the plot of *Rogue*, which dealt with an American submarine believed to be sunk by the Japanese with all hands lost. It turns out that the crew had mutinied against a deranged captain and realized their future lies behind bars if they returned to Pearl Harbor. Instead they allow themselves to be thought of as dead while they continue to fight the war on their own terms—as a phantom submarine prowling the Pacific.

Sid told it well and I jumped in with additional details. At one point Sid interrupted, "Barry, you're not taking notes." Which broke everyone up, including Diller himself, who yelled back, "I'm writing, I'm writing!" as he began scribbling furiously on his legal pad. It was an extremely pleasant meeting and Diller walked us out through his private entrance with his arm around me.

Need I add that Barry Diller did not buy my series for the Fox network. It budgeted out to be too costly a venture. Sid Sheinberg would eventually leave Universal to become an independent producer. He would always remain a loyal friend and supporter.

When I first met him, he'd been a frazzled young lawyer working on television contracts for Revue Productions, Universal's television arm, and labored in a small office in a metal Quonset hut located just off the studio's backlot. Peter Sabiston, with his uncanny ability to sense the potential in others, had told me, "This guy is going places. Let's take him to lunch." We had many enjoyable lunches with Sid well before he came to run the TV division and eventually the entire studio. He never forgot our early friendship. It's nice to know there's at least someone out there whom I haven't managed to offend.

In California I had never been part of the A crowd, but in New York, where filmmakers were harder to come by, we became socially desirable and the invitations began pouring in. We were asked to events four or five times a week, usually in the company of the same crowd, of which Andy Warhol was certainly the most prominent.

Andy always showed up looking frightful and carrying a tape recorder in which he was immortalizing every waking moment of his life. I used to tease him, saying, "Andy, somebody else has to give up their entire life to listen to your life," to which he would reply, "Well, that's exactly the idea."

I think he always enjoyed my jibes—everyone else treated him like a saint. I teased the hell out of him. One evening at Regine's, we were both invited to judge a Halloween costume pageant. Andy wanted to give the prize to a personal friend of his, but I wouldn't let him. "You can't do that Andy. It just isn't fair."

"Why not?" he pouted, accustomed to having his way. But I maintained my integrity as a judge. And so did Andy.

I hate to admit it but night after night in the VIP section at Studio 54 can become a dreadful bore. Some of the most sophisticated people in New York have the least to say. The truth is they only had me around because everybody wants to appear in a movie at least once, and I did give a few of them walk-ons. But after a while, we'd had enough of Halston and Jacques Bellini and began turning down these invitations. I must say we found the people in New York far more troubled and desperate than those we'd known in Hollywood. You'd meet a New Yorker once at a party and they'd begin calling you up every day. The women would hardly know Janelle before they'd proclaim her their very best friend and reveal their deepest secrets. These friendships ended as quickly as they began. We'd walk into a party with someone and they'd point to another guest across the room, whispering, "We used to be friends." People were too needy, too neurotic.

Bit by bit, Janelle and I began to change as well. When I first brought her to New York she claimed she could never live there. The city was too big, too intimidating. She swore she could never drive there, yet now she was zigzagging through the canyons of the city in her Jeep, bouncing fearlessly over potholes.

She'd found a composer to put music to her lyrics. She was writing a book. She was training as a gymnast with the Big Apple Circus along with Melissa and Jill. She was also providing counsel to a good many unhappy women. Everyone in the family was now seeing an analyst at least once a week. I attended with Janelle, then by myself, and then I was required to accompany Jill for her analysis after she experienced an outburst and smashed up the psychiatrist's office. He refused to see her unless a parent was present in the waiting room, and I was nominated. Life was not as carefree as I'd recalled it being back in good old Beverly Hills—or maybe this was mid-life crisis?

Since we were spending most of our time in Manhattan, it seemed like a good idea to rent the Coldwater Canyon house. Immediate interest came from *Hustler* magazine publisher Larry Flynt. Mom was kind enough to escort Mr. Flynt and his wife through the property and an offer was forthcoming. Larry wanted to build ramps to accommodate his wheelchair, and he also wanted an option to buy.

His offer was substantial, and I was about to close when I ran it past my attorney, Skip Brittenham. "Are you crazy?" Skip exclaimed. "Larry Flynt has about 60 lawsuits pending now. What are you going to do if he moves into your house and won't leave? Suppose he doesn't pay the rent? Are you going to take him to court? Get in line! You're not doing it, period."

Once again Skip saved my ass. You may recall that the FBI raided the Flynt residence—which would have been my house had the lease gone through. Flynt's wife was later found dead in the bathtub. I don't think I would've wanted her ghost haunting my place.

Eventually we got another offer from a Mr. Johnson, who turned out to be Rick James, famous for his recording of "Super Freak." With his dreadlocks and wild ways and his entourage of musicians and back-up singers, one might have thought he'd be a lousy tenant.

But I'd made a fortune on Blaxploitation pictures and my father had earned his living renting apartments in Harlem. Was I now going to refuse to lease my house to a black man? Absolutely not. Rick turned out to be a great guy. When I told him I intended to put my two dogs in a kennel, he wouldn't hear of it. He loved dogs and he'd look after them for me. Whenever Janelle and I visited Los Angeles, we were always welcome to come by the Coldwater house. He never resented it or saw it as an intrusion.

Rick loved the place so much that when he was interviewed for *Billboard* magazine, a full-page photo showed him standing in front of the house, which was described as his Beverly Hills home. He told everybody he owned it. A reporter commented on Rick's eclectic library of books—which were, of course, mine. Although Rick threw lavish parties every week, no damage was done to the property, and we got it back in excellent condition. Of course, for months afterward, people kept showing up late at night looking for a place to party.

I'd always relied a great deal on Janelle when I was making my films, so it came as a disappointment when she decided not to participate any longer. She had other commitments. Besides, she wasn't sure she liked the personality I assumed when I took the reins of a motion picture.

I'd be the last to deny it. It's hard for a nice guy to get a picture made, particularly when his own money is on the line. As director, I had to play the role of drill sergeant. Others may have the luxury of hiring a tough production manager to do their dirty work for them, but I was honest enough to do it myself, even if it meant clanking a few heads together. Still, I had the same crew members return time after time, so I assumed they enjoyed working with me. What was my wife complaining about? Janelle replied, "The rest of the crew doesn't have to go to bed with you!"

Once Janelle bowed out and I was back in Los Angeles alone, it took me almost no time to get into trouble. Prepping a movie, I was in my usual hyperactive state and requiring very little sleep. A long day's work would be followed by a night at the disco. It wasn't necessary to look for women—they simply walked into your life. There were just too many pretty girls who were agreeable. I hope it wasn't just because they wanted a part in a movie. Some of them weren't actresses. I knew I was wrecking my marriage, but I suppose that's exactly what I intended. Calling Janelle every day became a perfunctory chore, and we were continually more distant with each other.

When I flew back to New York to visit the family, I noticed she'd begun drinking in the afternoons. The half-empty wine bottle would always be there on the table between us. And since her father, sister, and brother were acknowledged alcoholics, perhaps there was a genetic disposition. Later she would tell me that she wanted to drink and that our deteriorating relationship simply gave her the excuse she needed. Everyone would feel sorry for her. It wouldn't be her fault. After 20 years in Alcoholics Anonymous she's mature enough to take this position. But I believe I bear the greater share of the blame.

To me, life in New York had become virtually intolerable. There was no fun left in it. Everyone else was changing while I remained the same lovable kid who never took matters seriously. What was there to be serious about if you had your health? Of course, I wasn't considering mental health. I was thoughtlessly inflicting pain on my loved ones and pretending otherwise.

Chapter 31
All About Laurene

I was primed for trouble when 21-year-old Laurene Landon walked into my life. She was a five-foot-ten blonde who looked like she'd stepped off a magazine cover. Unlike many young actresses she didn't have any bad angles, and she didn't have a mean bone in her body. I was as impressed with her sweetness as I was with her good looks when she showed up on the set of *Full Moon High*, which I was filming at Burbank High School. She'd come seeking a role in the picture and I told her she could go to work immediately. "Take a seat in the classroom and play one of the students," I suggested. To which she incredulously replied, "I'm sorry I can't because I have to go and read for a part somewhere else."

I couldn't believe she was turning down a firm commitment to go and seek a job elsewhere. Of course, it turned out she was simply nervous, and she returned the next day and went to work. During a break she invited me into the school auditorium to hear her play the concert piano and performed a number of her own compositions. I was even more impressed with her outrageous sense of humor. She seemed to be exactly what I was looking for. How could you turn down a beautiful girl who'd sleep in her car in your driveway simply because she wants to be near you? I seemed to be the most important thing in her young life, while back in New York I was being taken for granted.

I was about to make a major mistake. I hadn't been back home for more than a few days when I asked Janelle for a separation. She'd seen it coming and put on a brave front. I realize now how deeply hurt she was. All I could think of was getting back to California where I immediately rented a condo at the Malibu Outrigger on Carbon Beach and set up house with Laurene.

Within a week I knew it wasn't going to work. The attraction was still there but living under the same roof caused it to rapidly diminish. I'd been comfortable with Janelle from the beginning, but Laurene's daily habits proved to be a problem. She never hung anything up, clothes were tossed all over the floor, makeup was dropped and ground into the carpet, fake eyelashes were scattered around like insects. I immediately knew I was not going to get my security deposit back.

Mercifully, Laurene got a job that would keep her occupied elsewhere most of the day. Robert Aldrich was casting ...*All the Marbles*, in which Peter Falk was to play the manager of a pair of female wrestlers. Since Laurene was such an impressive physical specimen, he'd hired her along with seven other girls to train for a few months. Then he would pick two of them to star in the movie. I knew Laurene would get the role, and she did.

After that she left early each morning for MGM Studios where I visited her on the set several times. She was absolutely wonderful in the film and *New York Times* critic Vincent Canby singled her out for one of the best, most notable performances of the year.

Naturally Laurene came home exhausted at night and went right off to sleep. Suddenly I was feeling more lonesome than ever. I traveled back to New York, met with Janelle, and asked her to take me back. Perhaps we could make things work again. She would have none of it. She asked me for my key to the brownstone and I handed it over. I loved visiting with Melissa and Jill and hated having to leave them again.

It would be five years before Janelle and I actually divorced. Neither of us wanted to hurt the other. She was free to live her life as she pleased and I paid all the bills without question. I noticed with concern that many of them came from the local liquor store.

Janelle's drinking escalated until finally she bottomed out, finding refuge in Alcoholics Anonymous, through which she regained her physical and mental health. She became deeply involved in the program and went on to counsel others.

Over the years she's chaired many Alcoholics Anonymous symposiums. She even traveled to the Soviet Union to participate in the first Alcoholics Anonymous meetings ever held there. The Soviets' resistance to Alcoholics Anonymous was based upon their refusal to accept a higher power. Alcoholism, however, had become such a major social problem that the Russians were now willing to put aside any such objections and encourage the establishment of the recovery program which Janelle helped introduce. Over the years she's done so much good for so many people while I've continued to make movies, which I hope entertain people, but which I'm sure seldom help improve the human condition. From my perspective, Janelle is a much more successful human being than I am.

The great majority of Janelle's friendships and associations were now with people in the program. I always felt somewhat excluded when I accompanied her to meetings. The members were only interested in other alcoholics to whom they could relate. I was a total outsider.

Watching all the hugging and embracing of the members I realized I'd never get Janelle back. She'd entered a different world and probably a better one. It encompassed people from all walks of life, some extremely famous, others poor, but within this program they were all equals who'd suffered and were now unconditionally trying to help one another. I believe Alcoholics Anonymous is one of the finest organizations in existence. Unfortunately I can't be part of it.

Returning to Hollywood I was not about to give up on my relationship with Laurene. Not yet. I'd sacrificed too much for it. I wrote her an important role in my adaptation of Mickey Spillane's *I, the Jury*, which soon went into production in New York. Laurene would play Velda, Mike Hammer's secretary.

The lead role was played by Armand Assante, who took more than a casual liking to Laurene. His only problem was that I was in the way. We were all ensconced at the Mayflower Hotel near Central Park.

After the first week of production, I was fired. The fact that Assante was so agreeable to being rid of me was an important factor in my dismissal. If he'd resisted the idea I might well have remained.

Laurene was spirited off to The Pierre Hotel, so I'd be unable to reach her. They were afraid that she'd quit as a result of my firing, which was absurd. She was getting $75,000 for her role and it was an important career move. I wanted her to finish the film. I eventually located Laurene and went over and spent the night at The Pierre, running up a huge room service bill with

Laurene Landon in *I, the Jury.*

lobsters, steaks and champagne, and charging it to the production. I was soon working on my own film, Q, which meant
long grueling hours on the set away from her.

Laurene remained her usual irresponsible self, usually
leaving her $1,500 per diem lying around her hotel room and
finding it missing when she returned. She had such a good heart
she'd wander around the streets of the city giving $20 bills to
panhandlers, an act that I tried to discourage.

I was well into the production of Q when I got the distinct
impression that Laurene was keeping something from me. It
turned out that she'd been offered the lead in a movie which
was going to film in Spain. It had been written especially for
her and apparently the funding had been raised based on her
name. She was suddenly bankable. Moreover, the director of
the picture was an ex-boyfriend of hers, Matt Cimber, whom
she first met when she was a teenager playing Bo-Peep in a
Christmas pageant. Cimber, a former husband of Jayne Mans-
field, had ground out a few low-budget pictures of his own,
none of which had made any impression.

This venture, *Hundra*, was a *Conan the Barbarian* rip-off in which Laurene would play a warrior princess. It required plenty of stunts and swordplay, all of which she ended up performing herself, much to the frustration of her stunt double. It was eventually shot in Almeria utilizing the same fortress that had been built for *El Condor* many years before.

After Laurene left for Spain with her mother in tow, I felt relieved rather than frustrated. In the months to come I found single life very rewarding. It was a period of sexual liberation, long before anyone had ever heard of AIDS. Any girl who went out with you would go to bed with you, no strings attached. Fidelity was neither requested nor expected.

Meanwhile Laurene completed *Hundra* and soon went on to film *Yellow Hair and the Fortress of Gold*. She, of course, played Yellow Hair, a half-breed gunfighter, in a sprawling action movie which again was filmed on the original *El Condor* set with Cimber as director.

Laurene had allowed her mother to handle her finances. Since she'd earned over $100,000 from these two epics, she felt somewhat secure—until she discovered that her mother had been secretly endorsing the checks, transferring the money, and distributing it to Laurene's brother and sisters. Maybe she was afraid Laurene would squander the money or, worse yet, give it back to Cimber if the picture went over budget. In any case, by the time Laurene returned from Spain she was practically broke and in debt to the IRS. Now, after nearly two years away from Hollywood, her career had cooled off considerably. She'd signed with ICM but when she rejected a proposition from her agent, he buried her at the bottom of his client list.

Neither of the two Matt Cimber movies were released theatrically in the U.S. Laurene got one last chance, starring in a futuristic gladiator movie, *America 2000*, which was truly awful. She'd lost so much weight that she looked gaunt on the screen and her fiddling with her own makeup did nothing to enhance her appearance. My daughter Melissa and I traveled to Israel to visit Laurene on location where *America 2000* was being produced. I got there in time to learn she'd fallen in love with a focus puller.

I still considered her a friend and when she returned, I put her into several of the movies I either wrote or directed. Most notable was her comedic performance in *Wicked Stepmother* doing a take-off on *Wheel of Fortune* game show hostess Vanna White. She completely improvised her antics, demonstrating real comedic ability. I thought her performance might lead to a role in a sitcom, but nothing came of it.

While her career languished, she became involved with Marlon Brando's son, Christian, in what developed into an abusive relationship. Several times she reported that Christian had pointed a shotgun at her head. One night she was so fearful that she hid the weapon in the bushes outside their rustic home on Wonderland Drive off Laurel Canyon. Then she called Marlon, who came rushing over to spirit the shotgun away. A mixture of alcohol and drugs made Christian Brando an extremely dangerous individual. I was more than a bit uneasy when I realized that he was aware of my continued relationship with Laurene and might show up unexpectedly with a gun.

When I visited Laurene's apartment, she'd often play me messages which Marlon had left on her answering machine. These would drone on for as much as half an hour with the great actor's voice unmistakable as he rambled incoherently. Brando, Sr. had given himself the code name of Dr. Fungston. Laurene's code name was Vanilla. In one such message he instructed, "If you need me, call up and say Vanilla One. If it's an emergency say Vanilla Two. If it's a matter of life or death say Vanilla Three. But never say Vanilla Three unless you're in a critical situation." Then he went on to repeat this same information a half dozen times.

Laurene spent a great deal of time around Marlon, who'd cast admiring glances at her and say he wished he was young again. One of his principal hobbies now was using shortwave radio to communicate with strangers all across the globe. He'd assume aliases and establish long-term friendships with people who never knew they were talking to a famous movie star. Brando was comfortable with those who didn't know his identity. His favorite movie seemed to be *Saps at Sea*, starring Laurel and Hardy. He'd run the video again and again and laugh himself silly.

Brando confided his negative feelings about stardom to Laurene: "When you're a celebrity, everything happens in double-time—everybody speeding around you just because you made a few movies."

When Laurene had Thanksgiving dinner at Brando's house, he didn't sit at the table with everyone else but instead slouched in a chair, balancing the plate on his stomach and eating his turkey off his own built-in platform. As time went on, Brando began to rely on her. When his huge mastiff, Schlubba, had to be put to sleep, Brando couldn't face taking the dog to the vet. He begged Laurene to do it for him, and she agreed. It seemed odd to me that this girl who couldn't find work in Hollywood was constantly keeping company with the most respected actor of the century.

After Laurene suffered an appendectomy, I again tried to help her out by bringing her to New York for a cameo role in *The Ambulance.*

Naturally, she and her mother were invited when I screened the movie at the Writers Guild Theater some months later. By that time I was deeply involved with Cynthia. After the screening Laurene approached me in the aisle wondering if we were all having dinner together. I told her I'd made plans to be with Cynthia. She knew the score and she cheerfully left for home.

Not long after she and her mom arrived back at her apartment, Christian Brando pounded on the door. He had driven over from Musso & Frank's restaurant in Hollywood. His pregnant sister, Cheyenne, was waiting downstairs in the car. She had tearfully told Christian that her boyfriend Dag Drollet had been beating her up. This drove Christian into a frenzy of anger. Immediately upon entering Laurene's pad he went into the bathroom. From beneath the sink he retrieved a Colt .45 he'd stashed there without her knowledge. He left immediately and drove his sister up to Marlon's compound on Mulholland Drive. Drollet was waiting there, and minutes after Christian's arrival, a shooting took place. Marlon rushed in from the other room to find that Drollet had been shot in the head.

Christian was arrested for murder and brought to trial. Robert Shapiro successfully defended him, and he was sentenced to only six years in prison for the homicide. There is no question that had I taken Laurene and her mom out for dinner after that screening, the murder would not have taken place. No one would've been home to let young Brando in and retrieve the weapon. The tragedy did not end there. Some years later Cheyenne Brando committed suicide in Tahiti.

It occurred to me that if it hadn't been for Bette Davis, I wouldn't have met Cynthia, and, therefore, the Brando murder might never have happened. It seemed weird that Bette, who'd presented Marlon with his Oscar for *On the Waterfront*, should have had such a disastrous effect on his life simply by choosing to be in a movie. It seems as if every little action we take can have a ripple effect on so many others. It can do good or harm without ever meaning to.

Throughout the Christian Brando trial, Laurene regularly accompanied Marlon to the courthouse in downtown Los Angeles and was often photographed standing beside him. As she described it, Marlon's testimony in the case had its comedic aspects. As he rose from the spectator's section to take the stand, a button popped off his heavily stressed jacket. When he bent over to pick it up, a loud fart was heard. Moments later, he refused to take the oath because he denied the existence of God. Still, after being excused from the formality, he went on to preface many of his answers with "As God is my witness" and "So help me God."

Although she'd been questioned by the District Attorney's office, Laurene was never called as a witness during Christian's trial. It was bad enough that she'd become associated with the murder, and worse still when she was interviewed in front of the courthouse and stated lamely, "Christian is innocent." Nobody was claiming he didn't do it, except her. This was probably the final nail in the coffin of her career.

True to her gentle nature, Laurene had forgiven her mother and her siblings for absconding with her money. When her mother passed away suddenly, she fell into a deep depression. I couldn't allow her to be put into the psychiatric ward of a city hospital. Cynthia encouraged me to help her out and I paid for private care until she could regain her equilibrium. Laurene then began to focus on her father who lived in Vancouver and was suffering from cancer. She would eventually fly up there and remain with him for years, seeing him through several operations and providing him with loving support.

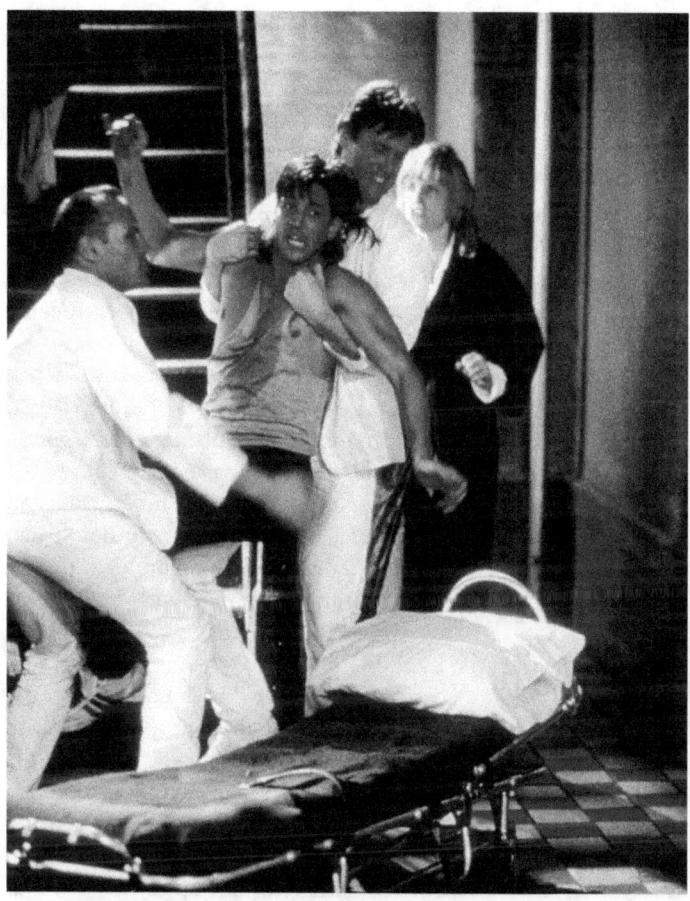

Laurene Landon's cameo alongside Eric Roberts in *The Ambulance*.

Laurene's career could have gone quite differently. Roger Ebert had raved about her performance in *Yellow Hair*, calling her "the greatest action star in movies since the original Douglas Fairbanks." He'd met her at the Cannes Film Festival, where she'd driven a stagecoach down the Croisette as a publicity stunt. He'd attended a dinner in her honor in which she publicly asked him if he was gay (which he isn't). Ebert thought her bluntness was hysterically funny and he became a huge fan. But unfortunate choices and a string of bad luck seemed to plague Laurene. Not to mention what an addiction to diet pills did to her health.

I still look back joyfully at the outrageous gags she pulled during the course of our relationship.

Once in New York we were having burgers at P.J. Clarke's when we noticed a large roach crawling up the wall beside our table. Most women might recoil from such a sight. Laurene simply flicked the roach with her forefinger, catapulting it across the restaurant. Instantly, we heard screams. The offending creature had landed on some woman's plate and guests were fleeing the table in all directions.

How can I forget the night at a New York drag show when she came on to one of the female impersonators? "I just wanted to see if I could straighten him out," she explained. Her appearance on the Johnny Carson show was a classic, particularly the moment when she scooped Dudley Moore up in her arms and ran around the stage with him. After the show Dudley began seeing Laurene, laying on her tales of his unhappy youth as a boy with a club foot who couldn't get a date with a girl. This apparently was Dudley Moore's technique with women. It didn't work with Ms. Landon.

Peter O'Toole had better luck. He'd met Laurene on the set at MGM and she invited him to our condo at the beach while I was away in New York. Before long she was giving the great actor a piggyback ride up Carbon Beach, and after his shirt became stained with tar, O'Toole left the premises wearing Laurene's fluffy pink sweater. She reported that he had been severely ill and that his lovemaking was not up to par, but that he was an awfully nice chap. Since *Lawrence of Arabia* was one of my favorite movies, I gave the relationship my blessing. Besides, she knew I had several girlfriends in New York and was equally permissive. Laurene and I seldom had to lie to one another.

But being with Laurene could get a guy into trouble. I ended up in the midst of a fist fight that nearly wrecked the Palm restaurant in Hollywood. Laurene had been flirting with a TV executive at the next table and it went too far. Eventually I slugged him, he slugged me back, tables were overturned, patrons were grabbing their steaks and fried onions and running for cover. Expensive bottles of wine shattered around us as my opponent and I wrestled one another to the floor. The waiters and busboys finally pulled us apart. My sparring partner turned out to be Leslie Moonves, shortly thereafter to become president of CBS. I got to be in a saloon fight straight out of a Western, compliments of Laurene Landon—but now I was sure to be persona non grata at CBS.

So many people in the entertainment business have only a brief taste of success—which is better than none. Many others never even get to first base. I know many talented writers and directors who've hardly worked in 20 years, not to mention performers whose careers dry up. An actress like Ronee Blakley, who was nominated for an Oscar, worked for me twice and has completely vanished. Michael Sacks (who appeared in *The Private Files of J. Edgar Hoover*) was the lead in *Slaughterhouse 5* and appeared in Spielberg's first picture, *The Sugarland Express*, but his career appears to have evaporated. Michael Moriarty's career came to a halt, probably because of his losing bout with alcohol. After time spent in recovery, he made a comeback. The truth is that the odds are heavily against survival in any creative area of show business.

Michael Moriarty in *Q*.

It's frightening to realize that even acclaimed talents like Frank Capra remained jobless for the last 30 years of his life. Likewise, Billy Wilder (whom everyone admired) found himself unfinanceable for nearly 20 years before his death. The industry even turned its back on the brilliant David Lean. Failure always seems to lie beyond success.

I suppose I should be thankful that for 45 years I've always continued to work steadily. In my case success was limited. I had a cult following and several box-office hits, but I had nothing much to live up to. I've had 36 feature films produced. Many of them are worth a second look. It'd be nice to see them finally get the attention they deserve. Whatever happens, I don't intend to see myself forcibly retired. Not ever.

Chapter 32
Terms of Endearment

I've been truly blessed by having a pair of fantastic wives. Though I'm only married to one, I still love both of them. People seem surprised when they learn that my ex-wife, Janelle, stays at our home whenever she visits California. I enjoy showing off photographs of her and Cynthia cooking Thanksgiving or Christmas dinner together. The fact is, they enjoy each other's company and often go out for lunch and shopping together.

If I couldn't get along with my producers, I certainly knew how to get along with my wives. The two women couldn't be more different from one another. Janelle is a 5-foot-3 Texas blonde who could ride and shoot and write poetry and songs. She brought five wonderful children into the world. Two of them were mine by birth, and the other three I just fell in love with. We had 17 great years of marriage, a three-year separation, and a friendly divorce. I suppose if someone told me that I could be guaranteed 17 years of happiness with any one person, I'd think that was a pretty good deal.

Janelle and I traveled everywhere, teamed up to make movies, and had homes in both Beverly Hills and New York. We lived for a year in London. That's where we almost lost Melissa when she fell off of a horse while riding in Hyde Park. We moved into the Westminster Children's Hospital for a week and held our breath while the doctors debated whether to remove Melissa's spleen. She pulled through without an operation and the ordeal only brought us closer together.

Janelle and I nearly lost our own lives in Tahiti when the outrigger canoe we were paddling was caught in a riptide and washed out to sea. I had to jump overboard with a rope tied around me and swim back to shore pulling the boat while Janelle paddled furiously. On this same ill-fated trip, a scuba diver was reloading his spear gun in the outrigger when he lost control of it. The spear sailed past my ear, parting my hair. A few inches the other way and this would have been a very short book.

Everywhere we went, Janelle and I seemed to experience some amazing adventure. In Tokyo we were adopted by a Japanese millionaire, who'd approached her in the lobby of the Imperial Hotel asking if he might touch her hair. After that he wined and dined us continually until we finally had to flee the country to get rid of him. In Bangkok, a Vietnamese Buddhist monk took us under his wing and showed us the countryside. Of course, he couldn't accept a cigarette directly from Janelle. She'd pass it to me, and I'd hand it on to the monk.

When the entire family visited Berlin, I took them through Check Point Charlie and into the Communist sector. One look at those East German guards with their submachine guns and dogs and the kids were on their best behavior all day. We'd been approached the night before in a small West Berlin café and offered a chance to make a small fortune by smuggling West German currency into the Eastern Sector. Fortunately, I turned the offer down. It turned out we were being set up and would've been arrested. It happened to other Americans in the weeks that followed.

Janelle and I were actually arrested in Moscow during a visit some years later. Instead of the usual travelogue, I had decided to make an 8mm spy thriller in and around the Kremlin. Janelle would star as an American tourist whose husband vanishes while touring the Russian capital city. I'd devised a scene where Janelle is rushing through the GUM department store searching for her missing spouse, of whom she's caught a brief glimpse.

I thought we'd get away with this under the guise of shooting a home movie, but suddenly we were surrounded by police and taken into custody. They herded us into a security office inside GUM (which actually was more like a huge multi-level mall than a department store). They wanted to know why Janelle was behaving so suspiciously. Fortunately, she was so damn charming that they released us after an hour. That was the last we shot of our spy movie.

All the way from Lapland to Nome, Alaska, Janelle was always at my side, willing to go along with anything. In my movies, she did props, wardrobe, casting—and even wrote songs. During the run of my stage plays, Janelle operated the food concessions in the lobby and made more money than the shows did. Once, flying low over the treetops of the Venezuelan jungles, Janelle prevailed upon the pilot to land on the banks of the Orinoco River, teeming with piranha fish, so that she could find somewhere to use the bathroom. Finally the pilot found a clearing and made a forced landing. I'm sure he never would have done it for anyone but Janelle. But she could be convincing.

My luck held the second time around. Cynthia is a fantastic wife, bubbling with humor and always unpredictable. She keeps me on my toes. Actress Colleen Camp (whom Bette Davis personally selected for a leading role in *Wicked Stepmother* after insulting her husband Samuel Goldwyn Jr.) recommended Cynthia for a job on the movie. She predicted I'd fall in love with this girl and marry her. You might say that if it wasn't for Bette, I wouldn't be married to Cynthia today. This marriage is the best thing that came out of that moviemaking experience.

From the first time Cynthia arrived to pick me up and drive me to Western Costume Company, I knew she was someone very special. I soon had her designing the sets and the wardrobe. Before long, she was casting many of the key supporting roles. Her original job was to drive me home after the shoot and I'd usually fall asleep en route. Though I was belted into my seat, I'd often feel her hands gently supporting my head when we came to an abrupt stop at a light. Pretty soon I asked her out, but she refused on the grounds that I was her employer. I threatened to fire her in order to get a date.

As soon as the production was finished, we began seeing each other seriously. Cynthia was not only a wonderful friend, she was also a terrific lover who was totally energized after a sexual encounter. While I'd lie in bed exhausted, I'd hear her downstairs playing Chopin selections on the grand piano.

I still had plenty of other girlfriends I felt responsible for, and it took me a long time to get free of these commitments and finally settle down with Cynthia. Her parents in Chicago were very traditional Greeks who naturally wanted her to get married. I resisted for quite a few years because I thought she only wanted marriage to placate her family. After a while, I realized I'd never find anyone better and the wedding was held in Chicago with a Greek band in attendance, of course.

When Cynthia and I visited Greece for the first time, I was still recovering from a head cold. Hoping not to become too clogged up on the flight, I took several antihistamine tablets. When we arrived in Athens, I was totally exhausted. She'd brought several suitcases full of clothes to give to relatives and I was pushing a cart so stacked up with baggage I could hardly see over it. We'd hardly gotten through Customs when several local relatives surrounded her and began chatting away happily in Greek. I found myself pushing the heavy baggage cart out of the terminal alone, expecting to see a car waiting, but the relatives hadn't brought one. There must have been 70 people queued up for taxis and the heat was intense. Suddenly I called out to Cynthia, "Something's happening…" A moment later I collapsed.

I was unconscious and happy. I saw myself walking down a country road. There was a cool breeze blowing and the trees formed a canopy overhead. I was totally at peace. After a while I woke up to see a crowd gathered around me. Apparently, they thought I'd had a heart attack. I slowly got to my feet and looked at those relatives who were staring with abject horror. I'm sure they were wondering why Cynthia had brought this dying man to her homeland. I also saw that we were a long way from getting a taxicab. The line still stretched forever. I didn't want to be there anymore. This time I didn't simply faint, I heaved first.

My last meal before boarding the airplane had been Tandoori chicken at an Indian restaurant, so you can imagine the result of my upheaval. Again I landed on the concrete in a heap. Again I was back on that idyllic country road in total serenity.

When they woke me up the second time, the crowd had parted and we were being allowed to take the next taxi. My suit was a complete mess. I don't know why the cab driver allowed me in the vehicle. Arriving at the Athens Hilton, I hid behind a potted plant while Cynthia registered. Once inside the room I took off my suit and threw it in the trashcan. We called the chambermaid and had her take it away. Minutes later, I realized all my traveler's checks were in that suit. Not without effort, we got them back.

We were to journey on to the town of Kiato, where Cynthia had dozens of relatives. I begged the few who had come to the airport and had witnessed my collapse to please keep the matter a secret. They promised they would. But when we arrived in the small seaside village on the Gulf of Corinth, half the town had come out to stare at Cynthia's new husband, who obviously didn't have much time on earth. I was already a legend—and a Greek tragedy.

Since that time we've made a number of other trips to Kiato and it's like a second home to me now. Anyplace where you can take 16 people for a huge dinner, including wine, and receive a bill for $110 (including tip), is my kind of town.

Cynthia has not only been wonderful to Janelle, she's also been a great stepmother to my kids. They call her Wickety (short for wicked stepmother, of course). With a great eye for furnishing, she's turned my home into a palace. Her skill with landscaping has transformed the property completely. I get to wake up in a beautiful place every morning next to a beautiful person. I always had trouble making new friends, but this is certainly no problem for Cynthia. She's opened up my life.

Contrary to rumor, neither of my children were the inspiration for the *It's Alive* baby.

I must admit my daughter Jill is a chip off the old block. She is positively fearless. A talented composer and singer as well as a designer of custom-made clothes, Jill is in awe of no one. Like myself, she has few inhibitions. Some years ago I took her to Paris on a trip and offered to set her up in an apartment in Montmartre. She had no connections in France but wanted to start life with a clean slate in a place where nobody knew her. There she could reinvent herself. In no time at all Jill was speaking fluent French, had several Parisian boyfriends, and was traveling around the city like a native. Then I got word that she'd injured herself during gymnastics and had landed in a Paris hospital. I immediately rushed over only to be greeted at the Charles de Gaulle Airport by Jill, looking absolutely fabulous in a large sunbonnet and seeming in perfect health. She claimed she'd escaped from the hospital and come to the airport to meet me. Whether this was all a ploy to get me over to Paris or not, we enjoyed a few fun weeks together.

We were seated at a sidewalk cafe near the Hotel Georges V when I noticed Roman Polanski strolling in our direction. I pointed him out to Jill, who immediately waved to Polanski, snapping her fingers and summoning him to our table. When he joined us, they began chattering away in French. I managed to remind Polanski that he'd been the chairmen of the jury that gave *It's Alive* a prize at Avoriaz, but his attention remained riveted on my highly animated daughter. After about 40 minutes, Polanski finally went on his way. I turned to Jill and asked, "How do you happen to know Roman Polanski?" She replied, "I didn't."

The following day she pulled virtually the same number with Jean-Paul Belmondo. At still another cafe, I noticed the international star entering with friends and called him to Jill's attention. When I turned back around, Jill was gone. Looking over my shoulder in the other direction I saw that she'd already captured the actor's rapt attention. Watching her operate was almost like watching myself in action. She had a knack of getting people to do what she wanted. As a kid she'd become quite an accomplished acrobat and when we joined a No Nukes demonstration in Washington, D.C., she did cartwheels and backflips all the way down Pennsylvania Avenue from the White House to the Capitol, a feat which she duplicated in the Macy's Parade on Thanksgiving Day in New York. As a teenager, she and her sister Melissa briefly joined New York's Big Apple Circus.

When I enrolled her at Sanford Meisner's acting retreat in the Bahamas, she not only mastered his techniques but was soon teaching it herself. She married Meisner's principal associate Martin Barter and helped him establish the Sanford Meisner Center in Burbank, where she performed in many of the early productions. Meisner was the best man at Jill's wedding, although he seemed quite wary of her, just as Bette Davis had been. Jill triggered some kind of warning system that made them back off. She's certainly been a most remarkable and entertaining child to have because she's always full of surprises. Life is never dull with my Jill nearby.

Her sister Melissa, a year her senior, is a statuesque beauty who seems to have inherited my dad's talent for photography — although with a surrealistic approach that is distinctly her own. No one Melissa photographs seems to keep their clothes on for long. Once naked, Melissa paints their bodies and then creates an environment, such as an artificial beach, bringing in colored sand. The results are astonishing. She's a true artist as well as one of my favorite traveling companions. The great thing about having two knockout daughters is that you always have a gorgeous date.

My baby sister, Ronni Chasen, grew up to be one of the most successful publicists in the motion picture industry. I'm proud to say I was her first client. When she was offered her first PR job in New York, it was predicated on her bringing in a client who'd contribute towards her weekly salary. I was nominated. When Ronni moved out to Los Angeles, I performed a similar function. Pretty soon she didn't need me as a client. She was handling some of the biggest names in the industry. I was lucky to get her back to do the publicity on *The Private Files of J. Edgar Hoover*, and she did such a fantastic job that American International invited her to come aboard as VP and Director of Publicity. She then moved on to Rogers & Cowan, one of the most respected firms in the entertainment business, where she was put in charge of the Motion Picture Division. She then headed up her own company, with a roster of clients who always seemed to bring home Oscars at the end of the year.

Ronni made a heroic effort keeping my mother alive for so many years when the doctors had given up on her. She was at the UCLA Medical Center day after day, asking all the right questions, making all the proper demands. Ronni never backed down and never allowed herself to be bullied. She got Mom the attention that was needed and certainly added many years to her life. I couldn't have done it, but she was fearless and dedicated and I'll always love her for it.

When I faced medical problems of my own, she was once again there, having taken up arms, ready to go into combat. As it turned out, I needed her. My surgery was a success, but the recovery almost killed me. Through Ronni's connections at the hospital, I received special care, which may have made all the difference. I suggested that she open a business as a patient's rep. Those entering the hospital really do need an advocate to fight their battles. Everybody needs a Ronni Chasen to look out for them.

Chapter 33
Making Waves

Some might argue that I have the knack of screwing up every opportunity that presents itself. Based on my experiences with director Sidney Lumet, I tend to believe this is true.

Lumet, with such astonishing achievements as *Network*, *12 Angry Men*, *Serpico*, *Dog Day Afternoon* and *The Verdict*, was one of my favorite filmmakers. He was the New York Director personified. His crews loved him. He worked short days and usually finished a week ahead of schedule. And the performances he got from actors were always superb.

When I heard that he was set to direct my screenplay, *Guilty as Sin*, I was elated. It was perfect casting. My initial meeting with Sidney was everything I had hoped for. He was complimentary about the script and said he would require only minimal changes. He said he'd like to rehearse the actors for at least a week and wanted me to be present and also make myself available to be on the set during the actual production.

During this meeting, in Jeffrey Katzenberg's office at Disney, it was decided to go after Paul Newman and Sean Connery for the male lead. Both of them had worked for Lumet before. The female lead was to be played by Rebecca De Mornay, who'd had an enormous success at the studio in *The Hand That Rocks the Cradle*.

The producer of the project was Martin Ransohoff, who would soon be eclipsed by Lumet. Eventually, when the picture was shot in Toronto, Mr. Ransohoff remained in Los Angeles and had no active role during the filming.

A few weeks after my first meeting with Sidney, Ransohoff and I flew to New York for additional meetings. It only took me one day to botch everything up. I had written a crucial supporting role in the film with my friend Red Buttons in mind. We had become great pals since the filming of *The Ambulance* and I'd hoped to get him a job on *Guilty as Sin*.

Lumet dismissed the idea. He intended to cast the very capable Jack Warden in the part. The only problem was that this was the typical Jack Warden role. He'd played it so many times before, often in pictures that Lumet himself had directed. Martin Ransohoff then came up with an excellent suggestion. It seemed that Jack Lemmon was between pictures and was willing to accept a good supporting role. He'd already agreed to do the part. I thought this was a marvelous idea and that it would elevate the entire production.

By this time, Newman and Connery had both turned down the lead on the grounds that they were too old to play it. We had to settle for *Miami Vice*'s Don Johnson, who was certainly adequate but not a major movie name. Lemmon would add luster to the cast, but Lumet was adamant about his decision to hire Warden. I suppose I pushed too hard.

Although the story was to take place in Chicago, Lumet filmed in Canada, both to take advantage of the currency exchange rate and to punish the New York unions who had angered and disappointed him on his last film. Despite the fact that he'd given so much work to New York crews, the guilds had made life difficult for him and he intended to teach them a lesson. Hence, Toronto.

I asked Lumet if he couldn't shoot at least a few days in Chicago—some street scenes, entrances and exits, perhaps some driving sequences, just to capture the color of the Windy City. Lumet dismissed any thought of it. I then came up with an idea for the main titles. A sweeping helicopter moving in over Lake Michigan and the city of Chicago, heading for one particular building and an open window. Then, as the camera draws closer, a woman would come tumbling out of that window and plunge out of camera range to her death. Lumet's response was, "I wouldn't know how to do a shot like that." I foolishly replied, "You don't have to shoot it yourself. A special aerial photographer can deliver the sequence." The suggestion was dismissed without further consideration.

Later, Lumet wanted to eliminate a comedic sequence at a bar where a pretty girl offers to buy Don Johnson a drink. He responds, "No thanks, but you can pay for the one I've got." Then he walks off. I objected to deleting this on the grounds that it would get a big laugh. Lumet immediately challenged me.

Don Johnson, Rebecca DeMornay and Jack Warden in *Guilty as Sin*.

"How do you know?" I told him I couldn't guarantee it, but I certainly thought it was a funny bit. After much pleading he retained the lines. It got one of the biggest laughs in the film.

Lumet had one odd request: he wouldn't shoot any scenes in a moving car. I pointed out he'd made an entire movie in a car, *Bye Bye Braverman*. He replied, "I guess that's why I hate car scenes now." Though this was clearly an arbitrary decision, I agreed to accommodate him.

When a point of logic in my script was challenged, never knowing enough to keep my mouth shut, I felt compelled to point out certain inconsistencies even in Lumet's own master-piece, *The Verdict*. One of the critical plot points in this excel-lent courtroom thriller made no sense at all. James Mason, a rival attorney, has hired Charlotte Rampling to spy on Paul Newman—an act which could have gotten Mason disbarred. Yet he paid for her services with a check bearing his own name. Any sensible person would have given her a counter check or cash. James Mason, in all his brilliance, would never have been so stupid. Conveniently, the check is found in her handbag and Newman discovers that she's been a spy. With a little thought, a much better plot device could've been devised.

Don Johnson and Rebecca DeMornay in *Guilty as Sin.*

Now, having totally alienated Lumet, I went on to bash Martin Ransohoff's hit thriller, *Jagged Edge.* Ransohoff, a brooding buddha of a man, glared at me through hooded eyes as I pointed out that in the opening sequence, the killer wears a mask to conceal his identity while his wife is tied to the bed awaiting execution and the maid lies dead on the floor nearby. There's nobody else there—so why is Jeff Bridges wearing a mask? Only for the benefit of the camera and the movie audience. And at the end of the film, after Glenn Close has discovered his identity as the killer, Bridges once again dons the mask when he comes to silence her. Since she already knows of his guilt, why the mask?

Now that I had done sufficient damage to both of my colleagues' egos, I came up with another brilliant proposal. The role of the judge was an important one and I had an innovative casting idea. Directors like John Huston had performed as well as the actors in their films. I knew there was a brilliant talent living in New York doing nothing at the time who'd had tremendous experience as an actor before he gave it up to direct. Why not offer Elia Kazan the part? Lumet pondered this for a moment, then smiled, "Gadge is one of my dearest friends. I wouldn't want to embarrass him."

I never understood what that meant. I suppose it meant to shut me up.

The script changes Lumet indicated were easy enough to accomplish within a few days. Cynthia and I returned to Los Angeles, where I eventually received a revised script. It appeared that Lumet had been tinkering with bits of dialogue himself. Oddly enough he had told me, "I can't write. The only thing I can write is cops." Yet he was monkeying around with the lines and, in some cases, the speeches were becoming awkward and confusing.

I thought I could smooth them out and clarify the ideas Lumet was attempting to express. I corrected this version of the script, putting notes in the margin for Ransohoff's attention only. I scribbled "badly structured dialogue" or "this line doesn't make any sense." Little did I realize that Ransohoff would deliberately forward a copy of my notes directly to Lumet. I certainly would not have been as brutal in my commentary had I thought the director would be seeing them. I believe Ransohoff did this deliberately to widen the rift between myself and Sidney. And he certainly succeeded.

All communication with Lumet instantly ceased. No longer would I be invited to rehearsals or to join the company in Toronto for the actual filming. Like Ransohoff, I was completely excluded. Maybe that's why Ransohoff did it. If he couldn't go, why should I?

Meanwhile, Sidney Lumet's most recent film, *A Stranger Among Us* was released to miserable reviews. The box-office returns were minimal. The film, which inexplicably cast Melanie Griffith as a New York detective working undercover in the Hasidic community in Brooklyn, was being ridiculed and dubbed "A Shiksha Among Us." Actually, none of Lumet's films since *The Verdict* had been at all successful at the box office.

Shooting began and the executives at Disney were unusually generous and invited me to attend the dailies. I accepted their invitation only once. I brought Jim Dixon with me, and we couldn't have been more disappointed. The coverage looked like something from a television series. There was virtually no choice of angles and no camera movement. When the lights came up, I waited for the Disney executives to make some negative comment, but they all happily left the screening room without a word. I never came back.

Eventually, many associated with the film would announce their displeasure, including Rebecca De Mornay, who nicknamed the film "Guilty as Sidney." The news filtering back from Toronto was that Lumet was wrapping up early every day, which wasn't difficult since he only went for a limited number of camera set-ups. The World Series was on, and Lumet was a great baseball fan. It seemed the games interested him far more than the film. I tried several times to phone him during the course of production but he never accepted my calls.

Some months later *Guilty as Sin* was previewed in Burbank. Cynthia and I attended. I was gratified to see that Michael Eisner, Chairman of Disney, was present, as was Jeffrey Katzenberg. Lumet and his editor had flown out from New York. I tried to engage him in pleasant conversation, which he tolerated, but I felt he was anxious to get away from me.

The picture was not a disaster. The narrative was strong enough to carry it along, even with the diminished production values. There was a love scene between De Mornay and Johnson that had been embarrassingly staged and needed to be cut, which it eventually was.

Don Johnson was excellent in a role not too far removed from his own persona—that of a handsome but shallow individual who thinks he's irresistible to women. De Mornay was good in her usual tough cookie mode, even if she didn't walk

Don Johnson with Sidney Lumet on the set of *Guilty as Sin*.

well in high heels. Cynthia kept complaining about the cheap shoes Rebecca was wearing and how awkwardly she moved in them. I thought some of the sets were abysmal. The bedroom of a rich woman's apartment looked more like a crappy mini suite at the Holiday Inn.

After the lights came up, we all gathered in the lobby to critique the film. Michael Eisner offered us the benefit of his expertise.

Eisner is generally accepted as a genius in the industry, so I expected some cogent notes. What I got was the lame suggestion that De Mornay should trap Johnson by hiding a tape recorder in her pocket and recording his confession. This notion was entirely flat and undramatic, certainly inferior to what we already had. As Eisner stood in the theater lobby expounding on this notion, Katzenberg was standing directly behind him, out of his view, rolling his eyes to the ceiling and making faces, clearly ridiculing Eisner's every word. I couldn't believe this top executive was acting like some high school kid. The rest of us facing Eisner couldn't ignore Katzenberg's grimaces. Finally, after Eisner departed, Katzenberg began referring to "the Eisner ending," making a total mockery of it. It was evident that the longstanding relationship between these two was wearing thin.

Maybe Eisner was a corporate genius, but story wasn't one of his strong points.

As was the policy at Disney, there were always re-shoots after a preview. Some of my suggestions were taken into account, others weren't. The picture that opened wasn't much different from what was previewed, but the reactions were better than I expected. Michael Wilmington's review in the *Los Angeles Times* was a rave and even Janet Maslin of the *New York Times* had some nice things to say. *The Nation* called the film "A fine bookend to *12 Angry Men* and *The Verdict*."

Guilty as Sin went on to become Lumet's most successful picture at the box office in ten years. It later became one of America's most profitable home video rentals and it's constantly played on cable and television. The Disney executives said they were extremely pleased with its reception. I knew it could have been a lot better.

This script led to my being assigned numerous other projects at Disney and brought me over a million dollars in additional fees. None of the other scripts ever got made.

I was soon back in the small time, accepting offers from director Mark L. Lester to adapt two novels, *The Ex* and *Misbegotten*, both of which were immediately filmed and went straight to cable. Mark wasn't much of a director and the scripts barely survived their treatment, but at least something was actually getting produced. I also not only penned *Maniac Cop* but also a *Maniac Cop* sequel for $250,000—a fact that I've tried hard to keep quiet.

It was then that Fred Williamson resurfaced in my life. We'd remained friends over the years, and he'd attended my marriage to Cynthia in Chicago. Fred and his wife, Linda, were producing a reunion film which would bring together all of the great Blaxploitation stars of the Seventies. It would eventually be called *Original Gangstas* and feature Pam Grier, Jim Brown, Richard Roundtree, Ron O'Neil and Paul Winfield. I was asked to rewrite the script and direct.

At first, I wondered if it was prudent for me to be directing the picture. After all, there were now plenty of black directors around. Why shouldn't one of them get the job? Fred

YOU HAVE THE RIGHT TO REMAIN SILENT...
FOREVER.
MANIAC COP
GLICKENHAUS FILMS, INC. LARRY COHEN WILLIAM LUSTIG "MANIAC COP"
TOM ATKINS • BRUCE CAMPBELL • LAURENE LANDON • RICHARD ROUNDTREE
WILLIAM SMITH • ROBERT Z'DAR SHEREE NORTH JAY CHATTAWAY
JEF RICHARD JAMES GLICKENHAUS LARRY COHEN WILLIAM LUSTIG
RECORDED IN
ULTRA•STEREO

countered, "Yeah, but I just don't like taking orders from black people." I couldn't think of an answer to that one.

I never actually believed Fred could raise the money to make the film. His independent projects had usually cost under half a million and this was a $3.5 million budget. In preparation, he took me to Gary, Indiana, the gang capital of the U.S. There were more per capita murders there than anyplace else in the country. Fred had grown up in Gary and his mother still lived there. He couldn't persuade her to leave her original home.

Fred's plan was to hire local gang members to work on the picture. I wasn't as worried about the ones we'd hire as the ones that we'd reject. Somebody might show up with an automatic rifle to express their dissatisfaction. Subconsciously I was hoping the money wouldn't come through, but when it did, I couldn't back out and leave Fred in the lurch. The financing seemed to be dependent upon my participation.

So off we went to Gary in the heat of summer. The temperatures rose to almost 110 degrees and sometimes even hotter inside buildings that had never seen air conditioning. Fred wouldn't spend the money to bring in cooling units and both Paul Winfield and Isabel Sanford ended up on oxygen. We cast well over a hundred gang kids to appear in *Original Gangstas*, and, amazingly, they all showed up on time and did their jobs with enthusiasm. Before our arrival, there were no sources of employment in Gary and there wasn't even a bank where a check could be cashed. During the weeks we were there, crime dropped to a new low. Everyone was working for us.

These homeboys would regularly show up at my trailer with bags of Famous Amos cookies, for which they knew I had a weakness. They took my direction without hesitation and gave a hundred percent. It was a tough shoot, which included the destruction of an entire city block. Fred had gotten permission to blow up a residential street lined with abandoned homes. They were dressed by the art department to look occupied, then they were rigged with explosives—perhaps too heavily. When I shouted action, the place went up like Nagasaki, and all of us watching from blocks away got sunburned. The stuntmen were actually propelled through the air by the force of the blast—no catapults were necessary. By some miracle, nobody got hurt.

Jim Brown taking care of business in *Original Gangstas.*

Despite such spectacular sequences I was bringing the picture in on budget, but I had always intended to spend the contingency money. Had this been left over, Fred would have pocketed it. Now that it was going up on screen, he wasn't at all happy. We weren't friends anymore. In the past he'd been working for me, now I was his employee—and he treated me like one.

Robert Forster and Frank Pesce in *Original Gangstas.*

The climax of the movie would bring all the stars together marching down the street like *The Magnificent Seven*, wreaking havoc on the bad guys. The only problem was that Jim Brown wouldn't be there. Fred hadn't told me that Jim was leaving, and I had no idea until he called my room to say goodbye. His contract was up. I begged him to stay on, but he had a commitment to appear at a political rally in New Jersey. I said "Suppose we hire a private jet and fly you there and then bring you straight back? Will you give me enough time to shoot the final sequence with you in it?"

Jim reluctantly agreed but limited me to three hours. Now I had to get Williamson to foot the bill for a private jet—another big dent in his contingency money. We finally did get Jim Brown back—just for 180 precious minutes—and I managed to get most of the coverage I needed. Under normal conditions I could've done so much more.

To demonstrate what I was up against, one day we filmed a drive-by shooting. The next day when we did additional coverage of the same sequence, I noticed that the gunman was firing from a different car. Fred had gotten in an argument with the owner of the original vehicle and had substituted another car that didn't match. I stopped production and insisted he go back and secure the proper car no matter what it cost. He glared at me—but he did it.

Every morning I'd sit in my trailer and rewrite the day's work to accommodate the missing props or unavoidable changes of location. Though we needed at least ten professional stuntmen, we had only four—which meant having to use the same guys over and over in different disguises, doing my best to hide their faces. Pretty soon I had gang members doing their own stunts. Despite weeks of preparation, nothing came off as planned. But in the midst of the chaos, I was in my element again and doing some of my best work.

Orion Pictures would be distributing the film, and several executives flew into Gary and began to pester me endlessly, following me around the set and eavesdropping on my every word. I finally kicked them off, knowing it was too late to fire me. I think they were worried that if they did, the gang would come after them before they could get out of town. Several of

Original Gangstas.

the kids did offer to rough the executives up or kidnap them, but I talked them out of it.

When we finally wrapped up it was time to say goodbye to these kids. They were really sorry to see us go. For five weeks they'd had a reason to get up in the morning. Now we were finished and were headed back to Hollywood, but they were staying in Gary with little chance of ever escaping. No jobs. No hope. They were trapped in a decaying community without skills, without education. They quickly returned to the only thing they knew: crime.

Within three weeks of our departure, the Indiana National Guard had to be called in to quell the resurgence of violence. I don't know how many of them ever actually saw the movie, as there was no theater in Gary. Maybe they caught up with it on television or video. Some of them are probably dead by now, either from bullets or from the drugs that permeated the community. We went there, we used them, and we left them behind. I don't feel very good about that, but I couldn't think of any solution, either. It had crossed my mind to bring some of them back to Hollywood and use them to intimidate the film community. With them I could've taken over the town. They would've eliminated anyone I asked them to. This sounds more like an idea for a Larry Cohen movie than reality.

Larry Cohen directing *Original Gangstas* in Gary, Indiana.

The picture turned out much better than either Fred or I imagined. The *New York Post* critic said it was "the best time I've had at the movies this year." Even *The New York Times* commented that it had important things to say. Orion had set the release date, but then moved it back two weeks so as not to open against another black film. Unfortunately the release of *Twister* was unexpectedly moved up by several weeks and we landed on the same date. *Twister* became the biggest opening of the year and *Original Gangstas* was overwhelmed. We had the second largest per-theater average, but we couldn't compete with a highly advertised blockbuster. Once again it was a distribution problem. And Orion didn't care to spend money to buy ads trumpeting our excellent reviews. They didn't consider it a review movie. Still, *Original Gangstas* was the sixth highest grossing independent movie of the year.

Now that it's long over, I'm glad I directed *Original Gangstas*. I enjoyed the people of Gary and eventually Fred and I patched up our differences. He and Linda worked their asses off to get this movie made and it was all Fred's idea. He found the locations and cast all of the roles. I suppose I'd work for him again, and I'm sure that just as before, we wouldn't get along. But we'd still make a hell of a film.

One of the most pleasant days of filming *Original Gangstas* was when Cynthia's mom and dad visited the set. They lived in Chicago, but her father had actually worked in the steel mills in Gary throughout World War II. In those days the mills operated 24 hours a day as part of the war effort. George Costas took every bit of overtime he could handle and saved every nickel he earned. The day the war ended he quit and bought a grocery store in Chicago. A few years later, he expanded to a large supermarket in Lincoln Park. He raised a large family and earned millions of dollars in the stock market. I actually wrote his story into the movie—that of a former steel mill worker who'd purchased a local grocery which is harassed by gang members.

I know Cynthia's parents had a wonderful day on location with us. I actually put her mother into a crowd scene only to have the Orion executives raise hell and demand that I re-shoot the sequence because a white woman appeared in a crowd of black people. Under pressure I finally cut Mrs. Costas out, but her picture appears prominently on the jacket of the Australian video release. So we had the last laugh.

Once again, the motion picture industry had undergone change. The advent of home video had given distributors an opportunity to recoup their investment without putting their movies into theatrical distribution. The cost of opening a movie had become phenomenally expensive. If you didn't have at least $10 to $15 million to promote your picture, you had virtually no chance at achieving any sizable box-office return. It was like a poker game. The major studios spent so much money on double-truck color ads and TV spots that the independents were outspent. The stakes had been raised so high that the smaller players had to cash in and walk away from the table. Once upon a time, distributors had no choice but to go for a theatrical release. There was no alternative. At least your movie got a shot at attracting customers. But those days were gone forever.

Being labeled "Straight to Video" was like having a curse placed on your film. Even if you had a good movie that was well reviewed, the stigma remained.

To me, having your movie premiere on home video was no worse than having your book published as a paperback. In the publishing world, hardcover books seldom showed a profit, while paperbacks did quite well. I didn't care how or where the audience saw my movie, as long as they had the opportunity to enjoy it.

Naturally, since I'd had a few theatrical hits, I always enjoyed visiting the theaters and seeing people lined up around the block waiting to get in. A video release didn't provide you with that pleasure, or the thrill of seeing your film in a packed house and hearing the crowd laugh or scream on cue.

Chapter 34
Three Leading Ladies

The most important thing was that I could go on making pictures, so when the USA cable network offered me a chance to write, produce and direct a thriller of my choice, I accepted the opportunity with enthusiasm. *As Good as Dead* was an excellent film noir vehicle. I set about casting it in the Century City offices of Wilshire Court Productions.

One of the young starlets who showed up to read for a role immediately caught my attention. I thought she was unusually photogenic. She turned out to be former porno star Traci Lords, who had scandalized the skin-flick industry when it was revealed that she was only 15 at the time of her screen debut. All of her pictures were withdrawn from circulation under the threat of prosecution. Now Traci was trying to make it as a legitimate actress.

Since she gave a much better reading than any of the other applicants, I wanted to offer her the job. My executive producers had other ideas. "She's been up here four or five times before, reading for parts. She's always good, but obviously we can't hire her."

This immediately irritated me. "You mean you keep bringing this poor girl back to audition with no intention of ever giving her a chance?"

After they explained that having Traci Lords headlining a show would be an embarrassment, I calmly informed them that I was exercising my prerogative to hire her on the spot, whether they liked it or not. I suppose they could have vetoed my decision, but I think they were afraid I might go public.

Traci Lords proved to be an excellent actress as well as a very poised and intelligent young woman. Every once in a while, some jerk would show up on set and attempt to meet Traci and tell her what a fan he was of her pornos, but I would always intervene and shoo the unwelcome admirers away. Traci was appreciative of my protectiveness, and we had many enjoyable

Traci Lords in *As Good As Dead*.

lunches and dinners together. But no romance. Cynthia and I were due to be married in a few weeks and I didn't want to screw it up.

Traci had a break of about a week between scenes and I was disappointed when she told me that she was leaving and would return later. Someone was making her feel extremely uncomfortable. Another of the actresses in the film had made a pass at her and wasn't taking no for an answer. Tracy was embarrassed by the situation and felt it would be best to vanish for a while.

Oddly enough, Traci's female admirer was outwardly a very proper young lady. She'd been working her way through the crew ever since we began production and was now obsessed with seducing Traci. Soon after Traci departed, she began coming on to me, but I strenuously avoided any involvement. When Cynthia visited the set, she would jump on my lap and cuddle up to me in an attempt to foment trouble. Cynthia was sharp enough to sense what was going on and kept a sense of humor about it.

Traci returned on schedule and completed her part. I'm afraid her reputation has kept her from getting the kind of roles she deserves. It's sad because she has an extraordinary presence in front of the camera, and she happens to be a very nice person.

One of the most interesting directorial challenges I faced was during the production of *Perfect Strangers*, aka *Blind Alley* as it was titled for release overseas. My principal actor, Matthew Stockley, was only two years old. He was still unable to speak—which was the whole point of the story. In this thriller a small child witnesses a murder. The assassin is unsure whether the little boy can identify him. He's reluctant to kill the child unless it's absolutely necessary. In order to determine if he's in danger of exposure, the killer strikes up an acquaintance with the child's mother and begins hanging around the kid, watching him carefully for some reaction.

Needless to say it was a demanding part. I knew what I was getting into when I wrote it. The question now was how to manipulate any two-year-old into actually performing the role. Matthew's parents accompanied him on the set at all times and

Matthew Stockley and Brad Rijn in *Perfect Strangers*.

he was extremely well behaved. Although he never uttered a word, I could see that he was interested in what was happening. I decided to direct him as I would any other actor.

Before each scene I sat him down and told him exactly what I wanted him to do. He showed no response, but when the cameras rolled, he invariably followed instructions to the letter. If he were to walk from the living room into the kitchen, I would position one of his parents in a hiding place close by his final destination. They'd call his name, and he would follow their voice. But sometimes there were nuances to the performance that defied logic. He gave me all the looks, pauses and reactions I needed. I don't believe anyone has ever directed a non-speaking child in such a complex role. Matthew always kept his focus on the other actors and when he was required to be afraid, he was convincing.

The role of the mother was portrayed by Anne Carlisle, whom I'd seen give an astonishing performance in a film called *Liquid Sky*, in which she played both the leading man and the leading lady. In one astonishing sequence she actually made love to herself. I thought she'd be perfect for the feminist activist who falls prey to the seductions of the professional hitman. She gave an excellent performance and displayed many of the

Anne Carlisle and Brad Rijn in *Perfect Strangers.*

qualities of a young Katharine Hepburn. The only problem was that there was a passionate love scene to be played naked in bed. Anne was openly gay, and her girlfriend accompanied her regularly to the set. Apparently, Anne's partner was extremely upset about the prospect of seeing her in bed with a man. When it came time to shoot the sequence I had to resort to an age-old directorial technique. Get the actor drunk. It took nearly an entire bottle of brandy to loosen Anne up enough to hop into the sack. Once she'd relaxed, she really got into the swing of things. Her girlfriend, however, became furious and stalked off the set. It took a while for them to reconcile.

Any movie set can be a dangerous place to work. Accidents do happen. Having a two-year-old child running around was nerve-wracking, to say the least. I instructed the boy's parents to keep him in sight at all times. Then one day in a Manhattan apartment I noticed them chatting together in a corner, while I could see no sign of Matthew. I rushed down the long hallway looking into each of the bedrooms. One of the doors was wide open. Lights had been placed inside to cast shadows on the opposite wall. As I caught sight of Matthew he was yanking on one of the cables and a light was tipping on its stand and about to topple directly onto him. It was red hot, and an instant later the child would have been badly burned. Fortunately I was able to catch the metal stand and prevent a disaster without burning my own hands. It would have been a tragedy and my arriving at that crucial moment certainly reinforced my faith in God.

Months after the filming was completed, I had a special screening of the picture for the Stockley family. I'd set up a video camera to record Matthew's reaction to his own performance. What would he think when he saw himself up there on the screen? The experiment proved a failure. He watched silently, demonstrating no form of recognition.

I filmed *Perfect Strangers* back-to-back with another low-budget picture also financed by Hemdale. This second film was entitled *Special Effects*, and I went out of my way to make sure there wasn't a single special effect in the entire picture, not even a fade or a dissolve. It was the story of a noted filmmaker on the decline who, after a series of huge flops, cannot get arrested. In a fit of anger and frustration he murders an aspiring young actress, and her death is inadvertently recorded by a movie camera hidden in his bedroom. The director decides to make a comeback movie about the murder and use the actual footage of the homicide intercut with fictional footage to blur the line between fantasy and reality.

The dual role of the murder victim and her look-alike was played by Zoë Tamerlis, who had gained renown as the star of Abel Ferrara's *Ms. 45*. Zoë certainly was a strange girl. Through the entire production we never had a home telephone number or an address for her. She would simply call in and be informed of the location and of the time she was expected to arrive. This kind of behavior is usually considered intolerable. The production staff needs to know where they can locate an actor at all times in case there are any last-minute changes. They came to me with their complaints. I asked them if she'd ever been late, and when they replied said no, I suggested that they simply leave her alone.

One day several crew members tried to follow Zoë to see where she lived. Apparently, she spotted the tail and changed taxi cabs to elude them. Each day she arrived toting an enormous

Zoë Tamerlis in *Special Effects.*

bag that she told me contained a screenplay she was working on. It was the only copy. I asked her why she didn't have some duplicates made and she replied that she didn't trust the employees at the Xerox stores. Someone might try to steal her script. The bag must have weighed a ton, and the script looked like it ran some 400 pages. Years later Zoë wrote the screenplay for *Bad Lieutenant*, which was also directed by Ferrara, and starred Harvey Keitel. It received sensational reviews. Zoë was one of the strangest young women I've ever met and yet there was a sweetness, an innocence, about her. She died in Paris, still in her thirties, long a victim of drug addiction.

For one scene in *Special Effects*, I needed 8mm home movie footage of a small farm in Texas. I immediately thought of Janelle's parents. I knew they had a camera, so I asked them to shoot some footage featuring a small child playing in front of a farmhouse. Grandpa and Grandma Webb became my second unit crew and the footage they sent was duly incorporated into the finished picture. They're both gone now and so is the farm, but every time I yearn for a nostalgic look, all I have to do is run *Special Effects*. George and Detta Webb were two of the kindest

SPECIAL EFFECTS

HEMDALE FILM CORPORATION
Presents
A LARRY COHEN FILM
"SPECIAL EFFECTS"
Starring ZOE TAMARLIS ERIC BOGOSIAN BRAD RIJN
and KEVIN O'CONNOR
Director of Photography PAUL GLICKMAN Edited by ARMOND LEBOWITZ
Associate Producer BARRY SHILS Music by MICHAEL MINARD
Executive Producer CARTER DeHAVEN
Produced by PAUL KURTA
Written and Directed by LARRY COHEN

and most loving people I've ever known. They continued to care about me even after my divorce from Janelle. I thought of them as mom and dad and always will.

Back in New York, I was polishing off *Special Effects*, adding a few more flourishes. Thanks to my friend Vincent Sardi, I was able to shoot a sequence in his famous theatrical restaurant. This was located at the heart of Teamsters territory. I thought we'd certainly be busted, but once again my luck held. Another non-union production showed up just across the street and was mistaken for us. They were closed down while we continued to film uninterrupted.

On that day I suffered a massive toothache and was fortunate to find a dentist who was also a movie fan. I continued to direct the picture while he worked over me on the set, removing a filling and applying a temporary. Though I've often worked in intense cold and in punishing rainstorms, I've never gotten sick during the production of a movie. As the temperature would drop, I would strip off my jacket and work in my shirtsleeves, much to the amazement of the crew, who were bundled up like Eskimos and complaining about the weather.

But immediately upon completing filming, I would inevitably collapse and be sick for a week. It's certainly proof that the human mind plays a decisive role in surrendering to illness. I was able to will myself to remain healthy as long as necessary.

How else can I explain my ability to stay on my feet for 18 hours a day, six days a week, for more than a month? I never felt better than when I was filming and never in more total control. For those who suffered under my manic behavior, I hereby tender my apology. I couldn't help myself. Of course, that's no excuse, but it's the best I can offer.

Chapter 35
Tricks of the Trade, Part 2

Everyone that knows me is curious about my aversion to driving an automobile. Not driving has actually brought me a great deal of good luck. I would never have met Cynthia had she not been hired to be my driver on the production of *Wicked Stepmother*. Many years before I talked Janelle into quitting her job at the restaurant in order to drive me around. After Janelle briefly put me behind the wheel, she soon gave up on any thought of honing my skills. Perhaps I deliberately drove badly to convince her. It was only an excuse to have her around, but it seemed logical to her that I needed someone to take me to pitch meetings.

All the time I was dating, girls would have to drive me home, and usually they'd be too tired to make the long journey back to their own pad, so they'd spend the night. Fortunately, none of the women I've known ever complained about having to drive. It gave them the freedom to come and go as they pleased, rather than be dependent upon the man to take them someplace. After my marriage, when we had five children running around the house, there was always some routine errand that needed doing. If I'd had a driver's license, I rapidly would have evolved into a full-time chauffeur. As it was, no one ever asked me to pick up anyone or to drop them off. I could spend all my time writing my scripts.

The fact is I'm constantly preoccupied with stories and my concentration is so deep I fail to focus on what's happening around me. Not a particularly good condition to be in if you're traveling at 65 miles per hour on a freeway. I must credit my relaxed nature and my youthful appearance to the fact that I've avoided the hazards of traffic. Being a New Yorker at heart, I still love taxis. In Manhattan I'm in and out of cabs all day. Of course, in Los Angeles, where everyone drives, I seem eccentric. Yet the pedestrians club boasts some distinguished members. There's author Ray Bradbury, director Joe Dante, and actor Michael Caine, among other fellow weirdos.

As a teenager I did have a learner's permit, but I failed the driving test because I used only one hand on the steering wheel. I never took the exam again. Of course, I have driven the car in emergencies but had to concentrate so much that it wasn't an enjoyable experience. Maybe my reluctance to drive stems from the recollection of how miserable my father was behind the wheel, cursing at other drivers and belittling them.

At this particular time in my life I have also developed an aversion to cellular phones, and avoid carrying one. I enjoy being unable to be reached. It's bad enough to come home and find all the messages awaiting you on the answering machine. The ideal answering machine would be one which collects all your messages and then erases them just before 6 pm so you have no calls to return.

I'm constantly asked what kind of computer I use. The answer is: none. If I ever hit the keys of a computer with the force that I employ on my Royal Standard typewriter I would smash the equipment the first day. Besides, I don't like to look at a printout of what I'm writing until I'm completely finished, and then I usually wait until the following day. I can't go back and correct while I'm writing because it breaks the rhythm. Once the characters begin speaking for themselves, I have to forge on.

To me, the simplest and most effective method of writing is longhand. Nothing beats pen and paper. I feel the dialogue running down my arm through the pen onto the page. My handwritten scripts are more concise and more fun to read. I tend to dispense with a preponderance of descriptive passages and tell the story through the dialogue. Since I can afford to have a secretary type the material up, I simply ship off the pages to Barbara Nelson and await their return. Reading over the manuscript, it's often like I've never seen it before. Once again, my subconscious has done the work for me.

Many years ago after cutting my hand and having it bandaged, I found it necessary to dictate. At the time I was writing virtually all the episodes for my *Blue Light* spy series for 20th Century Fox. The studio assigned me a team of secretaries and I would dictate a half-hour show each day, Act I in the morning, Act II in the afternoon. When the first secretary adjourned to do the typing, her alternate would take over. I found it enjoyable to perform all the parts aloud and the secretaries provided a good audience. Eventually I wore them both out and resorted to a tape recorder.

I would record the scripts like radio programs, playing all the roles, both male and female. I got to act the parts before any of the actors. When in New York, I'd often adjourn to Central Park where on a beautiful day I'd walk countless miles babbling into the handheld recorder. I've written at least a half dozen screenplays in the park while getting plenty of exercise. I found walking made the dictation even more pleasurable—it raised the level of nervous energy. People often stopped to stare at me as I ambled along talking to myself and apparently making faces. I never noticed anyone. Fortunately traffic is restricted in Central Park, or I certainly would have been run over.

I thoroughly enjoy the writing process. For others it's torture. I find it more difficult if the story is completely worked out. I love to create a premise and improvise on it, not knowing where the journey will take me. The characters begin to go off in their own direction as I struggle to keep up with them. I can't

Directing James Earl Jones in *The Ambulance.*

wait to get back to work the next day because I want to find out what will happen next. I become like a court stenographer taking down a transcript. Months later when I look over the material again, it's not uncommon that I can't recall the circumstances under which it was written. I forget where I was at the time. It's all a blank.

The same immersion in my work occurs when I'm directing. I've had friends remind me that they visited me on the set at a specific location and spent the entire day at my side. But I have no memory of their presence. My focus was entirely on the work. I could be cordial and even humorous, but I retained nothing of the experience.

In 2000, Paul Schrader, Peter Bogdanovich and I appeared at a symposium in New York to discuss screenwriting. I explained my modus operandi in detail:

> 1. Don't talk about your screenplay. Keep it bottled up inside of you. The more you talk about it, the less chance you'll write it.

> 2. You don't need to know what's going to happen next. It's perfectly alright to begin without knowing the ending. If you're lucky, the characters will assume control and start speaking for themselves.

> 3. Let your subconscious do most of the work for you.

When it was Paul Schrader's turn, he declared, "I couldn't disagree more with everything that Larry said. My method is just the opposite. When I have an idea, I tell it to anyone that will listen. I keep telling it, and if I get tired of it, I don't write it. If after all the telling I'm still interested, then I sit down and put it on paper."

Who am I to argue with the man who wrote *Taxi Driver* and *Raging Bull*?

Schrader then continued, "Sometimes I gather a large group in the living room, and I begin the story. Then, at a crucial moment, I just get up and go to the bathroom and leave them hanging."

I couldn't pass up the opportunity. "Paul, what do you do if you come out of the bathroom, and they've all left?"

Everyone in the auditorium roared with laughter—except Schrader. Maybe it actually happened to him.

The above just proves that everyone has their own way of working. Who cares, as long as it's good?

Chapter 36
The World's Smallest Movie

Nothing could have prepared me for the response that awaited my screenplay *Phone Booth*. For 25 years I had struggled to construct a movie that would take place entirely inside a solitary telephone booth. There were to be no flashbacks, no cutaways, no coverage of anyone other than the man in the booth. Everything had to be seen from his point of view.

He would enter the booth at the beginning of the film and not emerge until the end. In order to maintain the audience's interest, the story would require twists and turns to continually add new surprises. I had to come up with every possible variation on the theme.

I'd actually conceived this idea during my lunch meeting with Alfred Hitchcock at Universal. It seemed the perfect Hitchcock project. After all, he'd made a movie entirely in a lifeboat and perhaps his most enduring classic confined Jimmy Stewart to a wheelchair peering out into a courtyard of windows in *Rear Window*.

I knew he'd go for the idea, but neither of us could figure out how to flesh it out into a feature. Hitch sent me off to solve the puzzle. When I ran into him at the Hilton Hotel party after the *Frenzy* premiere, he asked, "How are you coming along on our phone booth movie?"

Long after I'd finally figured out the characters and plot and sold the script, I attended a Directors Guild event commemorating the issuance of an Alfred Hitchcock postage stamp. That night the director's daughter, Patricia Hitchcock O'Connell, made a few remarks on stage. She mentioned several projects her dad had always wanted to make—one of which, she said, was to take place entirely inside a telephone booth. Hitch had never forgotten my notion. It had been on his mind for years. I wish he'd still been around when I finally solved the puzzle.

Once I did, it took me only a week to write the script.

Almost immediately there was excitement within the industry such as I'd never experienced before. Jason Hoffs, the development head at DreamWorks, proclaimed *Phone Booth* the best script he'd ever read. Unfortunately his superiors didn't agree. But Jason had taken the script home and his wife, agent Jessica Tuchinsky, had read it and agreed that it was an extraordinary piece of work. Her agency, CAA, offered to package it. I retained Peter Sabiston as my manager and signed with Creative Artists. Soon everybody in town was reading *Phone Booth* and asking to meet me. I was the new kid on the block all over again.

Eventually, after it had been sold elsewhere, Steven Spielberg finally came across *Phone Booth* and briefly expressed interest in directing. When we met at an Oscar night party, he personally told me, "If Alfred Hitchcock were alive, he'd want to direct *Phone Booth*." Hearing that was reward enough for writing it. Nothing could ever top that moment.

CAA had brought in David Zucker and Gil Netter, their own clients, to produce the film after 20th Century Fox made a sizable offer. (Fox Chief Bill Mechanic told me, "The only contribution the Zucker and Netter made to this project was as messengers. They walked your script down the hall. For that they got a production deal.")

At that time, Joel Schumacher was ready to direct with Nicolas Cage starring. But soon after Fox finalized the deal, they began to think they might do better. Apparently, Mel Gibson showed interest in both starring and directing. Only Mel had a few creative ideas of his own.

After congratulating me on what a perfect script I'd written, Fox President Tom Rothman informed me that Mel wanted to change the principal character from a publicist to a lawyer. This would have meant a complete rewrite. Besides, I thought asshole lawyers had become a cliché. A hungry and desperate publicist on the make was far fresher. Rothman said he agreed, but added, "Let me play the devil's advocate." He attempted to justify Mel's suggestion. Neither of my CAA-appointed producers came to the defense of the original material, so I was odd man out. Finally, an appointment was made for me to meet with Mel and discuss changes. Our initial encounter occurred at the very private Cigar Club on Canon Drive to which I was accompanied by Elizabeth Gabler, an important Fox executive.

Mel didn't get up when I approached his table, but he was cordial, if a bit cautious. He kept studying me like I was from another planet. I tried to allay his suspicions—I didn't want this to become an adversarial relationship. But when he mentioned changing the character to an attorney, I quickly responded that it wasn't a good idea.

I noticed Elizabeth's mouth hanging open. Here I was telling the biggest name in Hollywood that he was wrong. Mel registered some surprise himself. Naturally, true to form, I'd already found a way to alienate my potential star.

Still, Mel invited me to join him at his office at Warner Bros. later in the week. We would spend the entire first day together kicking the story around. I think the fact that our relationship was one of give and take stimulated him. He was way too smart to want a yes man around.

When I arrived at Mel's ground-floor office near the backlot at Warners, I found him to be fully prepared. He'd sent a scout to the street corner in New York where the story was to take place. Wide angle photos had been taken from every direction and they were strung together so that there was a 360-degree view of the entire neighborhood. He'd also engaged a communications expert from the LAPD to join us to discuss the police procedures which were described in the script and to offer technical advice. It seemed like Mel was ready to go into production.

Still, he had problems about the leading character being a victim rather than a hero. The protagonist was confined to a telephone booth for the duration of the film, unable to hang up because his tormentor held him in the crosshairs of a telescopic rifle. If he dared terminate the conversation, he would die. When a street thug tries to drag Mel's character out of the booth, he is instantly gunned down. Mel is blamed for the killing and the police arrive, close down the street, and surround the booth from a distance. Our small-time publicist rapidly becomes the most famous man in the city as news coverage begins to focus on him in the booth. How he outwits his tormentor and turns the tables on him provides twists and turns that never lets the audience catch its breath.

Mel had some interesting ideas for added beats to the story. I told him, "Your suggestions are good. I'm going to use them whether you act in this picture or not," to which he was immediately agreeable.

We had a long and productive second meeting during which he never once mentioned changing the principal character to an attorney. Finally, at day's end, I asked, "What about that suggestion that we turn him into a lawyer?" Mel flopped back in his chair and said, "Don't pay any attention to me. Sometimes I don't know what the fuck I'm talking about!" That was the end of the lawyer problem.

Mel and I met for a third day at Warners and continued to get along famously. He seemed relaxed enough to volunteer personal information I really didn't need to know. In *Phone Booth* the main character uses the telephone booth to contact his girlfriend. He's afraid to use his own cell phone because his wife checks on the bill and might catch him cheating. Mel quipped, "That's exactly how my wife caught me. She went over all my phone bills, and she really nailed me."

But nothing prepared me for the burst of energy I witnessed when all at once Mel bolted from his chair in the midst of his story and without a word dashed out of the office into the parking lot and was gone. I took the opportunity to wash up and get some coffee. Mel stumbled back in, sweating and visibly out of breath. "Did you see her?" he asked. I didn't understand what he was talking about. "She was absolutely fantastic," said Mel. "I tried to catch up with her but she got in her car, so I chased her all the way to the Hollywood gate… but she got away."

I could just imagine the sight of movie icon Mel Gibson pursuing some anonymous girl all across the Warner Bros. lot with every ounce of strength he could muster. Even after we got back to work, Mel kept muttering descriptions of her and wondering who she might have been. "How the hell am I going to find her?"

I found Mel had a lot of pent-up anger. He was particularly pissed off at director-writer Brian Helgeland, of whom he said, "Some guys don't appreciate anything you do for them." It seemed odd that Mel expected any thanks since he'd just gotten Helgeland fired as director of their crime melodrama, *Payback*.

Mel had taken over and re-directed over a third of the film himself. He explained the situation to me in detail. "The way Helgeland had it, the main villain got killed off two-thirds of the way through the movie, so there was nobody left to root against. I created a whole new set of villains and brought them in, and I shot it all in ten days right here on the Warners backlot, but you'd never be able to tell the difference. It's seamless."

The truth was that anyone with a discerning eye could tell the difference between what Mel filmed and Helgeland's original footage, which was shot on location in Philadelphia. The Warners lot looked terribly phony. The entire enterprise was a shoddy piece of work for someone who had won the Academy Award for *Braveheart*. Both the sadism and violence were excessive. The only redeeming quality in *Payback* was Mel's performance.

Anyway, as Mel saw it, he'd done the director a great favor by canning him and taking over. He was also not a man who forgave easily. He was still carrying a grudge against the Teamsters up in New England who'd given him problems years before on his own directorial debut *The Man Without a Face*. Apparently, they had demanded all their perks and overtime which Mel begrudged them because he was making the picture on a tight budget. The fact that he usually collects $20 million a pop didn't seem to affect his attitude towards the crew members' salaries. Mel said the Teamsters had disliked him so much that when they drove him to work, they pulled over blocks from the set and made him walk the rest of the way on foot. He didn't dare argue with them, but he hated their guts.

I recall asking him at one point why he was so fucking angry. After all he'd succeeded in achieving all his dreams as a young actor. He sat back thoughtfully for a while, shrugged, and finally agreed that I was right. Why the fuck was he so pissed off?

In working together on a script, you often drift to unrelated conversations just as a break. When Mel discussed other actors, he didn't have much good to say. He'd met Marlon Brando once and was not impressed. As far as he was concerned Brando was okay in *On the Waterfront* and that was about it. He had no heroes. When I complimented him on his acting in *The Year of Living Dangerously*, with Sigourney Weaver, he dismissed the film as overrated. He did however, under my questioning, go into great detail about the filming of *Braveheart*, and how having a tighter budget actually made it a far better film. More money would have meant additional action scenes. As it was, the picture profited from concentrating on its dramatic elements. At first, he hated Paramount when they cut costs on him. But it turned out they did him a favor.

Meanwhile, other difficulties would arise. Business affairs at Fox would have to structure a complex deal with Mel. He wasn't just an actor, he was a studio unto himself. To lock him up would mean hiring his personal producer, Bruce Davey (whom nobody liked), and surrendering all controls to Mel's Icon Productions. Fox would be required to give up the rights to lucrative foreign territories. Zucker and Netter would be paid off and dumped. Eventually, this would prove too rich a deal. Especially when other important actors were suddenly clamoring to star in the picture. Their price would be far more reasonable (Will Smith was next up).

I found Mel to have excellent instincts when it came to the script. My final draft benefited from my association with him, and I regret losing him. I did deliver a set of rewrites to Mel and when I ran into him in Malibu at a shopping mall, he paused for a while to tell me how much he enjoyed those new scenes. But it turned out Mel was already committed to something else more traditional—*The Patriot*, an overblown epic that proved to be a disappointment. The idea of carrying a whole movie while trapped inside a telephone booth had piqued his interest for a time, but perhaps it was too much of a gamble. Stars are nervous about failure.

On the other hand, it was something of a relief when Mel's deal fell through because he'd begun talking about the wisdom of shooting the whole of *Phone Booth* on that same Warners backlot, which would've been a terrible mistake. Mel had convinced himself that the sets in *Payback* looked convincing. They might've been passable in a television episode, but not up there on a movie screen. I'm certain that the fake studio look would've ruined the picture, even with Mel in it.

I wasn't as shattered as I told everyone I was, particularly when Fox informed me that red-hot director Michael Bay would helm my picture and a meeting with him was scheduled at his Santa Monica offices. Elizabeth Gabler and Gil Netter accompanied me. Bay showed up late. This was indeed an ill omen. Michael's first words upon convening the meeting were, "Okay, how do we get this thing out of the fucking telephone booth?"

Michael Bay thought he'd need cutaways to the police and to the sniper. He wanted to go inside the sniper's apartment and get to know him. He was turning what was a totally original approach into a conventional melodrama. Just imagine taking *Rear Window* and cutting away to the inside of Raymond Burr's apartment across the courtyard for additional coverage. *Rear Window* only works from Jimmy Stewart's point of view, and that's what makes it brilliant.

Michael dismissed this argument. He wanted more bang for the buck, more hardware. I said, "You've already done all that SWAT team stuff in *The Rock*. Why would you want to do it again?" Looking over at Elizabeth and Gil I could see the expression on their faces. This director was clearly the wrong casting and fortunately they agreed. Bay would go on to direct one of the biggest blockbusters of the year, *Pearl Harbor*, instead of one of the year's smallest, *Phone Booth*.

I later discovered that Michael never had any intention of working with me on the project. Our meeting was a sham. He'd already decided to hire none other than Brian Helgeland to do a massive rewrite on my script, which would, of course, take it outside the reaches of the telephone booth. It would have begun in the offices of the Internal Revenue during an audit and gone on from there. Fortunately, everyone at Fox was appalled by Bay's concept, as well as the one-million-dollar rewrite fee Helgeland was seeking. No such deal was consummated, and Helgeland never wrote a single word, despite reports that may have appeared in the trades. Normally, a powerhouse director like Michael Bay could intimidate a studio into firing the original writer and starting anew from page one. I'm thankful that the Fox executives held their ground, although they did eventually succumb to insecurity and bring in other writers before returning completely to my material. What was finally filmed follows my revised screenplay religiously.

The star was still to be Will Smith. To further attract him, the Hughes brothers, who had a contract at Fox, had been brought aboard to direct. They had helmed *Menace II Society* and *Dead Presidents* and specialized in urban crime drama. I was invited to meet them and go through the script. As usual I was anxious to see what they'd have to say. Everyone I'd talked to so far had come up with some suggestions which sparked my creativity—even Michael Bay, who had recommended adding some kind of twist at the end of the story. He had nothing specific in mind, but it had taken me only one night to figure one out and incorporate it.

The Hughes brothers claimed to be huge fans of mine. They'd grown up on *Black Caesar* and had used James Brown's music from my films in their documentary on pimps. But as they went through the script, I realized these affable brothers had few suggestions, if any. They hadn't formulated any specifics on how to shoot the piece. The entire meeting amounted to a lot of pleasant socializing but no productive work.

I told them I had a few fresh ideas of my own. Since I was being honored at a film festival in Brisbane, I promised to send them a brand-new draft by Air Express. They indicated they'd be looking forward to receiving it—but again I was being conned. Cynthia and I vacationed in Tahiti for a week and then went on to Australia from where I mailed them my latest draft.

But even before I'd left town, 20th Century Fox had engaged another writer. It's become so embedded in studio policy to consistently recycle new writers that it's a difficult habit to break. The Hughes Brothers knew what was going on prior to our meeting. They were simply shining me on. Writers Guild regulations require the studio to notify the original author when he's being rewritten, but Fox simply decided to ignore the rules.

Having written *Rules of Engagement* and *Traffic* (still unreleased then), Stephen Gaghan was the flavor of the month. Fox paid him $450,000 to do a rewrite, which he was long in delivering. The studio was extremely unhappy with the result and gave him copious notes. Months passed and they received no further revisions. Finally, under immense pressure, he turned in a second draft which was in many ways worse than the first. He had reduced the suspense thriller to a talky diatribe. The sniper and his victim simply debated things back and forth while the momentum stopped cold. I know Gaghan is a better writer than that. I have to believe he simply threw the assignment away. After all, the man won the Academy Award for Best Screenplay for *Traffic*.

Upset as I was, I was even more surprised when Fox called and invited me back on the project. Elizabeth Gabler actually apologized for hiring Gaghan and agreed that it had been a big mistake. Would I please return and put the pieces back together? By this time Will Smith had also dropped out. The project was becoming an endangered species.

I spent my Christmas holidays executing still another set of revisions. I kept only two or three lines of dialogue from Gaghan's script and retained the many suggestions from Mel Gibson. I delivered a very solid shooting script. The studio seemed to agree.

I went to Chicago to visit with Cynthia's family and there I received a call from CAA. "Are you sitting down?" As it was, I was shopping in a furniture store at the time with my wife and mother in law. The call continued. "They've locked up a star for *Phone Booth*. It's going to be Jim Carrey with Joel Schumacher directing.

When I returned to Hollywood, I was stunned to learn that despite their praise, Fox had engaged still another writer. This time around it was Michael Leeson, who'd written *War of the Roses* and had done some uncredited work polishing Jim Carrey's notable hit, *The Truman Show*. I must say Leeson had the kind consideration to phone and tell me he'd been hired. He told me, "I think your script is great. I don't think it needs much work, but how can I turn down a job?"

Soon Jim Carrey was seen on television, touting *Phone Booth* as his next project. It appeared to be a fait accompli, but in the movie business nothing is ever certain. Within a month Jim Carrey was out! Joel Schumacher broke the news to me. "I'm one of his very best friends but I couldn't reassure him. He got scared of it. It's a straight dramatic part—something he's never done—and the whole picture depends solely on him. It was just too much of a risk."

I had now run the gamut of almost every important male star in Hollywood. Al Pacino and Dustin Hoffman were both rejected as too old, as was Robin Williams. CAA was beginning to bandy about lesser names, which scared me. Nearly two years had passed since I'd sold the script and I was tired of being asked, "What happened?" Nobody seemed at all pleased with Michael Leeson's polish so again they came back to me. I was no longer being paid by Fox for my additional work. I was just anxious to save the picture. I assumed somewhere down the line the studio would cough up the extra fifty thousand they now owed me—but they never did. They'd piss away over half a million on other writers who delivered nothing, then screw me out of my few dollars for work they actually used. Figure that one out!

Cynthia and I were in New York several months later when another call from CAA caught me on the sidewalk during the intermission of a play. "This time they're really going forward. It's a definite! Schumacher's directing as planned... and the film's going to star Colin Farrell."

"Who the hell is that?" I demanded.

"Just the hottest young actor in Hollywood. We represent him."

Colin Farrell in *Phone Booth*.

Forest Whitaker in *Phone Booth.*

Needless to say, this was not what I wanted to hear. *Phone Booth* was a small picture designed to be carried by a big-name actor. It was always envisioned as a major star vehicle. Now we had a virtual unknown. In a career plagued with mediocre casting, it seemed like the same curse had fallen upon me again.

But actually, it was a stroke of luck. As demonstrated in his film debut, Joel Schumacher's *Tigerland*, Colin Farrell is a brilliant actor with the kind of screen charisma that should make him a top star. Since playing the lead in *Phone Booth*, he'd been hired by Spielberg to star opposite Tom Cruise in *Minority Report*. He also starred in the title role opposite Bruce Willis in *Hart's War* and with Al Pacino in *The Recruit*. As predicted, he became one of the hottest young actors in movies today.

Colin was willing to take a chance on playing an entire movie inside a telephone booth. As Joel Schumacher said in *Premiere* magazine, "Success breeds fear, suddenly you have this amorphous thing called a career and the only way you got that way was by taking big risks. The minute you have a career you start thinking how do I protect it? Colin is at the beginning and has nothing to lose. That's what separates him from the high-profile talent who stepped in and out of *Phone Booth*."

The same *Premiere* article goes into some detail regarding the scripting of *Phone Booth*. Elizabeth Gabler, now promoted to head of Fox 2000, is quoted as saying, "We brought in Stephen Gaghan to make some revisions but that too fell apart. Steve had a more analytic take on what the characters were doing. It took away from the rapid-fire pace." Miss Gabler goes on to say, "Cohen's script, which chronicles the hero's attempt to escape the phone booth, was a house of cards. Once you pull one out, the whole thing starts to tumble. Once we realized this, we returned to Larry's original screenplay."

With Joel Schumacher on the set of *Phone Booth*.

Though conceived to be filmed in New York, *Phone Booth* would eventually be shot on a downtown Los Angeles street which was closed off and redressed to duplicate the Big Apple. Technically it was an excellent job. A few days of filming in Manhattan was completed to create additional atmosphere. I still miss the constant passage of buses, taxis and pedestrian traffic that are so much a part of New York. To me, the image of a man trapped in a phone booth with all this activity swirling around him was essential. He's a victim trapped in broad daylight in the most public of places. I didn't think the film could fully capture that on any closed-down street. Had I directed the film myself I probably would have stolen a great deal of footage by placing my phone booth on the busiest of street corners and shooting with hidden cameras which could circle 360 degrees around. But with the excitement surrounding the script I had long ago decided to step aside as director and segue into the so-called big time. The attention *Phone Booth* received did lead to many millions of dollars in other work, but if I'd kept the script so I could direct it myself, it would've been filmed years ago and already be in release.

I'd originally come up with the character of the hungry publicist on the make because one of my favorite movies had long been *Sweet Smell of Success*. I patterned Stu on the role played by Tony Curtis. When I was considering making the film myself, it dawned on me, "Why not get Tony Curtis?" I contacted Tony and asked, "What would Sidney Falco be like today?"

The idea fascinated Tony since it was probably his favorite role. I messengered over the script, and he loved it. We met for lunch at the Beverly Hills Hotel. Tony met me in the Polo Lounge, grabbed me by the arm, and dragged me downstairs to the much less expensive coffee shop. "I'm not letting you pay those prices."

Tony found the script to be a rare opportunity. Salary wouldn't be a problem. Tony Curtis wasn't a box-office star anymore but the publicity resulting from his return to one of his most iconic characterizations would draw tremendous attention to our movie.

Then Tony's manager informed me that the actor was worried about handling so much non-stop dialogue. Could he have cue cards or a teleprompter? I knew that wouldn't work. A performer must know the lines cold in order to improvise off of them. That's a prime requirement for working with me. I also had to shoot quickly and sometimes undercover. There was no way somebody could be holding cue cards in the middle of downtown Manhattan without attracting undue attention. It wasn't meant to be.

I probably cheated myself of a great opportunity by not directing *Phone Booth*, but it was a trade-off—an opportunity to move onto the screenwriting A-list.

Soon afterward I wrote *Cellular*, about a man trying to save a kidnapped woman who has managed to reach him on his cell phone. The victim doesn't know where she's being held and the hero must locate her before he loses the connection. I figured I'd direct this one instead, but it was immediately snapped up and produced by the team of Roland Emmerich and Dean Devlin, who'd made *Independence Day*. I was now getting as much money for a script as I was accustomed to receiving for delivering the entire movie.

Tom Rothman at Fox was upset that I'd written *Cellular*, which was really nothing at all like *Phone Booth* except that a telephone played a central role. In *Cellular*, the hero is racing all over Los Angeles and the plot and characters have no similarity.

Colin Farrell in *Phone Booth.*

Still, Fox threatened to make trouble until Devlin and Emmerich agreed to guarantee that *Phone Booth* would be released first. I still felt Rothman held a grudge and Schumacher confirmed it when he once asked me, "What've they got against you at Fox?" The studio had gone out of their way to keep me and Schumacher from getting together and having an ongoing working relationship.

Eventually I was invited to visit the set of *Phone Booth*, and Cynthia and I had a very pleasant time with Joel Schumacher, posing for pictures and chatting with the cast. Colin is not only a good actor but a terrific guy. He was quite charming even though he was physically exhausted. The picture was being shot in sequence and he probably hadn't slept in several days. I believe he denied himself sleep in order to make himself more haggard and actually live out the experience of the character he was playing. He staggered over to me, collapsed in my arms, and said, "Thanks a lot." Yes, I was the man responsible for his ordeal, having created such a demanding role.

As I watched filming progress I was disturbed by one critical detail—the telephone voice of the sniper. Schumacher had hired a very experienced actor, Ron Eldard, and placed him in the fourth-floor window of a building directly opposite the booth. In this way, Colin Farrell would have someone to play against. This was fine except that the actor's voice did not measure up to my expectations. It lacked a defining tone. I wanted a voice that was absolutely chilling.

I knew it would disturb Schumacher to offer any immediate criticism. I left the location early because I was afraid some facial expression might communicate my unhappiness to the directot, Instead, I took the matter up with Elizabeth Gabler and Gil Netter, both of whom completely agreed with my assessment. They promised to work on Schumacher, although they were both clearly intimidated by him. Eventually I took it upon myself to tell Joel how I felt. He simply replied, "Do you really think so?"—and then went on to follow my suggestion. Ron Eldard's voice was removed from the track, and he was replaced by Kiefer Sutherland, whom I felt was perfectly suited. He'd also acted for Schumacher in four previous films.

Since Colin Farrell had been cast in so many important roles elsewhere, Fox decided to hold off on releasing *Phone Booth* and allow the actor to become familiar to movie audiences. Sadly, *Hart's War* came out and bombed. We'd have to wait for Spielberg's *Minority Report* to firmly establish Colin. The wait was agonizing. Word around town was that *Phone Booth* was a superb thriller. My career as a writer was waiting to explode, but on a very long fuse.

Eventually, Joel screened *Phone Booth* for me and welcomed my input. I was generally pleased but, as always, had some notes which the Fox executives were again reluctant about passing on to Joel. So once more I took it upon myself. This time I was unhappy with the musical score and shortly thereafter, Joel hired a new composer.

Schumacher actually directed two other movies while waiting for *Phone Booth* to open. Once again, I was involved in a virtually unprecedented situation: a movie being held for nearly a year, not because it was bad, but because its star was on the verge of becoming huge.

The studio was highly enthusiastic over the marketing tests on the film and its reception at the Toronto Film Festival, which had been overwhelmingly positive.

Toronto is arguably the most important film festival in North America. It draws hundreds of stars and directors and is heavily covered by both domestic and foreign press.

Phone Booth was scheduled to be shown before an audience of over 2,400 people and Joel Schumacher was to attend along with Colin, Forest Whitaker and Kiefer Sutherland, who appears on screen for only a few minutes at the end of the film.

I had waited patiently for an invitation to attend the festival, but none was forthcoming. It seemed someone didn't want me there. I suspected that Fox Chief Tom Rothman was still peeved because I'd had the effrontery to write *Cellular* and sell it elsewhere. New Line now had it in pre-production. I assumed I was being punished by being uninvited.

I phoned Schumacher and asked him to intervene on my behalf. "Joel, if you want me there all you have to do is tell Tom Rothman that as your principal collaborator, I belong beside you on stage opening night."

Schumacher responded that the writer is never invited to these junkets, but since I persisted, he promised he would do his best to wangle me an invitation. Whether he did or not I'll never know. I doubt it. He'd gotten his way about everything else involving the film and I don't think Fox would have resisted his personal request that I accompany him and the actors to Toronto.

Finally Ronni, as both my publicist and sister, decided to mention the affront to my attorney, Skip Brittenham. Skip is extremely well connected and happened to represent Tom Rothman. Skip agreed that I'd earned the right to be at Toronto and take a bow. No matter how many times Fox had abused our relationship, I'd always turned the other cheek and come back to do additional work on the project, even without salary.

The real star of this movie was its concept: the outrageous idea of a whole movie that happens inside and around a telephone booth. It was an almost impossible stunt to bring off and yet I'd managed it. Everyone was excited about the film. Everyone agreed that it was a great script. And yet, I was absent from the guest list.

After a few choice words from Skip, I suddenly received a phone call from Fox informing me that two first-class tickets to Toronto would be arriving and a limo would be taking me to the airport. A suite had been arranged for me and Cynthia at the Four Seasons Hotel, and, of course, I'd be welcome on the red carpet on opening night to give interviews and share the spotlight with the stars and director on stage. It was a complete reversal.

Unfortunately, Cynthia didn't attend because she was completing her master's degree in psychology and couldn't afford to miss any of her classes. I journeyed to Toronto alone but fortunately Ronni would be there to keep me company. She was representing several other films that were showing in the festival.

The entire 24th floor of the Four Seasons Hotel in Toronto had been commandeered by 20th Century Fox for the purpose of promoting *Phone Booth*. Schumacher and the actors each had rooms which were completely outfitted with television cameras and lights. Journalists would line up outside and one by one be allowed into each of these inner sanctums for a period of ten minutes to do their interviews. No provision had been made for the writer to be interviewed, but I understood that these journalists were looking for star names whom they could present on their local television programs. This was a good way for Fox to get free publicity for the movie. I was a little less understanding when I was informed that I wasn't invited to participate at the press conference later that afternoon.

Schumacher, Colin Farrell, Forest Whitaker and Kiefer Sutherland would be up on the dais facing the crowd of reporters and fielding questions. I was welcome to watch from the audience.

At first, I wasn't going to attend, but finally curiosity got the better of me. I positioned myself between some of the video cameras, in plain view of Schumacher, who'd seen me earlier in the day and given me the perfunctory hug. He didn't seem particularly delighted about my presence but went through the motions. Now, when the press conference began, the very first question from the media was, "Where did the idea for this movie come from?"

Schumacher was quick to answer. "Well, this was a screenplay written by Larry Cohen that 20th Century Fox bought."

Since I was there in the room, he could easily have acknowledged me to the press, but he chose to completely ignore my existence. Then, as if to add insult to injury, he went on. "But, of course, I changed most of it." This, of course, was completely untrue. I don't know why he said it, but I'm sure he was sorry afterwards.

I felt like shouting out in my inimitable fashion and making an enemy out of everyone. But, for a change, I kept my yap shut. I figured we had to go through with this premiere and appear on stage together and I hesitated to create an incident. It was good that I did because prior to the opening event when we were all in the green room at the concert hall ready to go on, Schumacher took it upon himself to wrap his arm around me and announce to everyone, "I wouldn't have a job if it wasn't for this man," for which I received a round of applause. Maybe he was trying to make up for the earlier slight. I figured he was embarrassed.

Minutes later, we all came on stage together, took our bows, then sat down to watch the film along with the enormous audience that had shown up. I'd thoroughly enjoyed doing the TV interviews upon entering the theater, and the reception to the film that night certainly made the entire trip worthwhile. The crowd was riveted. The level of suspense was close to excruciating, but they laughed at all the right places and gave us thunderous applause. I quickly dialed Cynthia's cell phone back in Los Angeles so that she could hear the response, which went on for quite a while. Then the spotlight was thrown on the box in which Schumacher, the actors and me were stationed, and we rose to a huge ovation. A very nice party was staged at a chic Toronto club, and I took pictures with everyone. It was certainly a heartening experience and gave us all reason to expect a big hit when the picture opened.

I flew back to Los Angeles after the festival looking forward to rave notices in *Variety* and *The Hollywood Reporter*. I'd asked Ronni about the reviews, and she'd indicated they had not yet appeared. She wasn't telling me the truth. The reviews had already come out the day after the performance in Toronto. And they were rotten. I'd directed 20 movies based on my own scripts and never gotten any trade reviews quite as bad as these. Both critics slighted the film for being too short and criticized it for not making Colin Farrell a negative enough personality. He was being singled out by this sniper for special punishment when his actual crimes were negligible. He was simply a guy

On the set of *Phone Booth*.

who wanted to cheat on his wife. He hadn't even gone through with it yet. (In my version of the script, he had been screwing around fairly regularly.)

The reviewers complained that this fellow's principal crime was that he was a publicist and a bit of an asshole. Schumacher had added a beat to the story so that it now appeared that the sniper had previously killed a pedophile and a swindling corporate executive who cheated stockholders. Schumacher was pulling events out of the newspapers and inserting them into the movie. In my version, the sniper had also killed previously but simply picked his victims at random. He was doing this just for practice. Colin Farrell was always meant to be the main event. The sniper had become fixated on him after watching him day after day in his expensive suits, swaggering his way through life. Colin was a success whereas the sniper was an abject failure. He desperately wanted to be Colin but couldn't. His only other choice was to humiliate him and eventually destroy him.

It's amazing how adding only a few beats or a few lines of dialogue can alter the audience's entire perception of a story. What the critics in *Variety* and *The Hollywood Reporter* complained about was unfortunately valid. But it was not unfixable. We still had plenty of time. The entire picture had taken little more than two weeks to shoot. If we could re-shoot for one day at a minimum cost, we could repair every deficiency to which the reviewers had objected. I knew exactly how to do it, and upon reading the notices I sat down and drafted a memorandum to Tom Rothman. I assumed he would be the final arbiter. I explained that we needn't reconstruct the set in downtown Los Angeles. Everything that I suggested could be accomplished in close-ups using the existing New York street on the Fox lot which was convincing enough when seen on TV's *NYPD Blue*.

What I proposed was a dialogue sequence I'd written in conjunction with Mel Gibson. Mel had been of the same opinion as the critics. We needed more for the character to be guilty about. He had to have some inner secret, some terrible crime that he'd buried deep in his psyche, some guilt he wanted to deny but couldn't. Not just that he was a slick opportunist, not just that he put a wicked spin on things and misrepresented the truth. We had to have something deeper, more penetrating, more powerful, and a total surprise.

The way the picture currently played, we found out about Colin in the first five minutes and then learned all the same things about him later on when the sniper put him through an intense third degree. There was no sudden revelation to jolt the viewers' consciousness. That's what I proposed to do.

I sent Tom Rothman the memo and the four to five pages of dialogue which I'd written for Mel.

In this added sequence, Colin's character reveals how he'd been employed by a famous rock group, not only to do their publicity but also to occasionally procure young girls. One night he was summoned to their midtown hotel. A girl he'd brought them had overdosed. They wanted her off the premises and gone. Colin took the girl back to his Brooklyn apartment instead of a hospital emergency room. He was protecting the rock stars but in effect endangering the girl, who eventually died. When he called his employers, they simply told him to get rid of her, so he drove to nearby Prospect Park and dumped her body on a bridle path in the freezing cold. He still remembers the incident vividly and painfully, and yet has never revealed it to anyone else. If he'd acted responsibly, the girl might have lived. Not only did he fail to save her, but he disposed of her remains like she was a bag of garbage. Going through her coat he'd found some lyrics and poetry she'd written, hoping to impress the group. He tore up these pages and flushed them down the toilet. It was like killing her all over again.

His confession to all this is a forceful piece of drama. It would have given Colin Farrell a chance to really dig deeper into the character and expose layers of guilt and anguish. And it would have confirmed the sniper's instincts: that this young man was hiding some terrible crime for which he secretly wished to be punished.

Apparently, Tom Rothman didn't appreciate my suggestions. Not only did he ignore them, he even refused to acknowledge their receipt. I mailed these new pages and faxed them as well. When I got no response I sent them a second time, along with a note requesting that he at least confirm receipt of the material. He refused to do so. What more can be said?

I sent the same pages off to Joel Schumacher and got a similar response. Nothing. I realized that the film had received some excellent reviews from which the studio intended to cull quotes to appear in the ads. Perhaps they were satisfied with these good notices and refused to deal with the initial criticisms in the trade periodicals, regardless of the fact that the criticism was well founded.

Finally a date was set for the release. November 15, 2002. A perfect time to position a movie for academy consideration. But even more bizarre events were yet to unfold.

Chapter 37
A Sniper Intervenes

The publicity was out. The posters hung in theater lobbies every-where. The trailer was playing on thousands of screens in antic-ipation of our nationwide opening. A giant billboard dominated the Times Square area. And then the murders began.

On October 2, 2002, a 55-year-old man was shot while walking across a parking lot in Wheaton, Maryland. On October 3, another victim was shot while mowing his lawn in Bethesda, Maryland. Later that same day, a taxicab driver filling his tank with gas was shot in the chest and killed instantly. Still later that day the first female victim was shot while sitting on a park bench in Silver Springs, Maryland.

Again on October 3, a second woman was shot while vacu-uming her minivan in Kensington, Maryland. The nightmare was only beginning. A sniper was taking deadly aim, selecting victims at random and striking them down from distances as far away as three times the length of a football field.

I was shocked and sickened when I heard the news. I also knew that it would affect the project on which I had worked so hard for the past three years.

I thanked God that *Phone Booth* hadn't opened several months earlier and been blamed for putting the idea into this lunatic's mind. Bad enough that the coming attraction was centered around the sniper concept. It had been playing in theaters for several weeks now. It had been seen by hundreds of thousands of people. Could the sniper have been one of them? It was a question I didn't want answered.

The killer was only just beginning his rampage. Later on October 3, a man was shot while waiting for a bus in Wash-ington, D.C. The following day, another woman was wounded while loading packages into her car in Fredericksburg, Virginia. Then, on October 7 and 9, and again on the 11, the sniper struck with the same M.O.: going after complete strangers, selecting them at random, then vanishing.

The fate of my movie paled in comparison with the tragedy at hand. Certainly this movie didn't belong in theaters now. Whether or not the killer was apprehended, the gravity of the situation had cast a pall over the entire production.

When I first viewed the trailer in theaters, it had evoked a positive response from the audience. The idea titillated. It was a fun ride like *Speed* or *Die Hard*. For an hour and a half, the audience would be transported into a fanciful situation. They could experience almost unbearable suspense and anguish because they knew it wasn't real. But now suddenly it was.

I went back to the theaters and saw the trailer again. Now, the response was cold and fearful. A chill came over the audience. Perhaps the movie would be more powerful than before, more excruciating in its suspense. But it would never be the same.

It was anyone's guess how this series of horrific events would affect audiences' acceptance of *Phone Booth*. Some cited the success of *The Sum of All Fears*—released just nine months after 9/11—as evidence that a real-life event need not impede a strong box-office response. Apparently that picture was not at all harmed by the attack on the Twin Towers, although the film depicted the destruction of the Super Bowl by a nuclear device. Others pointed out that Schwarzenegger's film *Collateral Damage*, dealing with terrorism, had not fared well. But it wasn't a very good movie.

While the real-life manhunt continued, rumors soon reached me that 20th Century Fox was considering postponing the release. I'd been expecting this turn of events—and dreading it. After all, we'd been waiting for close to a year already for Colin Farrell to be seen in a number of other films, hoping that he would connect with the public and become a known quantity. His appearance in Spielberg's *Minority Report* had met with favorable critical response, but he had not emerged as a star in his own right. People remembered he was in the picture, but the impression he made was not overwhelming. No one was beating down the doors to buy tickets to a Colin Farrell movie. Not yet.

Then matters got worse. When the murder spree began, Fox had issued a statement to the press unbeknownst to me. When I received telephone calls at home requesting interviews,

I was caught unawares. Within a few hours, the *Los Angeles Times*, *Time* magazine and the Associated Press had all been in contact with me. I told them that I was deeply troubled by the sniper killings and wouldn't want any movie of mine to in any way upset or unnerve the families of the victims. Their loss was sufficient without having to see TV spots and advertisements about a movie centering around such events. I couldn't tell Fox what to do, but I certainly wouldn't ask them not to postpone the release.

I soon began to get frantic calls from the Fox press department, insisting that I not speak to the newspapers or TV reporters. This came a little late, since I'd already been quoted, and I felt that I'd spoken as a human being rather than as a mouthpiece for some corporate entity. By then I already suspected that Fox would indeed temporarily withdraw the film. On Saturday, October 12, the *Los Angeles Times* covered our dilemma in its news section in a footnote to the latest sniper reports. The headline was: "FOX OFFICIALS RETHINK RELEASE OF SNIPER FILM," complete with an interview by yours truly. It said in part:

> Cohen said he sees parallels between the fictional sniper in the movie and the real-life serial killer stalking innocent victims.
>
> "Both guys are fixated with the God complex," he said. "They both think they can control people's lives and strike them down at will because they feel they're omnipotent." He said he was grateful the film didn't come out before the killings began. "I realize movies can have an influence over people, particularly people who are mentally deranged."

This time I got calls from Ronni and even Skip Brittenham. Tom Rothman had asked Skip to shut me up. At least Rothman knew I was alive.

I felt I couldn't blow reporters off with a "no comment." I was heading to New York to appear at Lincoln Center and show several of my old horror films at an event sponsored by *The New York Times* and The Film Society of Lincoln Center. I'd be sure to encounter journalists and they'd be asking about

Phone Booth. As it was, the event in New York went over fabulously. *It's Alive* and *God Told Me To* were both screened to sell-out audiences. We received extensive press coverage and a photo of the *It's Alive* monster actually appeared on the front page of the *Times'* Sunday Arts and Leisure section. We also received a full-page color rendition of the *It's Alive* monster in *The Village Voice*, which designated the film a Choice of the Week. The once disreputable 1974 shocker *It's Alive* was now wildly heralded as a classic.

I was to appear with John Carpenter and Guillermo del Toro, two other eminent horror film directors, and they both proved to be affable companions. Guillermo, particularly, was a longtime fan and knew all of my films and even spoke of wanting to do a remake of *Perfect Strangers*. Of course, I couldn't avoid the questions about *Phone Booth,* so I simply spoke from my heart. I couldn't live with myself if I tried to rationalize the release of the movie at such a time. It's a great film and it will still be great two or three months down the line.

While in New York, I was informed that a huge *Phone Booth* billboard had been erected over Times Square. I grabbed a camera and rushed downtown with Janelle at my side. I wanted her to snap a few pictures of me in front of the gigantic sign. When we arrived, the cherry-pickers were there and our sign had just been taken down. There was nothing left of it. That was the capper. I'd never had a Times Square billboard for any of my previous movies and I never got to see this one. The studio hadn't wasted any time. I wondered if they'd erect another one or if the release of the picture would ever pick up the momentum it originally had. My greatest fear, of course, was that we'd simply be dumped on home video and cable. That would be a tragic conclusion and a total defeat.

At least if we had to wait several months to finally issue the film, we still had time to make those revisions in the picture that I felt were necessary. I would make still another pass at Rothman and Schumacher.

But there was a further concern. The way Joel had filmed the picture, the sniper escapes at the end. He'd killed two people before the picture begins, then slaughters two more on camera, and yet he walks away scot-free. He even comes off as

something of a hero. He warns Colin Farrell that if he misbe-
haves, he might well return to punish him further. He takes
on a godlike quality as he wanders off to lose himself in the
city, wryly commenting that, "When a phone rings, it must
be answered," indicating that he will soon mete out the same
torment to some other poor unsuspecting soul.

Certainly there have been movies in which the villain gets
away at the end, but I wondered how audiences would react to
the sniper in our film escaping unpunished, particularly if this
real-life sniper was never apprehended.

This wasn't the way I had ended the script. I'd written
many endings and in most of them, the sniper was killed.
Schumacher chose to take a more artsy, nihilistic approach.
There were complaints about this ending too in several of the
advanced reviews. I was never comfortable about letting the
sniper escape justice, although I had to admit it actually worked
when you saw it on the screen. Now I didn't think it was at all
appropriate.

While I was weighing all this up, a bus driver was shot
down in cold blood by the so-called one-shot sniper. The
nightmare was continuing. Eventually, on October 24, 2002,
the two snipers were found sleeping in their car and arrested.
Phone Booth was released on April 4, 2003 and proved a very
successful film with a long afterlife.

Chapter 38
It's Alive Lives Again

I'd originally intended to shoot *Captivity* myself as a re-entry into directing. It involved two principal characters in one location, and I thought we could make the picture for a price. Before doing it as a film, I tried it out on stage at the Beverly Hills Playhouse under the auspices of Milton Katselas. A friend of mine, Dick Weber, arranged for the production and it came off quite smoothly. Dick was kind enough to give the script to a producer acquaintance, which eventually found its way into the hands of Mark Damon, a foreign sales representative, who put the picture together with Russian money.

A story set in New York was going to be filmed in Moscow, and a somewhat prestigious British filmmaker, Roland Joffé, was engaged to direct. Joffé had made *The Killing Fields*, for which he was Oscar nominated, and then went on to direct Robert De Niro and Jeremy Irons in *The Mission*. This fellow had not had a successful picture in some time and was looking for something that might qualify as a hit to boost his career. Certainly a horror film like *Captivity* was not a good fit with his resumé, but I was flattered that he wanted to do the picture and thought that it would be well shot and well acted. Therefore, I stepped aside as director, took the money, and allowed them to go on with the project. Unfortunately, they ran it into the ground.

The production ran nearly 100 percent over budget, and even with only two characters and virtually one set, it took 55 days to film. Everything possible went wrong, including Joffé's insertion of a good deal of phony poetic nonsense to try and turn the picture into something that it wasn't, all of which was eventually removed. Elisha Cuthbert was hired to play the female lead. She'd had some success playing Kiefer Sutherland's daughter on *24* and had starred in a successful picture called *The Girl Next Door*. It wasn't a bad package, but unfortunately

Roland Joffé and Elisha Cuthbert on the set of *Captivity*.

the producers and director managed to jettison all the humor and human interest out of the first half of the movie, leaving us with characters with whom we really couldn't identify.

Captivity was well-shot by my long-time cameraman Daniel Pearl, who had been hired by coincidence. Daniel was very unhappy in Moscow. The crew came to work drunk, were hostile, and eventually Daniel was struck by a piece of pipe dropped from the catwalk above his head, which put him in the hospital. Let's hope it was an accident. Courageous as he always is, Daniel stayed on and finished the film, which turned out to be a calamity when screened for preview audiences. Nobody liked it. Especially me.

After one particularly gruesome screening in Hollywood, two focus groups were questioned and a suggestion was read to them for a new ending. Both groups rejected the new ending as ludicrous. The producers went out and shot the new ending anyway, completely overruling the audience testing results. When they previewed the picture a second time with the revised ending, the response was even more negative than it had been originally.

After four days of additional shooting and spending God knows how much money, they were in a worse situation than ever. And, of course, they would not listen to any suggestions from me, whom they now considered to be one of their harshest critics. I'd spent a good deal of time in the editing room trying to recut the picture with a very agreeable editor, whom they refused to listen to as well. And so the production continued on its road to hell.

Eventually, Mark Damon found a partner in After Dark Films, who had a distribution arrangement with Lionsgate, which had had great success with the *Hunger Games* and *Saw* franchises. The picture was scheduled to be released in May 2007. Someone named Courtney Solomon was now calling the shots. As President of After Dark, he instigated a new set of rewrites and a new shooting schedule. Half-way through this new shoot, Roland Joffé fled and Solomon took over directing some of the most horrendously explicit horror effects I've ever read on the printed page. Solomon then devised a billboard campaign which he put out all over Los Angeles and New York. The ads which appeared in 30 Los Angeles locations and on 1,400 New York taxi tops featured our frames with captions above each one. "Abduction" shows Elisha Cuthbert with a gloved hand over her face. "Confinement" pictures the actress behind a chain-link fence with a bloody finger poking through. "Torture" shows her face covered with gauze and tubes shoved up her nose. "Termination" shows her with her head thrown back, seemingly dead.

Elisha Cuthbert in *Captivity*.

The billboards met with huge negative response. A wave of protest swept over Los Angeles with demands that they be torn down. Although I've seen ads just as explicit for films like *Saw* and its sequels, I cannot deny that these billboards were clearly offensive to young people and no doubt to women in general.

The story made the front page of the trades. There were items about the ad campaign on CNN, on all the networks and on every local Los Angeles station. New York may be tougher, but the ads were removed from the taxis there as well. Of course, Solomon and his company received millions of dollars of free publicity and many suspected that he knew the ads would provoke protest and gain notoriety for the film. The Internet was teeming with items on this movie which was an unknown quantity just a week earlier. Perhaps there was some method in the madness. I only wish it was a better movie.

I was trying to decide whether I should remove my name and use a pseudonym. That said, I have seen some appalling movies in recent years that have gone through the roof and grossed great amounts of money. There is certainly an audience for that kind of violence and though it's not to my taste, I can't condemn people for what entertains them.

My 1974 Warner Bros. release *It's Alive* grossed around $39 million worldwide at a time when the average box-office ticket was about $2.50. Adjusted for inflation, that would be at about $120 million. With remakes like *Texas Chain Saw Massacre* and *The Hills Have Eyes* proving successful at the box office, I thought that the time had come for one of my own. Little did I know what I was getting myself into. The horror in *It's Alive* didn't come close to the horror of the deal-making. In my long career in Hollywood, this was the worst set of circumstances I'd encountered, and the deceptive practices and the devious behavior of the producers remains unparalleled in my experience.

Since Warner Bros. is seemingly reluctant to give up any property, my legal advisers had told me it was futile to approach them. Warners said they were not interested in doing a remake. I thereupon engaged an attorney named Marc Toberoff, who had successfully reacquired the rights to other old properties like *The Dukes of Hazzard*, *I Spy* and *The Wild Wild West*.

He was an extremely clever and persistent lawyer, and he was making a reputation for himself around Hollywood by seeking out the heirs and relatives of mainly deceased writers and reacquiring the rights for their families. Toberoff was successful in his negotiations with Warner Bros., probably because they were so sick of dealing with him in disastrous encounters over some of the other properties he had wrested from their grip.

We received the right to produce a single remake of *It's Alive* and set out to sell the property to another company. A producer with Joel Silver contacted me and offered me $500,000 for the *It's Alive* rights, which he decided he wanted to make back at Warners. But I thought that we could do better elsewhere.

Eventually, I wrote a spec screenplay updating the story to the present, redeveloping the characters and adding many new sequences. This spec script went on the market and fell into the hands of Bob Katz, who had produced my movie *The Ambulance* nearly 20 years before. Bob then took it to Moshe Diamant, and together they presented it to Nu Image, an Israeli-controlled company headed by Avi Lerner. So these are all the parties in the case—the cast of characters in one of the major screw-ups in my experience.

We made a deal (and Toberoff made a lucrative side deal of his own, earning him a producer credit and a lot more money than I did). Then the matter of a contract came into play. Weeks ran into months as the Nu Image people, Katz and Diamant, all took evasive action—anything to keep from finalizing the contract. Each time a draft would appear at my attorney's office, my lawyer, Steven Burkow, would call and say that they've omitted a paragraph, or they're trying to slip something else into the deal. And that's how it went. Continual stalling and changing of the deal so that we could never sign and never get paid.

All this time I waited to find out if the producers wanted me to do any rewrites and tailor the script for their production unit, which shot in Bulgaria. I had declined to direct the picture when I heard of the Bulgarian location because I didn't want to be out of the country for those many months and away from my family. But now I realized I was completely in the dark. Despite Writers Guild regulations requiring that the studio

Bijou Phillips in the remake of *It's Alive.*

offer me the opportunity to do the first rewrite, they had gone ahead with another writer whose name was withheld from me, and I was denied any access to the script that had been written. Subsequently, a second writer was hired and still the producer of record, Bob Katz, couldn't tell me the name of the writer because he couldn't remember it, and continued to claim that neither he nor anyone in Hollywood had a copy of the script. It was all Diamant's fault, and he was in Israel. I didn't believe any of this for a moment, but the charade continued.

With scripts being written behind my back and with my rights under the Guild being continually abused, I was further shocked to run into an agent with ICM, Jack Gilardi, who told me that his client, Josef Rusnak, had been hired to direct the picture. Since this was a special effects picture and a great deal of preparation was needed, I had the sneaking suspicion that they were in preproduction already. But Katz and Lerner both denied it.

More contracts came and went, more stalling, more changing of company titles. The producers couldn't seem to decide which WGA signatory company they wanted to picture to go out under. All the while, they were not only preparing the film, they had started production.

Once again from Gilardi, we were shocked to learn that the picture was already two weeks into production, with Bijou Phillips in the lead role, but that still no script was available. I'd made about ten requests for a script by now, to no avail. Finally, engaging a litigator and threatening to close down the picture, we were able to get a signed contract and get paid. By that time, the picture had been shooting for three weeks. Under threats of going to the Writers Guild, I finally was able to cajole the producers into supplying me with a copy of the screenplay. While many elements of my screenplay were used, a new concept had been added. In the original *It's Alive*, the infant is born as a monster and escapes from the hospital delivery room and eventually finds its way to its parents' home. It then escapes again and is hunted across the city and is finally eliminated in the storm drains of Los Angeles. The new concept was that the baby would be born looking like a normal child and would continually evolve into a monster and then revert to its infantile like state after each killing. So, like the Wolf Man, the baby would change into a monster, then change back into a human again. This concept might work or it might be ludicrous. The entire picture rests on the success or failure of this one concept. If the audience buys it, we might have a success. If not, the picture would be laughable, and quickly dismissed.

Instead of making the remake bigger and more spectacular, the producers made it smaller. I suppose they were just relying on the use of the title and decided to cut the budget and grab whatever income they could from the film's opening weekend. I'm proud to say that I had nothing to do with the making of the picture. I'm sad to say that I allowed the property to drift out of my hands and into those of people who had no respect for the earlier film, which had received some marvelous critical response and had an influence on many other films to follow. Naturally, we always hope for a hit. I don't like to badmouth one of my own projects, but the people who made this picture showed no respect for the property and no respect for the rules of the Writers Guild of America—and certainly no respect for me.

I could've closed the picture down, put everybody out of work, and the entire matter would've gone into litigation. The remake wouldn't have played and perhaps it never would have reached the screen. But I took the expedient course by accepting the money and letting them finish the film. In short order, the money will all be spent and the film will be around to haunt me for the rest of my life. I guess I'm more at fault than anybody.

I suppose beneath it all, I must admit that having made three *It's Alive* movies, I really wasn't that keen on making a fourth. I was curious as to what someone else might do with the property. But I was wrong. I had a responsibility to that little baby monster, and I let him down.

Chapter 39
Analyzing Larry Cohen

I must admit that I basked in my acceptance by my peer group, the other directors who seemed to understand and appreciate my efforts to work outside the mainstream.

One of these friendships was with André De Toth, for whom I'd previously written *El Condor*. We wanted to work together again so we took a meeting at Warner Brothers to pitch a sequel to *House of Wax*, one of André's great hits of the 1950s. After the meeting we strolled over to one of the soundstages where certain crew members who'd previously worked with André were currently shooting. When we came on the set that day, it was like the scene out of *Sunset Boulevard* when Gloria Swanson re-visits Paramount. The technicians immediately climbed down from the catwalks above. All production stopped as word went around that André De Toth was there. They gathered around him like some mythic figure. There was handshaking, hugging and such affection I'd never seen on any set. He was truly their hero, this legendary figure who'd directed battle scenes for *Lawrence of Arabia* and had recently supervised the flying sequences for *Superman*. Sadly, Warners did not share this enthusiasm for André and our pitch was rejected. André was simply not employable in the new Hollywood. He was much admired but never hired.

I continued my friendship with André until the night I screened *A Return to Salem's Lot*. Perhaps he was growing bitter because of the inactivity. Although my screening went quite well, André went out of his way to be cruel. He waited until after I'd received scores of compliments as the audience filtered out, then lashed out with "You're so talented, why do you make such shit?" I couldn't believe I was hearing these words from someone I adored and who seemed to have such affection for me. He was relentless. Well, at least Sam Fuller had praised the picture.

I saw André a few times afterwards, but the closeness was gone. He said he'd been devoting most of his time to sculpting and subsequently he was confined to a wheelchair. I prefer to dwell on the days in Almeria when André was my staunch supporter and the times in London when he entertained us so lavishly. André was a fabulous "expense account friend." When the studio was paying for everything, André was given to excesses—the food, the champagne, the limousines. Living out of his own pocket and without a movie to produce, some of André's great warmth evaporated. I suppose he truly wanted to hurt me that night. He succeeded. Or maybe he was just telling the truth.

I tend to avoid analyzing or discussing the content of my films because I hate second-guessing myself. There's a danger in becoming self-conscious about your own creative instincts. Soon you start imitating yourself. I've always preferred to let my unconscious do most of the work and leave the analysis up to the critics.

But it's clear that my overall tendency is to take generally mundane things and turn them into objects of menace: a newborn baby, ice cream, an ambulance, and even organized religion.

Most of my films operate on a number of different levels. They're thrillers, yet at the same time they're comedies. Still,

I play them absolutely straight, not as camp. The most important adage in creating horror is that the audience must truly believe. The humor comes as a welcome relief once the fear has passed. Then another even more terrible threat must arise. The audience is thereby kept off balance, never knowing what to expect.

I realize we're all products of our childhood, and I can trace the origins of the *It's Alive* concept back to my earliest recollections of Grandma Julie telling me of how my parents had sought an abortion prior to my being born. I can't imagine what possessed the old lady to reveal that kind of information to a kid. In those days it was difficult to terminate a pregnancy since it was illegal. The very fact that my own parents considered that certainly puts me in the same position as the persecuted *It's Alive* baby.

Growing up in a period when the extermination of the Jews had become a reality might also make a youngster fearful of being hunted down and murdered, just for the crime of being alive. I'd discovered my father had to work at the Davega Electronics store in Manhattan under a gentile name—this was a time when certain businesses would not hire Jews. The sense of

shame I felt may well have embedded itself in my psyche and led to my creating *It's Alive*, in which the authorities are attempting to locate and destroy an undesirable species.

If I became introspective enough to examine all of these details, I would drive myself nuts and probably never write anything again. Still I'm amused to read about it and flattered that others have taken the time to give my films such close scrutiny.

The first taste of real critical acceptance I'd received was from a young man who programmed the Z Channel, a popular Los Angeles cable station which carried movies exclusively. Jerry Harvey was an avid a fan who scheduled no less than four Larry Cohen Film Festivals. He showed just about every picture I'd ever made. Thanks to him, my films were made available to viewers who'd never seen them in theaters. Suddenly I wasn't just a B-picture filmmaker, I was an "auteur" to be taken seriously. I couldn't thank Jerry enough. Then one day I received word that he'd committed suicide after murdering his wife. Naturally there were the sordid jokes: Larry Cohen's movies certainly attract weirdos—and never turn your back on a Larry Cohen fan.

Still, I knew if I continued making my own movies, some critic would take notice of me. Little did I expect it would be Robin Wood, whose treatise on Hitchcock had served as a textbook for me in the construction of my thrillers. Robin's extensive article in *Film Comment* magazine in 1978 described me as the most underrated director in Hollywood. Suddenly, others were writing pieces about me and subjecting my films to critical analysis. I'd been discovered!

When Robin invited me to Canada for some speaking engagements, I was anxious to accommodate him. We flew in a blizzard to a suburban campus where one of the students surprised me with a unique analysis of my films. "I think there's a tremendously Jewish aspect to your work. For example, the scene in *It's Alive* where the milkman gets killed, milk comes pouring out of the back of the truck and is mixed with his blood. This invokes the Biblical taboo against mixing blood and milk."

I hadn't consciously thought of this, but maybe he had a point. He also zeroed in on the fact that the protagonist in many of my films deliberately undermines and destroys his God-like adversary. Isn't this like destroying the Messiah and re-enacting the role that Judas played?

I can't deny having had encounters with local bullies who'd accused me of having killed Jesus. At that point it was usually wise to throw the first punch, since the guy who hits first usually wins. Still, the accusation hurt more than the bruises I received in any schoolyard fight. Maybe this Canadian student had my number after all. In Q, the monster represents an Aztec god that's been reincarnated, and the hero ends up betraying and destroying this supreme being.

More recently, Elayne B. Graham Chaplin, a British academic, wrote a brilliant 276-page thesis on my films for her doctorate degree in philosophy. It's entitled "Monstrous Masculinity—Boys, Men and Monsters in the Films of Larry Cohen," and it's certainly an eye-opener, even to me.

And Tony Williams, who taught a college class on my work, wrote a critical examination of all my film and television work in his excellent book, *Larry Cohen: The Radical Allegories of an Independent Filmmaker*, published by McFarland Press. I admit I learned a lot about my own movies from reading his book.

Still, it's better not to think about it. Nothing will kill inspiration more than too much self-analysis. Another reason to keep away from psychiatrists. I find it more productive to get rid of my frustrations through my writing than by talking things out with an analyst.

Clearly, I'm obsessed with the subject of betrayal. While most television writers simply scribble unrelated episodes for whatever series is currently buying, I actually created a body of work with interrelated themes. In my early twenties I wrote what I call "The Treason Quartet" for *The Defenders*. These were four separate one-hour television plays, each a study of a traitor. In "The Secret," Martin Landau plays a nuclear physicist who refuses to surrender his discovery to the U.S. government. In "The Traitor," Fritz Weaver portrays a Soviet spy who allows himself to be arrested rather than commit espionage against the

U.S. In "May Day, May Day," Torin Thatcher plays the Admiral of the nuclear fleet who's put on trial for sedition—and he's been turned in by his own son. In "The Captive," Ludwig Donath is a captured Soviet spy being exchanged for an American businessman accused of espionage in Russia. We soon learn the Russian is to be executed upon his repatriation. I followed this up in NBC's *Espionage* series with "Medal for a Turned Coat," in which Fritz Weaver played a "good" German who goes back to Berlin to be honored for his heroic actions against the Hitler regime, only to confront the unpleasant truth about himself. All were produced by Herbert Brodkin.

Then, on CBS' *The Nurses*, another Brodkin series, I began writing teleplays which dealt with extreme sexual aberration. "Night Sounds" concerned a nurse sexually assaulted by one of her patients and the accusations that she led him on. "Party Girl," starring Inger Stevens as a high-priced prostitute, was originally titled "Call Girl" until the network's Standards and Practices department made us change it. The hooker, who has had a heart attack, comes into conflict with another hospital patient—a woman who has been admitted for a mastectomy—who feels she is being sexually mutilated by the surgery. Again the network interfered. A mastectomy was not permissible on television and so the woman had her leg amputated instead.

I followed this up with an episode of *The Defenders* called "The Unwritten Law" in which a sexually repressed husband murders his wife's lover when he catches them both in bed. That same season I wrote "Accomplice" for the NBC series *Sam Benedict*. It starred Edmond O'Brien and Eddie Albert as lawyers defending two homosexual lovers who are jointly charged with homicide. It was amazing that NBC telecast this episode at 7.30 pm. It never dawned on the censors that the relationship between the two men could be sexual in nature. Who'd have the nerve? To make it even more daring, one of the two men was black.

Topping this all off, I wrote, "My Name Is Martin Burnham," which starred James Whitmore as a convicted sex offender who's habitually re-arrested whenever such crimes are committed in his neighborhood. This show appeared on *Arrest and Trial*, a series that anticipates *Law & Order*.

With Sydney Pollack on the set of *The Defenders.*

In a period when sex was still taboo on television, I managed to examine many aspects of aberrant behavior and get away with it. Most importantly, I was able to do some of my very best writing. It's with great pleasure that I rerun these programs at the Museum of Television because they compare favorably with what is being done in the medium today. It seems inevitable that combining my interest in treason, obsessive government security and sexual deviation, I'd eventually be drawn to write and direct a movie bio of J. Edgar Hoover.

I still remember staying up all night writing these TV episodes, banging away on my typewriter with such force that all the periods would be pounded out of the paper and scattered like tiny dots all across my desk and on the surrounding carpet. I typed so hard that my pages felt like Braille. Usually writing up to 20 to 25 pages a night, I'd eventually collapse into total exhaustion. I couldn't wait to deliver a script and then get on to the next one. I approached each with total enthusiasm. Talk about TV's Golden Age. This was it for me.

To preserve these television programs, I have contributed prints of them to The Museum of Broadcasting and they can be seen in both the New York and Los Angeles branches. Just punch in the name Larry Cohen and the selection of shows will appear. I also recommend "Colossus," an episode of *The Defenders* in which Leo Genn plays a pioneer in leukemia research who stands accused of murdering his wife, and "The Gift," an episode of *The Nurses*, in which Lee Grant portrays a physical therapist trying to keep her suicidal patient from taking his own life. My *Defenders* teleplay "Go Between" is a thinly disguised retelling of the Charles Lindbergh story—that of a beloved American hero whose child is kidnapped. The intolerable behavior of both the press and the public help turn him into a dangerous neofascist.

One of my episodes of *The Defenders*, "Kill or Be Killed," which was directed by Sydney Pollack, was recently plagiarized by Paramount Television and remade into a two-hour movie for Showtime. The producers borrowed my teleplay and expanded it without giving me any credit. It took a Writers Guild arbitration to set the record straight. Paramount was forced to correct the credit and pay me nearly $100,000 in penalties. The remade version was called *The Defenders: Choice of Evils*, which goes to prove that the major studios are not above pulling any scam they think they can get away with. Even after losing the initial arbitration, Paramount failed to alter the credit on the video release. They put my name on the box but left the onscreen credit uncorrected. Again I had to appeal to the Guild for redress. Why should the studio give a damn? They've got plenty of money. If they get caught—so what?

Please don't get me wrong. It's still a great business.

Where could I have so much fun or made so much trouble?

Appendix
Memo (for the Internet)

CLINT EASTWOOD'S HOOVER BIO STARRING DeCAPRIO GETS IT ALL WRONG

Sadly, the new Warner Bros. epic is full of errors and misrepresentations.

Here's the real, never-been-told inside scoop on the celebrated FBI Chief.

from
LARRY COHEN
Producer/Director/Writer of the 1977 motion picture
THE PRIVATE FILES OF J. EDGAR HOOVER

Don't get me wrong. I'm a great fan of Clint Eastwood's… and I happen to like the guy. I worked closely with Clint on a screenplay some thirty years ago at Universal and again at Malpaso, his own company. Clint actually optioned *The Hostiles* twice in an effort to get it made with co-star John Wayne. Unfortunately, Duke did not sign on and Clint and I were both disappointed that the film never came to be.

Over the years, I've had several cordial encounters with Clint so I have no axe to grind with him personally. He's a great filmmaker and a fine fellow. Unfortunately, his new movie about J. Edgar Hoover is so full of untruths that I can't sit idly by without making comment.

I recently received a call from Leonardo DeCaprio's company, Appian Way, asking to see a copy of my movie about J. Edgar Hoover, which starred Broderick Crawford as Hoover and Dan Dailey as Tolson, with a splendid cast headed by Jose Ferrer, Celeste Holm and Rip Torn. It was a very well-regarded film, particularly in England, where it had a significant theatrical run plus two highly promoted telecasts on the BBC.

In America, the film was a victim of the fears of film distributors that the FBI would retaliate against them for releasing a picture critical of the Bureau, particularly at a time when the FBI anti-piracy seal was being affixed to every videotape put on the market. Still, the film was released by American International Pictures and received many terrific reviews.

After sending a copy of my film to Mr. DeCaprio, I got a call to schedule a meeting with him—but it was unexpectedly canceled and there was no follow-up. I could only assume that Leonardo had been advised by Warners attorneys or by Clint himself to steer clear of me. (I might add I consider Leonardo a most gifted actor and I wish him nothing but success in this new role.)

Shortly after I was privileged to read Clint's screenplay on Hoover, I received a call from Mr. Rob Aurins, who identified himself as Clint's producing partner. His message expressed sincere interest in discussing what elements I might add to the new movie, but after I returned the call, I never heard from him again. It's unfortunate, since the new movie is full of inaccuracies and outright misrepresentations.

The Eastwood film is based on a script by Dustin Lance Black, the gifted author of the highly acclaimed film *Milk*, a study of the life and death of the celebrated gay political leader. This time around, Mr. Black has chosen to portray J. Edgar Hoover as a closeted gay man. Unfortunately, while Harvey Milk's sexuality was an open book, the matter of Hoover's sex life is grossly distorted in this script. It's totally fabricated but will soon be accepted as fact unless someone contradicts it now. There have been previous assertions made over the years about the sexuality of the FBI chief and his number one aide, Clyde Tolson. Little attention is given to the era in which these two gentlemen grew up. They were both born before the turn of the century at a time when many men lived as "bachelors." It was traditional in those days for men to remain under their parents' roof, often for life, providing continued support by handing over their weekly paycheck. The fact that Mr. Hoover lived with his mother until her death was not at all unusual behavior. In fact, it was customary for his generation. We cannot judge Hoover by today's standards. He and Tolson never lived together and never shared bedrooms. They enjoyed sporting events, the racetrack, and Tolson served as Hoover's only full-time bodyguard. There is no doubt an emotional dependency developed, but no proof of any overt sexual activity. Even so, Mr. Black's first draft has a kissing scene between Hoover and Tolson.

It's true that there were many stories in publications unfriendly to Hoover, labeling him homosexual. I don't suggest there's anything at all wrong with an individual adopting a gay lifestyle. In fact, Hoover might've been a much better person if he'd had some outlet for sexual expression. But painstaking investigations never uncovered a single piece of evidence to indicate Hoover was anything but asexual. He did date actress Dorothy Lamour and Ginger Rogers' mother but for the most part, he remained celibate. I covered these allegations responsibly in my movie and tried to substitute facts for rumors. Still, oddly enough, I was the recipient of London's Gay Critic Award in 1978 for my depiction of the Hoover-Tolson relationship.

In some remote cases when something was published questioning Hoover's sexual preference, the authors were soon visited by FBI agents telling them to "put up or shut up." No one ever had any back up. Those high up in the Bureau who knew Hoover and Tolson closely never believed a word of it. However, years later a writer named Anthony Summers—seeking to write a scathing exposé-type book about J. Edgar Hoover—decided to include uncorroborated allegations by Susan Rosenstiel, an alcoholic woman who served time at Rikers Island for no less than perjury. This woman, the irrational ex-wife of one of Hoover's old friends, claimed that she had been taken by her husband to a party at the Waldorf Astoria Hotel, where she witnessed Hoover cavorting in drag, calling himself "Mary," and engaging in open homosexual activities.

The absurdity of this story is clear to any responsible historian and a great number of volumes have been published since which have totally discredited these falsehoods. Rosenstiel had a grudge against Hoover for helping her husband during a divorce action that she brought against him... and she wanted to get even. But a convicted perjurer is not a reliable source. And the absurdity that Mr. Hoover would have publicly displayed himself in women's clothes at a party defies credibility. Unfortunately, Clint and his screenwriter decided to compound this fiction by concocting a scene that no one in the world testifies to, that of Mr. Hoover trying on his mother's clothes soon after her death. It's unsubstantiated, irresponsible and exploitive. Long ago, television and nightclub comedians perpetuated the falsehood that Hoover was a cross-dresser to get laughs, calling him J. Edna Hoover. And even President Bill Clinton went so far as to make an unfortunate joke at a Correspondents Dinner in Washington, commenting that he had still not found anyone to fill J. Edgar Hoover's pumps. He got his laugh, but this unpleasant smear enraged certain people within the FBI who still retained allegiance and respect for J. Edgar Hoover for his forty-eight years of service.

It was soon after making this bad taste joke that Bill Clinton started to have his own troubles. A woman named Linda Tripp approached Monica Lewinsky and began pumping her for information, and Mr. Clinton soon found himself in the midst of the most embarrassing exposé in modern politics. He was eventually impeached—and acquitted. But he lost his license to practice law and, sadly, it tainted his illustrious career as Chief Executive. Perhaps he never should have told that bad joke because the FBI had used very similar tactics to retaliate and discredit its enemies throughout the Hoover Administration. And now Clinton himself was perhaps to bear the brunt of a resentment deep inside the Bureau.

Before making my Hoover movie, I'd spent years doing research—talking with long-time Hoover associates. Among them was William T. Sullivan, formerly the number three man in the Bureau. Sullivan took me into his confidence. He admitted personally writing the letter to Martin Luther King suggesting he commit suicide. But in Mr. Eastwood's movie, Hoover is depicted as writing the letter, which is a falsehood.

Another revelation from Sullivan was the identity of "Deep Throat," the Watergate informant who led to Nixon's eventual demise. In truth, the critical "leaks" to Woodward and Bernstein came from the very highest echelon of the FBI. We strongly indicated this in our film but were not allowed to specifically name Mark Felt as the informant. His identity was not to be revealed until thirty-five years later, with much hullabaloo.

In our original film, I included a shot of a headline that states: "Mark Felt denies he is Deep Throat," which is as far as the studio's lawyers would allow me to go. But there was much more to these revelations, since Felt was not acting simply of his own volition. After Hoover's death and Tolson's retirement, Felt moved into position as the number one man at the Bureau. He virtually ran the FBI. But the unanswered question remains: Why would Felt, a conservative, choose to leak info damaging to Nixon and aid Woodward and Bernstein? Simply because he was carrying out Hoover's explicit orders given shortly before his death to bring down the Nixon Administration. Mark Felt was never an initiator of policy—simply a functionary. He would never have acted except under Hoover's direct instructions.

This wasn't a random act. It was part of a carefully worked out program. The first step in Hoover's plan had been to remove Spiro Agnew as Vice President. There'd be no point in toppling Nixon only to have Agnew take his place in the White House. He was worse than Nixon. Hoover's resentment stemmed from the fact that Nixon was attempting to set up his own personal investigative unit, usurping the role the FBI had played under seven presidents. It was the Bureau that wiretapped people, broke into their offices and homes, and read their mail. These were code named "Black Bag Jobs," and ever since the Roosevelt administration, Hoover had claimed the exclusive right to carry them out.

The federal prosecutors who brought the case against Spiro Agnew for taking bribes in his Vice Presidential office admitted in their published book that they received their inside information from the very same source as Woodward and Bernstein. The press has never commented on the evidence that the FBI first brought Agnew down and then followed up with the destruction of the Nixon Administration. This was J. Edgar Hoover's final legacy—and it worked out exactly as he intended.

The news media chose to ignore the revelations in my film. After all, a moviemaker couldn't be taken seriously and the press preferred to make two Washington reporters the heroes of Watergate.

I had hoped that this information would finally be made clear in Clint Eastwood's new movie. He now had the full opportunity to include these facts as well as the strong indication that Hoover had ordered the copying of certain tapes that Nixon had recorded in the Oval Office. Learning they'd been duplicated, Nixon realized that if he erased the original tapes, there was always the chance that the duplicates would show up. These tapes—kept in Room 172½ of the Executive Office Building—had not been guarded. A few had even been removed by Ehrlichman and played at Washington parties. Hoover was well aware of the existence of these tapes because many of the Secret Service Agents servicing Nixon had formerly been FBI men. Once a G-man, always a G-man. This would finally explain why Nixon failed to degauze the tapes, which put the final nail in the coffin of his administration. This was all covered in my 1977 movie.

Moving on to other errors in Mr. Black's script that is so badly researched it even spells Tolson's name wrong:

He spends a good half an hour of the film focusing on the Lindbergh kidnap case, a crime in which J. Edgar Hoover had only the most peripheral involvement. Almost exclusively the New York and New Jersey Police Departments and Elmer Irey handled the investigation. Irey, the Chief of the Treasury Agents, supervised the passing of the traceable ransom money. Hoover personally had little to do with solving this crime, although he later tried to take credit for it.

Much is also made in the movie of Hoover's reluctance to pursue members of the Mafia. It's true that through certain contacts like Walter Winchell (the noted columnist), Hoover had a direct line to a number of Mafia chiefs—like Frank Costello. What isn't widely understood is that Hoover had worked out a secret "gentleman's agreement" with the organized crime bosses. He realized that prostitution, loan-sharking and gambling were vices that could never be eliminated, just as alcohol consumption had failed to be eradicated by prohibition. As part of the deal, Hoover had the top mobsters agree to severely limit narcotics traffic, which he realized was the most insidious threat to the public good. And over many decades, the drug trade was kept under strict regulation. It was only much later—after the break-up of the mob's national organization— that everybody who could purchase a plastic baggie got into the drug business for themselves. This new laxity opened the door for black gangsters, the Mexican Cartel and the Russian underworld to move into the drug trade, which then multiplied a thousand-fold into the national disgrace it is today.

Early in his career as FBI Chief, Hoover had personally arrested Louis "Lepke" Buchalter, the dreaded head of Murder, Inc., who had been forced to surrender to Hoover by the Mafia organization itself. This was not the simple capture of a criminal. This was a deal with the Cosa Nostra Organization to remove a vicious killer who had been bringing too much negative attention to organized crime. It marked the beginning of the "arrangement" with the mob bosses that Hoover felt was the lesser of evils. Heroin and cocaine traffic was kept to a minimum while Las Vegas flourished.

Over the years, Hoover broke many laws and violated the privacy of thousands of Americans. But every president he worked under was complicit in his actions. During the Korean War, it was Hoover who fueled Senator McCarthy and fed him information, instructing him exactly how to use it. In later years, when Hoover pulled the rug out from under McCarthy, the senator from Wisconsin was immediately discredited and destroyed. He'd simply been a tool of Hoover.

But there was a purpose to the creation of this demagogue. It was to instill fear of dissent during the Korean War, which was an extremely unpopular conflict. Red Chinese troops had entered the war and our troops were being slaughtered. Some 35,000 Americans died and there were hundreds of thousands of casualties. The losses in Iraq and Afghanistan pale by comparison.

And yet, at home there was little or no dissent on the streets or on the airwaves. There were few demonstrations and little public opposition. Controversy was silenced because fear was in the air, a fear which prevented criticism of the Korean intervention and eventually allowed a settlement to be negotiated that has endured for over fifty years. North and South Korea were divided at the 38th parallel. The United States managed to achieve its goal, which was made impossible in Vietnam by the huge public outcry. Hoover helped prevent a similar humiliating disaster during Korea and as despicable as many of his actions were, an unpopular war was brought to an acceptable conclusion. The McCarthy era was a national disgrace and a shameful period in our history. Yet the result was thousands of American lives were probably spared because the war was settled at the conference table and our soldiers could withdraw honorably instead of freezing to death in another incredibly bitter winter of combat. Shameful things were done to achieve a positive result and we can't excuse the despicable methods, but it explains the motivations behind the outrages that were perpetrated.

Finally, the hottest story that I could have added to the Clint Eastwood movie regards the Kennedy assassination and Hoover's belief, beyond any doubt in his mind, that the President had been assassinated under orders from Fidel Castro. The killer, Lee Harvey Oswald, an avowed Marxist who had fled to Moscow and then returned, had a long history of being associated with pro-Castro organizations and had quietly visited the Cuban Embassy in Mexico City just a few weeks before the assassination. Still, the government felt compelled to hide Castro's complicity from the American people. If it were revealed that Castro had directly ordered Kennedy's death, we would have had little choice but to invade Cuba. It might precipitate a world war—because the Soviet Union could intervene on Castro's behalf. Was it worth plunging the nation into a nuclear confrontation when Kennedy himself had provoked his own death by ordering Castro's murder? The Cuban leader was merely retaliating.

One might wonder why, in today's world—when we have had a rapprochement with Red China, when we have made peace with the Russians and Vietnamese, while we have dealt with numerous dictators—that we still refuse to recognize Cuba and to have any reconciliation with Castro or his brother. This is because every president that comes into office is soon apprised of the secret that Castro is the murderer of an American president and has gone unpunished. Only when Castro is finally deceased will the truth be revealed, but the Cuban leader seems to live on forever. And the truth remains unspoken. I can't prove the above is factual, only that it represents Mr. Hoover's belief. Somebody ought to check it out.

Many of Hoover's top echelon knew of his belief in maintaining the secret. It's been whispered but never openly discussed. I heard it thirty-five years ago during my research.

It's unfortunate that none of the above material will be seen in Clint Eastwood's movie version of Hoover's life. I certainly recommend that anyone seeing this movie also have a look at my film, *The Private Files of J. Edgar Hoover*, which MGM is releasing on DVD and can be purchased over Amazon and MGM Archives. It presents a much more accurate and full picture of Hoover's career and behavior, and Broderick Crawford is the precise image of Hoover.

When we shot at Hoover's home in Rock Creek Park outside of Washington, his elderly neighbor stepped outside to watch and saw what he thought to be two dead men, Hoover and Tolson, walking out of the adjoining house. The poor old fellow had a heart attack, collapsed on his lawn, and was taken away by ambulance. Fortunately, he survived.

In our film, which we shot in Hoover's actual office, Hoover's home, in Tolson's apartment and in all the real locales such as the Quantico Training Academy and the Justice Department itself (but without FBI censorship or approval), you will see the places where it really happened—with many of the real people that surrounded Hoover playing themselves.

I wish Clint Eastwood nothing but good luck and offer my continued friendship. It's just that I believe I have an obligation to the truth and to J. Edgar Hoover himself, who harmed a great many people, but did perform a unique service to his country for forty-eight years. There will never be anyone like him again. Thank God.

As my movie shows, they were all bad guys—the presidents, the politicians and the FBI director. There were no heroes—only ambitious men doing what was expedient. Hoover sacrificed the lives and reputations of many decent people in the interest of what he considered "the good of the nation." It's disgraceful and tragic, and it's got the makings of a great movie. I have hopes that perhaps a new version of the script has been fashioned since the draft I received. But certainly my disappointment in what could have been the definitive J. Edgar Hoover movie must be expressed. And I thank you for your time and attention in reading this—and hope that you'll pass it on to your friends and fellow movie fans.

Sincerely,
Larry Cohen